SPORT SCIENCE

Physical Laws and Optimum Performance

PETER J. BRANCAZIO

A TOUCHSTONE BOOK
Published by Simon & Schuster, Inc.
NEW YORK

Copyright © 1984 by Peter Brancazio, 1983 Lawrence Brancazio Trust, and 1983 David Brancazio Trust

All rights reserved
including the right of reproduction
in whole or in part in any form

First Touchstone Edition, 1985

Published by Simon & Schuster, Inc.
Simon & Schuster Building
Rockefeller Center
1230 Avenue of the Americas
New York, New York 10020

TOUCHSTONE and colophon are registered trademarks of Simon & Schuster, Inc.

Designed by Eve Kirch

Manufactured in the United States of America

10 9 8 7 6 5 4 3 2 1

10 9 8 7 6 5 4 3   Pbk.

Library of Congress Cataloging in Publication Data
Brancazio, Peter J.
   SportScience: physical laws and optimum performance.
   Bibliography: p.
   Includes index.
   1. Sports—Physiological aspects. 2. Human mechanics. I. Title.
RC1235.B73 1984   612'.76   83-20152

ISBN 0-671-45584-2

ISBN 0-671-55438-7 Pbk.

ACKNOWLEDGMENTS

This book has been shaped by the contributions of many people, and it is with pleasure and gratitude that I acknowledge their assistance. My editors at Simon and Schuster deserve special mention—namely, Robert Eckhardt, who first suggested the idea and later rode herd on my stylistic excesses, and Don Hutter, who shepherded the manuscript through the final stages of production. A number of my colleagues at Brooklyn College were particularly helpful. I wish to thank Professors Bonnie Berger, Sal Cannavo, Matthew Kleinman, Joseph Krieger, Donald Landolphi, Donald Michielli, Theodore Raphan, and Arthur Weston for their expertise and patience in answering my endless questions, and for guiding me to valuable sources of information. A special thanks goes to my good friend and fellow athlete Professor Richard Pizer for many stimulating and illuminating conversations. His obstinate refusal to try out my theory of basketball shooting is hereby forgiven. My research on the physics of baseball was enhanced considerably by several individuals who were especially generous with their time and interest—Bill Williams of Hillerich and Bradsby, Bill Allman of *Science 83*, Darrell Evans of the San Francisco Giants, and Frank Howard of the New York Mets.

Most of all, I am indebted to my family for their participation. My two sons, David and Larry (ages 16 and 13, respectively, as of this writing), contributed by gathering statistics, improving my computer programs, assisting in various experiments, reading parts of the manuscript, and providing numerous helpful suggestions and insights. My wife, Ronnie, supplied both emotional support and editorial advice. Indeed, her careful and attentive reading of the manuscript was a source of inspiration, in view of her lifelong indifference to all forms of sports and athletic activity.

For David and Larry
live long and prosper

CONTENTS

MATH BOXES

There is considerable scientific evidence that the healthy personality is one who not only plays, but who takes his play seriously.
—Dr. William Menninger

INTRODUCTION: SCIENCE AND SPORTS

This book represents the culmination of a long effort to come to grips with a split personality. When I was nine years old, I decided that I was going to be either a major league baseball player or a scientist; as it turned out, I had to settle for the latter. I was fortunate to grow up with a group of boys who shared a common love of sports. We spent countless hours playing all the popular urban games—stickball, touch football, basketball, and roller hockey were our favorites—and filled the rest of our time together in endless discussions of the relative merits of our favorite professional teams and players. Every school day I would rush home, do my homework, and then go outside and play until dark. On Saturdays, we would all meet early in the morning to go to the local park or playground, where we would choose up sides for a game of football or basketball and play until we were exhausted.

I was, at the same time, a closet intellectual. I showed great aptitude for science and mathematics, became interested in philosophy, and developed a love for classical music. I never discussed these matters with my friends, for those were the days when scholars were referred to as "eggheads," and I wanted desperately to maintain the friendships, the solidarity, and the spirit of the experiences that we shared as athletes. So when I closed my books and put on my sweatshirt and sneakers, I simply turned off one part of myself and turned on the other. I devoted equal time to mind and body, developing a scientist's inquisitiveness and a jock mentality, either of which could be called upon as the situation required, separate but equal.

I continued in this manner throughout high school, college, and graduate school. Despite the responsibilities thrust upon us by our work and our families, we still managed to get together on Saturday mornings and occasional evenings for football, basketball, or softball. On the same day that my Ph.D. thesis in astrophysics was accepted, our softball team played a crucial game, which I won with a clutch hit in the last inning. (I'm still not sure which of the two events of that day was more exhilarating.) Before the game began I made the mistake of confiding to one of my friends that I had just become a Ph.D. He thought about this for a moment, then replied begrudgingly, "I suppose now we have to call you *Doctor* Meathead." I was very fortunate to have friends who never allowed me to develop exaggerated feelings of self-importance.

It's been more than ten years since we last got together for a game. Only a few of us remain active athletes, although some have found new outlets coaching the teams on which their children play. In that time I've developed a great passion for basketball—a game whose elegance and subtleties are still being revealed to me. I play it two or three times a week, all year round, and I derive a great deal of emotional satisfaction from my participation. In fact, I will admit that I still get as much pleasure from my occasional athletic triumphs as I do from my accomplishments as a scientist and teacher. I've also retained my two personalities—one for academia, one for sports. And until a few years ago, it never occurred to me that there was any connection, any way of bridging or merging the two worlds, any way to apply what I had learned as a scientist to sports, or vice versa. And therein lies the genesis of this book.

I had been playing basketball on weekends with a new group of people who could be counted on to show up regularly in all kinds of weather. I was not a consistent shooter, and at 5' 9" I do not present an imposing figure on a basketball court, but I nevertheless managed to be reasonably competitive. One day, while we were sitting around talking after the game, someone asked me what I did for a living. When I admitted to being a college professor of physics and astronomy, they were rather taken aback. Finally, one of the players—a tough and earthy individual with great moves and a superb shooting touch—put it to me:

"If you're so smart, how come you stink at basketball?"

This comment stands out in my view as one of the most profound and illuminating questions anyone has ever directed at me. I was shocked into the recognition that my scientific curiosity, which, given my interest in astronomy, encompassed the far-flung reaches of the universe, had never extended to sports. It suddenly occurred to me that I should indeed be able to use the principles of mathematics and physics to analyze and improve my basketball skills. Within a few months, I had researched and written an article entitled ''The Physics of Basketball.'' Shortly after its completion, I presented my findings to a good-sized and enthusiastic audience at a meeting of the American Association of Physics Teachers, and my article was subsequently published in a scientific journal. Best of all, by applying the scientific principles I had deduced in my research, I was able to improve my shooting accuracy and other basketball skills considerably (I'll be describing some of my findings in a later chapter).

My success with basketball got me to thinking about whether other areas of sports were amenable to scientific analysis. Could one use physics and mathematics to figure out the best way to judge a fly ball or throw the discus? Could scientific principles be applied to optimize the design of a tennis racket, or to explain why a knuckleball is so difficult to hit? As I probed further into the subject, I became aware of a substantial body of scholarly research having to do with all aspects of sports and athletic performance.

A lot of people, it seems, take their sports very seriously. I know many professional people—teachers, doctors, lawyers, business executives—who are committed to making time in their schedules for a few hours of intense physical activity every week. Indeed, tens of millions of American men and women from all walks of life participate regularly in some sort of athletic pursuit—whether it be in competitive sports or in individual activities like jogging or skiing. Even greater numbers are involved in sports merely as spectators. The interest, emotional involvement, and even adulation that the majority of Americans profess for their favorite athletes and teams is rather remarkable. Yet this is definitely not a peculiarly American phenomenon; the attention given by whole countries to the progress of their national teams in World Cup soccer competition often borders on hysteria.

The emphatic role of sports in the life of the individual, the community, and the nation has stimulated much interest in the academic world. The past few decades have witnessed a steady multiplication of research, courses, and curricula dealing with all phases of sports. The focal point of these efforts has spread from physical education departments into the social sciences, the biological sciences, and even the physical sciences. To get some perspective on these developments, let's take a brief look at the evolution of the relationship between scholars and athletes in the United States.

The academic analysis of athletic activity dates back to the 1870s and 1880s, when the first departments of physical education were established at American colleges. At that time there were two conflicting approaches to athletics. The older of the two was an emphasis on participation sports and games, which is basically an English tradition that was brought to this country by the early colonists (the two most popular American sports, baseball and football, are both variants of older English games). The second approach, which stressed physical fitness through gymnastics, came to America with the German and Scandinavian immigrants of the nineteenth century. The founders of physical education advocated the latter, promoted various systems of gymnastic activities as a pathway to better health and physical fitness, and argued for compulsory physical education as part of the college curriculum.

By the end of the nineteenth century, interest in participation sports had expanded considerably. The introduction of tennis and golf to the United States in the 1870s and 1880s, the invention of basketball in 1891, and the revival of the Olympic Games in 1896 all contributed to this growth, as did the growing popularity of professional baseball and college football. One result was a shift in emphasis within physical education from formal gymnastics to instruction in competitive sports. The year 1895 marked the first appearance of a sports page as a regular feature in a newspaper—a notable milestone, considering the extent to which the interaction between sports and the media has evolved since then.

Undoubtedly, the most significant factor affecting the relationship between sports and the academic world has been the expansion of intercollegiate athletics in the twentieth century. At first, college teams were organized and run by the students themselves. However, their inability to maintain consistent standards of conduct, eligibility, and rules of play led the colleges to take over the administration of intercollegiate competition. This transition, completed by 1920, led within the space of a few decades to such excesses as the growth of huge athletic programs with multimillion-dollar budgets, the construction of 100,000-seat stadiums, and the massive recruiting of high school athletes with its attendant abuses. At many universities it would now seem that the tail wags the dog: these institutions of higher learning are better known for the successes of their football and basketball teams than for the quality of their academic programs, and the financial health of the school has come to depend on the ability of their athletic teams to maintain winning records. Although there is an occasional outcry against this state of affairs, there is little likelihood of any significant change—because it is generally agreed that colleges and universities have an obligation to provide entertainment to the American public in the form of intercollegiate sports, as well as to serve as a farm system for the professional leagues by seeking out and training the best young athletes.

The demand for colleges and universities to turn out highly trained athletes has greatly stimulated sports research. Coaches have been impelled to take a more scientific approach to their trade, and so they have called upon their research-oriented colleagues to supply them with the data and theories needed to develop more advanced coaching and training techniques. Another significant impetus is the ongoing "sports participation boom" that began in the late 1960s. A great many Americans—urged to "get into themselves" and to "discover their own bodies"—have become involved with physical fitness. In a parallel development, the women's liberation movement has encouraged women to take part in athletics. The growth of women's sports was also accelerated by a law, enacted in 1972, which had the effect of banning sex discrimination in college athletics. Public demand for more information about new performance techniques and exercise regimes, accompanied by a willingness to spend money on scientifically designed running shoes, tennis rackets, exercise equipment, or health-promoting foods and diets, has served to bring even more support to sports research.

In this book, I'm going to be chiefly concerned with the physical sciences and to a lesser extent the biological sciences as they relate to various aspects of sports. However, I feel that I should mention the fact that many social scientists also take a scholarly interest in the subject. Indeed, many interesting issues pertaining to the nature of sports and its role in society have been raised and explored by sociologists and psychologists. I don't propose to discuss these areas, as they are outside the intended scope of this book—but I do recommend that interested readers explore on their own the growing literature on these topics.

Sports research is organized into a number of wide areas of activity, with considerable overlap among them. One of these is *exercise physiology*, which studies the response of the human body to various levels of exercise and stress. Among the topics of particular interest are the effects of exercise on the cardiovascular system (i.e., the heart and blood vessels) and the respiratory system; the energy balance of the body during exercise; and the physiological consequences of various training regimes. A closely related field is *sports medicine*, which is concerned with the diagnosis, treatment, and prevention of sports-related injuries and illnesses.

Another broad area of study is *kinesiology*, which is defined as "the scientific study of human movement." Included under this umbrella is the analysis of *motor skills* and *motor learning*—the complicated neuromuscular processes through which our bodies acquire, develop, and maintain the coordination of the precise voluntary and reflexive movements required for athletic activity. Presently, the main thrust of research in kinesiology is in the field of *biomechanics*. Here the human body is viewed as a machine, a mechanical system, subject to the restrictions of the laws of physics. The body is broken down (figuratively speaking, of course) into a collection of body segments (forearm, foot, thigh, etc.) connected to one another and pivoting at the joints, and moved by muscular and/or externally applied forces. Very often, sports equipment—tennis rackets, golf clubs, etc.—is included in the analysis as part of the biomechanical system. The idea is to study the human body in action as it goes through some particular movement—swinging a golf club or throwing a javelin, for instance—in order to isolate the various individual motions that make up the activity, to measure the speeds of body segments and the forces that act on them, and in general to acquire accurate data on all aspects of the movement. The analysis can become quite complex—the golf swing, for example, involves nearly a hundred different forces acting on thirteen body segments—so sophisticated research equipment is a virtual necessity. Force gauges, bioelectrical sensors to measure muscle activity, frame-by-frame examination of high-speed moving pictures or video tapes, and computer analysis are all part of the repertoire of biomechanics research. Biomechanics had its beginnings in the late 1930s, but it has really blossomed in the past ten to fifteen years, a development that can be traced directly to the spectacular improvement in the speed, capacity, and availability of high-speed computers during the same period of time.

The *physics of sports* deals with the application of physical principles to diverse aspects of sports and athletic activity. Most of the underlying theory derives from *mechanics,* an area of physics that deals with forces and their effects on the motions of objects, living or inanimate. (The basic principles of mechanics are embodied in Newton's laws of motion.) Among the topics that have been analyzed by physicists are the flight paths of sports projectiles (baseballs, golf balls, the discus, etc.), the optimum design of a running track, and the forces developed in a karate blow. There is some overlap between the physics of sports and biomechanics (strictly speaking, biomechanics ought to be considered as an offshoot of the physics of sports), but the scientists that do research in biomechanics generally consider themselves as kinesiologists or physiologists rather than physicists. In fact, most of the research in the physics of sports has been done by physicists and mathematicians (many of them amateur athletes) as a diversion from their own specialties and major research interests. The majority of the articles in this field have been published in the *American Journal of Physics,* a respected journal devoted, not to the publication of major research findings, but rather to the "instructional and cultural aspects of physical science." Many of these articles contain interesting and useful discoveries and insights pertaining to sports, and I'll be discussing several of them later on.

While some sports research is motivated mainly by curiosity or the challenge of solving an interesting problem, much of it is done with a very practical goal in mind. We can group the major aims and accomplishments of sports research into four main areas:

1. *Improvement of health and physical fitness:* Research in exercise physiology yields data on the bodily changes brought about by exercise. This information can be used to design a regime of diet, exercise, and training to fit the specific needs and physical limitations of an individual—for the improvement of cardiovascular response, strength, stamina, flexibility of joints, and so on. Some of these findings have been especially useful in the rehabilitation of heart attack victims, for instance. Other research has been instrumental in testing the merits of various unscientific coaching theories, fad diets, and training programs.

2. Injury prevention: Biomechanical analysis of the stresses that result from different types of athletic movements, impacts, or equipment can reveal the basic causes of athletic injuries. This information can then be used to devise methods of protection and techniques to avoid these injuries. For example, a study of football-related injuries has led to the adoption of rules prohibiting specific tackling and blocking techniques that have been found to cause the most disabling injuries.

3. Equipment design: Sports research has been instrumental in the analysis, design, and engineering of all sorts of sports equipment —running shoes, skis, golf clubs, tennis rackets, ad infinitum. The popular new exercise machines (the Universal Gym and Nautilus) have been scientifically designed to improve the efficiency and effectiveness of weight-training and body-building programs. Biomechanics-based equipment research has also proven valuable outside of sports in the design of work environments and tools in industry, equipment for therapy and rehabilitation, and the development of artificial limbs.

4. Improvement of athletic performance: In the past twenty years we have witnessed a remarkable improvement in the performances of topflight athletes in virtually every sport. Track and field records have advanced at a surprising rate. The top athletes are bigger, faster, and stronger than their predecessors were. I am convinced that these changes can be attributed primarily to the fruits of sports research. One reason, as I've already mentioned, is the improvement in physical fitness brought about by a more scientific approach to exercise and physical training. Another is the advancement of coaching techniques in accordance with the results of physiological and biomechanical research.

In the past, athletes learned how to perform some particular activity or movement mainly through trial and error. They selected a particular technique because it worked best, or felt right, or was the one that the coach preferred to teach. Nowadays, intelligent coaches and athletes can make use of scientific findings to improve their methods of teaching and performing. Biomechanical analysis can pinpoint the most effective way to perform a given activity and can help to distinguish between effective and ineffective movements, productive and unproductive effort.

Some athletes are recognized by coaches and fans as being especially graceful. They seem to glide through their motions in the most economical and effortless way. Sports research points to the fact that the most efficient way to perform any movement, in terms of energy expended, is to eliminate all unproductive muscular effort—that is, to use only those muscles that are necessary for the movement and to relax the unneeded muscles. A graceful athlete is an efficient athlete.

Very often, one hears about an athlete who has gone into a sudden slump because he has lost his "rhythm." A smoothly performed motion—pitching a baseball or shooting a jump shot—suddenly feels and looks jerky and uncoordinated. In the past, an athlete might attempt trial-and-error adjustments, or simply ride out the slump until his rhythm returned, as mysteriously as it had disappeared. But today a more scientific approach is possible. Most athletic skills involve a sequence of several distinct movements; biomechanical principles can be employed to analyze the individual movements and determine the most effective timing of the sequence—the one that leads to the greatest force or highest speed, as the case may be. This information can be used to help an athlete find the proper rhythm for his performance, or to locate the "hitch" in the sequence that has caused him to lose his rhythm.

Biomechanical analysis is the wave of the future in professional and world-class amateur sports. An individual athlete is videotaped in performance; his movements are broken down and mathematically analyzed by computer; the results are compared with a predetermined computer simulation based in part on measurements of the athlete's physical characteristics; flaws in the athlete's technique, ways in which he can improve his effectiveness, can then be identified. A step in this direction has already been taken by one of the leading researchers in the field, Gideon Ariel, who has formed his own company (Computerized Biomechanical Analysis, Inc.) and established a research center in California. He works on a consulting basis with individual athletes, and has already had success with several Olympic-level shot-putters and discus-throwers. Until recently, the emphasis has been mainly on track and field events, but now the methods are being extended to tennis and golf. Football, basketball, and baseball—the last a sport where biomechanical analysis ought to be especially effective—cannot be too far behind.

There is a basic philosophical principle that permeates all the work that has been done in such fields as exercise physiology and biomechanics: *behind every successful technique is a fundamental scientific concept or natural law*. I stress this point because it forms the basis of what I hope to accomplish with this book—namely, to give the reader an understanding and appreciation of the scientific principles underlying all aspects of sports. My goal is to demonstrate to all those who are interested in sports how they can improve their performance as athletes or enhance their enjoyment as spectators—how they may watch or play with a new eye, with a new sensitivity to the subtleties of sports. I am writing for coaches, topflight athletes, weekend athletes, infrequent athletes, armchair quarterbacks, TV sports watchers, Little League parents—in fact, any intelligent, curious individual with an interest in sports who isn't afraid or unwilling to think scientifically about the subject.

There's no doubt that understanding the principles that support accepted performance techniques and being aware of the latest pronouncements of sports researchers can be of significant practical value to any athlete—up to a point. In the first few years of their existence, the New York Mets had a pitcher named Jay Hook, who had earned a degree in mechanical engineering and who understood and could explain in terms of aerodynamic principles exactly why a curve ball curves. It's difficult to say just how much Jay Hook was aided by this knowledge, considering that his career record as a major league pitcher was 29 wins and 62 losses. (He's now a vice president in charge of acquisitions for a large conglomerate.) Knowledge can go just so far; it's not a substitute for ability, and that's why we'll never see Cal Tech playing MIT in the Rose Bowl. Nevertheless, I'm convinced that knowledge of basic principles can give an informed and intelligent athlete an edge; it can guide him to recognize his own weaknesses and limitations and to make the best of his abilities. Moreover, anyone who understands and can explain the reasons behind the techniques is better qualified to pass his knowledge along to others. This applies not only to coaching but also to sports announcing as well. After years of having to put up with the traditional banal platitudes and bombastic nonsense, I find it a distinct pleasure to listen to the new breed of sports announcer—knowledgeable, articulate former coaches and athletes who feel an obligation to go beyond the statistics and personalities and educate their audience in the subtleties of performance.

This book is as much about science as it is about sports. A lot of people react negatively to the idea of learning about science; as a physics teacher I'm constantly confronted by students who are convinced that the subject is too abstract and beyond their comprehension. So there is a hidden agenda to this book, which is to demonstrate that scientific principles can be interesting in themselves and can be understood and used by the nonscientist. If there is one quality that characterizes every scientist, it's *curiosity*—the desire to know why things happen, to understand how the universe works. The nonscientific thinker, on the other hand, is more willing to accept things as they are, to move through life without asking questions. Yet curiosity is undoubtedly an innate human characteristic—and in this sense, there is a scientist lurking within everyone. By showing the advantages and pleasures of understanding the scientific principles behind sports, I hope that I'll be able to stimulate people to take a more positive attitude toward science.

Accordingly, my goal is to demonstrate to the general reader the value of a scientific approach to sports. This is not a book for specialists, and it is not intended to be an exhaustive compilation of the most recent advances in sports research. (I have, however, provided a bibliography of original sources and reference texts for any reader who might want a more detailed or technical discussion of some particular topic.) This is not an encyclopedic sport-by-sport survey, either. Instead, I will introduce the significant scientific principles— the law of gravity or the concept of energy, for example—and explain them in what I hope will be a comprehensible and nontechnical manner. I'll illustrate each principle with numerous examples from a variety of sports, and demonstrate ways in which the principle underlies different features of sports performance, as well as the role that it plays in sports research.

Mathematics is an essential part of any science and the ability to reason mathematically, to be able to solve problems by setting them up into equation form, is a skill that must be diligently learned and nurtured throughout life by constant practice. Unfortunately, most people who came through high school or college courses in algebra or trigonometry or calculus with flying colors have not found much use for these skills in their professions or in everyday life, and so their facilities for mathematical thinking may have gone to seed. In recognition of this situation, I have tried to keep the discussion as nonmathematical as possible. To satisfy those readers who are more at home with mathematics, I've set aside more quantitative treatments in "Math Boxes" throughout the book. They can be read and consulted independently of the main text, in accordance with the individual reader's predilections. However, there are some concepts in physics that can be stated or explained intelligibly only in mathematical terms, and these are, of necessity, treated as such in the body of the text. For those of you who feel anxiety at the very sight of any equation, my advice is not to panic. Try to keep in mind that an equation is really a shorthand version of a grammatical sentence; I've tried to treat them as such in the ensuing discussions. Also, with a little determination you ought to be able to follow the few simple algebraic manipulations that appear in the text.

Finally, a word about sexism and sexist language: it is my sincere belief that women should be encouraged to participate in athletics at all levels to the limits of their individual abilities. Accordingly, this book is written for and about both male and female athletes. My problem is entirely a technical one—the thorny issue of pronouns. I find the constant repetition of "he or she," "his or her," etc., to be tedious and clumsy. The alternating use of male and female forms on successive occasions or invented hybridizations such as "s/he" or "hes" are confusing and artificial. So I've decided to stick with history, tradition, and accepted grammatical practice by using the male forms exclusively. Therefore, please be advised that the words "he," "his," and "him," when used in a general sense, shall represent "he or she," "his or her," and "him or her," respectively.

1 / MAN IN MOTION

In Lewis Carroll's *Through the Looking-Glass*, the famous nursery rhyme character Humpty Dumpty appears, characterized as a rather cantankerous and pedantic philosopher. In his meeting with Alice, he comments on an important linguistic principle: "When I use a word," he says, "it means just what I choose it to mean—neither more nor less."

Most scientists would agree wholeheartedly with Humpty Dumpty's sentiments. Ambiguity is an important, perhaps essential, tool of the artist—but to the scientist, it represents the antithesis of proper scientific methodology. In the language of science, words have precisely defined and narrow meanings. This is a major reason why scientific writing may seem so cut-and-dried, technical, and difficult for the unscientifically trained reader. But it is a necessary evil of the profession, for without precise definitions, the communication of scientific information would be next to impossible. In this book we will come across a number of scientific terms—energy, work, acceleration, to name a few—that have become part of our everyday language. But in the process, the meanings of these words have broadened, taking on shadings that are not present in their scientific definitions. To utilize scientific terminology in the analysis of sports, we'll have to carefully define the precise meanings of such words—so that when we use them, they will mean neither more nor less than what scientists have chosen them to mean. Accordingly, I'm going to devote the first part of this chapter to defining and explaining the basic terminology used to measure motion, which is a fundamental element of sports. Then I'll illustrate the use of these terms in a scientific analysis of running times, an analysis that spotlights the differences between sprinting and longer-distance running and gives some insights into track performance and strategy.

Definitions are essential to scientific communication, and so is precision in measurement—you've got to be able to state exactly what it is you've measured and how you've measured it. Anyone who has tried to reproduce mom's apple pie from a recipe that includes such items as "a pinch of salt" or "a dash of cinnamon" knows that without exact definitions of the units of measurement, the results are not quite the same every time. Measurement plays a central role in science—and in sports also. Particularly in events where athletes are competing not only against other athletes but also against existing records, the accurate measurement of times and distances is a major concern.

Thinking Metric

Back in ancient times, every major civilization developed its own system of weights and measures. For example, the eastern Mediterranean peoples used the *cubit* to measure distances. In the *Book of Genesis* we learn that Noah's ark was 300 cubits long, 50 cubits wide, and 30 cubits high. Obviously, this means little to anyone who does not know how long a cubit is. (A cubit turns out to be about 20 inches long, so that Noah's ark, if built according to specifications, would have been about the size of a small cruise ship.)

But the accurate communication of scientific information requires agreed-upon standards of measurement. Surely, the multiplicity of systems of weights and measures that developed throughout history could not have been conducive to international relations. Imagine, for instance, the confusion that was caused by the fact that the French foot (12.8 inches long) was different from the English foot (12 inches). The turning point was the French Revolution. In the 1790s, the revolutionary government, in its zeal to wipe out all traces of the old order, imposed a new calendar and a whole new system of weights and measures. They even introduced decimal time—the day was to be divided into 10 hours, the hour into 100 minutes, and the minute into

100 seconds. Decimal time never caught on (though it does seem eminently reasonable); the revolutionary calendar (whose most interesting feature was a 10-day week) lasted for 13 years, until Napoleon reinstituted the church calendar as a part of an effort to win the support of the clergy for his empire. But the system of weights and measures, which differed little from the modern metric system, survived. Since then, one country after another has adopted the metric system. As of 1983, the only nations that have not gone metric officially are Burma, Brunei, Yemen, and the United States of America.

Why has the metric system been so successful? To appreciate its advantages, let's take a look at our own system of units, which is known as the U.S. Customary System. When I present this topic in my science classes, I usually open with the following dialogue:

Me: What is a foot?
Class: Twelve inches.
Me: Okay, now what is an inch?
Class: (After a pause) One twelfth of a foot!

This response is always followed by embarrassed laughter (it's amazing how predictable students are) as the class realizes the circularity of their answers. Then comes—

Me: But why are there twelve inches in a foot?
Class: (Silence. No one has an answer.)

Occasionally, one of the brighter students will respond, "Because that's the way it was defined." Fair enough, but why twelve inches? Why not ten, or fifty? And why was the mile established as 5280 feet, rather than some nice, round, easily remembered number?

The answer is that the major distance units of the customary system —the inch, foot, yard, and mile—were not defined in any unified way. The mile originated with the Romans as a distance equivalent to one thousand paces taken by a marching Roman legion (the word "mile" comes from *mille,* the Latin root for "thousand"). The yard was defined in the twelfth century as the distance from the tip of the nose to the end of the outstretched arm of King Henry I of England (try this measurement on yourself to see how big King Henry was). The foot was based, of course, on the size of the human foot, and has had a variety of lengths depending on the human used as the standard. The inch was established in the 1300s by King Edward II as the length of "three barleycorns laid end to end." When all of these different units were finally compared and standardized, it turned out that there were 12 inches in a foot (English), 3 feet in a yard, and 5280 feet in a mile. (There are also 16½ feet in a rod, 40 rods to a furlong, 8 furlongs to a mile, two kinds of mile—statute and nautical—plus a host of other even more obscure units for weight, volume, etc.)

Further subdivisions of these units lead to even more confusion. The inch is divided into halves, quarters, eighths, sixteenths—making measurement unnecessarily complicated and turning simple jobs like centering a picture on a wall into computational nightmares. (Where is the midpoint of a wall 17⅜ inches wide? If a recipe for eight calls for 1½ pints of milk, how many ounces are needed when making dinner for three people?)

The metric system, by comparison, is an oasis of rationality. Units are always subdivided decimally—into tenths, hundredths, etc.—rather than into fractions. In fact, all the units of measure are related by multiples of 10. For example, the basic unit of length is the *meter* (originally defined by the French as one ten-millionth of the distance from the equator to either pole). Longer distances can be measured in *kilometers* (the prefix "kilo" always means a thousand, so 1 kilometer = 1000 meters). Smaller lengths are usually measured in *centimeters* (1 centimeter = 1/100 meter) or *millimeters* (1/1000 meter). These same prefixes are used for all measures (e.g., 1 kilogram = 1000 grams; 1 milligram = 0.001 gram). The ridiculous set of units we use for measuring volumes—i.e., gallons, quarts, pints, cups, ounces, gills, ad infinitum—is replaced by one unit, the *liter,* and its various decimal multiples and subdivisions. Computations are relatively easy to do with these simple decimal relationships; it is obviously much easier to figure out how many centimeters there are in a kilometer than it is to calculate the number of inches in a mile. Furthermore, the simplicity of the metric system makes it easy to teach and easy to learn.

The natural superiority of the metric system is one of those rare matters on which virtually all the nations of the world, even the bitterest of enemies, are in agreement. It is all the more puzzling to them why a technologically advanced nation like the United States would resist metrication. Yet we are—at least officially—committed to a changeover. In 1975, Congress passed the Metric Conversion Act, which promulgated conversion on a voluntary basis. This legislation was lobbied against rather vigorously by the labor unions, who cited the cost and effort of retooling and retraining workers, and by small businessmen, who feared a flood of foreign imports once the United States had gone metric. However, it was supported very strongly by the large multinational corporations because metrication will improve their positions in the world markets.

Since then, metrication has proceeded with the speed of a glacier. The American public has been apathetic, if not hostile, to the idea. The U.S. Weather Bureau has attempted to get people accustomed to the Celsius temperature scale by giving its readings in both Celsius and Fahrenheit, but most people simply tune out the Celsius reading. The next phase of their plan had been to do away with the Fahrenheit reading, but this was never implemented. The Federal Highway Administration had planned to have all distances on road signs exclusively in kilometers by 1980—but abandoned the effort because of the strong protest against it.

Part of the opposition to metrication on the part of the general public may stem from the fact that the average person really sees no need to learn or use metrics. This attitude often changes if one travels to a foreign country. Many Americans who travel to Canada—which seems at first glance to be indistinguishable from the United States—are shocked to find that the country is almost entirely metric. Then they have to deal somehow with road distances in kilometers, posted speed limits in km/hr, and gasoline sold by the liter. Moreover, most Americans do not realize the extent to which they already use metric units. All of the standard electrical units—volts, amps, watts—are metric. Most prescription and over-the-counter drugs are measured in milligrams. Wines and soft drinks are now being sold in liter-unit containers. Also, a not unsubstantial portion of the populace has for many years been buying and selling substances such as cocaine and marijuana by the kilo. But for the measurements we encounter most frequently in everyday life—distances and sizes, weights, temperature—the vast majority of Americans still use customary units.

Taking a realistic view of the present state of affairs, I've decided to use customary units primarily in this book, citing metric equivalents wherever it seems appropriate. As a scientist, I'm strongly committed to metrication, but I suspect that most of my readers will be much more familiar with customary units, particularly in reference to sports. How many sports fans know Julius Erving's height in centimeters, or the speed of a major league fast ball in kilometers per hour?

Perhaps I should be using this opportunity to encourage people to think metric, but my main goal is to present the scientific concepts underlying sports performance, and it certainly won't help any reader to grasp these concepts if he has to deal with an unfamiliar system of units at the same time.

The progress of metrication in American sports has pretty much paralleled the general trend. Those areas of sports that are heavily involved in international competition, particularly the Olympic events, are well on their way to metrication, if not already there. American athletes in track and field, swimming and diving, skating, weight lifting, etc., are at a distinct disadvantage if they train for nonmetric distances or use nonmetric equipment. In the past, American athletes raced at distances that were measured in miles or yards —the 100-yard dash, the 220, the 440 (quarter-mile), the 880 (half-mile), and so on. But these traditional races have been abandoned in favor of the standard metric races—100 meters, 200 meters, 400 meters, etc. The reason for this change was the decision made by the International Amateur Athletic Federation in 1976 not to certify world records for races measured in customary units—with the sole exception of the one-mile run, which was retained for its historical value. The marathon, whose distance is set at 26 miles, 385 yards, also remains, but official records are not kept for this race.

All records in field events are now being listed metrically, so the 19-foot pole vault, the 75-foot shot put, the 29-foot broad jump will be relegated to history, replaced by their metric equivalents. Thus American track and field fans must become accustomed to the new metric distances and records. With time, they'll develop the facility to think metric—but for the present, many will prefer to convert metric values to customary units for comparison. Since this is a good opportunity to show how metric and customary units are related, let's look at some useful distance conversion factors.

Metric and customary units are related by the official National Bureau of Standards definition that 1 inch = 2.54 centimeters. (Yes, the United States legally defines the inch in terms of its metric equivalent.) From this we can get the following conversions (rounded to three decimal places):

$$1 \text{ foot} = 0.305 \text{ meter}$$
$$1 \text{ yard} = 0.914 \text{ meter}$$
$$1 \text{ mile} = 1.609 \text{ kilometers}$$

To convert from metric to customary units, use the following:

$$1 \text{ meter} = 39.37 \text{ inches}$$
$$= 3.281 \text{ feet}$$
$$= 1.094 \text{ yards}$$
$$1 \text{ kilometer} = 0.621 \text{ mile}$$

You don't have to be a math wizard to make use of these factors; a little common-sense reasoning (plus a pocket calculator) should do it. For example, it's easy to figure out that 100 yards is equal to (100 x 1 yard = 100×0.914 meter) = 91.4 meters. Thus we discover that the 100-yard dash is slightly shorter than its "metric equivalent," the 100-meter dash. The 1500-meter run is considered to be the "metric mile"; actually, since 1 mile = 1.609 km = 1609 meters, the 1-mile run is about 7% longer than 1500 meters. In 1981, the record for the pole vault surpassed 5.80 meters for the first time. The customary equivalent is 5.80×3.281 ft = 19.03 feet, or 19 ft ½ in.

How is the metrication of the United States going to affect sports? Eventually, distances on golf courses will be given in meters rather than in yards. Already, there are a few baseball stadiums that have distances from home plate posted in both feet and meters (American baseball fans probably ignore the meters, while the Canadian fans ignore the feet). I doubt seriously that critical and traditional dimensions like the 90-foot distances on a baseball diamond or the 10-foot height of the basketball rim will ever be changed. American football is deeply involved with the yard as a unit of distance, but it could be converted to the meter without changing the game too drastically (a 100-meter field, with 10 meters needed for a first down, might help the defense and cut down on scoring). The day may come when sports fans will speak knowledgeably about a 200-cm forward with a deadly 5-meter jump shot, or a tremendous 140-meter home run over the centerfield fence. But I suspect that most people will continue to "think customary" about many aspects of sports long after metrication comes about.

Measuring Speed

Measurements play a significant role in sports for two reasons. The first is *the need for standardization*—to make sure that all playing areas and equipment conform to the rules of the sport. The second reason is *to measure performance*. Athletes and sports fans need and want objective standards of performance in every activity. These enable athletes to set goals for themselves and to measure their accomplishments against those of other competitors. This information also provides fans with the fuel for endless analyses and debates about the abilities and relative merits of various athletes and teams, past and present. These measures of performance—the multitude of records for nearly every aspect of every sport—are at the very core of big-time sports, and they contribute much of the endless fascination and pleasure of being a sports fan.

Most of these measures of performance are merely statistical compilations—batting averages, shooting percentages, pass receptions in a season, total career home runs by a left-handed second baseman—the list is endless. Such records do not involve any real physical measurements. But in many sports, performance is judged through direct measurements of distances and times: the length of a javelin throw, the yards gained on a kickoff return, the time for a 100-meter dash. Here the traditional measuring devices are the tape measure and the stopwatch—although in recent years, sports officials and scientists have combined forces to produce more accurate measuring instruments such as electronic timers and laser ranging devices for precise distance measurement.

Speed is an important measure of performance in many sports. Although speed records are not reported in most sports—auto and speedboat races being the main exceptions—fans still find it interesting to know such things as the speed of a fast ball or a tennis serve. Football coaches in particular consider the running speed of a prospective player to be a significant indicator of his chances for success. Often a player will be described as being "quick" or having "good acceleration." Are these terms meant to be synonymous with speed? Some pitching coaches as well as announcers like to talk about the "velocity" of a pitch. Is this term also synonymous with speed, or does it have a different connotation? Here is a perfect example of the confusion that arises when the precise meanings of words are not made clear. So let us heed the words of Humpty Dumpty and learn the scientific definitions of the terms used to describe motion. The key words are *speed, velocity*, and *acceleration*—each of which has a separate and distinct meaning.

Speed is a direct measure of the *rate of covering distance* or *rate of motion* of a moving object. However, most objects, particularly in sports, do not always move at a constant rate. Therefore scientists have two measures of speed: the *average speed* and the *instantaneous speed*. The average speed is defined as follows:

$$\text{average speed} = \frac{\text{total distance covered}}{\text{time interval}}$$

Average speed can be calculated rather easily. (See Math Box 1, page 34, if you are not familiar with the rules for units of measurement.) If a racing car covers 600 miles in 4 hours, then its average speed is simply

$$\frac{\text{total distance covered}}{\text{time interval}} = \frac{600 \text{ miles}}{4 \text{ hours}} = 150 \text{ miles/hour}$$

Football players are traditionally tested on their speed over 40 yards (= 120 ft). A player who runs this distance in 4.6 seconds has an average speed of

$$\frac{\text{total distance covered}}{\text{time interval}} = \frac{120 \text{ feet}}{4.6 \text{ sec}} = 26.1 \text{ ft/sec} \ (= 17.8 \text{ mi/hr})$$

It is common practice, however, to report the player's time, rather than his speed. For example, the player in the preceding example would be described as "having 4.6 speed." A baseball player who has "3.6 speed down to first base" is considered to be exceptionally fast (assuming a running distance of 90 feet, this corresponds to an average speed of 17 mi/hr).

The average speed is not always a useful quantity by virtue of the fact that it is an average taken over the whole distance, and does not indicate the different speeds or changes in speed that may have taken place. This is where the *instantaneous speed* comes into play: as the name implies, this is *the speed of an object at a given instant of time*.

We can illustrate the difference between the two by turning to the proverbial race between the tortoise and the hare. The hare sprinted out to a huge early lead, then stopped to take a rest, fell asleep, and was passed and beaten by the slow but steady tortoise. When both of them were running, the hare had by far the larger instantaneous speed, but the tortoise had the greater *average* speed, since he covered the distance in a shorter overall time.

By its very definition, instantaneous speed is an abstraction—what do we mean by an instant of time? We may think of it as a "frozen moment of time," but time cannot be frozen except in our minds.

MATH BOX 1: UNITS OF MEASUREMENT

The units in which quantities are measured in science follow a specific system of rules. There are a small number of primary quantities (such as distance, time, mass, and temperature) whose units are defined according to very precise standards. All other quantities are derived quantities; that is, they are defined in terms of the primaries. A simple example of a derived quantity is speed, which is defined as distance/time. Consequently, speed is always measured in terms of a unit of distance divided by a unit of time. Any combination is legitimate—miles/hour (read as miles per hour and usually abbreviated as mi/hr or mph); kilometers/second (km/sec); millimeters/day (the speed of a microbe?); furlongs/century—whatever is useful and convenient.

Users of the customary system are most familiar with mi/hr as a speed unit, although feet/second (ft/sec, or fps) is actually more convenient for many calculations. Since 1 mile = 5280 feet and 1 hour = 60 × 60 = 3600 seconds, then

$$1 \frac{mi}{hr} = \frac{5280 \ ft}{3600 \ sec} = \frac{22}{15} \frac{ft}{sec} = 1.47 \ ft/sec$$

To convert a speed in mi/hr to its equivalent in ft/sec, multiply it by 22/15; to convert ft/sec to mi/hr, multiply the speed in ft/sec by 15/22.

In the metric system, speeds are usually measured in meters/second (m/sec) or kilometers/hour (km/hr). The following conversion factors may be used:

$$1 \ km/hr = 0.62 \ mi/hr$$
$$= 0.28 \ m/sec$$
$$1 \ m/sec = 3.28 \ ft/sec$$
$$= 2.24 \ mi/hr$$

A conversion chart graphically relating meters/second, miles/hour, and feet/second is reproduced in Appendix A.

Mathematically, an instant is an infinitesimally short interval of time —as short as you want to make it, but not zero. Yet even in so short an interval, the speed of an object may change. Therefore the instantaneous speed is, in effect, the average speed measured over an infinitesimally small time interval. If it turns out that an object is moving with a constant speed, then its instantaneous speed is the same at every moment, and its average speed is equal to its instantaneous speed.

There are instruments that can be used to get a good estimate of the instantaneous speed of a moving object. One very familiar device is the car speedometer, which operates by a gear system driven by the rotation of the car's wheels as it moves. Another of more recent vintage is the radar gun. A close relative of the radar units used by police to catch speeders, this device works on the basis of a physical principle known as the *Doppler effect*. A radar gun is a radio transmitter/receiver that sends out a beam of radio waves of a specific frequency. The waves reflect off the target, and the echo is picked up by the gun. According to the Doppler effect, the reflected waves should have a different frequency from the transmitted waves—higher if the object is approaching and lower if the object is receding. The faster the object is moving, the greater the change in frequency of the radio waves as they bounce off the object. The radar gun measures the difference in frequency between the transmitted and reflected waves, and electronically converts this difference to a speed, which it then displays. A radar gun is easy to use and is becoming increasingly popular with baseball coaches, scouts, and announcing crews who use it to measure the speed of pitched balls. In the past, players and fans debated endlessly who was the fastest pitcher; now these arguments can be settled scientifically. To date, only two pitchers have thrown balls with a measured speed greater than 100 mi/hr—Nolan Ryan (who holds the record of 100.9 mi/hr) and J. R. Richard.

Measuring Rotation

The definition of speed just presented applies to objects that are moving on a line (straight or curved) from one point to another. This type of motion is called *linear motion* (also referred to by physicists and mathematicians as *translational motion*). There are two classes of linear motion—*rectilinear,* or straight-line motion, and *curvilinear* motion, which is motion on a curved path.

Spinning objects—a bicycle wheel, a basketball balanced on a fingertip, the earth itself—exhibit a different kind of motion known as *rotation*. When an object is rotating (or revolving, or spinning—the words are all synonymous), every point of the object is traveling on a circular path about a common line, or axis—for example, in the course of one day every point on the earth's surface completes a circle about the earth's north-south axis. How, then, does rotation differ from curvilinear motion? The distinction is as follows: every point of a rotating object has curvilinear motion—all the points individually traveling on curved (circular) paths—but the object *as a whole* has rotational motion.

An object can, of course, possess both linear and rotational motion. The earth moves in its yearly orbit around the sun while it spins on its axis; a bicycle wheel spins and moves forward at the same time; a ball can spin in flight. One of the recurring topics of this book is how the combination of spin and linear motion strongly influences the strategies and course of play in virtually every sport in which a ball is used. Consider, for example, the importance of topspin in tennis, the rotation of a pitched ball in baseball, or the tumbling, end-over-end rotation of a kicked football. These and other effects of spin, and the physical principles that govern these effects, will be examined in detail in later chapters.

The rate of motion of a spinning object is described and measured differently from linear motion: whereas linear motion is measured in terms of distance, rotational motion is measured in terms of angles. As you doubtlessly remember from high school geometry, angles are measured in degrees, based on the division of a circle into 360°. Thus one full rotation corresponds to motion through an angle of 360°, a half-rotation is 180°, a quarter-rotation is 90°, and so on. Because it is measured in terms of angles, rotational motion is also referred to as *angular motion*. (There is another unit for measuring angles known as the *radian,* which is very useful for trigonometric computations—see Math Box 2, page 38.)

The measurement of rotation in degrees appears only occasionally in sports terminology. One example is a spectacular move in basketball known as a "360": a player driving to the basket leaps into the air, spins his body a full turn (360°), and releases his shot—preferably with a resounding slam dunk—before landing. Particularly in the acrobatically oriented sports, maneuvers are more commonly described in terms of the number of rotations the athlete makes—for example, there's the springboard diver's forward 1½ somersault, or the figure skater's triple axel (three spins in midair).

Note that in these examples it's only the *number* of rotations, rather than the rotation *rate*, that we're referring to; the time required to make the maneuver is not being considered. The rate of rotation is defined as the *angular speed,* and just as the linear speed is the distance covered in a unit of time, the *angular speed is the angle tra-*

versed in a unit of time. For example, the earth makes one 360°
rotation in 24 hours—hence its angular speed is 360°/24 hours = 15°/
hr. Angular speed is measured in units of angle divided by time—i.e.,
degrees/hr, degrees/sec, radians/sec, etc. A more familiar measure of
the rotation rate is the number of revolutions (full 360° turns) made in
a given time interval. In these terms, the rotation rate is measured in
units of revolutions per minute (rev/min or rpm) or revolutions per
second (rev/sec). Physicists call this measure of rotation rate the *angular frequency* or *rotation frequency* to distinguish it from the angular speed.

A record player is an illustration of the everyday use of the rotation
rate concept. Everyone knows that stereo records come in two forms
—33⅓ and 45 (some of you may even be old enough to remember the
78). These numbers refer to the proper rotation frequency, in rpm, for
playing the record; that is, a 33⅓ is designed to be played on a turntable that is making 33⅓ revolutions per minute. Another example is
a *tachometer,* an instrument found on the dashboards of racing cars,
airplanes, and power boats which gives the rotation rate of the engine
crankshaft in rpm (the dial is usually labeled as "engine rpm"). The
rotation frequency of the engine is considered to be a more accurate
measure of engine output than the linear speed of the vehicle in miles
per hour, since the latter is affected by such items as friction and air
resistance.

All parts of a rotating object have the same angular speed: every
point moves through the same angle, and makes the same number of
revolutions, in the same period of time. A 33⅓ record, for instance,
makes 33⅓ revolutions in 60 seconds, so the time for one revolution
is then 60 sec/33⅓ revolutions = 1.8 seconds per revolution. Thus
every point on the record makes a full revolution of 360° in 1.8 seconds. During this time interval, every point travels on a circle around
the center of the record—but some points travel in bigger circles than
others do; a point at the outer edge covers a greater distance in one
revolution than another point closer to the center. It follows that the
point on the edge has a greater *linear* speed than the one nearer the
center, even though they have the same *angular* speed. Therefore on
any rotating object *the farther a point on the object is from the center
of rotation, the faster the point is moving.* In other words, the linear
speed of any point on a rotating object is in direct proportion to its
distance from the axis of rotation (see Math Box 2, page 38, for the
mathematics of this relationship).

Math Box 2: Measurement of Angular Motion

1. Measurement of Angles in Radians

Angles may be measured in *degrees*, with 360° to a circle. Angles may also be measured in *radians*, based on the definition that a circle has 2π radians. (This definition is based on the fact that the circumference of a circle is equal to 2π times the radius of the circle.)

Degrees and radians are related as follows:

$$360° = 2\pi \text{ radians} \quad 1° = \pi/180 = 0.01745 \text{ radians}$$
$$180° = \pi \text{ radians} \quad 1 \text{ radian} = 180/\pi = 57.3°$$
$$90° = \pi/2 \text{ radians}$$

2. Measurement of Rotation Rate

There are two ways to measure the rate of rotation. They are defined as follows:

angular speed, ω (the Greek letter, omega):

$$\omega = \frac{\text{angle traversed}}{\text{time interval}} \quad \textit{Units:} \text{ degrees/sec; radians/sec}$$

angular frequency, $f = \dfrac{\text{no. of revolutions}}{\text{time interval}}$ *Units:* rev/sec; rev/min

When ω is measured in radians, ω and f are related by the following equation:

$$\omega = 2\pi f$$

3. Linear and Angular Speed

Consider a point on a rotating object located a distance R from the axis of rotation: in each rotation, the point traces out a circle of radius R. Since the circumference of any circle is equal to 2π times the radius of the circle, it follows that the point travels a distance $2\pi R$ with each revolution. Since

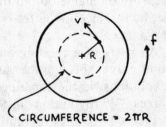

CIRCUMFERENCE $= 2\pi R$

$$\text{speed} = \frac{\text{total distance}}{\text{time interval}}$$

$$= \text{distance per revolution} \times \frac{\text{no. of revolutions}}{\text{time interval}}$$

$$= 2\pi R \times \text{angular frequency}$$

or

$$v = (2\pi R)f$$

The angular speed ω (in radians) is $\omega = 2\pi f$, so

$$v = R\omega$$

This equation relates the linear speed of any point on a rotating object to the angular speed of the object.

This means, for example, that when a golfer swings his club in a large arc toward the ball, the clubhead is moving at a higher speed than the golfer's hands are. In a properly executed tennis serve, the server tries to hit the ball at the top of his swing, with his arm and the racket fully extended in a straight line. This maximizes the distance between the impact point and the axis of rotation (the server's shoulder) and thereby gives the largest possible linear speed to the ball. As another example, consider a baseball and a basketball both spinning with the same rotation rate of 5 rev/sec. Since a basketball is about 3¼ times larger in diameter than a baseball, it follows that the linear speed of any point on the surface of the basketball will be 3¼ times larger than that of any point on the surface of the baseball, even though their angular speeds are the same.

Rotational motion is a rather common and important feature of sports—it appears in gymnastics and diving, pitching and batting, swinging a golf club or tennis racket, and many other activities. The relationship between linear speed and rotation rate proves to be quite useful in the analysis of these actions.

Velocity

Although the words *speed* and *velocity* are used interchangeably in everyday language, they have different scientific meanings. Very simply, the difference is that *velocity is speed in a given direction.* In other words, the velocity of an object is equal to its speed *and* the direction in which it is moving. For example, a car moving northward at 50 mi/hr has a speed of 50 mi/hr, and a velocity of 50 mi/hr north. Another car moving southward at 50 mi/hr has a velocity of 50 mi/hr south; it has the same speed as the first car, but a different velocity. By the same principle, the velocity of a car going on a circular track at 50 mi/hr is clearly quite different from that of a car going at 50 mi/hr on a straight road. In order for two objects to have the same velocity, they must be moving with the same speed and in the same direction. As we will discover later on, there are good reasons why this distinction between speed and velocity has been made.

From the definition of velocity, it follows that to have a constant velocity requires both constant speed *and* constant direction. If *either* the speed *or* the direction (or both) is changing, then the velocity is considered to be changing. To maintain a constant direction an object must move along a straight line. Consider, for example, motion on a circular path: you're going north at one point, east at another, west at another—so your direction is constantly changing. Thus a car driven in a circle at a steady 50 mi/hr has a constant speed, but not a constant velocity, because it's not keeping a fixed direction. In short, constant velocity can be translated as "constant speed on a straight-line path."

A similar distinction is made for angular motion. Angular speed and angular velocity are two distinct entities—namely, *angular velocity is angular speed in a given direction.* Now the labeling of the direction of angular velocity poses a bit of a problem. All rotations are seen as having only two possible directions, either clockwise or counterclockwise. "Seen" is the key word here. The same rotation can appear to be clockwise when viewed from one direction and counterclockwise when seen from another direction. The hands of a clock are moving counterclockwise—if viewed from inside the clock (or behind its face). The earth's rotation is counterclockwise as seen looking down on the north pole and clockwise as seen looking down on the south pole. The spin of a curve ball is clockwise to the pitcher, counterclockwise to the batter and catcher. So in identifying the direction of the rotation, *we must specify the viewpoint*—i.e., "clockwise as seen from above"; "counterclockwise as seen from the right"; etc. It is standard practice to represent the direction of angular velocity pictorially by drawing an arrow along the axis of rotation. By convention, the arrow is drawn pointing away from the observer if the rotation is seen as clockwise, and toward the observer if the rotation is seen as counterclockwise (Fig. 1.1).

Velocity is one example of a special kind of quantity used in mathematics and physics known as a *vector.* This is another word that

COUNTERCLOCKWISE ROTATION

Angular velocity points
toward viewer

CLOCKWISE ROTATION

Angular velocity points
away from viewer

FIGURE 1.1   The direction of angular velocity.

sometimes appears in everyday usage, so let's see what it means. A vector is any *directed quantity*—that is, a quantity that always has a direction associated with it. Any quantity that does not have a direction, and can be represented by a single number, is called a *scalar*. By direction, I mean a *direction in space*—north, west, southeast, up, down. We can think of time as going forward or backward—but its "direction" is not a direction in space, so time is a scalar rather than a vector. Scientists also distinguish *distance,* which is a scalar, from *displacement* (distance in a given direction), which is a vector. The definition of displacement and velocity as vectors is particularly useful in navigation to describe the position, motion, and/or path of a ship or plane. Air-traffic controllers and pilots often speak of "vectoring" a plane to a specific destination.

Vectors follow a special kind of arithmetic which proves to be very useful. For example, suppose that a plane, headed due north at an air speed of 500 mi/hr, encounters a 200 mi/hr crosswind blowing west to east. What will the actual speed and direction of the plane be as a result? The plane's velocity can be found by adding two velocities— 500 mi/hr north and 200 mi/hr east. Any two vectors may be added graphically by representing them as arrows of appropriate length and direction, drawn to scale; the two vectors to be added are then joined to form a triangle (Fig. 1.2).

The line that completes the triangle then represents the sum of the two vectors. By direct measurement on the diagram, or by using basic geometry and trigonometry, it is possible to calculate the new size and direction of the resultant sum vector.

By reversing this process, it becomes possible to break up or *resolve* a single vector into two perpendicular vectors or *components* (Fig. 1.3).

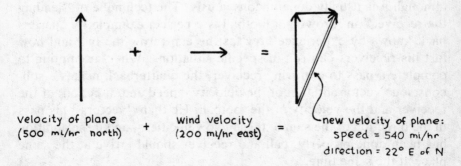

velocity of plane   +   wind velocity   =   new velocity of plane:
(500 mi/hr north)   (200 mi/hr east)   speed = 540 mi/hr
                                                            direction = 22° E of N

FIGURE 1.2   Addition of vectors.

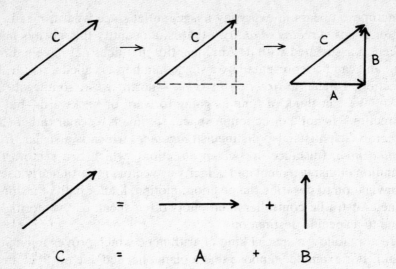

FIGURE 1.3 Resolution of a vector into its components.

Note that the sum of the two components A and B (each of which is a vector in its own right) is equal to the original vector C. This technique is often used to analyze motion in two or three directions. For example, the velocity of a projectile (such as a baseball or a discus in flight) can be broken down into its *horizontal component* (its velocity parallel to the ground) and its *vertical component* (its velocity perpendicular to the ground). The two velocity components can be examined separately, then added back together using the rules for vector arithmetic. We will return to this procedure later on when we look at projectile motion in more detail.

The procedure for the addition of vectors is common in sports, although it is usually done unconsciously. The technique of "leading the receiver" in throwing a football is a perfect example. A quarterback knows by experience how fast he can throw the ball and how fast his receivers can run in specific situations. When attempting to complete a pass to a moving receiver, the quarterback makes a subconscious vector addition of the velocity (speed and direction) of the receiver and the velocity of the football. He then "vectors" his pass in the direction of the sum of these two velocities—and if the addition has been done properly, ball and receiver should arrive at the same place at the same time.

Acceleration

Now we come to the third key word used in the description of motion—*acceleration*. This is a much-used term which denotes an important quality: a car or an athlete with "good acceleration" is always much admired. The scientific definition of acceleration is very straightforward: *acceleration is equal to the rate of change of velocity*. In equation form,

$$\text{acceleration} = \frac{\text{change in velocity}}{\text{time interval}}$$

Thus "good acceleration" is not the same as being fast. Rather, it measures *the ability to change velocity quickly*. For example, a car that goes from zero to 40 mi/hr in 5 seconds has a better acceleration than one that goes from zero to 60 mi/hr in 10 seconds. In other words, a runner may be fast, but not have good acceleration ("he's fast, but not quick"); he may run at a higher speed than most other runners, but he takes a longer time to get up to top speed. (See Math Box 3 for a discussion of the units used to describe acceleration.)

MATH BOX 3: UNITS OF MEASUREMENT, CONTINUED

Since velocity is defined as speed in a given direction, its units will be those of speed plus direction—mi/hr north; ft/sec east; etc.

The units of acceleration are a bit more complicated. Acceleration is defined as "change in velocity over time." Therefore its units will be those of velocity/time or speed/time plus a direction. In turn, speed/time = (distance/time)/time. (We won't concern ourselves with the direction of acceleration here.) Therefore acceleration may be measured in such units as mi/hr/sec (read as miles per hour per second); km/min/sec (kilometers per minute per second); ft/sec/sec (feet per second per second); or any such combination. Note that an acceleration of, say, 10 mi/hr/sec signifies that "the velocity is increasing by 10 mi/hr every second."

The acceleration unit "ft/sec/sec" is very commonly used in customary system calculations. It is often shortened to "ft/sec^2" (read as feet per second squared). Of course, there is no such thing as a squared second; this is just a kind of shorthand used by physicists. An acceleration stated as 10 ft/sec^2 is equivalent to 10 ft/sec/sec, which indicates that the velocity is increasing by 10 ft/sec every second.

Acceleration can be positive or negative, depending on whether the velocity is increasing or decreasing. A negative acceleration, which occurs when the velocity is decreasing, is also known as *deceleration*. Thus the concept of acceleration takes into account the ability to slow down—"good deceleration"—as well as to speed up. Every automobile has an accelerator and a "decelerator"—the brake pedal—to bring about changes in velocity.

Note that acceleration is defined as the rate of change of *velocity,* rather than speed. (Acceleration, incidentally, is a vector quantity—but this is a subtlety that we can safely ignore here.) A change in velocity signifies a change in *either* the speed *or* the direction, or both. A racing car or a sprinter moving on a straight track—and thus in a constant direction—accelerates by changing speed; so in this case good acceleration refers to the ability to get up to top speed in a short interval of time. However, if the motion is on a curved path, acceleration also takes account of the change in direction. For example, a car being driven at a constant speed on a circular track is accelerating because it is changing direction. Legendary football runners like O. J. Simpson or Gale Sayers had the ability to "stop and go"—make sudden changes in speed—and make sharp cuts (changes in direction) enabling them to run through holes or elude tacklers. The same ability is essential to making the fakes and moves needed to be a good one-on-one basketball player. All of these skills fall in the category of "good acceleration."

Acceleration itself may be constant or changing. A *constant* acceleration indicates that *the velocity is changing at a steady rate*. This is the simplest kind of accelerated motion to deal with mathematically; fairly simple equations can be used to calculate velocity and distance (see Math Box 4, page 45, for details). A changing acceleration means that the rate of change of velocity is itself changing. One example of this type of acceleration is the motion of a car that accelerates from a start, but then levels off to a constant velocity. The acceleration is greatest (there is the largest change in velocity) at the beginning of the run; then the acceleration decreases (the rate of increase of velocity gets smaller) until the velocity is no longer changing.

Unaccelerated motion (zero acceleration) is equivalent to constant-velocity motion—motion in a straight line at a constant speed. Thus we can say that there are only two basic kinds of motion—*constant-velocity motion* and *accelerated motion*. When we look into the

MATH BOX 4: THE EQUATIONS OF MOTION

The following equations are used in calculations involving distance, speed, and acceleration.

If an object is moving at a constant speed v (the letter "v" is traditionally used as the symbol for speed and velocity), then its instantaneous speed and average speed are the same. The distance d covered by the object in a time interval t follows from the definition of average speed = distance covered/time interval:

$$v = \frac{d}{t} \quad \text{or } d = vt$$

This equation also applies to constant-velocity motion.

The equations for accelerated motion are more complicated. The simplest situation occurs when the object is moving in a straight line and the speed is changing at a steady rate—that is, the acceleration is constant. We assume that the moving object starts off with a speed v_1, which changes (increases or decreases) to a speed v_2 after a time interval t. Since

$$\text{acceleration} = \frac{\text{change in velocity}}{\text{time interval}}$$

and since the direction is constant, the change in velocity is equal to the change in speed. Thus

$$a = \frac{v_2 - v_1}{t}$$

If v_2 is greater than v_1, the object is accelerating; the acceleration, a, will be positive. If v_2 is smaller than v_1, the object is decelerating; the acceleration, will be a negative quantity. This equation can also be stated in the following form:

$$v_2 = v_1 + at$$

The distance covered by an object while accelerating (or decelerating) in a straight line with a constant acceleration can be calculated by using the following equation (which I will not bother to derive):

$$d = v_1 t + \tfrac{1}{2}at^2$$

The last two equations can be combined mathematically to give a third equation which does not include the time:

$$v_2{}^2 = v_1{}^2 + 2ad$$

If the object starts from rest ($v_1 = 0$), these equations take on much simpler forms:

$$v_2 = at$$
$$d = \tfrac{1}{2}at^2$$
$$v_2{}^2 = 2ad$$

causes of motion in the next chapter, you'll understand the significance of this simple division of all motion into two categories.

Rotation is by its very nature a form of accelerated motion, since all parts of a rotating body are moving on circular paths. In addition, the rate of rotation—as measured by the angular velocity—can increase, decrease, or change direction. Hence there is also an *angular acceleration,* which is defined as *the rate of change of angular velocity.* For example, a bicycle wheel has an angular acceleration whenever the rider speeds up, slows down, or turns a corner.

See How They Run: The Kinematics of Sprinting

In the past few pages, you've been introduced to the science of *kinematics,* the study of motion. Kinematics is one of the most basic areas of physics; in fact, its definitions and methodology provide the foundation on which most of physics rests. If you understand, even in a nonmathematical way, the basic properties of and distinctions among speed, velocity, and acceleration, then you should have no difficulty with the following examination of the kinematics of running.

We are, as everyone is well aware, in the midst of a running craze. The streets are filled with joggers, sporting goods stores are replete with an abundant variety of running outfits, and bookstores display countless paeans to the psychological benefits and inner meaning of the running experience. One of the most popular movies of 1981 was *Chariots of Fire,* a dramatization of the lives of two Olympic runners, Harold Abrahams and Eric Liddell. The movie probed the different psychological forces that motivated each of these men toward their ultimate goal—an Olympic gold medal. It emphasized the long hours and months of training and preparation, the sheer physical effort and determination to push one's body beyond its natural limits—all for an event that is over in a matter of seconds.

Abrahams and Liddell were sprinters, and so the nature and purpose of their running were wholly different from the typical runner's. Sprinters possess the rare physical ability to run fast, and they train to expend all their physical resources in an all-out effort to run at top speed for a short period of time. Long-distance runners, on the other hand, train for endurance—to run for as long as they can at a comfortable pace by spreading out their effort as evenly as possible over the entire distance. Although they are usually lumped together under the common heading of "track," sprinting and distance running are rather different activities, physically and psychologically. We'll begin our analysis by taking a look at the kinematics of sprinting.

Over the years, a number of scientists have tried to measure the *velocity curve*—the way that the sprinter's velocity changes from start to finish—or, in mathematical terms, the graph of velocity vs. time. (Actually, it's more appropriate to call it a speed curve, since changes in direction are not considered.) One of the earliest efforts was made by the British scientist Archibald V. Hill, who was awarded the Nobel Prize in 1922 for his pioneering work in the physiology of exercise. Hill was really more interested in the physiology of running—the way that the body generates the muscle responses and energy needed for this effort—but he contributed some important insights into the kinematics of sprinting in the process. Hill proposed a simple mathematical model to represent the velocity curve, and subsequent observations involving direct measurements of sprinting have confirmed this model. Thus the measured velocity curve for any sprinter can be represented by a relatively simple mathematical equation. It should be emphasized, however, that most sprinters conform fairly closely—*but not exactly*—to this idealized mathematical model. A graph of a typical velocity curve is shown in Figure 1.4.

At the start of the race, the sprinter is at rest (v = 0); when the gun is fired he accelerates. (Due to the athlete's natural reaction time, there is a brief delay of about 0.1 second between the firing of the gun

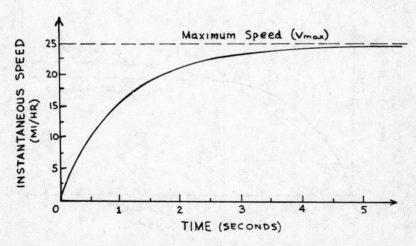

FIGURE 1.4   Velocity curve for sprinting.

and the actual start of motion.) Note that the speed increases rapidly at first, but then levels off toward a constant value—in this case, of 25 mi/hr. This means that the acceleration is decreasing—the change in speed is greatest at first, but it gets steadily smaller toward the end of the run. What this reveals is that a sprinter cannot increase his speed indefinitely. The faster he runs, the more difficult it becomes for him to increase his speed. Every sprinter has a maximum running speed, and his goal should be to reach this speed as quickly as possible. The best sprinters typically accelerate to 90% of maximum speed within 2 seconds and reach 99% of maximum in 4 seconds.

Two factors characterize each sprinter—his maximum acceleration at the beginning of the race and his maximum speed at the end. Figure 1.5 shows a comparison of the velocity curves of two hypothetical sprinters. Sprinter A has the better acceleration, but sprinter B has the greater maximum speed. Sprinter A reaches top speed in a shorter time, so he has the advantage over B in a shorter sprint. But in a longer sprint, A's early advantage is lost, and B will eventually overtake him. There is also a third factor to contend with—namely, the need to maintain maximum speed until the end of the race. In the longer sprints, fatigue begins to set in, and the sprinter may begin to lose speed near the end. To be an outstanding sprinter, an athlete must have excellent acceleration, high maximum speed, and the ability to maintain top speed to the finish line.

What is the fastest *instantaneous* speed that any human has at-

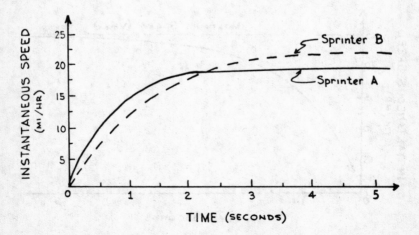

FIGURE 1.5 Velocity curves for two different sprinters.

tained? Since direct measurements of instantaneous speed have never been made during competition, we cannot answer this question definitively. We do know that the fastest *average* speed attained to date in an officially sanctioned race was set by Tommie Smith, who ran 220 yards in 19.5 seconds in 1966. His average speed for this race was 33.8 ft/sec, equivalent to 23.1 mi/hr. The record for the 100-yard dash of 9.0 seconds, set by Ivory Crockett in 1974 and equaled by Houston McTear in 1975, comes out second best with an average speed of 22.7 mi/hr. All things being equal, we would expect a sprinter to have a greater average speed in a longer race because he spends more time running at top speed than in a shorter race. Unfortunately, we don't have the information we would need to calculate the maximum speeds attained by Smith, Crockett, or McTear, so we can't determine which of them actually ran the fastest. However, we do have sufficient data on another race.

In 1963, Bob Hayes—who was later to become an outstanding football player for the Dallas Cowboys—set a record of 9.1 seconds for the 100-yard dash. Hayes, who was known to be a slow starter with exceptional speed, was reported to have covered the distance between the 60- and 75-yard marks in this race in 1.1 seconds. This information can be used to derive Hayes' velocity curve, and from this it is possible to calculate Hayes' maximum speed. It turns out to be 28 mi/hr—which is generally considered to be the highest instantaneous speed ever attained. Because of his slow start, Hayes' velocity curve for this race resembles curve B in Figure 1.5—and even though their average speeds were greater than Hayes', it seems unlikely that Smith, Crockett, or McTear achieved a higher instantaneous speed.

Long-Distance Running

Turning to the longer-distance races, the data we have to work with consist of the world record times for races covering distances from 100 meters to the marathon. This information, shown on Table 1.1, provides some interesting and surprising insights into several aspects of long-distance running. The table lists the world men's and women's records for a number of running distances as of December 1982. For comparison I've included the men's records as of December 1957, twenty-five years earlier. For the record, I've also listed the *average* speed (the total distance divided by the time) for the race. It is easiest to calculate and work with the average speed in meters/second—but since this is an unfamiliar unit of measurement for most people, I've calculated and listed the equivalent average speed in miles/hour. (Many distance runners like to judge their speed by the number of minutes it takes them to run a mile, so a conversion chart relating minutes/mile to miles/hr and m/sec appears in Appendix A.) You'll also notice that I've listed records in Table 1.1 for metric distances only (except for the mile); this is because records are no longer being kept for races in yards or miles.

Like most scientists, I fervently believe that a graph is worth ten thousand words—so in Figure 1.6 you'll find the average speeds plotted against the distances. (Don't be bothered by the peculiar compressed scale used for distance—this is so all the distances can fit on one graph. For those of you more familiar with mathematics, this is actually a graph of average speed vs. the logarithm of the distance.) As you can see, the points for each set of records all fall on a surprisingly smooth curve. Each curve shows a peak at a running distance just below 200 meters. This is the highest average speed on the curve, and it represents the longest distance that can be run at top speed. To

	MEN (1982)		MEN (1957)		WOMEN (1982)	
Distance (meters)	Time	Average Speed (mi/hr)	Time	Average Speed (mi/hr)	Time	Average Speed (mi/hr)
100	9.95s	22.5	10.1s	22.2	10.87s	20.6
200	19.72s	22.7	20.0s	22.4	21.71s	20.6
400	43.86s	20.4	45.2s	19.8	48.60s	18.4
800	1m 41.72s	17.6	1m 45.7s	16.9	1m 53.42s	15.8
1000	2m 12.18s	16.9	2m 19.0s	16.1	—	—
1500	3m 31.36s	15.9	3m 40.8s	15.2	3m 52.47s	14.4
1 mile	3m 47.33s	15.8	3m 58.0s	15.1	4m 17.44s	14.0
2000	4m 51.40s	15.4	5m 02.2s	14.8	—	—
3000	7m 32.10s	14.8	7m 52.8s	14.2	8m 26.78s	13.2
5000	13m 06.20s	14.2	13m 40.6s	13.6	15m 00.42s	12.4
10,000	27m 22.47s	13.6	28m 30.4s	13.1	31m 35.30s	11.8
20,000	57m 24.20s	13.0	59m 51.7s	12.5	—	—
25,000	1h 13m 55.80s	12.6	1h 16m 36.4s	12.2	—	—
30,000	1h 29m 18.80s	12.5	1h 35m 01.0s	11.8	—	—
Marathon (42,195 m)	2h 08m 13s	12.3	2h 17m 39.4s	11.4	2h 25m 28s	10.8

TABLE 1.1: WORLD TRACK RECORDS

the left of the peak, the average speeds are lower because the runner spends proportionally more time accelerating and less time running at top speed. To the right of the peak, the average speeds are lower because the runner cannot go at top speed over the entire distance; the greater the distance, the lower the average speed that can be maintained over that distance. This peak is sort of the "continental divide" of racing—it divides the sprints to the left from the runs to the right.

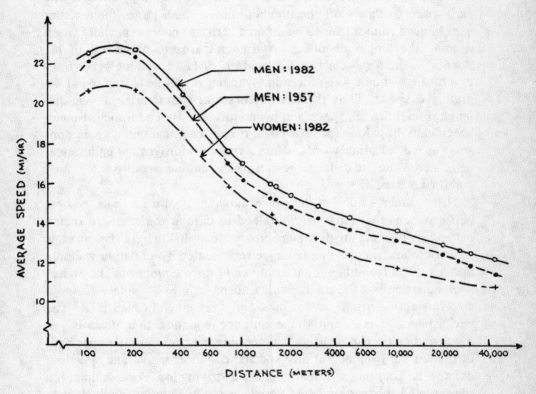

FIGURE 1.6   Running performance curves. The average running speed for world record performances is plotted against the distance. For distances greater than 400 meters, the performance curves follow the endurance equation $v_{avg} = K/D^n$, where K and n are constants. Specific values are as follows (v_{avg} = average speed in mi/hr; D = distance in meters):

$$\text{Men (1982): } v_{avg} = 29.91/D^{0.085}$$
$$\text{Men (1957): } v_{avg} = 29.66/D^{0.089}$$
$$\text{Women (1982): } v_{avg} = 28.32/D^{0.093}$$

The strategy for distance running is different from that for sprinting. As we've already noted, a sprinter tries to accelerate rapidly and run at his top speed for the entire race. On the other hand, the best strategy for running a long-distance race is to run at a constant speed (we'll learn why this is so later on). There is, of course, a brief period of acceleration at the beginning of the race, and—if the runner has any reserve left for a final "kick"—a burst of acceleration at the end. Often a competitor wants to run a tactical race, aiming to win and not necessarily to set a record, and will employ some stratagem like holding back to let someone else hold the lead, or possibly setting a fast early pace to throw off the competition. By and large, though, the experienced runner tries to maintain a constant pace, especially when running the longer distances. A runner learns to make use of his "splits"—the times for the first quarter, or half, or some other fraction of the distance—to determine whether or not he is running at his preferred speed. Thus the two factors that characterize a long-distance runner are his speed and his endurance. By endurance, I mean specifically how long (or how far) a runner can maintain a given constant speed. In other words, when a runner improves his endurance, he is increasing the distance he can cover running steadily at his most comfortable speed.

The "runner's side" of the curve shown in Figure 1.6 links the best performances that have been attained to date at the standard racing distances. In fact, for distances greater than 400 meters the curve is so smooth and regular that it can be represented by a relatively simple mathematical formula known as the *endurance equation*. (The endurance equation has the mathematical form $v_{avg} = K/D^n$, where K and n are constants. Specific values of K and n are given in Figure 1.6) The performance curve, and the endurance equation that describes it mathematically, can be used to determine the present-day upper limit of human performance at any specific distance or average speed. It defines the goal that a runner should be striving for. For example, if a runner can run steadily at an average speed of 13 mi/hr (equivalent to a 4:37 mile), the performance curve tells us that the longest distance he can expect to run at this average speed is about 20 km. Alternatively, a runner who chooses to run 5-km races can discover that to achieve the standard set by the performance curve he would have to run at an average speed of 14.2 mi/hr (equivalent to a 4:13 mile). In either case, a runner who aspires to world-class performance can set his goals in terms of either greater speed or greater endurance.

The performance curve can also be used to establish standards for distances that are run infrequently. For example, the record for the 50-km run is 2h 51m 32s, which corresponds to an average speed of 10.9 mi/hr. According to the endurance equation, this race should be run by world-class athletes at a speed of 11.9 mi/hr, corresponding to a time of 2h 36m. Perhaps at this long distance, the best runners cannot attain the same standards as at shorter distances. But the most likely reason for the relatively poor showing at 50 km is the lack of top-class competition. For the somewhat shorter marathon (42.2 km) —which certainly draws plenty of top-class competition—the best time to date (2h 08m 30s) is slightly better than the time of 2h 10m projected by the endurance equation. The 50-km run is clearly a distance at which a new world record could easily be set.

Now let's turn to women's running. I had originally planned to list the women's track records for 1957 in Table 1.1—but was surprised to discover that there was virtually no women's track in 1957. Competitions at distances greater than 880 yards were rarely, if ever, held. Women were denied permission to compete in the Boston Marathon because they were deemed physiologically incapable of completing the distance. But the women's movement has brought about some welcome changes. The past decade has seen a tremendous growth of women's track, particularly in the area of long-distance running.

The performance curve in Figure 1.6 based on the present women's world records shows that the average speed for longer distances drops off at about the same rate for women as it does for men. This indicates that while women runners cannot run as fast as the men, they have the same endurance capabilities, to the extent that the *relative* speeds for longer vs. shorter races are virtually the same for women as for men.

As the cliché goes, records are made to be broken. The endurance equation represents the *present-day* limit of human performance, and as new records are set, the equation must be changed to reflect these higher performance standards. Figure 1.6 shows the substantial improvement in running performance that has taken place over the past twenty-five years. Races are now being run at average speeds that are from 4% to 10% faster than in 1957. But even more dramatic than the increase in speed is the increase in endurance. The top runners now go up to twice as far at a given average speed as they did in 1957. The 10,000-meter run is now being covered at an average speed of 13.6 mi/hr, the same average speed that was used to set the record at 5000 meters in 1957. This constitutes a 100% increase in endurance at this speed. At shorter distances (and higher average speeds) the improvement in endurance is not quite as large, but it is still substantial; for example, the speed for 800 meters in 1957 is now the speed for 1000 meters, representing a 25% improvement. The explanation for these increases in speed and endurance can be traced to more runners, more competition and, above all, better training methods.

What can we predict for the future? Let's suppose that speed and endurance continue to improve at the same rate for the next twenty-five years. The average speed for the mile run has increased by 4.7% since 1957, and if the same rate of increase prevails, we can expect to see a 3:37 mile by the year 2007. Similarly, if the marathon is run at the average speed now used to run 20 km, we can predict a marathon run in 2 hours flat within twenty-five years.

It should be kept in mind, however, that these predictions are based on the assumption that the present improvements in speed and endurance will continue into the future at the same rates. To be honest, we have no assurance whatsoever that this assumption is valid. Obviously, the trend cannot continue indefinitely; there is undoubtedly some physiological limit to human speed and endurance. But it's not certain how close today's athletes are to that limit.

In the early 1950s, it was believed by some that a 4-minute mile was beyond human capability; it supposedly presented a physiological barrier that could not be crossed. I remember rather clearly that when Roger Bannister ran his 3:59.4 mile in 1954, he collapsed at the finish line—and we were led to believe that Bannister (who was a physician) had used his medical knowledge to extract every possible bit of his available energy for the race. Today, as everyone knows, 4-minute miles are run routinely; races are run in which the last-place finisher does 3:55. It turned out that the 4-minute mile was a psychological barrier, rather than a physiological one. This episode points out the futility of prognostication when it comes to human performance. It may be fun to make projections based on past performances and trends, but they often turn out to be wrong.

Why should this be so? Our predictions for the future are based on the observed changes in the performance curve over a period of time. But each performance curve is nothing more than a table of data, a pictorial representation of the world records at a given time. It is remarkable that all of these records, set by different individuals, actually follow a precise mathematical relationship. What is even more impressive is that similar performance curves of comparable accuracy can be constructed based on the records for long-distance events in swimming, cycling, speed skating, race walking, and even horse racing. But why are all these performances so magically linked?

We've reached an impasse here, created by the fact that the endurance equation merely *describes* performance at long distances, but doesn't *explain* it. If we don't understand why long-distance running times are related as they are, if we can't explain their improvement over the past twenty-five years in anything but vague terms, then how can we expect to predict the future with any confidence?

What we need is a *scientific explanation* of the performance curve in terms of more fundamental concepts. Such an explanation might be based on the physics of running—an examination of the forces that are needed to propel a runner, for instance—or on a biomechanical analysis of the human body to determine limitations on running speed, or on a physiological study of the way that the body assimilates and delivers energy to the muscles during running. Any of these approaches, alone or more likely in combination, might enable us to explain why the performance curve turns out the way it does, and then we would be able to predict future trends with much greater understanding and success. Later on we'll consider the physics and physiology of running, after we've first examined the scientific principles behind them. For now we have learned how to *describe* motion in scientific terms, but we have not yet learned about its causes.

2 / WHAT MAKES THINGS MOVE?

We're about to embark on a brief philosophical analysis of a rather fundamental and deeply metaphysical question: *what makes things move?* But first of all, let me justify this inquiry. An excursion into metaphysics might seem out of place in a book about sports. But in fact, this question gets right to the heart of the matter, for *virtually every aspect of athletic activity deals with the creation and control of motion.* If an athlete is to know *how* to command motion effectively and skillfully, he has to understand *why* motion takes place. There are, to be sure, many great athletes whose movements come automatically through instinct, sheer natural ability, and experience. Yet the athlete who, in addition, can understand and articulate the mechanics of his performance is somehow on a higher plane. Indeed, he is twice blessed: he can appreciate his own efforts intellectually, and he also stands a good chance for a successful career as a TV sports analyst after he retires from competition.

The Causes of Motion

Motion is such an inherent part of our existence that we hardly ever think about it. Most people know enough to say things fall because of gravity. But what keeps an airplane up in the air? How does an automobile move? Well, you turn the ignition key, release the brake, step on the gas . . . and it goes! I suspect that a rather small percentage of licensed drivers really understand what happens under the hood to make an automobile move.

The question of the cause of motion is an extremely old one. In ancient times, people believed that living things move because they will themselves to do so. But what about inanimate objects? What makes the sun move across the sky, or rivers flow to the sea, or arrows fly through the air? It was generally believed that these motions were guided by the deities—the sun god, the river god, the arrow god—and we can understand the need for so many gods in ancient religions simply by the fact that there was so much for them to do.

The intellectuals of ancient times eventually came to seek more naturalistic explanations for motion. The Greek philosopher Aristotle (384–322 BC) wrote extensively on the subject and devised a system for explaining motion that shaped and influenced all subsequent theories. As we will see, Aristotle's system contained some contradictory features, and it was the efforts of later scholars to resolve these contradictions that led to our present-day concepts.

Aristotle classified all motions as being either *natural* or *violent*. Natural motions proceed because of some power inherent to or contained within the object, whereas violent motions require an external force that acts on the object. In keeping with his belief that the earth is at the center of the universe, Aristotle divided the world into a terrestrial realm (the earth) and a celestial realm (the heavens). In the celestial realm, all motions are natural; the natural motion of every celestial object—sun, moon, planets, stars—is to move on a circular path at constant speed around the earth.

On the earth, however, both natural and violent motions exist. Aristotle considered all vertical motions (toward or away from the earth) to be natural. The tendency for an object to rise into the air or fall to the earth was thought to be the consequence of an inherent power that returns the object to its natural resting place. He believed that everything on the earth is made from four basic elements—earth, water, fire, and air. The natural resting places of earth and water are at the earth's surface; thus an object will tend to fall if either of these elements predominates in its makeup. If the predominant element is air or fire—whose natural resting places are above the earth, in the sky—then the object will naturally rise. An object moving in opposition to its natural motion—a stone moving upward, for example—constitutes a violent motion, requiring an external force. Moreover, no object can have a natural tendency to move horizontally—i.e., parallel to the earth's surface—hence any horizontal motion must also be a violent motion.

In Aristotle's system, a violent motion will continue only so long as an external force is acting in direct contact with the object. Once the force is removed, the motion must immediately cease. This brings us to a major point of controversy: consider the motion of some projectile such as a ball thrown through the air. While the ball is still in the thrower's hand, it moves because it is being pushed by the thrower. But why does the ball continue to move after it has been released? Aristotle could only conclude that the air itself has the power to exert a force on any object that moves through it. The power either is transferred to the air by the thrower, or comes about through the action of the projectile itself: the projectile pushes the air aside as it moves, and the air immediately returns and pushes the projectile forward. Aristotle also proposed that the speed with which any object moves through air or any other medium depends on the resistance offered by the medium. The smaller the resistance, the greater the speed; thus stones naturally fall faster through air than through water because air offers less resistance to their motion. Empty space, a vacuum, can offer no resistance to motion; hence, Aristotle reasoned, an object would naturally travel through empty space at infinite speed —an obvious impossibility. He thereby concluded that a vacuum cannot exist; all space must be filled with a medium of one kind or another.

Modern scientists, of course, no longer accept Aristotle's theory of the causes of motion. The belief that earth, air, fire, and water are the four basic elements has long since been disproved; the fundamental building blocks of matter are now believed to be protons, neutrons, and electrons. Aristotle's distinctions between celestial and terrestrial motions, between horizontal and vertical motions, have also been rejected. However, we should note that Aristotle's theory was accepted as correct for more than two thousand years, and its overthrow was not easily accomplished.

Despite their general acceptance of Aristotle's system, medieval philosophers were puzzled by some of its specific details. How does the air have the ability to both resist the motion of a projectile and impel it forward at the same time? Why do streamlined objects like javelins and arrows travel so fast, when they obviously push aside very little air as they move and hence should not be pushed very hard in return by the air? By the 1300s, a number of scholars had come to the conclusion that the motive force resides in the projectile itself. New questions arose: Is this force transferred to the projectile by the thrower, and if so, how? Is the force used up during the motion, or does it permanently reside in the object?

The first radical departure from Aristotle's ideas came about through the work of Galileo in the early 1600s. Galileo, one of the great figures in the history of science, is probably most famous for his vigorous defense (in the face of strong opposition from the Catholic Church) of the theory that the earth moves around the sun. For his efforts, Galileo was condemned by the Church and forced to renounce his beliefs. To most scientists, however, Galileo is more than just a martyr to the conflict between science and religious authority: Galileo argued for the primacy of observation and experimentation over faith and reason, and for this he is regarded as the founder of modern experimental science.

Throughout his life—both before and after his conflict with the Church—Galileo did experiments on various aspects of motion in an ongoing effort to describe it mathematically and explain its causes. In a later chapter, we'll see how his experiments on the motions of falling bodies came into conflict with Aristotle's theories. Galileo also rejected the idea that horizontal motion is a violent motion requiring the constant application of a force to maintain it. In contrast, Galileo concluded that an object once set in motion has an inherent tendency to keep moving, and it will stop only if its motion is *opposed* by a force. Thus an object moving horizontally should continue to move indefinitely, provided all obstacles are removed from its path. In other words, while Aristotle believed that any moving object, if allowed to move freely, will naturally come to rest, Galileo believed that any moving object allowed to move freely will maintain its motion indefinitely.

Historically, Galileo's view came to prevail because of the work of Isaac Newton, who incorporated Galileo's concept into his own philosophical system. Newton's theory of motion turned out to be hugely successful and brought to an end Aristotle's influence on scientific thought. Newton was born in 1642, the same year in which Galileo died. He made many of his important scientific discoveries when he was in his twenties, but did not reveal them until many years afterward. The publication of his book *The Mathematical Principles of Natural Philosophy* (more familiarly known as the *Principia*) in 1687 astounded the scientific community. In the *Principia,* Newton introduced his theories of motion and of gravitation, and used them to account for a host of astronomical and terrestrial phenomena. Quite simply, Newton changed forever the way in which we view the universe.

Newton certainly ranks among the most influential thinkers in human history, and has come to be regarded as a figure of almost mythic proportions. He was hero-worshipped even by his contemporaries; his close associate, Edmund Halley, wrote a long poem of tribute to Newton which ended with the words, "Nearer the gods no mortal may approach." Alexander Pope's lines

> Nature and Nature's laws lay hid in night,
> God said: "Let Newton be!", and all was light.

reflected the popular belief of the time that Newton had been chosen by God as a vehicle through which the secrets of the universe would be passed on to mankind—a view with which Newton himself found no argument. Since then, attempts to humanize Newton have met with little success. He was actually a rather austere, humorless, and rigid individual. He was unable to tolerate opposition or criticism of his ideas, and demanded complete loyalty from his supporters. He could be extremely autocratic and vindictive. Were he alive today, Isaac Newton might well have become a successful football coach.

In putting together his theory of motion, Newton borrowed and synthesized ideas from his predecessors. (In an uncharacteristically modest mood, he once wrote: "If I have seen farther, it is by standing on the shoulders of giants.") He adopted Aristotle's basic framework in which all motions are considered as being "natural" or "violent." However, Newton greatly simplified Aristotle's system of classification by making the sole basis of distinction between natural and violent motion depend upon whether or not the motion is accelerated. Newton distinguished between them as follows:

> *Constant-velocity motion is natural motion.*
> *Accelerated motion is forced (violent) motion.*

A natural motion, according to Newton, is one that proceeds without any outside influence; it is due to some innate property or inherent tendency of the object itself. Thus an object moving with a constant velocity (in a straight line at constant speed) should continue this motion of and by itself until it is opposed or altered by some external influence. (As you may have guessed, this is an idea that Newton borrowed from Galileo.) For an object to accelerate—i.e., change speed or direction—an external force must be continually applied. When this force is removed, *the object does not stop moving*; rather, it reverts to natural motion and continues to move with whatever velocity it had at the instant when the force was removed.

We can see immediately one advantage of Newton's theory of motion; it is much simpler than Aristotle's. Newton rejected the need for different rules for horizontal and vertical motions; both kinds could be explained under the same principle. More significantly, he abandoned the separation of the terrestrial and celestial realms. By this time, the theory that the earth is one of the planets moving around the sun had been well established, and Newton could see no reason why the earth should obey different laws of nature than the other celestial bodies. The idea that the laws of nature are the same throughout the universe constitutes one of Newton's most profound and powerful contributions to scientific thought.

Our metaphysical analysis of the causes of motion is very nearly at an end, and we will be returning to the more comfortable world of sports very shortly. At this point, though, it is worthwhile to reemphasize the major philosophical difference between Aristotle's and Newton's conceptions: Aristotle believed that it is the natural tendency of moving objects to come to rest, whereas Newton (and Galileo) believed that it is the natural tendency of moving objects to keep on moving. Both of these views seem fairly reasonable, so on what basis do we choose one over the other? If we observe the motions of actual objects—a book sliding along a tabletop; an automobile coasting with its engine shut off; a golf ball rolling on a green—we find that they do tend to come to a stop of their own accord, as Aristotle had proposed. But Galileo and Newton both recognized the reason why such objects come to a stop—namely, that their motion is being opposed by friction. The more we can reduce the amount of friction between a moving object and the surface on which it lies, the farther the object will travel before coming to a stop. For example, an automobile will come to a stop much sooner on a dry surface than on a wet or icy one; a spinning bicycle wheel will coast to a halt in a much shorter time if its axle is not fully lubricated or mounted on ball bearings. It is reasonable to assume that if we could do away with friction or other resistance forces entirely, then moving objects would never come to a stop. You may wonder why the same idea did not also seem reasonable to Aristotle—but remember, he lived in a time of very simple technology; vehicles were propelled by animal or manpower on stone or dirt roads, and nearly frictionless motion was rather rare. With the growth of technology and the development of friction-reducing devices and more powerful methods of propulsion, Newton's concept has come to be seen as a more effective and simpler way to understand the causes of motion.

Inertia

Now let's take a more practical, nuts-and-bolts look at Newton's theory and see how it can be used to explain the motions that we see in everyday life and in sports. We'll begin with the concept of "natural" motion, which can be stated as follows:

It is the natural tendency of any object to maintain a state of constant-velocity motion, which can be changed only by an externally applied force.

This natural tendency of objects to remain in motion is considered to be an innate property of all matter, and it has been given the name of *inertia*. It is common usage to say that objects "possess inertia"— meaning that they have the ability to stay in motion in the absence of external influences. Inertia is a rather useful word, both within and outside of science, and we will make frequent use of its various connotations.

One common use of the word "inertia" is to describe the tendency of an object or the desire of a person or group of individuals *not to move*—and when used in reference to people, this can mean mentally as well as physically. For example, we might have to deal with the problem of "overcoming inertia" in order to get something moving or to gain acceptance of a new idea. This aspect of inertia arises from an interesting feature of Newton's theory—specifically, that he made no distinction between objects at rest and objects in constant-velocity motion. The key idea here is that *a stationary object is moving with a constant velocity*—namely, a velocity of zero. Thus inertia also represents the tendency of an object at rest to remain at rest until it is acted on by an external force. When used in this sense, the word "inertia" signifies "resistance to change."

One very good illustration of the concept of inertia has to do with the use of seat belts in automobiles and airplanes. If you're sitting in a car that is moving at 55 mi/hr, you are *not* at rest; you and everything else in the car are also moving over the ground at 55 mi/hr. Now suppose you are unfortunate enough to be in an accident in which the car collides with some other object and rapidly decelerates. The force of the impact or the rapid action of the brakes acts directly on the car itself, but not on its occupants. Because of inertia, you would continue to move forward at 55 mi/hr—until your motion is opposed by the dashboard or the windshield. The advantage of a seat belt is that it firmly attaches you to the car and acts to oppose you inertial tendency, so that if the car suddenly decelerates, you will also decelerate at the same rate. Even in lower-speed collisions (at 15 or 20 mi/hr, for instance) a seat belt can make a big difference, particularly for the occupant of the front passenger seat. In a low-speed collision, the driver may be able to brace himself against the steering wheel, but a surprised passenger may have no such opportunity to overcome his inertia—and the result is usually an uncontrollable collision with the windshield.

Wearing a seat belt in an airplane isn't going to do too much for you in a crash at several hundred miles per hour, but it is of significant value in protecting against the effects of the sudden bumps and jolts that occur when a plane is flying through turbulent air. On rare occasions a plane may encounter a sudden downdraft or unexpected "air pocket" (a region of low pressure) and may lose considerable altitude in a short time. Unbelted passengers have been known to fly out of their seats and collide with the cabin ceiling in such instances. The explanation is simply that the plane is being accelerated downward, while the passenger is maintaining his inertial motion—forward at constant speed in a straight line—until the top of the cabin drops onto his head.

The motion of a projectile, so difficult to explain in terms of Aristotle's theory of motion, can be easily understood in terms of inertia. Any thrown or batted object starts from rest and is accelerated by the force that launches it. But once it loses contact with the launching force, the projectile continues to move because of its inertia. However, a baseball or golf ball in flight clearly does not move with constant velocity; it travels on an arc and changes speed and direction. The explanation is that a projectile in flight is still being acted on by other forces—namely, air resistance and the force of gravity pulling it toward the earth. We will look at projectile motion in more detail later on to see how the interplay of inertia, gravity, and air resistance shapes the path of flight.

An interesting use of inertia is the "run-up" that is used by a thrower before launching a projectile. In the javelin throw, for example, the thrower typically runs about 75 feet with the javelin before he throws it; thus the javelin is first set in motion and given speed in the run. Because of inertia, it maintains this speed when it is released, and is given additional speed by the throw. Thus a javelin thrown on the run will be released at a higher speed than if it were thrown with the same arm action from a stationary stance. The thrower must be certain not to come to a stop before the throw, since this would defeat the whole purpose of the run-up. In the same manner, high jumpers and long jumpers take a run-up before they leap so that their inertia will carry them forward as they rise and fall, and outfielders who have to make a particularly long throw will run forward a few steps before releasing the ball.

Inertia, needless to say, plays a significant role in all areas of sports. Ice hockey is a game that proceeds at tremendous speed because of the relatively low friction; hence the players and the puck move along with little resistance to their motion, without the more rapid loss of speed that would occur on rougher surfaces. On the other hand, there are situations in sports where inertia turns out to be more of a hindrance than a help. In baseball, a runner sliding into a base at high speed sometimes is tagged out because his inertia carries him past the base. Another example—one with which I am painfully familiar—has to do with the layup shot in basketball taken by a player who is driving toward the basket. The main idea in basketball shooting is, of course, to aim the ball at the basket. But when the shooter is moving, the ball is already in motion *before* it is shot. Therefore the shooter must correct for the inertial motion of the ball when he puts up his shot. To take a shot while moving toward the basket, the trick is to shoot the ball *vertically upward* and let the ball's inertia carry it forward into the basket. But if the ball is pushed toward the basket, the speed acquired by the ball from the act of shooting will add to the forward speed that it already has, and it will overshoot the basket. When this shot is taken properly—you have to judge your speed and moment of release rather carefully—and the ball floats smoothly through the hoop, it's a pretty sight to see. Unfortunately—even though I understand the physics of it perfectly—I've never been able to master this move, and I manage to miss embarrassingly easy layups with frustrating regularity.

What Is a Force?

According to Newton, an object cannot change velocity unless it is under the influence of an external force. One of the many advantages of Newton's concept is that it provides us with a clear definition of a force:

A force is any action that can cause an object to accelerate.

Forces are not things that can be seen. But we can see (or feel) their effects. Any time an object accelerates, we know that a force is at work. (Please note that acceleration, as I refer to it here, includes both positive and negative kinds. Deceleration—negative acceleration—signifies that a force is acting in opposition to the motion.) However, the application of a force does not necessarily produce acceleration, because there may be another force at work to counteract the effect of the first force. For example, a person trying to push a large, heavy weight across the floor may not be able to exert enough muscular force to overcome the opposing friction force, so no motion occurs. In a tug-of-war, the groups on opposite ends of the rope may be pulling with equal forces, so there is no acceleration. Thus an object that is in inertial (constant-velocity) motion could have two or more exactly counterbalanced forces acting on it, or no forces at all. But an object that is *not* at rest or is not moving in a straight line at constant speed *must* have an unbalanced force acting on it.

The forces that exist in nature may be classified in a number of ways. The most common type is the *contact force,* which encompasses all the pushes and pulls that are exerted by one object in direct contact with another. We can exert such forces on other objects by using parts of our bodies directly or by using various devices such as ropes, sticks, baseball bats, tennis rackets, and so on. *Friction* is a contact force; this is the resistance that an object experiences when it is moving and in contact with the surface of another object. Another contact force is *air resistance:* when an object is moving through air (or any other medium, for that matter) it collides with the molecules of the air and experiences a retarding force as a consequence.

A force is exerted by any object that has been distorted from its natural shape. This is known as an *elastic* force and is another type of contact force. Every solid object is elastic to some degree: when its natural shape is changed (stretched, squeezed, or twisted) by some outside force, the material exerts a counteracting internal force that tends to restore the object to its natural shape. When a rubber ball strikes a surface, the impact distorts its shape, and the elastic restoring force (which is rather substantial in rubber) is what makes the ball spring back. High-speed photographs show that even a baseball, a seemingly rigid object, distorts when it is hit by a bat, so that part of the force that accelerates the ball when it is hit is the elastic restoring force generated internally by the ball itself. Elastic forces are also generated by springs when they are stretched or compressed. They have a wide variety of uses—in scales, windup watches, automobile suspensions, trampolines, to name a few. Elastic forces play an important role in the operation of many different kinds of athletic equipment—from bows and arrows to vaulting poles to the stringing of tennis rackets. Later on we will learn more about how the scientific analysis of elastic forces has brought about advances in the design of such equipment.

Our bodies have various ways of sensing contact forces. The skin contains various receptors that are sensitive to contact and contribute to our sense of touch. There are also specialized cells in our muscles that register the extent to which a muscle is being stretched. The semicircular canals of the inner ear, which provide us with a sense of balance, are responsive to accelerations of the head. These various sensors generate nerve impulses that are transmitted to the brain and make us aware of the pressure, pain, or sudden acceleration caused by a contact force.

In contradistinction to the contact forces are the *action-at-a-distance forces*. As their name implies, these are forces that are exerted by objects that are not in direct contact with each other—in fact, these forces can act even when the objects involved are separated by perfectly empty space. The most familiar action-at-a-distance force is *gravity*. Any object released in midair and allowed to fall freely always accelerates as it falls—indicative of a force pulling it toward the earth. Newton identified this force as the earth's gravitational attraction for the object—and it is evident that the object experiences this force even though it is not in direct contact with the earth. Newton demonstrated that the motions of the moon around the earth and the earth and other planets around the sun could also be attributed to the force of gravity, thereby showing that this force can be transmitted over rather vast distances of virtually empty space.

If the ends of two magnets are brought near to, but not in contact with, each other, they will very noticeably attract or repel each other. This demonstrates that magnetism is also an action-at-a-distance force. So is the electrical force between electrically charged objects. Yet another action-at-a-distance force is the *nuclear force,* the force that binds protons and neutrons together in the nucleus of the atom.

Over the past century or so, scientists have pieced together a grand and all-encompassing picture of nature showing how the action-at-a-distance forces direct the organization of matter in the universe. All matter is made of atoms, and atoms owe their stability to the electrical force between the negatively charged electrons and the positively charged nucleus. (As we have already mentioned, the stability and structure of the nucleus depends on the nuclear force.) Atoms are attracted electrically to other atoms, and the strength of these inter-atomic attractions determines whether the atoms organize themselves into a solid, a liquid, or a gas. In a solid, the interatomic forces are relatively strong, which explains why solid matter maintains its rigid shape. In liquids and gases, the interatomic forces are progressively weaker, and their properties can be accounted for accordingly. Thus the familiar objects of our terrestrial existence—chairs and tables, basketballs and hockey sticks, even our own bodies—are held together by electrical and nuclear forces. The largest objects in the universe—planets, stars, and galaxies—have shapes and motions that are controlled by the force of gravity. The reason why the earth, the sun, and other celestial bodies are round is because the mutual gravitational forces of the matter in these bodies pull everything toward the center, thereby forming a spherical shape.

The atomic picture of matter reveals another interesting aspect of forces—namely, that *all contact forces arise from interatomic electrical forces.* Friction is caused by the electrical attraction of the atoms at the surface of one object for the atoms at the surface of the other. The elastic forces that are generated when an object is distorted represent the interatomic forces working to restore the atoms to their normal, equilibrium positions. The common "push-and-pull" forces are the result of the interatomic forces in one object acting to oppose the effects of the interatomic forces in another. The surprising conclusion is that there are very few, perhaps only three or four, *fund-amental* forces in nature—that is, forces that cannot be explained in terms of other forces—and all of these are action-at-a-distance forces.

But how do these forces work? How can one object exert a force on another when they are separated by empty space, when there is no physical link? Consider the fact that during a solar eclipse, when the moon is in a direct line between the sun and the earth, the sun's gravitational force on the earth is unabated (the earth, after all, does not fly off its orbit when this event occurs). The force seems to "pass through" the moon, as if it weren't there. How can we understand this? More than 2300 years ago, Aristotle came to the conclusion that action-at-a-distance forces could not exist. He stated that all forces had to be transmitted by direct contact—but nowhere in all his writings does he clearly explain how gravity causes objects to fall. Isaac Newton refused to speculate publicly about the nature of gravity—"The cause of gravity is what I do not pretend to know," he confided to a friend. Early in our own century, Albert Einstein framed the general theory of relativity to explain gravity in terms of such esoteric ideas as four-dimensional non-Euclidean geometry and space-time curvature. He succeeded with gravity, but was not able to extend his theory to encompass the other action-at-a-distance forces.

The fact of the matter is that after several millennia of speculation, theorizing, and experimentation, scientists still do not understand— not as thoroughly as they would like to—the fundamental forces of nature. Yet we have used our limited knowledge of these forces to develop a remarkable, bewildering, almost uncontrollable technology —spacecraft to the moon and planets, electronic computers, nuclear weapons, and similar wonders of our times. How do all these devices work? At the most basic level, we do not pretend to know. The lesson here is just that even if we don't understand what forces are, if we can just close our eyes to our ignorance and concentrate on the *effects* of forces, we can accomplish quite a bit.

Forces and Motion

Forces can also be classified in terms of their effects. A force that acts on an object but does not produce motion because it is counter-balanced by other forces is a *static* force. Our muscles exert static forces when they are pushing against an immovable object or support-ing a weight. Our own body weight acts as a static force on the floor or whatever surface we're standing on. In contrast, a force that is not counterbalanced and thereby causes acceleration is called a *dynamic* force.

Different types of static force are shown in Figure 2.1. *Tension* forces act to stretch an object, and *compressive* forces, as the name clearly implies, tend to squeeze or compress. Bodies that are subject to tension or compression resist through their internal interatomic forces, and every material has some upper limit of tension or com-pression that it can resist before breaking. Some substances can sup-port one but not the other—for example, a rope can support tension but not compression (you can use a rope to pull, but not to push). When an elongated object like a board or a pole is bent, one side of it is subject to tension and the other side to compression. *Shear* forces act perpendicularly to the axis of an elongated object. Graphite, a form of carbon that is used as the "lead" in lead pencils, is very weak against shear forces, so when it is slid along a piece of paper, it breaks off in very thin sheets that deposit on the paper—as words, punctua-tion, or mathematical symbols. Many of the common athletic injuries are the result of *torsional* (twisting) forces, to which joints are partic-ularly susceptible. Research on how various materials respond to these different types of forces has obvious value in the design of all kinds of structures. In sports, such information is extremely useful for determining how bones and muscles respond to different forces, as well as for the design of athletic equipment.

Turning to dynamic forces—forces that produce an actual acceler-ation—our main concern is to learn how much acceleration is pro-duced by a given force. One fairly obvious relationship is that the bigger the force, the greater the resulting acceleration. But what hap-pens when the same force is applied to two different objects?

To answer this question, we have to go back to the idea of inertia as an object's resistance to a change in its state of motion. Scientific observations, experiments, and just our general experience all clearly indicate that some objects are more difficult to accelerate than others —it takes a lot more effort to lift a piano than a flute; more force is needed to accelerate a Cadillac as compared with a Honda; the same throwing effort will send a baseball a lot farther than a bowling ball. One way to describe this state of affairs is to say that *some objects have more inertia than others*. This makes inertia more than just an

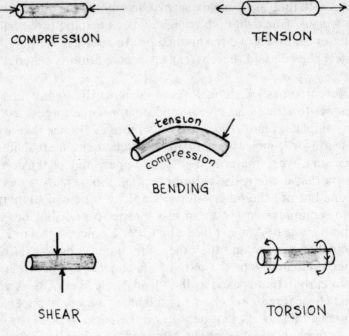

FIGURE 2.1 Types of static force.

innate tendency: it turns it into a quantity—that is, different objects possess different *amounts* of inertia.

The measure of any object's inertia is its *mass*. The more mass an object has, the more inertia it has—and the more difficult it is to accelerate. The mass of an object is not the same as its weight, although the two are closely related. Weight is a force—specifically, the gravitational force acting on an object. Since the force of gravity is not the same everywhere (for reasons that will be discussed later), the weight of an object will depend on its location. The mass of an object, which is a measure of its inertia, is a more fundamental quantity which does not change with location. However, at any given place, the more mass an object has, the more it weighs. There is a precise mathematical relationship between weight and mass, which is based on ideas related to the theory of gravity. A full discussion of this subject may be found in Appendix B.

In the metric system, the mass of an object is measured in *kilograms*. The kilogram—or kilo, for short—is a commonly used everyday unit in metric countries, where commodities are measured, bought, and sold by their mass in kilos rather than by their weight. (Many an American tourist who has done food shopping or tried to weigh himself in a foreign country has been surprised to find that the scales record mass, rather than weight.)

In contrast—and adding to the confusion caused by two systems of measurement—in the United States and other countries still using customary units, commodities are measured by their weight rather than their mass. The weight of any object is given in pounds, since weight is a force and the pound is the customary unit of force. There is also a customary unit of mass, although it is hardly ever used and rarely appears outside of physics books. It is called the *slug*. (This rather graceless name derives from the word "sluggish," which is descriptive of an object with a lot of inertia.)

Since I've chosen to use customary units in this book, I'll be using the slug as a unit of mass on occasion. The easiest way to visualize it is to remember that any object with a mass of 1 slug weighs 32 pounds on the earth's surface—about the weight of a typical 3-year-old child. For completeness, I should point out that there is a corresponding unit of force in the metric system; following a tradition of naming secondary units after famous scientists, the metric unit of force has been named the *newton*. One newton is slightly less than a quarter of a pound. (Refer to Appendix B for a complete summary of the conversion factors relating weight and mass units in the customary and metric systems.)

The definition of mass as a measure of inertia or resistance to force enables us to relate force to acceleration. It's easy to see that the more mass an object has, the more force will be needed to give it a specific acceleration—or that a given force will provide greater acceleration to an object with less mass. What is needed, though, is a mathematical statement of the relationship.

Newton's theory of motion is normally encapsulated into three basic principles or laws of motion. We have already discussed the first law without identifying it as such. It deals with the concept of natural motion, and is commonly known as the *law of inertia*. One way to state this law is as follows:

A body will remain in a state of constant-velocity motion (at rest, or moving with constant speed in a straight line) unless acted on by an unbalanced force.

Newton's second law is an equation that relates force, mass, and acceleration. This rather simple relationship is as follows:

$$F = ma$$
$$\text{force} = \text{mass} \times \text{acceleration}$$

In metric units, the force (measured in newtons) is equal to the mass of the object in kilograms multiplied by the acceleration in m/sec² (meters/second/second). In customary units, the force in pounds equals the product of the mass (in slugs) and the acceleration (in ft/sec²).

In this equation, F stands for the *net* force acting on the object in question—that is, the sum of all the forces involved. If all the forces on an object exactly counterbalance, then the net force is zero. From the equation, we see that if F is zero, then the acceleration, a, must also be zero (since m, the mass, can't be zero). Zero acceleration corresponds to constant-velocity motion, so if there's no net force, there can't be a change in velocity. If you think about this a bit, you'll see that Newton's first law is really included in Newton's second law.

In adding up all the forces acting on an object to determine the net force, we obviously have to take the direction of action of the forces into account. For instance, if two people are pushing a heavy crate in an eastward direction with a force of 10 pounds each, then the net force is 20 pounds to the east, and the crate will accelerate in that direction (Fig. 2.2a). But if one person pushes to the west while the other pushes to the east—both with 10-lb forces—then the two forces counterbalance, and the net force is zero (Fig. 2.2b). What happens if one of our pushers now changes direction, and pushes to the north? It's evident that force is a vector quantity—so to get the net force in this case, the rules of vector arithmetic must be used (the net force turns out to be 14.1 lb, northeast, as shown in Figure 2.2c).

Newton's second law is a scientific principle of inestimable power and value. We will refer to it time and time again in our analyses of sports activities and performance. Let's take a look at some demonstrations of its role in sports. First, let me remind you of several important points. Acceleration is defined as the rate of change of velocity or as the change in velocity over time. Remember also that a large acceleration does not necessarily imply a large change in velocity per se; rather it indicates a large *rate of change* of velocity—a small change in velocity over a very short time interval will do. Moreover, a large force is not necessarily needed to produce a large accel-

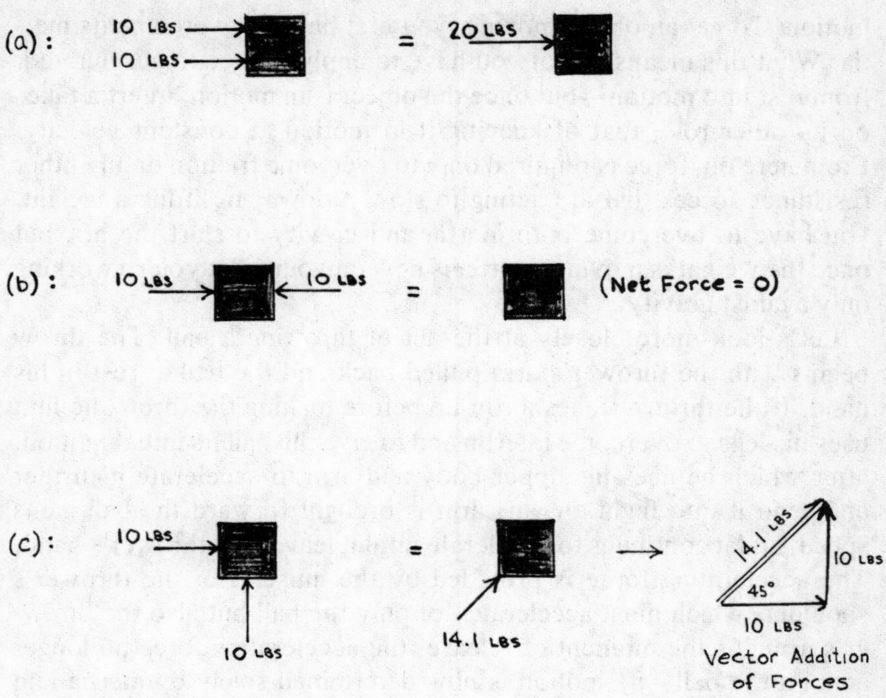

(a):   10 LBS → ▮   = 20 LBS → ▮
       10 LBS →

(b):   10 LBS → ▮ ← 10 LBS   =   ▮   (Net Force = 0)

(c):   10 LBS → ▮   =   ▮ ↗   →   14.1 LBS ↗ / 45° / 10 LBS
       ↑ 10 LBS   14.1 LBS   10 LBS
                                    Vector Addition
                                    of Forces

FIGURE 2.2   Vector addition of forces.

eration; according to the second law, the mass of the object being accelerated must also be taken into account.

One example of the role played by mass is provided by the relationship of size to function in football players. A lineman has to be very massive, because he is often called on to be immovable—defensive linemen to turn back a running play, and offensive linemen to protect the quarterback on a pass. The more mass the player has, the more force his opponent has to exert to move him. But since linemen are often called on to run, they can't be *too* heavy; otherwise they won't be able to accelerate their own body effectively. Running backs and defensive backs must have good acceleration—the ability to make rapid changes in speed and direction—so lower body mass acts to their advantage; the smaller their mass, the smaller the force they must generate in order to accelerate their own body.

Anyone who has tried weight lifting knows that in lifting a weight, more effort is needed to get the weight in motion than to keep it in

motion. To get an object moving, you first have to overcome its inertia. What this means is that you have to apply a force to accelerate it
from rest into motion—but once the object is in motion, intertia takes
on its other role, that of keeping it in motion at constant velocity.
From here on, force is required only to overcome friction or any other
resistance forces that are acting to slow it down. In lifting a weight,
you have to overcome both inertia and gravity to start the lift, but
once the weight is moving, inertia is now on your side; you're working
only against gravity.

Let's look more closely at the act of throwing a ball. The throw
begins with the thrower's arm pulled back and the ball at rest in his
hand. If the thrower takes a run-up before making the throw, he first
uses his legs to overcome intertia and to give the ball its initial motion,
after which he uses his upper body and arm to accelerate it further
and send it into flight. As his arm is brought forward the ball gains
speed, and it continues to accelerate until it leaves the thrower's hand.
The accelerating force is provided by the muscles of the thrower's
shoulder, which must accelerate not only the ball but also the thrower's arm. At the moment of release, the accelerating force no longer
acts on the ball—its motion is now determined solely by inertia and
gravity—but the shoulder muscles still have the job of decelerating
the thrower's arm to a stop.

What factors decide the speed of the ball at the moment of release?
The launching speed depends on the acceleration, which in turn depends on the net accelerating force and the mass of the ball, in accordance with Newton's second law. The accelerating force is set by the
thrower's muscular strength and throwing technique, and to simplify
matters we'll assume that he's throwing as efficiently and with as
much force as he can muster. For a given throwing force the acceleration will then depend on the mass of the ball; the more mass it has,
the less acceleration (and launching speed) will be attained. This explains in scientific terms the rather obvious fact that you get better
distance throwing a lighter ball than a heavier one, assuming that air
resistance does not significantly affect the flight of the ball after its
release.

Now let's move to the other end of the throw. A ball or some other
projectile is approaching at a given speed, and the receiver's job is to
decelerate the object to a stop. To do this, he must apply an opposing
force to the projectile using some part of his body, preferably his
hands, and the idea is to use as little force as possible so as to reduce
the chance of pain or damage to the body.

One factor, of course, is the mass of the projectile. The greater its mass, the greater the force needed to bring it to a stop; but once the projectile is in motion, there's nothing the receiver can do about its mass. The only way to reduce the force, then, is to reduce the size of the acceleration (actually, it's a deceleration we're talking about, but Newton's second law doesn't make any distinction between positive and negative acceleration). This can be done by consciously bringing the projectile to a stop *over a longer interval of time*. The basic technique—one that most people learn by experience—is to pull the hands backward while making the catch, thereby taking more time and decelerating the projectile at a slower rate. This is precisely the same principle as that of "rolling with a punch"—by decelerating your adversary's fist over a longer distance and time, the decelerating force (supplied by your head) is made smaller. However, there are some situations in sports where there is no choice but to decelerate the projectile as rapidly as possible—a first baseman stretching for a throw, or an infielder on a tag play, for instance. Wearing a glove serves an important purpose here because the ball is decelerated as it compresses the glove material, thereby reducing the intensity of the force that has to be supplied by the fielder's hand.

In these few illustrative examples, we've seen how Newton's second law can be used to explain some of the things athletes have learned to do by experience. In later chapters, we'll be making more specific and detailed use of this valuable principle.

Action and Reaction

As we've seen, the ideas that Newton put to use in formulating the first two laws of motion are not entirely original. Even his theory of gravitation contained elements that were borrowed and synthesized from the work of others. But in Newton's third law we have a really original idea that sprang entirely from Newton's imagination, an elegant and surprising concept with remarkable explanatory power.

Newton's third law is the famous principle of action and reaction. Let me first state it in its unadorned, scientific form:

If one object exerts a force on a second object, the second object exerts an equal and opposite force on the first object.

Several important ideas are contained in this statement. The first is that a force never acts in isolation: if object A pushes on object B, then B automatically exerts a push on A; every force invokes a counterforce. Secondly, the force and counterforce—the action and reaction—*each act on a different object*. Consequently, they cannot counterbalance or cancel each other out, because each of the two forces has its own separate effect. Another consequence of the third law is that a force can never exist as a single entity; forces always come in pairs. Forces are *interactions* between two objects: although we may tend to think of one force (the action) bringing on the second force (the reaction), the two forces must exist simultaneously or not at all. In many instances there is no real distinction between the two. Consider a book lying on a table: the book presses down on the tabletop, and the tabletop presses upward on the book. Which is the action, which is the reaction?

The symmetry of action and reaction is preserved by another feature of the law—namely, that the forces are equal and opposite. This means specifically that the forces have the same strength, but act in opposite directions (if A pulls B to the right with a force of 10 pounds, then B pulls A to the left with a force of 10 pounds). This feature leads to some thoroughly unexpected (and initially unbelievable) conclusions. The moon travels in an orbit around the earth, and we know that it remains in orbit because of the earth's gravitational pull on the moon. According to Newton's third law, the moon must also exert a gravitational pull on the earth. Question: which is larger—the earth's pull on the moon, or the moon's pull on the earth? Intuitively, one might think that the earth exerts a greater force because it is a larger body. But according to the third law, the moon and earth must pull on each other with *equal* force! This conclusion seems entirely contrary to our intuition and our expectations—but Newton could not have fully explained the orbit of the moon without it.

The key to understanding (and coming to believe) this strange conclusion is to recognize that while the forces in an action-reaction pair are equal, their *effects* are not necessarily the same. The effect of a force depends on the mass of the body on which it acts—the larger the mass, the smaller the acceleration—and the two members of the action-reaction pair each act on a different object. Thus while the earth and moon exert equal gravitational forces on each other, the effect of the earth's pull on the moon is greater than that of the moon's pull on the earth, because the moon's mass is so much smaller than that of the earth. As a consequence, the moon has a much greater orbital acceleration. (If the earth and moon had the same mass, they would orbit each other.)

To clarify this point further, think of an apple falling from a tree: we all recognize that the apple falls because of the earth's gravitational pull. But the third law tells us that the apple must be pulling upward on the earth with the *same* force that the earth is exerting on the apple. However, the effect of the apple's pull on the earth is insignificant because of the comparably huge mass of the earth; the apple accelerates noticeably toward the earth, whereas the earth's acceleration toward the apple is totally undetectable.

We can illustrate this principle on a more mundane level by analyzing the consequences of a punch in the nose. The third law requirement is that the nose must exert the same force on the fist as the fist does on the nose—yet one would much rather be the puncher than the punchee. Once again we have to realize that while the action-reaction forces are equal in strength, their *effects* are different—in this case the difference arises from the fact that a nose is more likely to suffer damage and pain from a given force than a fist is.

The value of the third law extends well beyond its capacity to surprise us with interesting explanations. As we will soon see, the third law plays a pivotal role in helping us understand and analyze athletic activities. Its particular importance to this end arises from its use in explaining virtually every form of locomotion or self-propulsion, from walking to space travel.

The basic problem of self-propulsion may be outlined in very simple terms. An object, initially at rest, is to be set in motion—a motion whose speed and direction can be controlled and monitored. According to Newton, an object at rest can be set in motion only by an external force acting in the direction in which the object is to move. It makes no difference whether the object is a person or something inanimate; the problem is still the same—how to get some external entity to apply a force in the right direction.

Obviously, the problem of locomotion can't be too difficult—after all, people learn to propel themselves before they're a year old. But our concern here is to explain how it takes place in scientific terms. Let's begin with walking, the most basic form of locomotion. Think carefully for a moment about how you walk: the basic action is to press *backward* with your foot on the floor. For every action, there is an equal and opposite reaction—so if you push backward on the floor, the floor automatically pushes forward on you. This forward push is precisely the force (exerted by an external object, the floor) that accelerates you forward. Whether you're walking, or crawling on hands and knees, or running, the principle remains the same—push backward on the ground, and the ground pushes forward on you.

What kind of force do we generate by this action? Surprisingly, the propelling force is friction—a force that we normally think of as a retarding force. But it is just that aspect of friction that propels us, for friction prevents the foot from sliding backward when it is pushed in that direction, thereby creating the forward reaction force on the foot. Try to walk or run on ice, a highly waxed floor, or any other low-friction surface—your feet simply slide out from under you. Running on a sandy beach is a difficult and tiring activity because the sand gives way underfoot and provides very little resistance or forward-directed force.

Effective locomotion also calls for the ability to decelerate as well as accelerate. To slow down when walking or running, we again make use of friction—in this case by pushing *forward* on the ground with our feet. In reaction, the ground pushes backward, providing the force that resists and decelerates our forward motion.

In order for us to move effectively, the more friction the better, and athletic footwear is specifically designed to create as much friction and surface contact as possible. Sneakers have soles made of rubber —a high-friction substance—with a pattern of grooves or bumps designed to increase the amount of surface contact. Cleats and spikes, by digging into the surface, prevent the foot from sliding and provide the traction needed for rapid acceleration and deceleration. Football players have a particular problem because of the many different surfaces they play on in the course of a season: soft or frozen ground, dry or wet grass, a variety of artificial surfaces. Accordingly, they are provided with several different kinds of footwear to choose from, depending on the field conditions.

There are a few sports that take place on rather slippery surfaces— notably skiing, ice skating, and ice hockey. How do the participants manage to accelerate and decelerate? Ice skaters use the edge or tip of the skate blade, digging it into the ice to produce a surface to push off (hockey players sometimes prefer to push off each other). In downhill skiing the idea is to move as rapidly as possible, and waxing the skis is one way to reduce friction. The external accelerating force is provided mainly by gravity, but the skier also uses the ski edges and especially his ski poles to produce desired changes in speed and direction on his run. One of the lesser-known forms of skiing competition is speed skiing, in which, as the name implies, participants try to attain the highest possible speed on a downhill run. Accelerating mainly by gravity (the course is inclined at a 50° angle), skiers have achieved speeds as high as 125 mi/hr.

The use of friction in locomotion leads us to an interesting hypothetical question: if you were standing out in the middle of a perfectly hard and frictionless sheet of ice, how would you get yourself to the edge? Without friction, you can't get yourself started—walking, running, crawling simply leave you in the same place. And you can't dig into the surface (it's perfectly hard) to give you an edge to push off. What can you do? As you might have suspected, Newton's third law provides a solution. Since you can't push off the surface, you have to push off something else. You could, for example, take off a shoe and throw it with as much force as you can. As you push the shoe to throw it, it pushes back on you—and once your body is accelerated (in the opposite direction from the throw), you should glide smoothly across the frictionless surface to the edge. Incidentally, this brings up an important aspect of throwing any projectile: the projectile is pushing backward on the thrower with as much force as the thrower is exerting to accelerate it. This is why it's more difficult to throw while jumping or running, and why it's important to "plant your feet" before launching a throw—by digging in, you provide another force to counteract the effect of the backward-acting reaction force of the projectile.

At the end of the last chapter, we learned that the ideal sprinter accelerates only in the first few seconds of a race; his acceleration, which is maximum at the start, tapers off rapidly, and he runs at constant speed thereafter. Why is there a limit to running speed? Newton's laws can supply an answer.

When you walk, at least one foot is always in contact with the ground, and at one point in your stride both feet are on the ground simultaneously. In fact, a basic rule of race walking is that the participant must make simultaneous contact with the heel of one foot and the toe of the other in every stride. (The peculiar hip-waggling motion that race walkers use keeps them from bobbing up and down excessively as they move.) On the other hand, when you run, both feet never touch the ground simultaneously, and your body is airborne for a significant part of the time. In a running stride, first one foot is planted on the ground; then the trailing leg is swung forward and the runner's body becomes airborne; finally the other foot, now in front of the body, strikes the ground. A runner in full stride at top speed typically has a stride length (measured from footprint to footprint) that is about 20% greater than his body height, so stride lengths of 7 feet or more are not unusual. If we multiply a runner's stride length by his stride frequency (the number of strides per second), we get his running speed. So the secret to running fast would seem to be: take long strides, as rapidly as possible. But it's not that simple.

A runner cannot accelerate while he is off the ground because he has nothing to push against—in fact he decelerates because of air resistance. Thus the runner must use the contact time—the time interval when one foot is on the ground—to push backward on the ground so that the reaction force will accelerate him forward. (The runner also exerts a downward force with his foot to support his weight and decelerate his body vertically when it lands.)

The start of a race is the point of maximum acceleration, and this is the moment when the runner must push backward with as much force as possible. By starting in a crouch, with his legs nearly parallel to the ground, the runner can direct most of his leg thrust horizontally backward (Fig. 2.3). Sprinters are provided with angled blocks, anchored to the track, to give them a firm surface to push off. (In the past, sprinters were allowed to dig holes in the track to set their feet in at the start.) After the start, the first few strides are relatively short (providing proportionally more contact time), and the sprinter inclines his body forward to increase the horizontal (backward) component of his force against the ground.

As a runner gains speed he straightens his body to increase his stride length—but he soon finds it more and more difficult to run faster. One reason is that the faster he moves, the less time his feet spend in contact with the ground. In addition the force of air resistance increases with speed. Ultimately, though, there is a limiting speed because the runner simply cannot move his legs fast enough. With each stride, he must bring up his trailing leg and plant it in front of his body, putting it down so that it will push backward on the ground on contact. The faster he runs, the less time he has in which to do this. At a certain running speed, the runner finds that his muscles simply cannot accelerate his leg forward as rapidly as needed. He may find himself having to put down his foot while it is still going forward, in which case it creates a decelerating force on his body. The mass of the runner's leg is also a factor here—the more mass it has, the more

FIGURE 2.3   The sprint start. Maxie Parks is shown practicing his starts at the 1976 Olympic Games in Montreal. The low angle of his body enables him to push off the starting blocks with a nearly horizontal force. The reaction to this force accelerates his body forward *(UPI photo)*.

muscular force needed to accelerate it. (Thus heavy-legged athletes generally do not make good sprinters.) Eventually, the runner settles into a stride length and frequency that he can maintain comfortably.

Since human beings have only two feet, they must necessarily stride by alternating from one foot to the other. But think of all the options that four-footed animals have available to them! It's interesting to watch a four-footed animal in full run and try to follow the sequence of how his feet hit the ground; each of the different gaits of horses—trot, canter, gallop, etc.—has a different sequence.

The various ways that we have of propelling ourselves in water can be easily understood through the third law. A swimmer uses his hands and arms to push backward on the water, and the water exerts a reaction force that pushes him forward. Pushing downward on the water—as one does in the "dog paddle"—causes the water to push upward; this helps to keep a person afloat but does not propel him forward. In rowing a boat, the rower uses the oars to push backward on the water; the larger the blade surface, the greater the force will be.

Finally, let us consider for a moment what is often regarded as ancient mankind's greatest invention—the wheel. Long ago, our ancestors discovered that when you are using an animal, slave, close relative, or (as a last resort) yourself to drag a heavy object, it's much easier to do if the object is first placed on a carrier with wheels. The reason, as we now understand it, is because there is less friction to overcome; as a rule, the rolling friction between any two surfaces is always less than the sliding friction between them. In its earlier uses, the wheel was a passive device, attached to something that was being pulled or pushed. But over the past few centuries the wheel has acquired additional application as a more active propulsion device. In this new role, the wheel is forcibly rotated, whether it be by the legs of a bicyclist or by the engine of an automobile or locomotive. As the wheel is turned, the friction between the wheel and the surface it's resting on creates an action-reaction pair of forces—the wheel pushes backward on the surface at the point of contact, and the surface pushes forward on the wheel. It is this second force that accelerates the wheel forward. To stop a turning wheel, we apply the brakes—and what they do is to slow down and then lock the wheel so as to prevent it from turning. Now the wheel is forced to *slide* forward on the surface, creating a retarding friction force that decelerates it to a stop. Strictly speaking, what makes an automobile go forward is not the engine, but the friction between the tire and the road. The engine simply spins the wheel—but if there's no friction, the wheel will not go forward. Similarly, the brakes do not directly stop an automobile; they stop the wheel from turning—but on an icy road a car with its brakes engaged and wheels locked can still travel quite a distance.

This completes our introduction to the basic concepts of Newton's theory of motion, as embodied in his three laws. In this chapter, we considered a few examples of how these principles can be used to help us understand, analyze, and predict various features of sports and athletic performance. In the next chapter we will examine some more specifically sports-related applications of Newton's laws.

3 / MORE ABOUT FORCES

It seems fairly certain that Sir Isaac Newton did not like sports. His biographers tell us that "instead of playing among the other boys, when from school, he always busied himself in making knick-knacks and models of wood" and that he "was always a sober, silent, thinking lad, and was never known scarce to play with the boys . . . at their silly amusements." Nevertheless, I like to think that Newton would not have objected too strenuously to seeing his principles used to explain the flight of a golf ball or the collision between a bat and a baseball. After all, it was his intention to show that *everything* in the universe obeys the same natural laws. He achieved this goal, as we well know, with spectacular success.

To Newton, the physical universe consisted of nothing more than material objects and the forces between them. Given the initial position and speed of any object and the forces that act upon it, the laws of motion predict its future motion with considerable precision. The "objects" that I constantly refer to in this book could be stones, or baseballs, or living human beings—it makes no difference at all; the laws of motion apply to all things, animate or inanimate.

In this chapter I'm going to present a few more ways in which Newton's laws can be used to explain common occurrences in everyday life and in sports. First we'll look at some of the phenomena associated with circular and rotational motion; then we'll turn our attention to see how the human body, acting as a Newtonian "object," creates and responds to forces.

Going in Circles

According to Newton's laws, circular motion cannot be considered as a natural form of motion. Since motion on any curved path involves a change in direction, it is necessarily accelerated motion and therefore requires a force. Thus no object can naturally travel on a curved path; a force must act to thwart its natural tendency to travel on a straight line. An object traveling on a curved path, even if it has a constant speed, is being accelerated away from a straight line. The force that is causing this acceleration must therefore act to push or pull the object away from a straight line and toward the inside of the curve (Fig. 3.1).

Let's consider an object that is moving in a circular path at constant speed. At every point on its path, the object has a natural tendency to continue off in a straight line. To keep it moving in a circular path, an inward-acting force must be applied—one that changes the *direction* of its velocity but not its speed. A detailed analysis of this situation (one that can be found in any introductory physics text, if you're curious) demonstrates that *the force must always act toward the center of the circle*. This kind of force is known as a *centripetal* (literally, "center-seeking") *force* (Fig. 3.2).

The strength of the centripetal force (F_{cent}) needed to sustain circular motion can be calculated from the equation

$$F_{cent} = \frac{mv^2}{R}$$

where m is the mass of the object, v is its speed and R is the radius of the circle it's traveling on. This equation defines the precise amount of force required to keep an object moving in a circle at constant speed. If the actual force on the object is less than the prescribed strength, the object will curve outward, away from the circle; if the

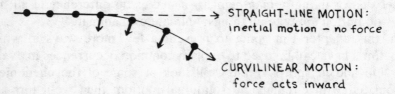

FIGURE 3.1   Motion on a curved path.

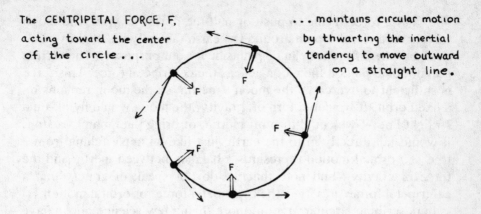

The CENTRIPETAL FORCE, F, acting toward the center of the circle... ...maintains circular motion by thwarting the inertial tendency to move outward on a straight line.

FIGURE 3.2   Centripetal force.

actual force is greater than required, the object will spiral inward. The equation shows the following relationships:

1. The greater the mass of the object, the more force is needed to keep it on a circle (as m increases, F_{cent} increases)
2. The greater the speed of the object, the greater the force needed (as v increases, F_{cent} increases)
3. The smaller the radius of the circle, the greater the force needed (as R decreases, F_{cent} increases)

To clarify these features, let's look at the specific example of a car being driven on a circular track. The centripetal force that keeps the car on the circle is the friction between the tires and the track. If there is insufficient friction, the car will curve outward; that is, it will skid to the outside of the track. There are several aspects of negotiating a curve or turn, following from the centripetal force equation, that are familiar to any driver. For example, a heavier car is more likely to skid outward than a lighter one; a car is more likely to skid outward if it's driven at a higher speed; the car is more likely to skid on a sharp curve or a tight turn (corresponding to a smaller radius of curvature) than a wider one.

To understand the concept of centripetal force, you must keep in mind that circular motion is *not* a natural motion, but a balance that has been struck between inertia (the tendency to travel on a straight line) and a force trying to push or pull the object inward. The moon travels on a circular path around the earth (actually it's slightly elliptical, but the difference can be put aside for our purposes). The earth's gravitational pull on the moon acts as the centripetal force. This force is sufficient to overcome the moon's inertia, so the moon remains on a fixed orbit. If we could turn off gravity, the moon would fly off on a straight line; if we could turn off inertia, or bring the moon to a stop, it would fall directly in to the earth, just like an apple falling from a tree. *All* orbital motion represents a balance between inertia and the force of gravity—and note that we do not speak of gravity *and* a centripetal force; gravity *is* the centripetal force for orbital motion.

In describing circular motion, more than a few science books have made the concepts more difficult to understand by confusing *centripetal* force with *centrifugal* force. A centrifugal ("center-fleeing") force is supposed to arise in circular motion to push objects off the circle, away from the center, according to the incorrect view. Actually, this centrifugal *tendency,* as it should more properly be called, is nothing more than inertia. Objects tend to fly away from a circle, not because of an outward-acting force, but because of their natural tendency to move on a straight line. Orbital motion is sometimes incorrectly described as the result of a "balance between the inward centripetal force and the outward centrifugal force"—but if this were true, and there were two exactly counteracting forces, then there could not be an orbit: the object would experience a net force of zero and would have to travel on a straight line.

The spin-drying action of a washing machine can be used to illustrate this point further. At the end of the spin-dry cycle, the clothing is found flattened against the wall of the basket and all the water has been spun out. This is *not* the result of an outward, centrifugal "force," but of inertia. Once the basket begins to spin, the wet clothing starts to move on a straight line—but then it collides with the wall of the basket. The wall exerts an inward, *centripetal* force on the clothing that prevents it from moving on a straight line, and keeps it going in a circle. The water, on the other hand, escapes because it can continue to move inertially by passing through the small holes in the side of the basket.

The use of circular motion and centripetal force as a device for launching a projectile is a feature of a number of sports. The prototype for this action is a weight being spun around at the end of a string. The centripetal force that keeps the weight moving on a circle is the inward pull exerted by the string on the weight. In accordance with Newton's third law, the weight must exert an equal and opposite— i.e., outward—pull on the string, a pull that is in turn transmitted by the string to the hand of the person swinging the weight. (This outward reaction to the centripetal force is identified by some physicists as the centrifugal force. This a legitimate definition—provided it is made clear that the centrifugal force *does not act on the circling object,* but on whatever is creating the centripetal force.) To make the weight circle at greater speed, a larger centripetal force is needed, and at some point the reaction force on the string may be so great that it either breaks the string or causes the person holding the string to release his grip. When this happens, *the centripetal force no longer exists*—therefore the weight will revert to its natural, inertial motion and take off on a straight line.

Two athletic events that make use of this principle are the discus and hammer throw. In each of these, the athlete first spins his body several times to gain speed. He then releases his grip on the projectile, which consequently flies off on a straight line. The hammer throw is a particularly interesting event because of the throwing speeds attained and the amount of force required, so we'll have a more detailed look at it later. A similar motion is used in the windmill-style softball pitch: the pitcher starts the ball above his head, swings his arm in a wide arc, and releases the ball when it is a little past the bottom of the circle. In each of these examples, the centripetal force is being supplied by the muscles in the thrower's hands, arms, and shoulders that help to pull the projectile onto a circular path before it is released.

A less obvious use of centripetal force is in swinging a tennis racket, golf club, baseball bat, or a similar piece of equipment. These all travel on circular arcs when they're swung, so the holder must provide a centripetal force to make them go in a circle. As a good demonstration of this principle, think about what happens when the bat slips out of a hitter's hand during a swing—namely, it flies off on a straight line out into the field. The knob on the end of a baseball bat helps to prevent this from happening. In addition, batters have a variety of ways to increase the friction between their hands and the bat handle. A traditional method for professional players is the use of pine tar to make the bat handle stickier. One of the great rituals of my youth was the wrapping of the handle of a newly purchased bat with adhesive tape to give it a better grip. In recent years, batting gloves have become increasingly popular for this purpose.

Racing a high-speed vehicle or running on a curved track presents a specific problem for the competitor, because he must in some way provide a centripetal force to overcome his inertial tendency to continue on a straight line. For a turning car or bicycle, the centripetal force is supplied by the friction exerted by the ground on the tires—a force that is angled toward the center of the curve when the wheels are turned in that direction (Fig. 3.3). But, as noted before, the friction developed between the tires and ground may not give sufficient force at high speeds or on sharp turns to keep the vehicle from skidding outward. One way to increase this force is by improving the design of the tire surface to create greater traction. But the most effective way to provide additional centripetal force is by banking the track. The track surface actually exerts two forces on any vehicle—a friction force, parallel to the surface, and an upward force (perpendicular to the surface) to support the weight of the vehicle. On a flat track, only the friction force can contribute to the centripetal force. But if the surface is banked, then the upward force acts partially inward (in vector terms, it has a component acting toward the center of the curve), as shown in Figure 3.4. Consequently, a banked track can exert a centripetal force even without any friction. In effect, the angled surface of the track acts somewhat like the wall of the basket in a washing machine, exerting an inward force to prevent straight-line motion.

The angle at which the track is banked is chosen to provide sufficient centripetal force, without the aid of friction, for a given speed

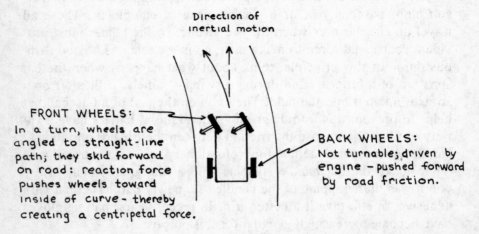

FIGURE 3.3 Centripetal force on a turning car.

FORCES ON A WHEEL —
FLAT TRACK

FORCES ON A WHEEL —
BANKED TRACK

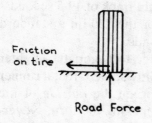

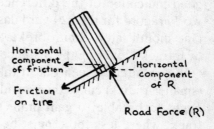

Centripetal force = friction

Centripetal force =
horizontal components of
friction and road forces

FIGURE 3.4 Centripetal force on a banked track.

and curve radius. For a curve of, say, 500-feet radius, the proper banking angle is 26° at 60 mi/hr, and 63° at 120 mi/hr. Friction then provides the driver with an additional safety margin that allows him to negotiate the curve at a somewhat higher speed. Drivers can also increase their margin of error by using the technique of "taking a wide turn" or steering to the outer edge of the curve. This increases the radius of the curve, thereby decreasing the centripetal force required to make the turn.

Running tracks, particularly outdoor ones, are normally not banked. An exception is usually made for wooden indoor tracks in small arenas, to compensate the runner for the shorter straightaways and the greater number of turns he has to make on a small track. To turn a curve on a flat track, a runner must push outward on the surface to generate an inward-acting reaction force. Thus a runner leans inward on a turn and uses his legs and feet to push in an outward direction on the track surface. (The next time you ride a bicycle, notice how you automatically tilt the bike inward on a turn—the principle is the same.)

On a straightaway, a runner pushes downward and backward on

the track, creating a reaction force that accelerates him forward. But on a curve, a runner must also push outward—in other words, some of the force normally used to change speed must be used to change direction. This diversion of effort means that a runner cannot increase his speed on a curve as much as he can on a straightaway. Here's a good indication of the difference: in May 1966, Tommie Smith set a world record for the 220-yard dash on a straight track of 19.5 seconds. One month later, Smith broke the record for the 220 on a standard oval track, covering the distance in 20.0 seconds.

We've already seen that it takes more force to negotiate a tighter (smaller-radius) curve than a wider one. It follows, then, that a runner ought to be able to gain more speed running on the *outside* of the track, where less force must be diverted to making the turn. Nevertheless, the strategy of "getting the inside track" is so well established that the phrase has become an idiom of the language. Is there a contradiction here?

The main advantage of the inside track is simply that it is shorter. If you keep to the outside on an oval track, you have to run a longer distance to complete a lap. In longer-distance events (400 meters and up) the runners do not have to stay in their lanes. They try to get the inside track because it's a shorter run, and also to force a trailing runner to travel on a longer path in order to pass. But in sprint races, the contestants must stay in their lanes. If the race is not being run on a straight track, then the starting positions must be staggered to compensate for the greater length of the outside lane. (In a 200-meter dash, the differences in distance are compensated for in the first 100 meters.) Thus in sprint races with a staggered start, since everyone must run the same distance, the advantage—perhaps as much as a tenth of a second—lies in running on the *outside* track. Nevertheless, most sprinters still prefer the inside track! In a staggered start, the sprinter on the outside starts out ahead of everyone, and cannot see his competition for the first 100 meters. The one who draws the inside lane starts farthest back. Even though there is no self-pacing or strategy involved—everyone simply tries to accelerate as rapidly as possible to top speed—sprinters claim that there is a psychological advantage to being on the inside lane, where you can see all the other runners and catch them from behind.

The Center of Gravity

Many objects move linearly and rotate at the same time. Of course, Newton's three laws apply with equal validity to both kinds of motion. Under what conditions will an applied force cause linear motion as opposed to rotation? How can a force be directed to emphasize rotation at the expense of linear motion, or vice versa? Common experience tells us that to make an object rotate, you have to apply an off-center force: to spin a wheel, or throw a curve ball, or launch a Frisbee, a force must be applied to the edge of the object—and the farther from the center the force is applied, the more effective it is. It's easy to see that if a force is applied so that it acts through the center of an object, the object will not rotate.

What specifically do we mean by the center of an object? If the object is a circle or a sphere, then the center is the point that is the same distance from every point on the circumference. The center of a regular geometric figure like a rectangle or a cube is equidistant from its corners. But where is the center of a chair, or a baseball bat, or a human body? Clearly, this is not so easy to define. But from the physicist's point of view, insofar as the effects of forces are concerned, the "center" of any object, regardless of shape, is a specific point known as the *center of gravity*.

There is a very precise mathematical definition of the location of the center of gravity of any object, but it's too abstract to be presented here. Instead, I'll try to give several descriptive definitions that ought to give you a good sense of the meaning of this concept. The center of gravity is the balance point of any object—if you support an object at its center of gravity, it will not tip over of its own accord. In this sense, we can think of the center of gravity as the point about which the mass and weight of the object are evenly distributed. A somewhat more precise statement is that an object reacts to applied forces (including gravity) as if all its mass were concentrated at this point. In other words, if the line of action of a force passes through the center of gravity of an object, the object responds as if it were a "point mass"—a hypothetical, dimensionless entity with all of its mass located at its center of gravity. This concept, as we will see, greatly simplifies the analysis of forces and motion in many instances. (The center of gravity is also referred to as the *center of mass*. Actually there's a very subtle difference between the two, but it's of no concern to us here, and we can use the terms inter-changeably.)

The center of gravity (I'm going to call it "the CG" from here on) of an object is not necessarily the same point as its geometrical center, the reason being that the object may not have a uniform composition throughout (imagine a ball with one hemisphere made of iron, the other of wood—its CG would be shifted from the geometrical center into the iron side of the ball). Also, the CG doesn't have to be inside the object—for example, the CG of a donut is located in space, in the center of the hole. This definition of the CG as the balance point of an object gives us a simple procedure for locating its position. Very often, it's possible to find the approximate position of the CG by trying to balance the object on the tip of a finger. Try this with a baseball bat, for example. It's easy to demonstrate that the CG of an aluminum bat is several inches closer to the handle than on a wooden bat of the same length. (The explanation: an aluminum bat is hollow, while a wooden bat is solid, so the latter has relatively more weight at its upper end.)

To study how the human body creates and responds to forces, it is obviously very useful to locate its CG. Of course, the location of any individual's CG will depend on age, sex, and build. Moreover, the location of your CG changes with every move; if you bend at the waist, raise an arm, extend your leg, it changes the spatial distribution of body mass and thereby the position of the CG. A great many studies have been done to develop techniques to locate the CG for human bodies of various sizes, shapes, and configurations. (Much of this research has been done by and for the Air Force and NASA, ostensibly to design more comfortable equipment for pilots and astro-nauts.) Here are some of the more interesting and significant findings:

1. The vertical position of the CG for a person standing erect with arms at sides is typically about 55% of the person's height mea-sured from the floor, independent of the person's actual height or weight. This point is located about an inch below the navel.

2. Although the body is not symmetrical in the front-to-back direc-tion, the differences are not very significant. Thus the CG lies midway between one's front and back. (This rule may not hold for individuals who spend many hours drinking beer in front of the TV.)

3. The CG is slightly (about 1%–2%) higher in men than in women,

mainly because women tend to have a proportionally smaller upper body, heavier pelvis, and shorter legs.

4. The CG is up to 5% higher in children's bodies because of their proportionally larger heads and shorter legs. (One group of researchers came up with the interesting statistic that the CG remains at about 6 inches above the crotch throughout one's lifetime.)

5. Movement of the arms and legs can shift the position of the CG by several inches. For example, when you raise both arms vertically overhead, your CG rises 2 to 3 inches. With the body bent in a "U," with hands to toes (the "pike" position in diving and gymnastics), the CG may actually be located outside and in front of the body.

Having defined the center of gravity, we can now answer the question on the conditions under which a force will produce linear or rotational motion. The answer, very simply, is this: *If the line of action of the force passes through the center of gravity, the force will produce only linear motion.* The object will respond to the force as if all its mass were concentrated at the CG. If the force does not act through the CG, then it can produce both a linear motion and a rotation about the CG.

The act of kicking a football gives a good demonstration of the difference between these two outcomes. If the kicker's foot hits the football below its CG, the result will be an end-over-end kick. The football will rotate about its CG as it travels through the air. However, if the kicker's impact point is in line with the CG, the football will travel without tumbling—usually for a greater distance.

Following the Bouncing Ball

The use of spin plays a significant role in the tactics and techniques of virtually every sport that involves the use of a ball. It is no exaggeration to say that success or failure in many sports depends upon how well an athlete is able to control the speed and direction of spin on a ball when he hits or throws it. To do this, he must apply a force to the ball with his hand or with whatever implement he's using (tennis racket, paddle, etc.) so as to give the ball both a forward motion and a rotation about its center. Different grips and/or strokes must be mastered to give the ball a backspin, topspin, or sidespin, as desired.

We'll be discussing the importance of spin in several places in this book. Later on, we'll learn how spin stabilizes the flight of a ball, and also how air resistance makes a spinning ball curve, sink, or rise in flight. At this point, though, we will focus on the action that occurs when a spinning ball strikes a surface.

The physics of the situation is fairly easy to understand. When a ball hits a surface, it remains in contact with the surface for a brief period of time before it rebounds away. During this time the ball is skidding along the surface, creating a friction force. Normally, the ball will be pushing forward on the surface, and the surface will push backward on the ball. The result is a slowing of the forward speed of the ball. The amount of speed lost by the ball will depend on the size of the friction force, which in turn depends on the kind of ball, the surface, and the speed of the ball at the point of contact.

If the ball is spinning when it hits the surface, the rate and direction of its spin will alter the effect of the friction force. Thus the speed and direction of a spinning ball after it bounces may be quite different from the "normal" bounce of a ball with little or no initial spin. The higher the spin rate and the slower the linear speed of the ball, the greater will be its tendency to take an unusual bounce.

Let's begin by considering what happens when a ball that has been given backspin hits a surface. The ball's motion can be pictured as a combination of a forward linear motion and a rotation around its center, as shown in Figure 3.5. At the point of contact—where the ball touches the ground—the two motions are in the same direction and combine: in the example shown, the tennis ball has a forward speed of 30 mi/hr and a rotation speed at its edge of 2 mi/hr (corresponding to a spin rate of 5 rev/sec), so the bottom of the ball strikes the ground with a speed of 32 mi/hr. As a consequence, the friction force at the point of contact (Fig. 3.6) has more of an effect than if the ball had no spin. The result is a greater-than-normal loss of speed; the ball will then have a lower forward speed and will take a lower bounce.

If the initial forward speed is fairly small and the spin rate high—as it is in a well-executed backspin lob in tennis—the ball may even reverse direction entirely when it bounces. When hit correctly, a golf ball can be given a good backspin. Sometimes you'll see a golfer loft an approach shot over the flag, seemingly overshooting his target, but then the ball takes a nice backward bounce toward the hole when it

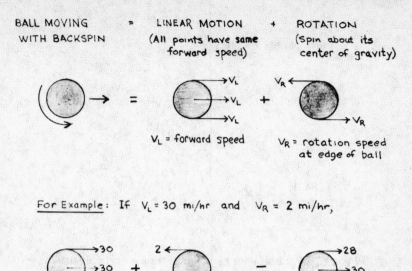

BALL MOVING = LINEAR MOTION + ROTATION
WITH BACKSPIN (All points have same (Spin about its
forward speed) center of gravity)

V_L = forward speed

V_R = rotation speed
at edge of ball

For Example: If V_L = 30 mi/hr and V_R = 2 mi/hr,

the bottom of the ball has the largest instantaneous speed.

FIGURE 3.5   Motion of a ball with backspin.

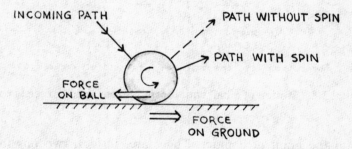

FIGURE 3.6   Effect of friction on a ball with backspin.

hits the green. When a ball strikes a vertical surface (Fig. 3.7), as it does in wall sports, backspin will cause the ball to be deflected more sharply downward by the friction force created on contact.

Hitting a ball so as to give it a topspin produces an entirely different result. Now the direction of rotation is opposite to that of the linear

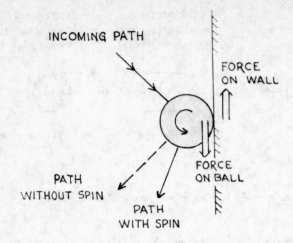

FIGURE 3.7   Ball with backspin hitting a vertical surface.

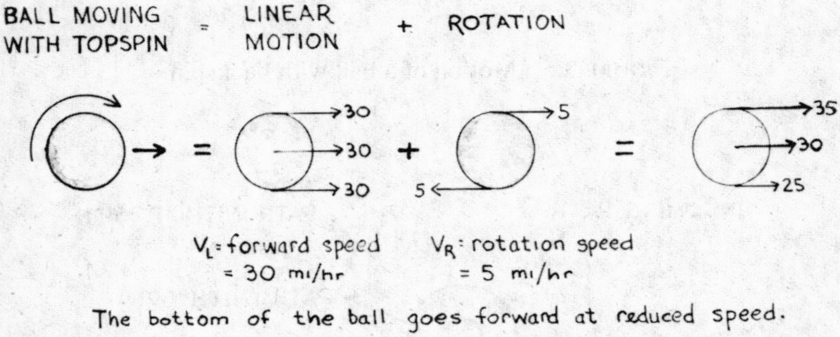

BALL MOVING WITH TOPSPIN = LINEAR MOTION + ROTATION

V_L: forward speed = 30 mi/hr V_R: rotation speed = 5 mi/hr

The bottom of the ball goes forward at reduced speed.

FIGURE 3.8   Motion of a ball with topspin: linear speed exceeds rotational speed.

speed at the point of contact. There are, in fact, two possible outcomes. In the first example (Fig. 3.8), the linear speed is greater than the rotation speed, so the ball is going forward at the point of contact, but at reduced speed. This lessens the effect of friction, so that the ball does not lose as much forward speed when it bounces as it would if it had no spin. A well-hit topspin shot will take a higher bounce and seem to jump toward you when it bounces—but it has not gained speed on the bounce; it simply has lost less speed than you expected it to.

The second example (Fig. 3.9) shows a slowly moving ball with a lot of topspin. Its rotation speed is greater than its linear speed, so that it will be going backward at the point of contact, like a wheel does. On contact, the ball will actually be *accelerated* by the friction force, and will thereby *gain speed* on the bounce. The topspin lob is a very difficult shot to make in tennis, but a very effective one, because the ball unexpectedly jumps up and away after it bounces.

Giving a ball sidespin when you hit it is often a good strategic maneuver. Depending on the direction of spin, the ball will veer sharply right or left when it bounces: if the ball is made to spin clockwise (as viewed by the server) it will veer to the server's right (receiver's left) when it bounces; a counterclockwise spin will, of course, veer the opposite way. One of the many sports where this technique is used is the English game of cricket. The bowler in cricket serves the same function as the pitcher in baseball. A bowler makes his

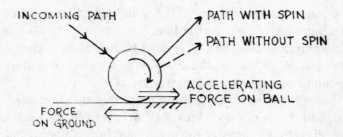

FIGURE 3.9 Motion of a ball with topspin: linear speed is smaller than rotational speed.

delivery with a stiff-armed overhand motion—but he is allowed to take a long run-up before releasing his throw, and he is also allowed to throw the ball on a bounce. Thus the bowler uses various types of spin to make the ball bounce or "pitch" at sharp angles toward or away from the batsman. Spin is also used strategically in the various forms of billiards, where it is known as "English." The spin on a ball is controlled by hitting it above, below, or to either side of its center with the cue. The expert billiards player knows how a ball with a particular kind of spin will react when it hits the rail or the other balls on the table, and makes use of this information every time he selects and lines up a shot.

Many a baseball game has turned fatefully on a "bad bounce" taken by a batted ball. Most of the time, a bad bounce results from the ball hitting some irregularity on the playing surface. Batted balls normally travel with linear speeds that are much greater than their rotation speeds (for a baseball, a rotation speed greater than about 15 mi/hr, corresponding to about 1700 rpm, is highly unusual), so spin is normally not a factor. Occasionally, though, a weakly hit ball coming off the end of the bat may have a rotation speed nearly the same as its linear speed, and it is likely to take an unpredictable bounce if it hits the ground.

Table tennis is another game where significant bounce effects arise because the rotation speed of the ball can be as large or even greater than its linear speed. When I was in my first year of college, I got seriously involved in the game—enough to cut an occasional class to play—and I got to be fairly good at it. Like most players at the time, I used the traditional pimpled-rubber-surface paddles. But my skills were quickly made obsolete by an unexpected technological advance —the sponge paddle. This paddle has thick, soft, foam-rubber surfaces, so the ball literally sinks into the surface when it hits, producing more friction and a longer contact time, and making it possible for the player to put a lot of spin on the ball. Anyone who could master the use of a sponge paddle had a great advantage, because it was so difficult to follow and return the shots. Wisely, and fortunately, I gave up table tennis for more intellectual pursuits.

A basketball can easily be given a large spin rate in comparison to its speed, and the use of spin does play an important role in basketball shooting. Players who master the art of banking a spinning ball off the backboard can make layups from seemingly impossible angles. One of the secrets of good basketball shooting is to give the ball a backspin by making the ball roll off your fingertips when releasing the shot. We've already seen that a ball loses the most speed when it hits a horizontal surface with a backspin. A basketball shot with backspin that hits the rim will lose a lot of its speed on contact, and is likely to drop into the basket. In shooting free throws, there's a significant advantage to using the underhand technique (the ball is gripped with one hand on either side, and the shooting motion starts with the ball between the player's knees). The ball can be thrown with a lot of backspin from this position, and the shot is more likely to go in if the ball hits the rim or backboard. However, only a few college or professional basketball players use this style. The most notable underhand free-throw shooter was Rick Barry, who had the highest career free-throw percentage of any NBA player. The main reason few players use this style, despite its advantages, is that most players prefer to shoot free throws with the same motion they use to take game shots, and an underhand shot is not very likely to be used during the course of play.

Yet another sport where spin and friction play a crucial role is bowling. Because of the spacing and arrangement of the pins, it is difficult to get strikes consistently by throwing a straight ball. In order to get the best sequence of collisions among the pins, the ball has to curve into the pocket. To make this happen, the ball has to be given a sideways spin, so that when it starts to slide down the lane the friction will deflect it sideways. A right-handed bowler naturally throws a ball that rotates counterclockwise. At the point of contact the ball will be pushing the floor to the right, so the floor will push the ball to the left. A left-handed bowler throws a clockwise-spinning ball, so the friction force will act to make the ball curve to the right. The amount of curvature of the path depends on the forward speed of the ball, the rate and direction of the spin, and the amount of friction between the ball and the lane surface. The greater the friction, the more the ball will curve, so lanes that are used in competition must be carefully cleaned and and uniformly oiled to maintain standard conditions. Yet no two lanes are ever exactly alike, so the bowler must adjust his throwing style to the particular lane.

The motion of a bowling ball can be subjected to a detailed mathematical analysis. In fact, in 1977 an article on this topic was published in the *American Journal of Physics* by D. C. Hopkins and J. D. Patterson, both physics professors at the South Dakota School of Mines. By making a few simplifying assumptions—that the ball doesn't bounce, and that the friction between ball and floor is constant—they were able to show in detail how the path is related to the launching velocity and spin. A bowling ball will always slide at first, and then begin to roll as it slows down. During the sliding phase, the curvature of the path gradually increases as the ball loses speed; but once the ball begins to roll instead of slide, it travels on a straight line. The authors contrasted their results with the "folklore" of bowling—specifically, that there is a difference between a hook (which is supposed to start out straight, then break sharply at the end) and a curve (which has a curved path from the beginning). The difference between bowlers' perceptions of curvature and the theoretical predictions could be due to a number of causes—including optical illusions, uneven friction on the lanes, or an oversimplified theoretical analysis. In any case, those of you who are bowlers ought to test out the theory on your own. Try different spin speeds and directions, and watch the curvature closely.

Keeping Your Balance

We've seen that if the line of action of a force passes through the center of gravity of an object, the force will produce a purely linear motion. To give an object a spin, it has to be hit off-center. Thus the effect of an *eccentric* (off-center) *force* is to set an object into rotation or, if the object is already rotating, to create a change in its rate of rotation. In the physicist's language, an eccentric force produces an *angular acceleration*—a change in the angular velocity of the object. Angular acceleration and rotational motion are central to much of athletic performance, and they will be examined more thoroughly in Chapter 4. For now, we're going to focus on another aspect of eccentric forces—their ability to disturb the balance or equilibrium of a stationary object.

The effect of an eccentric force does not depend only on its strength; the more "off-center" the force is, the greater its rotational effect. The "center" I'm referring to here is the pivot point or axis of rotation of the object in question. An object that is completely free to move rotates automatically about its CG when acted on by an eccentric force. But if one point of the object is fixed in place, it must, of course, rotate about that fixed point. For instance, when a force is applied to a door, it is constrained to rotate about its edge—where the hinges are—rather than about its CG. A baseball bat is forced to pivot at the handle when it is being held, but if you throw a bat, it will rotate naturally about its CG. Accordingly, the effect of an eccentric force depends on the distance from the point where the force is being applied to the pivot point. Called the *moment arm* of the force, this is defined as *the perpendicular distance from the line of action of the force to the pivot point* (Fig. 3.10).

The effectiveness of an eccentric force is equal to the strength of the force (F) times the length of the moment arm (d_m). This quantity is called the *torque* or *moment* of a force. The equation for torque is

$$T = Fd_m$$

torque = force × moment arm

The validity of this concept can be readily tested. Go to the nearest door and try to open it by pushing at a point close to the hinges. Not so easy, is it? Now push at a point farther from the hinges (thereby increasing the moment arm): now much less force is needed to make the door move. By making the moment arm as large as possible, the amount of force that you must apply to rotate the door becomes smaller. This is why doorknobs are placed at the edge of the door; they would look much nicer placed at the center, but then it would require twice as much force to open or close the door. A wrench

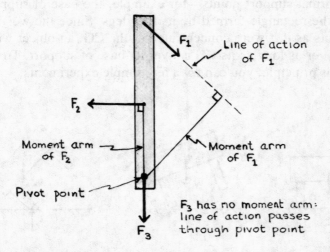

FIGURE 3.10   The moment arm of a force. The moment arm is the perpendicular distance from the line of action of a force to the pivot point.

operates on the same principle. To loosen a tight nut, you push as hard as you can on the end of the wrench handle—and if that doesn't work, use a wrench with a longer handle. Again, we see how the length of the moment arm determines the rotational effect of a force.

The key to understanding the concept of torque is to recognize that *a torque is not a force*. Rather, it is a measure of the *effectiveness of a force for producing rotation*. The same torque can be achieved by using either a small force with a long moment arm or a large force with a short moment arm.

Now let's see how torques affect stability. Consider the table shown in Figure 3.11: its weight is supported by the upward force exerted by the floor at its legs, and the table is in a stable equilibrium. In *b* the table has been tipped slightly. Its weight is now supported by only one set of legs, and the table can pivot about the axis passing through the two points of support. The line of action of the weight force passes to the left of the pivot points, and so it produces a counterclockwise "restoring" torque that acts to rotate the table back to its more stable, four-legged position. But if we tip the table until the line of action of the weight is to the right of the pivot *c,* its torque will now cause the table to rotate clockwise, and the table will fall over.

Here then, in a nutshell, is the principle of maintaining balance: *keep the line of action of the weight of the object inside its normal base of support*. The base of support is specifically the area enclosed by its normal support points—for example, the base of support of a table is the rectangle formed by its four legs. Since the weight of an object acts as if it were concentrated at the CG, an object will resist tipping over as long as its CG is over its base of support. To demonstrate this principle, you can try a few simple experiments.

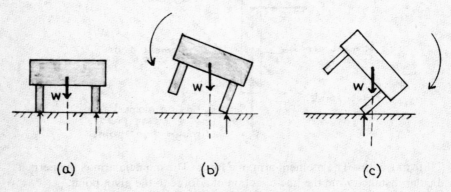

(a)   (b)   (c)

FIGURE 3.11   Torque and stability.

1. Try to balance a pencil on end. You'll find this extremely difficult, if not impossible. To achieve balance you have to get the CG of the pencil directly over the base of support—which, for a pencil, is virtually a point.
2. Try to balance yourself on your right foot. This is a lot easier to do—just keep your CG over your foot (if you have big feet, so much the better). You'll find that it's a lot more difficult to balance just on the toes of one foot, because it's not as easy to keep your CG over the smaller base of support. Notice also that if you lean too far to the right, you'll reflexively lift your left leg outward (this shifts the position of your CG to the left).
3. Now stand on both feet, keeping them fairly close together. Maintaining your balance takes almost no effort—as long as your CG remains over the region between your two feet. But if you lean too far forward or to one side so that your CG is outside this region, you'll lose your balance and be forced to take corrective action. Usually it's to move one foot forward or to the side to establish a new base of support, one that encompasses the line of action of your weight. Notice that if you stand with your feet farther apart (creating a wider base of support) you can lean a lot farther to the side without losing your balance.

Another aspect of maintaining balance is having a low center of gravity. In Figure 3.12 we see two objects, one with a high CG, one with a low CG, having the same base of support. To make either one tip over, we have to rotate it so that the CG is outside the base. It is easy to see that the object with the lower CG must be turned through a much larger angle before it will tip over. As a general rule, it requires a much greater effort to tip over an object with a lower CG. This is the reason why racing cars are built low to the ground with a wide wheelbase.

Once you come to understand how stability is maintained against destabilizing torques, you'll begin to see the reasons behind the actions that you take automatically to keep your balance in different situations. Here are a few examples:

When you're carrying a heavy weight, such as a pail of water, with one arm, why do you hold your free arm out horizontally? The reason is that this action shifts the CG of your body away from the weight, making it easier to keep your CG over the base of support.

Why do you lean forward when you're walking into a strong wind? The main reason is that the force of the wind, acting horizontally

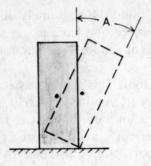

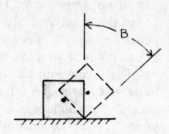

Object with high CG must be rotated through angle A to make it unstable (the CG is not over the base of support)

Object with lower CG (but same base) must be rotated through a larger angle (B) to make it unstable.

FIGURE 3.12   Stability and position of center of gravity.

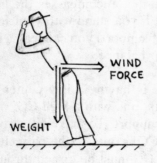

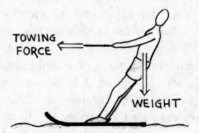

WIND FORCE

TOWING FORCE

WEIGHT

WEIGHT

FORWARD LEAN:
Counterclockwise torque of weight balances clockwise torque of wind force.

BACKWARD LEAN:
Clockwise torque of weight balances counterclockwise torque of towing force.

FIGURE 3.13   Body weight as a source of balancing torque.

through your CG, creates a torque which tends to rotate your body backward about its pivot point at the ground (Fig. 3.13). By leaning forward so that your CG is in front of your feet (outside the normal base of support) your weight creates an opposing torque that tends to rotate your body forward. By leaning at the appropriate angle, you can make these two torques counterbalance.

Why does a water skier lean backward when being towed? The forward pull of the towrope produces a torque that tends to rotate the skier's body forward, tipping him over. By leaning backward, the skier uses his weight to generate a countering torque (Fig. 3.13). The same technique is used in a tug-of-war to prevent a participant from being pulled off his feet.

The ability to maintain one's balance is essential to an athlete. In baseball, basketball, and football, players are taught to stand with feet spread apart, crouched forward with knees bent. As we've learned, this is a position of great stability—feet spread apart to give the widest base of support, and knees bent to keep the CG as low as possible. In this position, it's easy to keep your CG over your base of support and more difficult to lose your balance. In baseball and basketball, where a player must react quickly and reflexively to movement, this stance enables him to change direction from a position of stability. Thus the first reflexive reaction of a fielder to a batted ball or of a basketball player to the moves of the man he's guarding will be less likely to throw him off balance. The wide, squat stance is particularly suitable to football players and wrestlers because it makes them more difficult to topple.

A boxer's stance—one foot forward, one foot back—is different because he is responding to forces coming from his front rather than his side. When hit with a punch, he has to keep his CG between his two feet to prevent him from toppling over backward. A boxer who staggers backward when hit is trying to get his back foot behind his CG so that he can regain his stability.

A skier has a different problem because of the low friction and high speed that he encounters. He leans forward to counteract wind resistance, and crouches down to lower his CG. The skis provide a long, wide base of support to keep him from toppling forward or backward. By shifting the position of his CG between the two skis, a skier can vary the weight supported by each ski, and can thereby control his speed and direction.

Wrestling is a sport that makes full use of the basic principles involving torques and maintenance of balance. Wrestling throws generally involve maneuvers that force the opponent's center of gravity to shift outside of his base of support, accompanied by the use of one's body to create large torques so that the opponent can be thrown. Perhaps the most sophisticated form of wrestling is judo. This is a sport that developed in Japan (the word means "the gentle way" in

Japanese) from jujitsu, a form of unarmed combat used by samurai warriors to cripple or kill their opponents. Judo techniques in particular make effective use of the torque principle to enable an individual to throw a bigger and stronger opponent. For example, in a properly executed hip throw, the thrower uses his hip as the pivot point and tries to maneuver his opponent's center of gravity above this pivot (Fig. 3.14). The torque created by the thrower's pull on the arm of the opponent rotates him over the thrower's hip—and the opponent has no effective way to produce a countertorque against this rotation.

Compared with the subtle techniques of judo, professional wrestling is nothing more than a sham (notice how the matches are always referred to as "exhibitions"). Professional wrestlers must be skilled actors as well as athletes; the fun of watching them is to observe the skill with which they deliver their faked blows and take their falls without injuring themselves, while giving the impression that they are committing serious mayhem on each other. Their theatrical performances are in sharp contrast to amateur free-style wrestling competitions, which involve a great deal of careful maneuvering for favorable positions and holds.

In sumo wrestling, which is extremely popular in Japan, a match ends when one of the participants touches the mat with any part of his body other than his feet; contests are usually over in a matter of seconds and are invariably much shorter than the rituals that precede them. Sumo wrestlers weigh 300 pounds or more, for strength and

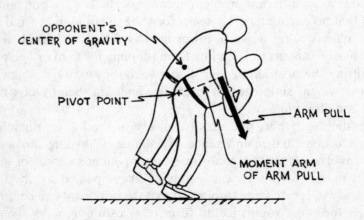

FIGURE 3.14   The judo hip throw.

size are their greatest attributes; the more mass they have, the more difficult it is to move them. If there is one key physical principle underlying sumo wrestling, it is the principle of inertia.

We could go on through a long list of sports giving more examples of how athletic movement is related to the positioning of the center of gravity. But I feel that the illustrations I've given here ought to be sufficient to get the idea across. The next time you watch some sports event on TV, particularly if it's a competition that involves good balance, like gymnastics, try to look for the subtle tricks they use to maintain balance, in the light of what we've just discussed.

There's one other way in which the torque concept can be of service to us: it stands as the basic principle behind that very ancient and useful invention, the lever. A lever is known to physicists as a "simple machine"—a device that is designed to alter the strength or direction of an applied force. To make a lever, all you need is a long, relatively rigid object (such as a metal bar) and a fulcrum, or pivot point. To use a lever we require a resistance—a weight to be moved or a force to be overcome—and an applied force to do the work. There are three different ways to set up the lever (see Fig. 3.15).

A lever essentially is set up for one of two purposes: either to reduce the force needed to overcome the resistance or to increase the range of movement of the resistance. Now here is where the torque concept comes in: to rotate a lever around its pivot point at the fulcrum, you must supply a torque greater than that created by the resistance. We've learned that a torque is the product of a force and its moment arm—the perpendicular distance from the line of action of the force to the pivot. Let's call the moment arm of the applied force the *effort arm, EA,* and the moment arm of the resistance the *resistance arm, RA,* as shown in Figure 3.16. We can determine the force,

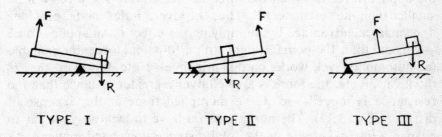

TYPE I   TYPE II   TYPE III

FIGURE 3.15   The three basic types of lever.

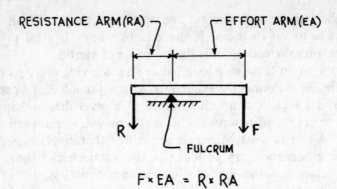

FIGURE 3.16   The principle of the lever.

F, needed to turn the lever by setting the two torques equal to each other:

$$F \times EA = R \times RA$$

so that

$$F = \frac{RA}{EA} \times R$$

$$\text{applied force} = \frac{\text{resistance arm}}{\text{effort arm}} \times \text{resistance force}$$

This gives the amount of force F needed to keep the lever in balance. To make the lever rotate, you must apply a force greater than F; the greater the force, the faster the lever will turn. It's not too difficult to see from this equation that if the effort arm is larger than the resistance arm—i.e., if the resistance is closer to the fulcrum than the applied force is—then the force needed to turn the lever will be smaller than the resistance, R. Thus the lever, in this mode, provides a mechanical advantage by multiplying the effect of an applied force —you can lift a 100-pound weight with a 10-pound force, for example (an automobile jack works on this principle). Note, however, that as the lever pivots, the force is applied over a greater distance than the resistance is moved—so we've multiplied force at the expense of distance (Fig. 3.17). The next time you have to jack up your car to change a tire, take note of the total distance your hand moves back and forth at the jack handle, just to lift the car a few inches off the ground.

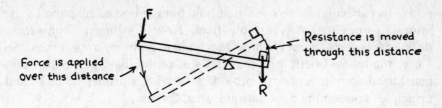

FIGURE 3.17   The lever: multiplying force at the expense of distance.

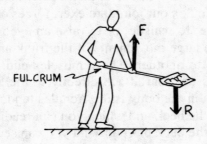

FIGURE 3.18   The shovel as a lever.

Levers of types I and II can be used to multiply forces, but what about a type III lever, where the resistance arm is necessarily larger than the effort arm? Here a force *larger* than the resistance must be used to rotate the lever—we're trading force for distance; by moving a larger applied force over a shorter distance, we move the (smaller) resistance through a larger distance. When you use a shovel to lift snow or dirt, you're using a type III lever; one hand (at the handle) acts as the fulcrum, while the other hand (on the shaft) exerts the effort (Fig. 3.18). A relatively small movement of the hand on the shaft produces a considerably larger movement of the shovel blade and the load it contains—but as a trade-off, the lifting force must be greater than the weight of the load. While it may seem that type III levers represent the least useful application of the lever principle, they in fact play an exceedingly important role in the workings of the human body, as we shall now discover.

Muscle Force

This chapter has concentrated on forces. We've talked about what forces are, and how to identify them, and especially about their effects. In particular, we've learned how human bodies respond to the various forces that may act on them. Now it's time to consider a different aspect—namely, how the human body *creates* forces. So I'm going to dip briefly into the ABCs of physiology, neuroanatomy, and kinesiology in order to provide you with a primer of facts and principles concerning how muscles exert forces.

Muscles are involved in many human bodily functions, including blood circulation and digestion. However, we're mainly interested in the skeletal muscles, the ones responsible for body movement. The skeletal muscles—there are several hundred of them, all told—allow us to stand erect, to flex our joints, to exert forces on external objects —and also to smile, to whistle, or to raise an eyebrow. The muscles responsible for the large movements of the trunk and limbs generally go from one bone to another. These muscles end in *tendons*—very strong, cordlike tissues that attach directly to the bone. Perhaps the best known tendon in the body is the Achilles tendon, which attaches the calf muscle to the heel, and which you can readily feel at the back of your ankle. On the back of your hand you can see the long tendons that attach your fingers to the muscles in your forearm that move them.

A skeletal muscle may serve one or more functions. It may act to move a part of the body, to stabilize a bone against the pull of other muscles, or to restrain excessive movement (such as the hyperextension of a joint) caused by the action of another muscle or an external force. All of these functions are performed in essentially the same way—*by contraction of the muscle*. Muscles are like ropes in that they can pull, but not push; they can exert force only by contracting or attempting to contract. A muscle can be stretched by an external force, but it cannot stretch itself. However, as it lengthens, a muscle can create a tension force as a resistance to being stretched (this process of exerting force while being stretched is known as *eccentric contraction,* as contrasted with *concentric contraction*—the exertion of force through contraction of the muscle). A muscle may also exert a tension force even without changing its length. This occurs when the muscle is being pitted against an immovable object, or is exerting force without moving, as in a tug-of-war or in arm-wrestling. (This exertion of force in the absence of a length change is known as *static contraction.*) The tension force generated by a muscle is not constant, but varies according to its change in length. Generally, a muscle produces its greatest tension in eccentric contraction, when it has been slightly stretched. Moreover, the faster the movement (the rate of contraction or lengthening) of the muscle, the smaller the tension it produces.

I'll clarify all this terminology with an example. Suppose that you're holding a 10-pound dumbbell in your hand (with your forearm horizontal and your palm facing up) and you want to lift it by bending your arm at the elbow—a maneuver known to body builders as a *curl*. The two major muscles involved in this action are the biceps, on the front of the upper arm, and the triceps, located on the back of the arm. These muscles are attached to opposite sides of the lower arm near the elbow. When the biceps contracts, it flexes (bends) the arm at the elbow; when the triceps contracts, it extends (straightens) the arm.

Simply holding the dumbbell stationary against the force of gravity requires muscle action, so the biceps is in static contraction, creating a tension force that keeps the forearm from being pulled down by the weight of the dumbbell. But to curl the dumbbell, the biceps must contract (a concentric contraction). As the arm bends, the triceps is stretched (eccentric contraction). When the dumbbell is slowly lowered by extending the arm, the roles reverse; the biceps is stretched as the triceps forcibly contracts. The biceps and triceps are known as *antagonistic* muscles, in the sense that each causes the opposite motion of the other. A similar pair is formed by the quadriceps, on the front of the thigh, and the hamstrings on the back. These muscles attach to the top of the lower leg and control the bending of the knee joint.

It's interesting to see how muscles produce the enormous variety of motions of which our bodies are capable. The processes by which we bend our arms, legs, and other joints are, in fact, based on the principle of the lever. It turns out that almost all the levers in our bodies trade force for distance, so that muscles exert forces many times larger than the resistances they must overcome. Figure 3.19 is a schematic of the forearm, which is pivoted about the elbow by the contraction of the biceps or triceps. The biceps is attached to the two forearm bones (the radius and ulna) a few inches in front of the actual pivot point of the elbow, where the humerus is hinged to the ulna, while the triceps is attached (to the ulna) right behind the pivot point. (Note: this is a simplified picture; there are actually several other muscles involved in the action.)

The resemblance of this arrangement to a lever is easy to see. When

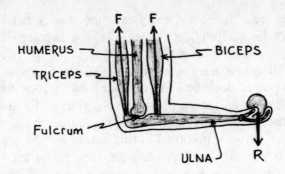

FIGURE 3.19   The forearm as a lever. Note that the resistance arm (the distance from the fulcrum to the resistance, R) is much larger than the effort arm (the distance from the fulcrum to the point of attachment of the muscle).

the biceps contracts, it pivots the forearm so as to flex the arm; when the triceps contracts it pivots the forearm the other way and straightens the arm. (You might find it instructive to verify that the forearm acts as a type III lever when it's being flexed by the biceps and as a type I lever when it's being extended by the triceps.) For either muscle, the effort arm is much shorter—anywhere from five to ten times shorter—than the resistance arm. Thus with relatively short contractions of the biceps or triceps, we are able to bend our arm through a much larger distance. The price that we pay for this privilege, however, is that these muscles must exert a force of contraction that is many times larger than the actual weight to be moved.

As the forearm pivots and the angle between the upper and lower arm changes, there is a corresponding change in the angle that the muscle makes with the bone at the point of attachment. Moreover, a muscle does not produce a constant tension when it is contracting or being stretched. As a consequence of these two factors, a muscle does not generate a constant torque. The biceps, for example, supplies the greatest torque when the arm angle is about 120°.

One other example: the diagram in Figure 3.20 shows the foot of someone standing on his toes. His foot is acting as a type II lever: the toes are the fulcrum; the resistance is the person's weight, transmitted through the leg bones onto the bones of the foot at the ankle joint; and the applied force, stabilizing the foot in this position, is the upward-acting tension in the Achilles tendon, attached at the heel. Again, we see that the effort arm is shorter than the resistance arm. To allow us

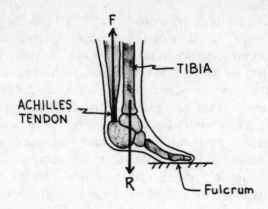

FIGURE 3.20 The foot as a lever.

to stand on the toes of one foot, the Achilles tendon must withstand a tension force about two or three times our body weight. When someone's Achilles tendon is damaged to the extent that it cannot provide the required tension, it becomes painful or even impossible for him to walk or run in a normal manner. This is the reason why a torn Achilles tendon is perhaps the most feared injury among athletes.

How does a muscle actually contract? To answer this question, we'll have to examine the structure of a muscle at a microscopic level. The basic unit is the *muscle fiber*—a rod-shaped cell a few millionths of an inch in diameter and several inches in length. Generally speaking, a skeletal muscle consists of many bundles of fibers, lined up in parallel along the length of the muscle (only a few individual fibers actually extend the entire length). Muscle fibers contract in response to a nerve impulse. This is a minute electric current which travels along a motor neuron directly from the spinal cord to the muscle fibers. The impulse causes a "twitch"—a momentary contraction and relaxation of the fiber. A single twitch may last anywhere from 50 to 500 milliseconds (1 millisecond = one thousandth of a second). However, a rapid series of nerve impulses can cause the individual twitches to merge into a single, sustained contraction at a constant level of tension. A single nerve impulse may trigger as few as five to as many as several hundred fibers into simultaneous contraction, the number of fibers triggered by a single neuron being smallest in muscles that control very fine movements.

A single motor neuron and its attendant muscle fibers are called a *motor unit.* The number of motor units in a given muscle depends upon the size and function of the muscle. When a muscle is first stimulated to contract, only some of its motor units are triggered, but if a greater effort by the muscle is required, then more motor units are called into use. Every muscle contains receptors, called *muscle spindles,* that respond to the movement of the surrounding muscle fibers by sending a nerve impulse back to the spinal cord. These receptors provide a feedback system that coordinates the number and rapidity of impulses sent to the muscles via the motor neurons.

An individual muscle fiber is rather flexible, and can contract or be stretched by as much as 50% of its normal length. A single fiber can exert a tension force of about 100 pounds per square inch of cross-sectional area. Hence the thicker the fiber (the larger its diameter), the more force it can exert (the cross-sectional area of a single fiber is, of course, exceedingly small). The more motor units being fired at any given instant, the more individual fibers that are contracting—and the greater the force exerted by the muscle as a whole.

Muscles contain a mixture of two different types of muscle fiber: *fast-twitch* and *slow-twitch.* Fast-twitch fibers respond more quickly to a stimulus and provide a stronger contraction of relatively short duration—a sharp pulse of force. Slow-twitch fibers respond more slowly with a less forceful but somewhat longer-lasting contraction. The ratio of fast-twitch to slow-twitch fibers varies according to the function of the muscle. Those muscles in which fast-twitch fibers predominate are useful when a burst of intense effort is needed, but these muscles tend to fatigue more quickly. Muscles having a majority of slow-twitch fibers are more amenable to sustained, steady effort, and are more fatigue-resistant. The ratio of fast-twitch to slow-twitch fibers also varies from individual to individual, and apparently is genetically determined to some degree. If the thought has just struck you that perhaps long-distance runners have more slow-twitch fibers while sprinters are fast-twitch types, you're not far from the truth. However, the distinction is not all that clear-cut. There seem to be a few different kinds of fast-twitch fibers, some of which can be made to become more fatigue-resistant through training. With regard to fatigue: scientists have learned quite a bit about the chemistry and energy requirements of muscular action. When we discuss the concept of energy later on, we'll learn about the energy transformations that take place in a muscle, and why you get tired when you exercise.

Incidentally, slow-twitch fibers tend to be darker in color (they receive a greater blood supply), while fast-twitch fibers are lighter-colored. The difference between the "dark meat" and "white meat" in chicken and turkey stems from the fact that the dark meat is muscle that contains mostly slow-twitch fibers, while the white meat is muscle that has mainly fast-twitch fibers. Ducks and other birds that fly long distances require a preponderance of fatigue-resistant, high-endurance slow-twitch muscles to sustain flight, and so they tend to have more dark meat on them.

Muscles generate heat when they're working, and warm muscle is stronger and more flexible than cold muscle. These facts underscore the importance of "warming up" and stretching the muscles before taking part in strenuous activity. Stretching is an important aspect of baseball, for example, a game in which the players experience long periods of inactivity. Practice swings taken by a batter before stepping up to bat and the pitcher's windup both serve to stretch muscles just prior to their use, to increase their strength and flexibility.

The Science of Muscle Building

Among the many fascinating things about muscle fibers is the way they respond to exercise and weight training. The prevailing theory is that the actual number of fibers in a muscle is fixed before birth, and never changes throughout one's lifetime. *Exercise does not increase the number of fibers; rather it increases the size of the ones that already exist.* The individual fibers increase in diameter, and since the strength of an individual fiber is about 100 lb/in^2 of cross-sectional area, as the fiber diameter increases, its overall strength increases. Thus the bulging muscles you see on body builders do not have more muscle fibers than normal, just thicker ones. Thickening the muscle fibers also increases their mass, so the muscle becomes heavier as well as stronger. The development of stronger, more massive arms and legs may be to an athlete's advantage in some sports, but not in others. A heavily muscled arm or leg is not as easy to accelerate, so athletes whose specialties depend on good arm or leg speed—i.e., runners, baseball pitchers, basketball players—generally do not have heavily developed arms or legs.

To build a muscle, i.e., thicken the fibers, you have to subject the muscle to a force that it doesn't experience normally: you have to overload the muscle. This calls for a systematic program of *weight training*—using specific muscles or muscle groups to overcome the resistance offered by heavy weights as a means of developing muscle strength, size, and endurance. Years ago, weight training was the exclusive domain of body builders and weight lifters. But in recent years, as techniques have become more scientific, more sophisticated, and more specifically tailored to individual needs, weight training has grown considerably in popularity among athletes and physical fitness enthusiasts at all levels.

There are several different bases for weight training programs, each of them having ridden at least one wave of popularity. *Isometric* training involves exercises in which the muscles undergo static contraction —that is, they are stressed without undergoing a change in length. An isometric exercise consists of straining against an immovable object —pushing on a wall, pressing against the floor, or pitting one muscle against another. Charles Atlas, whose advertisements adorned comic books and magazines for many years, offered hope to the "98-pound weakling"—the one who had sand kicked in his face at the beach— through his method of dynamic tension, which was simply another name for isometric exercise.

Isometric training enjoyed a vogue of popularity in the 1950s. It was attractive because it required a minimum of equipment and time; a busy executive could do many of the exercises at his desk in a few moments of spare time. However, minimum effort usually leads to minimum results: it has since been shown that isometric exercise, while producing some improvement in muscle strength, is the least effective means of weight training.

An *isotonic* exercise is one in which the muscle must overcome the resistance of a constant force. Lifting a barbell is the most basic form of isotonic exercise and is the most widespread type of weight training. Isotonic exercise involves both contraction and stretching of muscles, and it does lead to improvements in strength and endurance. However, there is a basic flaw in the method, arising from the fact that muscles produce neither constant tension nor torque. Thus the effort exerted in raising or lowering a fixed weight is variable, being greatest when the moment arm of the muscle force is smallest, and less taxing at all other points in the movement. Thus the muscle is not required to exert maximum effort throughout the exercise.

In recent years, a variety of sophisticated exercise machines—the Universal Gym, Nautilus, Cybex, etc.—have been developed to compensate for the shortcomings of isotonic exercises. These machines all make use of *variable resistance*—that is, they are designed to vary the load so that the muscle must exert maximum effort throughout the movement. For example, a Nautilus machine makes use of eccentric (noncircular) pulleys and cams to vary the moment arm of the resistance, so that the force required to move the resistance changes systematically throughout the range of motion of the exercise. Each machine is specifically designed to work a particular muscle or muscle group, and a complete set of machines is quite expensive. Thus to be able to work out regularly on a Universal or Nautilus, you have to be a member of an athletic team or else join a gym or physical fitness center.

Different schemes of weight training seem to affect different kinds of fibers. It is generally accepted that lifting very heavy loads tends to develop the fast-twitch fibers and gives the muscle more overall strength. Exercising with somewhat lighter loads but with more repetitions of the exercise tends to develop the slow-twitch fibers, providing more stamina and endurance. Speaking from experience, I can say that this does seem to work, and also that it's never too late to start. When I reached my late 30s, I found that I was tiring too quickly playing basketball, and couldn't keep up with the younger competition. Desperately seeking a remedy, with a midlife crisis staring me in the face, I turned to weight training. I went out and bought my son a barbell and weights for Christmas (he was much too young to use them) and began a regular program. I decided to work with smaller weights—60 pounds, tops—and do a lot of repetitions of each exercise. I kept this up for about a year, with great success. My muscles didn't bulge, but my stamina improved tremendously.

The foregoing description of how muscles generate force is an intentionally simplified and superficial treatment of a topic that is actually rich in interesting details. I must say that as an astronomer, dealing with the universe on a grand scale, I used to be overwhelmed only when I thought about the enormity of it all—the incredible numbers of stars and galaxies that exist, and the vast distance between them. I had never been too stimulated by biology—the earth and its inhabitants being little more than a flyspeck on the scale of the universe. But in recent years, as I've learned more and more about how muscles work, I've come to be overwhelmed just by thinking about the complex of processes that takes place whenever I decide to wiggle a finger.

4 / ROTATING BODIES

When I was in the eighth grade, my phys ed teacher tried to teach me some basic gymnastics. He began with the simplest of all exercises—the forward roll. The experience terrified me; I was convinced that I was going to break my neck. I had similar problems with diving. Despite the best efforts of an army of summer-camp swimming instructors, every attempt that I ever made to jackknife cleanly into the water always ended up in a resounding, stinging belly flop. I have long since resigned myself to entering a swimming pool feet first.

To this day, I am humbled by any kind of acrobatic performance. How does anyone develop the courage to throw his body into the air to do flips and twists and somersaults, in full confidence that he will come down safely? In my wildest fantasies I see myself slipping between Julius Erving and Moses Malone for a reverse layup, or striking out Reggie Jackson with a tantalizing knuckleball—but never turning a cartwheel.

Actually, I suspect that acrobatic maneuvers aren't quite as difficult as they look. You've got to have the right kind of body build—lean and limber, which certainly doesn't describe me—and a great deal of self-discipline. More importantly, gymnasts and divers get a lot of help from the laws of physics. There's one principle in particular, known as the conservation of angular momentum, which underlies most of the techniques used by gymnasts, ice skaters, and divers. An understanding of this and other principles that relate to rotational motion in general should help you to enjoy and appreciate some of the subtleties of athletic movement—and possibly even convince you to try a few tricks yourself.

Torque Is Not Cheap

The basic definitions and concepts pertaining to rotational motion may not be so familiar to someone who has never taken a formal course in physics. However, only a rudimentary comprehension of such terms as angular velocity, angular acceleration, and torque is required to understand the scientific principles that we'll be examining here. These topics have all been discussed previously, but a brief review of the most important facts to remember about them will be useful.

1. The rate of rotation can be described in terms of the angular velocity (ω) measured in degrees/sec or radians/sec, or the angular frequency (f) measured in revolutions/sec.
2. All points on a rotating object have the same angular velocity and angular frequency. However, the linear speed (v) of any point on a rotating object (measured in ft/sec, mi/hr, etc.) is in proportion to its distance (R) from the axis of rotation. (The exact equation linking these quantities, from Math Box 2, page 38, is $v = R\omega = 2\pi Rf$.)
3. Angular acceleration is the *rate of change of angular velocity*. Accordingly, an object has an angular acceleration whenever there is a change in either its rate or direction of spin.
4. An object can be made to pivot around any fixed axis—but if it is not fixed and is spinning freely, then it will rotate naturally about its center of gravity.
5. In order to set an object into rotation, an eccentric force must be applied, a force whose line of action does not pass through the axis of rotation. An eccentric force generates a torque, which is the product of the force and its moment arm ($T = Fd_m$), the moment arm being the perpendicular distance from the line of action of the force to the axis of rotation. Remember that a torque is not the same as a force, but rather a measure of the rotational or twisting effect of a force. Specifically, *a torque produces angular acceleration*. Thus a torque can set a station-

ary object into rotation, increase or decrease the spin rate of an already spinning object, or change the direction of the spin.

A bicycle wheel nicely illustrates a number of basic ideas about torques. Three different torques act on the rear wheel of a bicycle, as shown in Figure 4.1. There are two *decelerating* torques that result from friction—one caused by friction between the tire and the ground, the other resulting from friction between the axle and hub of the wheel. The third torque is an *accelerating* torque provided by the drive chain which connects the pedals to the rear wheel. The force exerted by the cyclist's feet on the pedals is transmitted through the chain to create this torque.

If the accelerating torque created by pushing on the pedals is greater than the sum of the two decelerating torques, then the wheel will experience angular acceleration—that is, it will turn at a faster rate. If the two decelerating torques exceed the accelerating torque, then the wheel will lose rotational speed. To keep the wheel turning at a constant rate, the rider has to push on the pedals with sufficient force so that the accelerating torque transmitted by the drive chain exactly balances the decelerating torques due to friction.

On a multispeed bike, the rear wheel has a series of toothed wheels (sprockets) of different sizes mounted on its axis (the gear-shift mech-

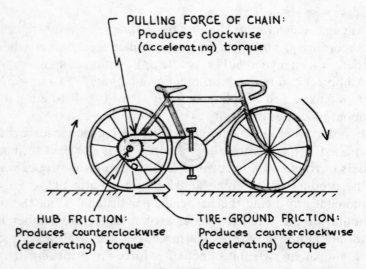

FIGURE 4.1   The torques on the rear wheel of a bicycle.

anism, the derailleur, allows the drive chain to move smoothly from one set of sprockets to another). The larger the sprocket diameter, the greater the moment arm of the pulling force exerted by the chain. In other words, the same pulling force from the chain produces different torques, depending on the diameter of the sprockets on which the chain is riding—the bigger the diameter, the bigger the torque.

On a ten-speed bike the lowest-numbered gear usually corresponds to the largest-diameter sprocket. Thus a given pedaling force produces the greatest torque when used in the lowest-numbered gear, so this is the gear that gives you the best advantage when climbing a hill.

To produce a given amount of torque, the smallest amount of force is needed when you are in the lowest gear because it has the largest moment arm. However, a gear system works much like a lever, in that you trade off distance for force; thus in low gear you don't have to exert as much force, but you do have to turn the pedals at a faster rate as compared with the higher gears. In high gear, you're trading force for distance—you don't have to pedal as rapidly to maintain a given speed, but you do have to exert more force to turn the pedals. A ten-speed bike can be the source of many interesting observations related to the torque concept; it's definitely worthwhile to spend some time studying and experimenting with the gear system with this in mind.

Now let's go one step further to see how the size of the torque is related to the angular acceleration it produces. It seems fairly obvious that a bigger torque should produce a bigger acceleration, and it does —but how are these two quantities related? The relationship between torque and angular acceleration exactly parallels the relationship between force and linear acceleration described by Newton's second law.

As we learned previously, Newton's second law (F = ma) relates force and linear acceleration through the concept of mass. The mass of any object is a measure of its inertia, or tendency to maintain constant speed in a straight line; the more mass an object has, the more force required to give it a specific linear acceleration. However, the parts of a rotating body do not move on straight lines. Their natural inertial tendency is thwarted by the internal interatomic forces that hold the object together and maintain its shape, thereby restricting its parts to move in circles about the axis of rotation.

Accordingly, to describe the relationship between torque and angular acceleration (taking into account the constraining effects of the interatomic forces), a modified version of Newton's second law had to be derived. The resulting equation, which may be thought of as a "rotational version" of Newton's second law, looks like this:

$$T = I\alpha$$

In this equation, T represents the *net* or *unbalanced* torque—the sum of all the torques acting on the object, taking into consideration whether the individual torques are accelerating or decelerating the object (accelerating torques are considered to be positive, decelerating torques are negative). The symbol α (the Greek letter alpha) is used to represent the angular acceleration. Finally, the letter I stands for a quantity known as the *moment of inertia*. As we'll soon see, the moment of inertia is the key to a sound understanding of rotational motion.

The preceding equation is, I'm sure, unfamiliar to anyone who has not taken a college-level physics course. We won't be using it for any calculations, so I haven't bothered to discuss units of measurement or any of the other complications that attend its use. The important thing, as far as we're concerned, is to recognize its similarity to Newton's second law. Let me write them both out in words:

> *F = ma (for linear motion):*
> net force = mass × linear acceleration

> *T = Iα (for rotational motion):*
> net torque = moment of inertia × angular acceleration

We can see right away that torque plays the same role in rotational motion that force does in linear motion—the bigger the torque, the bigger the angular acceleration. If there is an equilibrium of torques (if all the positive and negative torques exactly balance) or if there are no torques whatsoever, then there can be no angular acceleration. This means that the object in question either will not rotate at all or will continue to rotate at a constant angular velocity. We have here a rotational version of Newton's first law: *an object maintains a constant angular velocity unless acted on by an unbalanced torque.* There are some exceptions to this rule, as we'll learn later on when I state a more general form of this principle and give some illustrations of its use.

Completing our comparison of the linear and rotational versions of Newton's second law, we find that mass and moment of inertia play parallel roles, and it is important to understand the analogy that re-lates them. In basic terms, the mass of an object is a measure of its tendency to maintain a constant velocity, whereas the moment of inertia of an object is a measure of its tendency to maintain a constant rotation. Mass measures resistance to linear acceleration; the moment of inertia measures resistance to angular acceleration. Thus the mo-ment of inertia can be thought of as a measure of the "rotational inertia" of an object. If the same torque is applied to two different objects, the one with the larger moment of inertia will have the smaller angular acceleration.

The Moment of Inertia

What exactly is the moment of inertia? It is a quantity that depends partly on the mass of the object and partly on the way that mass is distributed—that is, the moment of inertia depends on the positioning of the mass with respect to the axis of rotation. Consequently, both the mass and the shape of a given object are determining factors.

Let me give you some specific examples. The simplest moment of inertia is that of a small body spinning in a circle at the end of a relatively long and lightweight string (see Fig. 4.2a). Here all of the mass is essentially at the same distance from the axis of rotation, that distance being L, the length of the string. The theory of rotational motion states that the moment of inertia is equal to ML^2, where M is

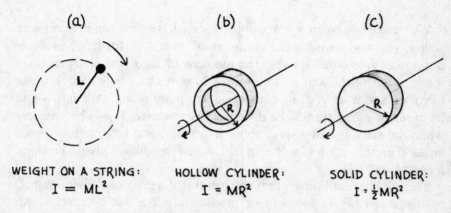

FIGURE 4.2   The moment of inertia.

the mass of the body. Note that the moment of inertia depends directly on the length of the string (or, more specifically, on the square of its length). Shorten the length and the moment of inertia decreases; increase the length and the moment of inertia gets larger. In other words, a circling body—a ball being swung around on the end of a chain, for instance—becomes more resistant to angular acceleration (requiring more torque to accelerate it) when the chain is made longer.

Figure 4.2b shows a hollow, cylindrical wheel, whose mass is concentrated along its rim. The wheel has a total mass M and a radius R. Since all of the mass is essentially the same distance from the axis of rotation, the wheel resembles a collection of small weights (whose total mass is M) all spinning in the same circle. Consequently, the moment of inertia of the wheel is equal to MR^2. But now contrast this with a solid wheel of the same mass and radius: here different parts of the wheel are at different distances from the axis of rotation. There is no simple way to deduce the moment of inertia; what is required is a complicated summation process to total up the contributions of each part of the wheel according to its distance, and the methods of calculus must be used. The final result, however, is fairly simple; a solid wheel turns out to have a moment of inertia of $\frac{1}{2}MR^2$, exactly half that of a hollow wheel. Even though the two wheels have the same total mass, the solid wheel has a smaller moment of inertia. Accordingly, it will be easier to set in rotation, easier to accelerate or decelerate than the hollow wheel. The same torque applied to each of the two wheels will thereby cause the solid wheel to spin at a faster rate. Incidentally, the moment of inertia is always measured in units of mass × $length^2$—i.e., $kg\text{-}m^2$ in metric units and $slug\text{-}ft^2$ in customary units.

We've just seen how two objects can have the same mass and shape, yet possess different moments of inertia. A further complication arises from the fact that the moment of inertia also depends on the location of the axis of rotation. A long stick or pole can be made to rotate about its end, its center, or any point along its length—and its moment of inertia will be different in each case. It will be smallest when the stick is being spun about its center, and largest (four times larger than the smallest value, in fact) when the stick is pivoted around its end (Fig. 4.3).

The upshot of all this is that the rotational inertia of a given object, as measured by its moment of inertia, is not a fixed quantity. An object may be accelerated more easily around one axis than another.

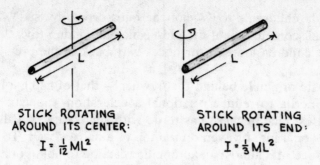

STICK ROTATING
AROUND ITS CENTER:
$$I = \frac{1}{12}ML^2$$

STICK ROTATING
AROUND ITS END:
$$I = \frac{1}{3}ML^2$$

FIGURE 4.3   The moment of inertia depends on the axis of rotation.

Moreover, the moment of inertia of a flexible object (e.g., a human body) can be changed by altering the mass distribution within the object. By shifting material closer to the axis of rotation, the moment of inertia can be made smaller; moving mass away from the axis thereby increases the moment of inertia. With these ideas in mind, let's look at some of the practical consequences of the basic theory of rotational motion.

Any well-designed steam or gasoline engine, including the one found under the hood of the family car, contains a little-known and well-hidden device known as a *flywheel*. A flywheel is a large wheel—more specifically, a wheel with a large moment of inertia—that is mounted on the main drive shaft of the engine. The explicit purpose of a flywheel is to "smooth out" the rotation of the drive shaft. The reason it is needed is that the forces that turn the drive shaft are usually not constant. In a gasoline engine, the explosion of the gas-air mixture in the cylinders drives the pistons up and down; the pistons are connected by a mechanical linkage that uses their up-and-down motion to rotate the drive shaft. Since there are only four or six (sometimes eight) cylinders in an automobile engine, the sequence of explosions produces bursts of force that would give a jerky motion to the drive shaft—if not for the flywheel. Since it has been designed to have a relatively large amount of inertia, the flywheel resists sudden fluctuations in its rotation. Because of its tendency to keep turning at a constant rate, the flywheel will keep the drive shaft turning smoothly. Moreover, if the driving force is suddenly cut off—as might happen if you were to run out of gas—the flywheel will continue to turn and will coast relatively slowly to a stop. Flywheels are found even inside children's toys—not the ones driven by six D batteries and a small computer, but the old-fashioned windup toys that somehow kept children amused for hours way back in the pre-solid-state past.

The basic principle behind the flywheel—that of using a large moment of inertia to reduce rotational acceleration—appears in many other guises. One of these has to do with such feats as walking on a tightrope, on a log, or even on the top of a narrow wall. To maintain your balance, it's almost an automatic reaction to hold your arms out horizontally to the side. When walking on a very narrow path, you tend to lose your balance very easily because it is difficult to keep your center of gravity over the support point. Your weight (acting through your CG) creates a torque that tends to set your body into sideways rotation. Holding your arms out horizontally serves two purposes: one is to provide a means of shifting your CG back over your support point (this is the goal of the frantic arm-waving that you do when you feel you're about to topple over). The second purpose is to increase your rotational inertia. Raising your arms shifts mass away from the axis of rotation, increases the moment of inertia, and reduces the angular acceleration created by a momentary imbalance. In fact, holding your arms vertically overhead increases your moment of inertia even more, but in this position you can't use your arms as easily to shift your CG, so the horizontal position is preferable.

Circus performers on the tightrope and high-wire often carry a very long, horizontally held pole (sometimes with a close friend or relative dangling from each end) as they walk. The illusion is that this makes their act even more difficult. In reality, it makes it *easier* for them to walk on a tightrope, because a long, downwardly curved pole (especially one with weights on each end) increases the moment of inertia and lowers the center of gravity of the performer-pole combination.

The idea of increasing rotational inertia to reduce angular acceleration is now being put to conscious use in the design of tennis rackets. A tennis racket has an axis of rotation running through the handle and along the center line of the racket head. When a ball strikes the racket off-center, to either side of this line, its impact creates a torque that tends to twist the racket in the player's hand. Racket designers have tried to counter this tendency by increasing the moment of inertia of the racket around this axis. One way to do this is by adding weight to the rim of the racket; another is simply to increase the size of the head, so that the rim is farther from the center line. Since official tennis rules place no restrictions on the weight, size, shape, or construction materials of a tennis racket frame, both of these techniques are currently used by racket manufacturers. In recent years, in fact, racket manufacturers have taken a much more scientific approach to racket design, and have introduced radical changes in shape and construction materials. We'll learn a bit more about what they've done, and why, in a later chapter.

The golf swing is another example of rotational motion in sports that has undergone considerable scientific analysis. A golf club—especially the driver, with its long, slender shaft and weighted clubhead —has a relatively large moment of inertia. The golfer's basic task is to provide an angular acceleration that gets the clubhead to the ball with the right arc and with as high a linear speed as possible at the moment of impact. High-speed cinematography has revealed that the clubhead can be traveling at speeds of 100 mi/hr or more in a well-executed swing. A golf swing is actually not a single rotation, but rather a coordinated sequence of rotations involving the hips, shoulders, and wrists. After planning his shot and addressing the ball, the golfer begins his motion with a backswing, which brings the club to a momentary rest position generally above and behind his head. The backswing prepares the golfer's body for the downswing of the club. The same muscles that are used to decelerate the club at the end of the backswing are the ones that initiate the downswing. In particular, the backswing serves to stretch those muscles whose contractions accelerate the club on the downswing—of importance because the force of contraction is greater when a muscle has been stretched.

A long backswing also gives the golfer a greater angle through which to accelerate the club on the downswing, thereby enabling him to give more speed to the clubhead at impact and/or to compensate for a lack of strength. However, a long backswing also serves to multiply any positioning errors that may arise from slight deviations in coordination and timing on the downswing. A short backswing affords more accuracy but less time to develop the angular speed of the club. Unless the golfer compensates with more force and torque on the downswing, he will not get as much distance on shots using a short backswing.

The Swing of a Bat

A golfer at least has the advantage of swinging at a stationary object; moreover he can begin his swing at a time of his own choosing.

A baseball player, who is trying to hit a ball approaching on a curved path at speeds of 80 mi/hr or more and which is in flight for a fraction of a second, has a much more formidable problem. In fact, batting is considered by many observers to be the most difficult task in sports. A good argument for this assertion is that the very best batters hit the ball successfully only about 33% of the time.

A critical look at traditional baseball batting techniques leads to some interesting questions. Why does a right-handed batter grip the bat with his left hand below his right? What is wrong with a "cross-handed" grip (right hand below the left)? And why does a right-handed batter stand with his *left* side facing the pitcher, with his head and eyes turned to the *left*? The standard batting stance is such an ingrained part of baseball technique that we never stop to consider the reasoning behind it. The stance seems odd when you think about it in the abstract, yet perfectly comfortable and natural when you use it. Why is this the most effective way to hit?

The underlying reason is simply that batting requires more accuracy than strength. It's important, of course, to swing hard so as to achieve a high bat speed in a short period of time. But a powerful swing is worthless if you don't make contact with the ball. The ultimate goal of the swing is to guide the bat to the point where the ball will be when it crosses the plate—or, as Einstein might have said, to position the bat correctly in space and time. A right-hander naturally has more precise control and positioning accuracy when using his right hand for any task. In swinging at a pitch, a batter *pulls* the bat with his left arm, and *pushes* it with his right; thus the left arm supplies more of the accelerating torque, while the right arm steers. With a cross-handed grip, it's more difficult to steer the bat—the left hand can't easily steer and pull the bat at the same time, and the right hand can't steer effectively with the left hand gripping the bat above it.

Thus a right-handed batter, in order to hit effectively, must stand with his left side to the pitcher and rotate his body to the left to meet the pitch. He must use his left arm to accelerate the bat, aided in great measure by the trunk muscles that rotate the hips and shoulders. A natural right-hander who tries to bat from the opposite side of home plate must stand with his right shoulder closer to the pitcher (as a natural left-hander does) and must be able to steer and position the bat with his left hand, which is held above the right on the bat handle. There are a number of ballplayers who are sufficiently ambidextrous to bat well from either side; being an effective switch-hitter is, of course, a great advantage to a baseball player.

In the general population, right-handers outnumber lefties by about nine to one. In their daily lives, left-handers must contend with constant petty annoyances arising from the fact that many of the artifacts of modern life are designed specifically for use by right-handers—scissors, can openers, windup wristwatches, writing desks (and the act of writing itself), to name just a few. But in baseball a left-handed batter has a distinct advantage in that he is several steps closer to first base when he hits the ball. Also, a curve ball thrown by a right-handed pitcher is much easier to hit if you're left-handed (we'll discuss the specific reasons why in a later chapter), which is another advantage for the lefty hitter, since most pitchers are right-handed. However, left-handed batters are at a disadvantage against lefty pitchers. In order to be prepared for all the possible righty-lefty confrontations, a baseball team ideally ought to have equal numbers of righties and lefties, both hitters and pitchers. As it turns out, though, most players are right-handed (another advantage for the lefty hitter). A careful survey of the major league ballplayers of 1982, completed by my younger son (a baseball fanatic and statistics junkie) revealed the following: Of the pitchers, 70% were right-handed and 30% left-handed. Of the batters, 56% were righties, 30% were lefties, and 14% were switch-hitters. (In general, most switch-hitters are natural right-handers who have learned to bat left-handed.) Thus the proportion of left-handers in major league baseball is three times higher than in the general population. Yet despite their advantages, only 26% of the top fifty hitters were left-handed! Does this mean that unqualified individuals are being hired to play major league baseball simply on the basis of their left-handedness? The foregoing results are based only on a single season, so I invite the sports statisticians among you to consider the data and come up with your own conclusions.

In baseball lingo, a left-handed pitcher is known as a "southpaw," and there is a scientific explanation for this term. Baseball games—those that are still played in the daylight—take place in the afternoon, when the sun is in the western half of the sky. So that the batter does not have the sun in his eyes when he is at bat, baseball stadiums are traditionally laid out so that the batter faces east and the pitcher and fielders face west. (This, of course, places a burden on the fielders, who sometimes must look up into the sun when trying to catch a high fly ball.) With this alignment, first base is on the south side of the stadium, third base on the north side. A left-handed pitcher's deliveries always come from the first-base or south side of the field—and so he is a southpaw.

It is now time to contemplate a piece of athletic equipment that, if placed in appropriate hands, can be an implement of skill, of artistry, or of awesome power. I am speaking, of course, about the baseball bat. Any serious baseball player, from the Little Leagues to the majors, takes great care in selecting a baseball bat. In choosing a bat that feels right, a player considers its weight, its length, the thickness of its barrel and handle, and also, quite without realizing it, its moment of inertia.

The swing of a baseball bat is, of course, primarily a rotational motion. Allowing for the time that it takes for the ball to travel from the pitcher's hand to home plate (almost always less than a second and sometimes as short as 0.4 second) and for the batter to decide whether or not to swing, it turns out that the bat must be accelerated through an angle of more than 90° (from the batter's shoulder to a horizontal position across the plate) in about a quarter of a second or less. Postponing as long as possible the decision to swing gives the batter a better idea of the path of the pitch—but the longer the batter waits, the faster he must then accelerate the bat. Motion picture studies of major league ballplayers taken some years ago showed that the very best hitters—Ted Williams, Hank Aaron, Willie Mays, and Stan Musial were among those studied—could complete a swing in 0.23 second or less, whereas the average batter took about 0.28 second. Hank Aaron in particular was renowned for his "quick wrists," a term that describes his ability to accelerate his bat exceptionally quickly.

How does the moment of inertia of the bat enter into this consideration? Swinging the bat requires rapid angular acceleration. The torque needed to accelerate the bat is supplied by the batter's hips, shoulders, arms, and wrists, each of these rotating in a proper sequence that builds one rotation on another. The amount of torque created in this manner naturally depends on the batter's size, strength, and coordination. However, the effect of this torque—i.e., the angular acceleration it produces—is determined by the moment of inertia of the bat. It is to the batter's advantage, at least in this respect, to use a bat with as small a moment of inertia as possible.

As with all objects, the moment of inertia of a bat depends on its total mass and how that mass is distributed. A long, top-heavy bat has a relatively high moment of inertia. A short bat with a slender barrel and thick handle has a lower moment of inertia. The latter can be swung more easily, and should therefore be preferred. But there are other factors to consider. For one thing, there are disadvantages to using a short bat. The batter must be able to reach any pitch that crosses the plate, so he has to stand close to the plate to cover the strike zone with a short bat. This makes it more difficult to hit inside pitches, which will come in near the handle rather than the fat part of the bat.

Another factor to consider is what happens when the bat makes contact with the ball. The speed with which the ball rebounds off the bat depends on many different factors, one of the most important being the speed of the bat at the point of contact. In a rotational motion, all parts of the rotating object have the same *angular* speed. However, the *linear* speed of any point on a rotating object is proportional to its distance from the axis of rotation. Accordingly, it is to the batter's advantage to use a long bat and to hit the ball near the end of the bat where the linear speed is greatest, in order to get a high bat speed at the point of contact. But a longer bat has a larger moment of inertia, so it is more difficult to accelerate to a high speed.

Later on, we'll be looking at the ball-bat collision in more detail to see how the weight and length of a bat affect the speed with which the ball rebounds when hit. At that point I'll have more to say about the science of choosing and using a baseball bat.

Gyroscopic Action

Earlier I took note of what I referred to as "a rotational version of Newton's first law." I had expressed it in the following way: if there is no net torque on a rotating object—either because of an equilibrium or because of a total absence of torque—then there cannot be any angular acceleration. Hence there is no change in the angular velocity; both the rate of spin *and* the direction of the spin axis remain unaltered. As stated, this is strictly true only if the object is completely rigid and its moment of inertia doesn't change. We'll assume for now that the moment of inertia does remain constant—and return later to consider what happens if it does not.

One immediate consequence of this principle is that if an object is given a spin and then allowed to move freely, its spin axis will stay pointed in the same direction. This is the principle behind the *gyroscope,* a device that has many important technological uses. A basic gyroscope consists of a rotor, which is essentially a flywheel on a shaft, mounted on frictionless bearings in a supporting frame (Fig.

4.4). If the rotor is made to spin at a high and constant rate, and if there are no torques acting on the rotor, the direction of its spin axis will not change. Thanks to the frictionless bearings, there won't be any sideways forces or torques on the rotor when the supporting frame moves; thus the frame can be turned in any direction, and yet the axis of the rotor will always be aligned in the same direction.

The ability of a gyroscope rotor to maintain a constant direction makes it especially suitable for use as a compass. Unlike a magnetic compass, which must align itself with the earth's magnetic field, a gyrocompass can be oriented in any preset direction—and once it is set spinning, it will always point in the chosen direction. Gyroscopes and gyrocompasses are used in ship navigation; they guide the controls of the automatic pilot on an airplane; and they are especially valuable in space flight, where they serve to maintain a spacecraft in a fixed orientation in space. Any deviation between the direction of an airplane or spacecraft and the preset direction indicated by the axis of the gyroscope can be used to initiate an automatic course correction.

The tendency of a rotating object to maintain a constant spin axis is often referred to as *gyroscopic action*. One feature of gyroscopic action is particularly intriguing, though a bit difficult to understand. We know that a spinning body maintains a constant angular velocity (rate of spin and direction) when it is torque-free. But what happens when an unbalanced torque acts on a spinning body? The result is a motion known as *precession,* in which the spin axis begins to pivot around in a circle.

The classic demonstration of precession is provided by the motion of a child's top. If a top is given a very rapid spin, it will stand on its end and with its axis straight up. But as it loses speed, or if you gently

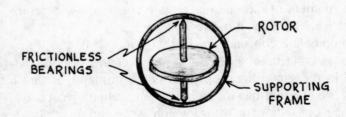

FIGURE 4.4   The simple gyroscope.

try to tip it over, it will begin to swing around in a circle, as shown in Figure 4.5. When a top is vertical, the line of action of its weight passes through its pivot point (i.e., its center of gravity is directly over the pivot point), so its weight does not produce a torque and the top maintains its balance and its spin direction. But if the top is tilted, the weight force does produce a torque around its pivot point. If the top were not spinning, it would immediately fall over; but because of its spin and rotational inertia, the top resists being tipped over, and it responds to this torque by swinging sideways and precessing.

The mathematical analysis of gyroscopic action—the motion of a top in particular—is one of the more complicated subjects in mechanics. (Back around the turn of the century two German physicists, Felix Klein and Arnold Sommerfeld, collaborated on a book entitled *The Theory of Tops*—in *four* volumes—which, as you might expect,

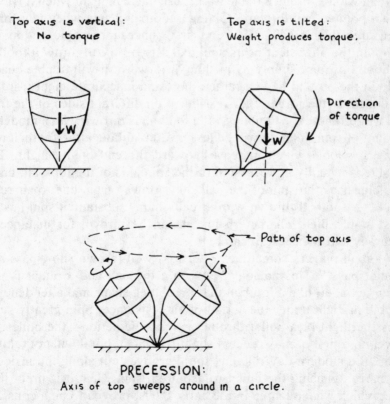

FIGURE 4.5   Precession: the gyroscopic action of a top.

tells you more than you would ever want to know about the subject.) Despite its seemingly esoteric nature, the phenomenon of gyroscopic action makes its presence felt in a variety of everyday circumstances, including sports. The basic principle here is that *spin stabilizes the motion of an object through gyroscopic action.* When an object is launched into the air, the path of its center of gravity is determined by inertia and by the forces acting on it—gravity, air resistance, etc. If any of these forces is eccentric (i.e., doesn't act through the center of gravity), the object may begin to rotate or tumble in flight. However, giving the object a spin helps it to resist eccentric forces through gyroscopic action.

Certainly the best and most familiar illustration of this principle is the flight of a football. Anyone who has ever tried to throw a football immediately discovers that the ball must "spiral" in flight—that is, it must be thrown with a good deal of spin. Given its oblong shape, a football will experience the least air resistance in flight when it travels with a pointed end forward. Giving a football a spin when you throw it ensures that it will travel end first, since gyroscopic action will maintain the alignment of its spin axis. If you try to throw a football without any spin, simply by pushing it forward, it will tumble chaotically in the air and have a rather short and inaccurate flight (torques produced by the force of air resistance on different sides of the football will promote the tumbling). If a football is thrown with a moderate amount of spin, its path will be less erratic, although the football may show a wobble which increases toward the end of the flight. This wobble is actually a precession of the spin axis of the football, and it gets bigger as the spin of the ball slows down (again due to air resistance). A football thrown with a really hard, substantial spin has the most stable flight characteristics; it can be thrown for distance or accuracy and is easiest to catch.

Football players sometimes refer to a well-thrown short pass as a "bullet pass." This analogy between a football and a bullet is well taken: a bullet, like a football, has an oblong shape and a tendency to tumble in flight under the action of air resistance. Spin greatly stabilizes the flight of a bullet through gyroscopic action—the bullet will travel nose first or may precess slightly in flight, but it will not tumble. Thus, the modern-day rifle has spiral grooves cut along the inside of the barrel, causing the bullet to acquire a spin when it is fired. (The rifle, which was invented in the early 1500s, proved to be a considerable improvement over the firearms that existed prior to that time;

these so-called *smooth-bore* weapons were totally inaccurate for distances greater than 100 yards or so.) Spin is now used to stabilize the flight of artillery shells, missiles, rockets, and spacecraft as well.

Regarding the distinction I made earlier between right-handed and left-handed athletes, it's worth noting that there have been very few left-handed quarterbacks in the college or pro ranks. Yet there's no real advantage (or disadvantage) to being one or the other. There are certain relatively minor accommodations that a team must make to a left-handed quarterback. For one, a ball thrown by a left-hander comes to the receiver spinning clockwise, while a right-hander's pass arrives spinning counterclockwise, so the pass receivers must adjust their catching techniques accordingly. In addition, a right-handed quarterback throws better moving to his right, while the reverse is true for a left-hander, so the offensive plays must be designed with this in mind. Probably because it is somewhat confusing and less efficient to set up an offense for a team that has a right-handed starting quarterback and a left-handed backup (or vice versa), some coaches have found it best to avoid using the left-handers.

The Stability of the Bicycle

Yet another familiar object whose stability depends on spin and gyroscopic action is the bicycle. If you try to balance a top on its point *without* giving it a spin, it will immediately fall over. The same is true of a bicycle: a stationary bicycle will topple rather quickly, while a rolling bicycle can be kept upright rather easily. Even a riderless bicycle, if given a good push, will roll for several seconds before it becomes unstable and falls over.

But the stability of a bicycle, and the ease with which an individual can learn to ride one, are not easy to explain. As any bike rider knows, the faster you go, the easier it is to maintain your balance. Moreover, a bicycle has a very narrow base of support, so it's fairly clear that balancing on a bicycle is *not* just a matter of keeping your center of gravity over the base of support.

In fact, physicists have yet to come up with a simple and clear-cut explanation of bicycle stability. Think for a moment about how you balance on a bicycle—and if you can, go for a ride on one to refresh your memory. When the bicycle feels like it's going to tip over, your instinctive reaction is to turn the front wheel in the direction that you're going to fall. Instead of toppling over, the bicycle will now travel on a curved path; the tilt of the bicycle now serves to generate the friction that provides the centripetal force needed for the turn. Thus turning the wheel acts to stabilize the bicycle against falling over, and you can then get back on your original path by shifting your weight and steering the wheel appropriately.

It is generally agreed that an important contribution to bicycle stability is made by gyroscopic action of the wheels; by acting to maintain a fixed direction of a wheel's axis of rotation, gyroscopic action serves to keep the bicycle upright. If the bicycle begins to lean to one side, the front wheel will react to the change in direction by automatically turning its axis in the direction of the lean—an action similar in principle to the precession of a top—thereby preventing the bicycle from immediately toppling over. Thus the gyroscopic behavior of the front wheel maintains the stability of a riderless bicycle.

However, the stability of a ridden bicycle is another matter. About fifteen years ago, a British scientist named David E. H. Jones became intrigued with bicycle stability, and attempted to test the accepted theories by building an unridable bicycle. To verify the importance of gyroscopic action, Jones mounted a second wheel right alongside the front wheel, raising it slightly so that it could spin freely without touching the ground. By spinning the free wheel in the opposite direction of the front wheel, Jones could cancel out their combined gyroscopic effects. As predicted, this bicycle was unstable when riderless and very quickly fell over when pushed off on its own. But much to his surprise, Jones discovered that this supposedly unstable bicycle could actually be ridden fairly easily. This demonstrated that gyroscopic action is not the only cause of bicycle stability.

Jones eventually did succeed in building an inherently unstable and virtually unridable bicycle. To understand how he did this, we have to take a look at what is called the "steering geometry" of the front wheel of a bicycle. This wheel is mounted on the front fork, which swivels when the handlebars are turned. The fork is angled from the vertical and curves forward near its end at the axle. The angling of the fork is needed to provide clearance between the frame and the front wheel so that the wheel can turn freely—but why is the fork curved forward at its end? The curvature is not merely a matter of design esthetics; it actually plays a key part in determining the maneuverability and stability of the bicycle.

As shown in Figure 4.6, a straight line drawn along the fork and

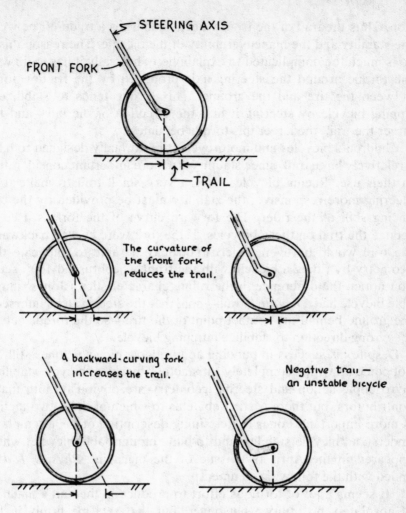

STEERING AXIS

FRONT FORK

TRAIL

The curvature of
the front fork
reduces the trail.

A backward-curving fork
increases the trail.

Negative trail —
an unstable bicycle

FIGURE 4.6   The trail of a bicycle.

extended downward intersects the ground in front of the point where
the tire makes contact with the ground (this line represents the steering axis around which the front wheel rotates). The tire makes contact
with the ground at a point directly under the axle. The distance between these two points is known as the *trail* of the bicycle. It turns
out that the larger the trail, the more stable (but less maneuverable)
the bicycle becomes. A bicycle with a large trail is very easy to balance, but it responds fairly sluggishly to attempts to change its direc-

tion. Thus the trail of the front wheel establishes a trade-off between the stability and the maneuverability of the bicycle. The reason this is so is much too complicated to explain here; basically it has to do with the torque around the steering axis produced by the friction force between the tire and the ground. This torque tends to stabilize a tipping bicycle by steering it into the direction of the fall—and the larger the trail, the larger this torque becomes.

Children's bicycles and motorcycles are normally designed to have a relatively large trail, since stability is a more important consideration in their use. Racing bicycles have a very small trail to make their steering more responsive; the stability must be provided by the balancing skill of the rider. The forward curve of the fork is used to reduce the trail on these bicycles. If the fork were curved backward, the trail would be even larger. (You may be able to duplicate this geometry by riding a bicycle with the front wheel turned 180°; see if you notice the difference in the riding characteristics.) Jones' unridable bicycle had a *negative* trail—note that the steering axis intersects the ground behind the contact point of the tire—so the torque acts in the wrong direction to stabilize a tipping bicycle.

Despite his success in building an unridable bicycle, Jones still did not come up with a completely satisfactory theory of bicycle stability. Gyroscopic action and steering geometry are obviously both major contributors, but there is still debate as to which of these two factors is more important. Jones' entertaining description of his attempts to understand bicycle stability and to build an unridable bicycle, which appeared in the April 1970 issue of the magazine *Physics Today,* ended with the following comment:

"It seems a lot of tortuous effort to produce in the end a machine of absolutely no utility whatsoever, but that sets me firmly in the mainstream of modern technology. At least I have no intention of foisting the product onto a long-suffering public in the name of progress."

Rotational Action and Reaction

So far our examination of rotational motion has focused on rotational equivalents of Newton's laws of motion. We've already discussed the equivalent of the second law ($T = I\alpha$ instead of $F = ma$) and the first law (the angular velocity of a rigid object is constant in torque-free motion). Now we'll take a look at a rotational version of Newton's third law, the principle of action and reaction.

The third law dictates that if object A exerts a force on object B, then B exerts an equal and opposite force on A. However, the rotational version (if A exerts a torque on B, then B exerts an equal and opposite torque on A) is not necessarily true. Remember that a torque is equal to a force multiplied by its moment arm. Thus it is possible for two equal and opposite forces to create different torques if they have different moment arms. For example, one of the two forces of an action-reaction pair might act through the center of gravity of an object, thereby producing no torque. But if an action-reaction pair of forces have identical moment arms, then the torques would necessarily be equal and opposite. Such a situation arises if the forces act on two objects that are rotating around a common axis. If this is the case, we can state a modified action-reaction principle for rotational motion:

If object A exerts a torque on object B, then B exerts an equal and opposite torque on A, provided that A and B are rotating about the same axis.

This principle has several interesting and surprising consequences, some of which can be demonstrated in a simple and convincing manner. To start with, think about all the different ways that you can rotate your fingers, arms, legs, hips, etc. Every joint in the human body is the site of a rotation about at least one axis. Some joints permit rotation around three different axes, although there is usually more flexibility in some directions than in others. For example, you can rotate your leg at the hip in three different directions, around three different axes. It can be rotated forward-backward, as in walking (around a side-to-side horizontal axis); in a sideways, left-right direction (around a front-to-back horizontal axis); and also twisted (around a vertical axis). Of these, the first has the greatest flexibility and range.

The action-reaction principle comes into play every time you rotate a part of your body. For the purpose of analysis we can think of the body as two distinct entities, one on each side of the joint involved in the rotation. Consider, for instance, rotation of one arm in a vertical circle: the arm becomes "object A"; the rest of the body is "object B." Thus the muscles that are used to rotate the arm in one direction supply an equal and opposite torque that acts to rotate the rest of the body in the other direction. Keep in mind that equal torques do not necessarily create equal rotations, because the relative moments of inertia must be taken into account: the larger the moment of inertia, the smaller the rotation (more specifically, the angular acceleration) produced by a given torque.

Here are a few demonstrations that you can do to convince yourself of this principle:

1. Stand erect, with both arms stretched vertically upward. Now jump vertically—and *after you have left the ground,* swing your arms forward and downward. Notice that your legs swing slightly forward as a result (Fig. 4.7). The forward motion of your arms is a rotation (clockwise as seen from the right) about a horizontal axis through the shoulders. The reaction will be a counterclockwise rotation of the rest of the body about the same axis. But since the body has a greater moment of inertia than the arms about this axis, it will not swing forward through as great an angle (if you swing your arms through a complete circle, your body will rotate forward approximately 20° to 30°). If you are sufficiently flexible, agile, and daring, try to bring your hands to your toes in midair by swinging your whole upper body forward, bending at the waist. The moments of inertia of the upper and lower body about a horizontal axis through the waist are more nearly equal, so they will rotate toward each other through approximately the same angle.

Swinging your arms forward and downward
after your feet have left the ground
will make your lower body swing forward.

FIGURE 4.7   Rotational action and reaction: vertical arm swing.

2. Now stand with your right arm extended horizontally to the side. Jump vertically, then swing your arm forcefully across your body to the left (I should emphasize the importance of initiating all of these movements *after* your feet leave the ground; otherwise the rotation will be counteracted by the frictional forces between your feet and the ground). Notice that your body twists slightly to the right (Fig. 4.8). This works even better if you hold a heavy object in your hand; this increases the moment of inertia of your arm so that you must use a larger torque to accelerate it. The motion of your arm constitutes a rotation (counterclockwise as viewed from above) about a vertical axis through your shoulder. The reaction is a rotation of your body in the opposite direction.

3. The last demonstration is similar to the first, but this time swing only one arm forward and downward, keeping the other fixed at your side. You'll notice that your legs come forward as before, but in addition your body will also twist about a vertical axis. Swinging one arm forward is a more complicated motion which involves rotation of the body about two axes— one vertical and one horizontal. To perform this motion, you might imagine yourself throwing a ball in midair (again, it's important to initiate the arm movement *after* your feet leave the ground). If you throw right-handed, the forward motion of your right arm twists your shoulders from right to left (counterclockwise, as seen from above), so the rest of your body will twist slightly to the right (clockwise) in reaction. This is

Swinging your arm horizontally in one direction
will make your body twist in the other direction.

FIGURE 4.8   Rotational action and reaction: horizontal arm swing.

one reason why is is difficult to throw a jump pass with a football; the thrower does not have his feet planted to absorb the reaction forces generated by the throwing motion, and the twisting of his lower body makes it harder for him to regain his balance after the throw. In baseball, an identical situation arises when an infielder tries to make a throw while jumping to avoid the feet of a sliding runner. Getting off an accurate throw in this situation is one of the more difficult plays in baseball, and it is magnified by the danger of losing one's balance in the process. Skiers undergo a similar response whenever they make a turn; the rotation of their skis in one direction causes a counterrotation of their shoulders in the other direction.

You might think of these demonstrations as simply amusing examples of physics at work, but the fact is that they are fundamental movements, integral parts of our daily activities. Consider the simple act of walking: why do we swing our arms when we walk? Try walking or jogging with your arms pinned to your sides or your hands in your pockets, and you may begin to understand why, in the light of the last demonstration. The forward swing of each leg in walking causes the upper body to rotate in reaction—the shoulders twist slightly to the right when the right leg is swung forward, to the left when the left leg is swung forward. This twisting motion is small when you're walking at an easy pace, but it becomes quite noticeable when you're walking briskly or jogging.

We can counteract this rotation of the shoulders simply by swinging our arms to produce a counterrotation. By swinging the left arm forward and right arm back at the same time that the right leg is stepping forward (and vice versa), the rotations of the body that each produces are effectively counterbalanced. As an experiment, try to walk swinging the arm and leg on the same side together—i.e., swing your right arm forward with your right leg, your left arm in unison with your left leg. It's hard to maintain this motion—your arms will very soon return to their normal rhythm if you don't concentrate—but if you can do it, you'll find your shoulders twisting very noticeably as you move. Arm swinging is particularly important in running because of the forceful rotation of the leg in each stride. Runners have to pump their arms rather vigorously when sprinting to keep their shoulders from twisting (Fig. 4.9). It is uncomfortable, if not difficult, to run with any speed without moving your arms.

FIGURE 4.9   Good running form: vigorous arm-pumping is needed to maintain rotational stability in running. Arms and legs are flexed to reduce their moments of inertia. Shown above are Sebastian Coe (6) and Rob Harrison of Great Britain running in a 1000-meter race *(UPI photo)*.

While we're on the subject of running, there's one aspect of it that can be nicely explained in terms of rotational inertia: namely, why does it seem easier to run with the arms flexed (bent sharply at the elbow) rather than extended? The answer is simply that the moment of inertia of the arm is smaller when it is flexed (its mass is kept closer to the axis of rotation through the shoulder), and so it takes less effort (specifically, less torque from the shoulder muscles) to swing your arms when they are bent. The difference is not negligible—the moment of inertia of a flexed arm is about three times smaller than that of a fully extended arm. The same explanation applies to the leg in running: during that part of the running motion where the runner brings his trailing leg forward, he bends his leg at the knee, with his heel almost to his thigh, to lower its moment of inertia, thereby reducing the muscular effort needed to swing it forward at high speed.

The principle of balancing the rotation of one part of the body with a countering rotation of another part shows up in other activities as well. Hurdling, a track event that requires excellent coordination as well as speed, is a good example. Hurdlers are sprinters who must be able to time their steps so that they can clear the hurdles without breaking stride (the high hurdles are 3½ feet high; low hurdles are 3 feet high). The hurdles are cleared one leg at a time; the hurdler first extends his leading leg over the hurdle, foot first, then sweeps his trailing leg over in a roughly horizontal motion, knee ahead of foot (Fig. 4.10). The swing of the trailing leg tends to rotate the body about a vertical axis, so the hurdler balances this motion with a countering arm movement. He holds one arm—the one on the same side as his trailing leg—in front of his body at shoulder height as he clears the hurdle. As he sweeps his trailing leg forward, he counters its rotation by forcefully swinging the arm horizontally backward. The significance of this rather subtle movement is not often recognized by sports fans, but hurdlers and their coaches know that it is essential to their success.

Anyone who tries roller skating or ice skating for the first time usually has a lot of difficulty keeping his balance. One common technique used by beginners to keep themselves from falling over is to "windmill" their arms—swing them in vertical circles—as a means of keeping their feet from sliding out from under them. As Figure 4.11 shows, windmilling your arms (both arms circling in the same direction) in a backward direction—with your arms moving backward at the top of the circle—produces a backward (clockwise as seen from the right) rotation of the lower part of the body. Windmilling your arms forward tends to rotate the lower part of your body forward. If your feet are moving faster than the rest of your body, as is often the case on skates, windmilling your arms backward will help you to regain your balance.

FIGURE 4.10 Olympic hurdler Michael Shine demonstrates proper hurdling form at the Montreal games. His left arm is prepared to swing backward as he brings his trailing leg over the hurdle. *(UPI photo)*.

There are few events more evocative of the spirit of the American frontier than a rodeo. The participants take considerable risks in the course of the competition, and they even manage to demonstrate some scientific principles in the process. Usually, the most exciting and dangerous events are the saddle bronc and bull riding competitions, in which the cowboy tries to stay on the animal for an allotted period of time while holding on to the saddle or a rope with one hand. If you ever get to see these events—occasionally they're shown on

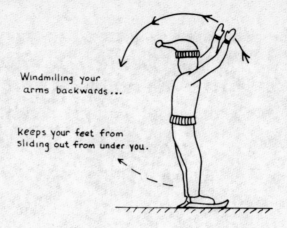

Windmilling your arms backwards...

keeps your feet from sliding out from under you.

FIGURE 4.11 Rotational action and reaction: keeping your balance on skates.

the weekend TV sports shows—notice how the cowboy uses his free arm; he extends it outward and upward, waving and circling it in different directions (Fig. 4.12). The purpose, of course, is to produce opposing rotations to counteract, through action and reaction, the twists and turns imparted to his body by the gyrations of the animal he's riding.

Angular Momentum

Many of the movements I've just described are an essential part of the repertoire of any athlete who performs gymnastic or acrobatic stunts. Their performances also include maneuvers that are considerably more complex than the ones we've looked at so far. Behind their complexity is the fact that *the moment of inertia of an object is not necessarily a fixed quantity:* it can be altered either by shifting the mass within the object toward or away from the axis of rotation, or by changing the axis of rotation itself. Thus rotational motion is more varied and complex than linear motion simply because the mass of an object is constant but its moment of inertia is not. One object whose moment of inertia can be varied with relative ease is the human body, and it is this simple fact that underlies the ability of divers, gymnasts,

FIGURE 4.12 Rotational action and reaction: keeping your balance while bull riding. Ed Kutz uses his free arm to counteract the rotations of his body caused by the motions of the bull. His large hat increases the moment of inertia of his free arm *(UPI photo).*

and other acrobatic performers to startle, mystify, and please their audiences with the dexterity and swiftness of their movements.

Our survey of the principles underlying rotational motion up to now has not taken the variability of the moment of inertia into account.

For example, in explaining gyroscopic action we made use of the idea that torque-free motion must have a constant angular velocity. When the changeability of the moment of inertia is taken into account, however, this principle is no longer strictly true. Nevertheless, this does not invalidate our discussion of gyroscopic action, since all the objects we've looked at so far—gyroscopes, footballs, wheels, etc.—have a fixed moment of inertia.

It is possible to arrive at a more general principle for rotational motion which allows for changes in the moment of inertia. This all-encompassing principle—by itself sufficient to describe virtually every aspect of rotational motion—centers on a quantity known as *angular momentum,* which is defined as the product of the moment of inertia and the angular velocity:

angular momentum = moment of inertia × angular velocity

Symbolically,

$$L = I\omega$$

Starting from Newton's laws of motion, an equation linking torque and angular momentum can be derived (I'll spare you the details). This relationship can be stated in words as follows:

net torque = rate of change of angular momentum

This equation takes into account any changes in the moment of inertia that may occur, since a change in angular momentum can be brought about by changing either the moment of inertia or the angular velocity, or both. If the moment of inertia is fixed, then, of course, only the angular velocity can change. In that case,

net torque = rate of change of angular momentum
= moment of inertia × rate of change of angular velocity

But since angular acceleration is defined as the rate of change of angular velocity, the above becomes

net torque = moment of inertia × angular acceleration

As you can see, this is the equation $T = I\alpha$. What I've shown here is that the general statement "the net torque equals the rate of change of angular momentum" encompasses the equation $T = I\alpha$ as a special case when the moment of inertia is constant. If you've followed this argument so far, then you should have no difficulty with the following statement:

If there is no net torque acting on an object, its angular momentum is constant.

This is known as the *law of conservation of angular momentum.* The angular momentum of a torque-free object is "conserved" in the sense that it does not change. Conservation laws of this type hold great significance to physicists. The most famous conservation law—the conservation of energy—is one that we'll be examining and putting to considerable use later on.

For our purposes, the most important point to understand is that *a constant angular momentum does not imply a constant angular velocity.* If the moment of inertia increases and the angular velocity decreases by the same factor (or vice versa), the angular momentum (which is the product of the two) will still be the same. To summarize:

1. If a spinning object has no unbalanced torques acting on it, its angular momentum cannot change.
2. If the moment of inertia of the object increases while it is spinning, then its angular velocity must decrease (it will spin at a slower rate). If the moment of inertia decreases, then the angular velocity must increase (the object will spin faster) in proportion to the change in the moment of inertia (see Math Box 5, page 150).

The Science of Acrobatics

When an athlete is spinning freely—if there are no major unbalanced torques acting on his body—his angular momentum is fixed. However, *he can increase or decrease his rate of spin by consciously changing his moment of inertia.* He can do this by moving some part of his body toward or away from his axis of rotation.

Before we go to the specific details, I'd like to underscore the importance of the principle of conservation of angular momentum by making a list (undoubtedly incomplete) of activities in which it plays a prominent part.

MATH BOX 5: CONSERVATION OF ANGULAR MOMENTUM

The definition of angular momentum (L) is

$$L = I\omega$$

where I is the moment of inertia of an object, and ω is its angular velocity. If there are no unbalanced torques acting on an object, its angular momentum is conserved (stays constant). However, its moment of inertia can change (through an internal rearrangement of its mass) without changing its angular momentum. Let us assume that the initial moment of inertia of the object is I_1, and it has an angular velocity of ω_1. The moment of inertia is then changed to I_2, resulting in a new angular velocity, ω_2. Since the angular momentum is not affected by the change,

$$L = I_1\omega_1 = I_2\omega_2$$

We can also express this relationship in terms of the more familiar angular frequency (f), measured in revolutions/second, using the equation $\omega = 2\pi f$ (from Math Box 2, page 38). Thus

$$L = I_1(2\pi f_1) = I_2(2\pi f_2)$$

which simplifies to

$$I_1 f_1 = I_2 f_2$$

The new angular frequency f_2 is

$$f_2 = \left(\frac{I_1}{I_2}\right)f_1$$

In other words, the angular frequency will change in inverse proportion to the change in the moment of inertia. For example, if the moment of inertia is tripled ($I_2 = 3I_1$) then

$$f_2 = \left(\frac{I_1}{3I_1}\right)f_1 = \frac{1}{3}f_1$$

The angular frequency will now be one third of its original value; that is, the object will make one third as many revolutions per second as it did before its moment of inertia changed.

Springboard and platform diving
Gymnastics (horizontal bar, balance beam, trampoline, horse, floor exercises)

Track and field (long jump, high jump, pole vault)
Figure skating
Skiing
Ballet and modern dance
Circus acrobatics
Cheerleading
Space travel

Perhaps you're surprised by the inclusion of space travel on this list. But since astronauts are in a gravity-free and resistance-free environment, floating freely inside or outside their spacecraft, they are able to rotate and orient their bodies in any direction. In fact, much of the research on the measurement of the moment of inertia of the body under different conditions has been done by or for NASA in preparation for the Apollo, Skylab, and Space Shuttle programs.

The human body can rotate freely and stably about three principal axes of rotation. These axes are mutually perpendicular (that is, each one makes a 90° angle with the other two), as shown in Figure 4.13. They coincide with the lines of symmetry of the body and intersect at the center of gravity. They're normally identified as follows:

1. The *longitudinal* axis is a vertical, head-to-toe axis. A rotation around this axis is called *twisting*.

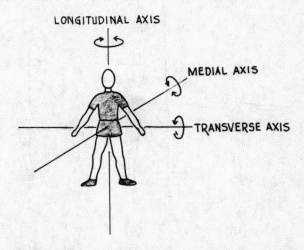

FIGURE 4.13   Principal rotation axes of the body.

2. The *transverse* axis is a horizontal, side-to-side (left-right) axis. A rotation around this axis is called a *somersault* or a *flip*.
3. The *medial* axis is a horizontal, back-to-front axis. A rotation around this axis is called a *pinwheel*.

For any given configuration of its parts, a human body has different moments of inertia around each of these three axes. The moments of inertia around each axis increase or decrease whenever the configuration is changed by selective bending of the arms, legs, and/or the entire body at the waist. Precise measurements of the moment of inertia of the body in different positions are difficult to make. But by determining the relative weights and centers of gravity of various parts of the body (dissecting cadavers to obtain their data), researchers have been able to calculate approximate moments of inertia. The results naturally depend on body size and build, and vary significantly among individuals.

Some general conclusions can nevertheless be drawn. The moment of inertia is smallest about the longitudinal axis, since most of the body mass is concentrated close to this axis. Hence twisting is usually the easiest body rotation to perform. The moment of inertia relative to this axis can be increased by extending the arms or legs to the front or side, by bending at the waist, or by any combination of these. Figure 4-14 shows a number of different positions used in various activities (most notably in ice skating) to perform rotations about the longitudinal axis. I've arranged the diagrams so that the moment of

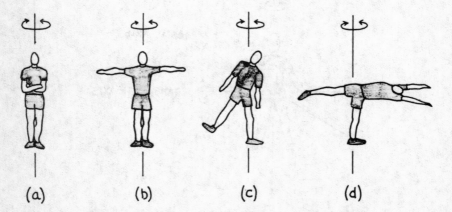

FIGURE 4.14   Rotations about the longitudinal axis.

inertia increases from left to right. A performer who has a fixed amount of angular momentum about his longitudinal axis will spin or twist most rapidly with his body in position *a*. An ice skater can increase his spin rate rather dramatically by shifting from positions *d*, *c*, or *b* to *a*. The moment of inertia in position *b* is about three times larger than that of *a*, so a skater who changes from *b* to *a*, simply by pulling in his arms, will triple his spin rate. The position shown in *d* is one version of the *arabesque* position in ballet; a twist around the longitudinal axis in this position is known in figure skating as a *camel spin* (the association of camels with Arabs—as in "arabesque"—is probably not a coincidence). A skater's moment of inertia in position *d* is about six times greater than for *a*, so a change from *d* to *a* will bring about a sixfold increase in spin rate (Fig. 4.15).

Relative to the transverse axis, the body's moment of inertia is greatest when the arms and legs are fully extended in a line, and smallest when the arms and legs are folded close to the body, as shown in Figure 4.16. The moment of inertia is smallest in position *a*, the *tuck* position. It is approximately 1½ times larger in the *tight pike* *b*, 3 times larger in the *loose pike c*, and 5 times larger in the *layout* position *d*. The somersault is the most popular acrobatic maneuver; it is a common part of the repertoire in gymnastics and diving. Obviously, a somersault is done most easily and rapidly in the tuck position, as is well known to anyone who has ever seen this stunt performed.

Up to now we've considered only free or unsupported rotations of the body, which automatically take place about an axis through the center of gravity. Somersaults (rotations about the transverse axis) and twists (rotations about the longitudinal axis) are familiar maneuvers. On the other hand, rotations around the medial (front-to-back) axis are considerably less common. They appear most often in trampoline routines, where they are known as *turntables*.

In addition to performing free rotations, an athlete can also pivot his body around any fixed point of support. For example, in doing a cartwheel the performer pivots about the points where his hands touch the floor; he is rotating in the same way as in a trampolinist's turntable—i.e., about a front-to-back axis—except that the axis passes through his support points (his hands) rather than through his center of gravity. Of course, the moment of inertia is different for a cartwheel than for a turntable, because the rotations are each made around a different axis.

FIGURE 4.15 Figure skater Rosalyn Sumners performs a tight spin by reducing her moment of inertia. Note the effects of centripetal force on her clothing and hair *(UPI photo).*

In gymnastic routines on horizontal bars the athlete can rotate about a side-to-side axis extending along the bar and through his hands. The "giant swing," where the gymnast pivots around the bar with his body fully extended, is thus equivalent to a somersault, but it uses an axis that parallels the gymnast's transverse axis. In fact, a gymnast will often dismount from a high bar by a somersault in the

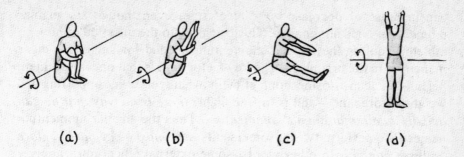

(a)   **(b)**   **(c)**   **(d)**

FIGURE 4.16   Rotations about the transverse axis.

tuck position. The angular momentum that he acquires in the giant swing remains constant after he releases his grip from the bar, but it is transferred to his transverse axis—in other words, the gymnast, now turning freely, will automatically begin to rotate about a parallel axis through his center of gravity. Moreover, the moment of inertia of the body about an axis through the hands is quite large—more than twenty times larger than in the tuck position. So in coming out of a giant swing into a tucked somersault, the gymnast can increase his spin rate by a factor of twenty, thereby making it possible to complete two or three somersaults before hitting the ground.

A similar maneuver is performed by a circus acrobat on the flying trapeze. He swings back and forth on the trapeze, hanging by his hands, to build up his angular momentum. When he lets go of the trapeze, his angular momentum is automatically transferred to his transverse axis for somersaulting. The somersaults must be timed so that the performer's wrists can be grasped as he flies by the "catcher," who is hanging from his knees on another swinging trapeze. The more angular momentum the acrobat acquires, the more somersaults he will be able to complete during his flight, but his greater rotational speed increases the difficulty of making the catch. Most circus aerialists can perform a double somersault fairly routinely, but only a few performers have ever managed a successful triple somersault from a trapeze. In July 1982, Miguel Vasquez, now performing with the Ringling Brothers circus, accomplished the first *quadruple* somersault—four spins in the air from one trapeze to the other. This feat requires incredible timing and strength on the part of the flyer and the catcher, considering that the flyer is going about 70 mi/hr when he is caught.

So we have seen how an athlete, by changing his moment of inertia, can increase or decrease his rate of spin, even though his angular momentum does not change. This brings us to the question of how an athlete acquires the angular momentum needed for some particular maneuver in the first place. The key factor here is that once the athlete begins his leap—losing contact with whatever was supporting his weight beforehand—and is in free flight, *there is no way that he can acquire additional angular momentum.* Thus the angular momentum he needs to perform twists, somersaults, etc. *must be acquired before he loses contact.* In other words, some external object must apply a torque to the athlete's body in order to change his angular momentum. There are various ways to do this, according to the particular activity.

To dive or jump off a springboard or platform, the athlete must use his feet to push downward on the surface. This action creates an upward reaction force on his body. If the athlete is standing erect so that the line of action of the force passes through his center of gravity (Fig. 4.17a), then the force will not produce a torque, and his body will not rotate. If, however, he leans his body to shift his CG forward (Fig. 4.17b), then the upward force generates a torque which will give his body angular momentum while he is in flight. In addition, the force of gravity (the diver's own weight) also sets up an angular-momentum-creating torque. If you simply lean over so that your CG is in front of your base of support, your weight force produces a torque about a

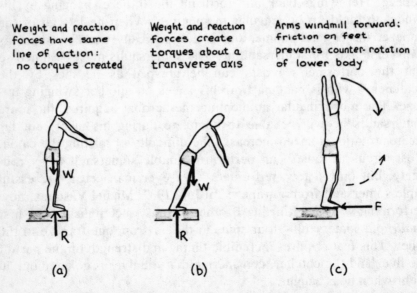

Weight and reaction forces have same line of action: no torques created

Weight and reaction forces create torques about a transverse axis

Arms windmill forward: friction on feet prevents counter-rotation of lower body

(a)   (b)   (c)

FIGURE 4.17   Gaining angular momentum from the diving board.

pivot point at your feet. Thus by merely toppling off the edge of a platform or board, a diver gains angular momentum. His rate of spin will be very slow at first, because the moment of inertia of his body around the pivot point will be large, but his spin rate can be increased by going into a tuck or pike position.

Another technique used by divers to generate additional torque is to windmill their arms forward just before jumping. As we learned earlier, this action normally causes the lower body to rotate forward in reaction. However, this motion is prevented by the friction between the diver's feet and the board (Fig. 4.17c). Because the reaction is thwarted, the angular momentum of the diver's arms in the windmilling motion is transferred to his entire body when he jumps.

To make his body twist or spin about his longitudinal (vertical) axis, a performer must obtain angular momentum about this axis from the ground before he begins his leap. The procedures are essentially the same as those used to gain angular momentum for somersaulting— that is, they are based on the action-reaction principle. For a right-to-left (counterclockwise as seen from above) spin, the performer pushes his feet sideways (to his right) against the ground as he jumps. He can also swing his arms in a horizontal circle from right to left before he leaves the ground. This generates angular momentum about the longitudinal axis in the same way that a forward windmilling of the arms produces angular momentum about the transverse axis.

Twists and spins are especially common in figure skating and ballet performances. Part of the beauty of ballet is the effortless way in which the dancers perform their movements, especially the more acrobatic ones. The positioning of arms and legs in ballet movement is carefully designed to provide the torques needed to initiate spins, as well as to produce the appropriate changes in body moment of inertia needed to increase or decrease the rate of spin. If you watch carefully, you can see how physical principles have been incorporated into the classic techniques. For example, if you see a ballerina performing a series of pirouettes, notice how she plants one foot firmly on the floor to push off during each turn, and raises and lowers her arms to decrease or increase her rate of spin. A traditional movement for the male dancer is the *tour en l'air:* he leaps vertically from a stationary position, completes one or more spins in the air, and lands in the same spot. Notice how the dancer begins this movement by twisting his body slightly in the opposite direction, then swinging his arms horizontally to generate angular momentum before he begins his leap.

It is also possible for an athlete to rotate his body in flight *even if he has no angular momentum.* Zero-angular-momentum twists and turns are performed by using the principle of action and reaction, turning one part of the body against another. To turn your body to the right while in midair, for example, you have to perform two movements in rapid succession. The first movement is to rotate your upper body to the right by twisting at the waist. (Because of action and reaction, this will cause your lower body to counterrotate to the left.) The second movement is immediately to rotate your lower body to the right, an action that will cause your upper body to counterrotate to the left. Doesn't this counterrotation cancel out the rotation from the first movement? Not if the movements of inertia of the upper and lower parts of the body are changed in an appropriate manner. In the first movement, the counterrotation of the lower body can be made small by extending the legs to increase their moment of inertia; in the second movement, the arms are extended to increase the moment of inertia of the upper body and reduce its counterrotation. During these maneuvers the total angular momentum of the body remains at zero, and at the end the body is at rest. In other words, this maneuver can be used to rotate the body through any angle, *but it does not initiate continuous rotation.*

Cats are famous for always landing on their feet. If you hold a cat upside down by his feet and release him, he can perform a zero-angular-momentum twist and rotate his body 180° in about ⅓ second, falling not more than 1½ to 2 feet in the process. (If you happen to have a cat handy, you can test out their remarkable ability to turn over in a short distance, but I must warn you, from personal experience, that cats prefer not to cooperate in scientific research.) As they fall, they turn first the front half, then the rear half of their body, using their paws and tail to vary the moments of inertia in the proper way. In their honor, this maneuver is known as a *cat twist.* Rabbits can also perform this maneuver, but dogs do not have the flexibility for it. Humans can perform cat twists without difficulty (though not as fast as a cat does). One particular group of humans who have learned how to make zero-angular-momentum rotations about any principal axis are the members of the astronaut corps, who must use such maneuvers to orient their bodies in any given direction when floating freely in space.

The law of conservation of angular momentum is used, consciously or unconsciously, by athletes in a variety of ways through a wide range of sports activities. I've given only a small sampling here; in later chapters I'll discuss a few more examples. I've endeavored to focus on the basic principles—namely, (1) how the body's moment of inertia can be changed to increase or decrease the spin rate; (2) the conditions in which angular momentum remains constant; (3) the techniques used to change one's angular momentum. With these ideas in mind, one can watch gymnastics, diving, or figure-skating competitions or go to the circus or ballet with a new frame of reference, a heightened sensitivity to the subtleties of technique, and a much deeper appreciation for the skill, discipline, and artistry involved in the act of spinning the human body.

5 / ENERGY

Of all the scientific terms that have passed into common language, the most conceptually useful, and by far the most familiar, is energy. The principles describing energy transformation and conservation have provided scientists with an extremely powerful and effective tool for analyzing the processes and interactions that occur in a complex system—whether it be an automobile engine, a human body, or an economic community. As a consequence, the concept of energy has become so thoroughly embedded in political and economic models of the functioning of human society, and in the scientific visualization of the universe itself, that it comes as a great surprise to discover that energy did not become a part of the scientific vocabulary until well into the nineteenth century. The energy concept was unknown to Newton, and does not appear in the *Principia*. In fact, the validity of the principle of conservation of energy was still being debated in the 1850s.

Most people have some intuitive idea of energy. It is usually visualized as some kind of mysterious substance; objects are said to "possess energy." It is known that energy can be stored or transferred from one object to another; when an object "runs out of energy," its supply can usually be replenished. It is generally believed that energy comes from certain sources—food, gasoline, coal, the sun. Yet anyone who is asked to give a definition of energy, to complete the sentence "Energy is . . . ," usually finds it rather difficult to give a coherent answer. For energy, as we will soon discover, is not a "thing," not a substance, but a mathematical abstraction, a convenient and useful abstraction which has taken on a life of its own. In this chapter, we'll look into the scientific definition of energy and show how it evolved within the past century to attain its present-day position as the most powerful and central concept of science. In this framework, we can then consider the human body as an energy-conversion system, an analysis that will be enlightening and valuable to every athlete and sports fan.

Work and Power

Historically, the energy concept evolved from attempts by physicists to find different ways to measure the effect of a force. One such measure is the motion that a force produces—specifically, the distance an object moves under the action of a force. The product of force and distance is a useful physical quantity which has been given the name of *work*:

$$\text{work} = \text{force} \times \text{distance}$$
$$W = Fd$$

In the customary unit system, work is measured in *foot-pounds* (ft-lb). The metric unit of work is called the *joule* (rhymes with *tool*), named for James Joule, who contributed to the discovery of conservation of energy (more about him later). The foot-pound is a slightly larger unit than the joule: 1 ft-lb = 1.356 joules.

Work is done by a force only when an object is moving and its motion is influenced by the force. If a force acts on an object and doesn't make it move, then no work is being done because there is no motion; the distance is zero. Thus a weight lifter who is holding a 350-lb barbell overhead is doing no work. Of course, the weight lifter would undoubtedly be inclined to dispute this contention, since he finds the task to be tiring and painful. To hold up the barbell, he must maintain his muscles in a state of tension, an action that requires a considerable expenditure of energy. But in the strict sense of the definition, he is doing no work on the barbell while holding it stationary. However, he did do work in the act of lifting it: in raising a 350-lb barbell a vertical distance of 6 feet, the weightlifter does 350 lb × 6 ft = 2100 ft-lb of work.

A muscle does work whenever it contracts or stretches in response to a force. According to the definition, the work done by any single muscle is equal to the tension force in the muscle multiplied by the distance the muscle contracts or stretches. Thus a muscle that contracts 3 inches (¼ foot) under a tension of 400 lb does 100 ft-lb of work while it is contracting. However, a muscle in static contraction—one that is exerting force without a change in length—does no work in the process. In everyday language we use the word "work" to describe various kinds of physical and mental effort, usually done for financial or personal gain, and in contrast to "play." As we've seen, the scientific definition of work is much more narrow and specific; a lot of work is done in the course of play.

The work done by large-scale forces falls roughly into two categories. One of these is *work against inertia*—work done by a force that is being used to accelerate or decelerate an object (here the force doing the work is acting to overcome the natural tendency of any object to maintain a constant velocity). This kind of work is done in throwing a ball, putting the shot, or swinging a baseball bat—the work done against inertia being equal to the strength of the force multiplied by the distance through which the object moves while it is being accelerated (about 90 ft-lb of work are done in throwing a baseball at 90 mi/hr, about 200 ft-lb in swinging a bat, and about 500 ft-lb in launching a shot with enough speed to go 70 feet). Work is also done by any force that decelerates rather than accelerates. In such instances, however, the force must naturally oppose the motion, so the work that is done is considered to be negative. Negative work is done by a tackler in bringing down a ball carrier, by air resistance in slowing the flight of a football, by friction in bringing a rolling automobile to a stop.

The other category of work done by large-scale forces is *work done to counteract another force*. When an archer stretches his bowstring or a pole vaulter bends his pole, he is doing work against the elastic forces of the string or pole. To push a heavy carton or a piece of furniture across the floor, we must do work against the opposing force of friction. Any time we lift an object we are doing work against the force of gravity; whenever we jump vertically, climb a ladder, do a chin-up or run up a flight of stairs, we are using our muscles to do work against our own weight.

Before we get into the connection between work and energy, however, we should consider the concept of *power*—a quantity that is often confused with both force and energy, but is quite distinct from both of them. Very simply, power is the *rate of doing work;* that is, it takes into account the time required to do a given amount of work. Thus

$$power = \frac{work\ done}{time\ interval}$$

Since power has the units of work/time, we might expect customary system measurements to be in ft-lb/sec. However, the standard unit of power turns out to have a familiar name: *the horsepower.* By definition, 1 horsepower (hp) is equivalent to 550 ft-lb/sec. The credit for the naming and measurement of this unit belongs to the Scottish inventor James Watt, who employed it to show how the output of one of his steam engines compared with that of a horse performing the same task (specifically, turning a winch to lift heavy weights out of a well). As it turns out, the power output of a horse at top effort is actually much larger than one horsepower. The metric unit of power has been aptly named the *watt* in his honor (1 watt = 1 joule/sec). The watt is a very familiar unit, since it is commonly used to measure the output of electrical appliances such as light bulbs, toasters, and stereo amplifiers (objects that do no work in the way we have defined it). It is just another facet of the confusion with unit systems in the United States that we measure the output of our electrical devices in metric units (watts) but of our machines and engines in customary units (horsepower). Incidentally, the horsepower is a much larger unit of power than the watt: 1 hp = 746 watts.

As I've already noted, power is often confused with force, energy, strength, or even ability ("the power to cloud men's minds"). A power hitter in baseball or a power forward in basketball (a player who concentrates on rebounding rather than scoring) is really displaying strength rather than power in the scientific sense, for power is actually a combination of speed and strength—the capacity to do a given amount of work as rapidly as possible. A 200-hp engine does not necessarily produce twice as much work or go twice as fast as a 100-hp engine; rather it does the same amount of work in half the time. The main advantage of a high-horsepower automobile engine is its acceleration: it can get the automobile up to a chosen speed more quickly than a lower-power engine can.

Kinetic and Potential Energy

Having clarified the definitions of work and power, we can now introduce the concept of energy. This concept arises from an analysis of the work done against inertia by a force—that is, a force that acts to accelerate or decelerate some object. Suppose that the speed of the object changes from v_1 to v_2: an application of the basic equations (W = Fd, F = ma, $v_2^2 = v_1^2 + 2ad$) produces an equation for the work done by the force. The equation looks like this:

$$W = \frac{1}{2}mv_2^2 - \frac{1}{2}mv_1^2$$

The quantity $\frac{1}{2}mv^2$ that appears in this equation is called the *kinetic energy* (it was first given this name in 1807). We can read the above equation as follows: *the work done by a force on an object is equal to the change in its kinetic energy.*

What exactly is kinetic energy? From the equation (KE = $\frac{1}{2}mv^2$) we can see that the kinetic energy of an object depends on both its mass and its speed. A stationary object has no kinetic energy (since v = 0); the kinetic energy of a moving object grows as its speed increases. When we say that an object "has kinetic energy," we mean simply that the object is in motion, the amount of its kinetic energy depending on both the mass and the speed of the object. Kinetic energy is measured in the same units as work is—joules (metric) or foot-pounds (customary). Table 5.1 lists representative kinetic energies of a few objects familiar to sports enthusiasts.

Work done on an object changes its kinetic energy. This principle can be looked at from another angle: a body possessing kinetic energy can be made to do work. A swinging hammer, landing on the head of a nail, transforms its kinetic energy of motion into work, exerting a force on the nail that drives it a small distance farther into a piece of wood. The moving hand of a karate blackbelt transfers its kinetic energy to a concrete block, bending it enough to make it crack in the middle. A fullback, running headlong into a stationary defender, uses his kinetic energy to drive the defender backward several feet when they collide. Examples of this sort—wherein a moving object uses its kinetic energy to do work on another object—abound in nature, and

TABLE 5.1: KINETIC ENERGY IN SPORTS

This table gives approximate values for the kinetic energies (measured in joules) of projectiles and athletes when they are moving at speeds typical of top-level performance.

Object	Kinetic Energy (joules)
Baseball pitch (fast ball)	120
Basketball (15-foot jump shot)	15
Bowling ball	230
Football (forward pass)	150
Golf ball (hit by driver)	110
Hammer throw	2700
Hockey puck (slap shot)	170
Karate chop	60
Shot put	680
Tennis ball (serve)	75
200-lb fullback (open field run)	2600
140-lb sprinter (top speed)	3600
140-lb swimmer (top speed)	125

this has led physicists to propose a simple definition of energy: *energy is the capacity of an object to do work.*

I would not be surprised if this statement leaves you unmoved and uninformed; it conveys a lot more meaning to a physicist than it does to the layman. Actually, it's not as important to be able to state what energy is as it is to identify and understand its transformations, for the value of the energy concept lies in the fact that *virtually every process or change that occurs in nature can be analyzed in terms of a transformation of energy from one form to another.* To really appreciate the significance of this statement, we must first learn about the different forms of energy, kinetic energy being only one of many.

The discovery—or perhaps I should say the invention—of other forms of energy came about when scientists began to examine the effects of work done to counteract other forces (the second category of work described earlier). Consider, for example, work done to counteract the force of gravity: in order to lift any object, we must exert an upward force that is greater than its weight. As we lift it, we exert a force through a distance, and so we are doing work on the object. If we then release the object and allow it to fall freely, it will accelerate toward the ground, increasing in speed—and kinetic energy—as it falls. Thus an object lying motionless on the ground tends to remain at rest; it has no potential for movement. But if we raise an object above the ground, *it now has the potential for motion,* for when we let it go, it immediately begins to fall.

This simple act of lifting and then letting go of an object can be understood in an energy context as follows: by doing work on the object as we lift it, we are giving it *potential energy*—the higher we lift it the more work we do, and the more potential energy it has. When the object is released and allowed to fall, its potential energy is gradually changed into *kinetic* energy (energy of motion). It is attractive to think of potential energy as *stored energy*—energy that does not dissipate and can be exchanged for kinetic energy at any time. If, for instance, you take a basketball and put it on the shelf in your closet, you do work, and thereby give the basketball potential energy, in raising it to the level of the shelf. For as long as the basketball remains on the shelf, it has the same amount of potential energy. If at any time thereafter the basketball rolls off the shelf, its stored potential energy is immediately available for conversion to kinetic energy.

The process of exchanging potential energy for kinetic energy can be reversed; that is, it is possible to convert kinetic energy to potential energy. When a ball is thrown vertically upward, it starts out with the kinetic energy imparted to it in the launching process. As the ball rises it loses kinetic energy (slows down) but gains potential energy. At the top of its trajectory, all the kinetic energy has been converted to potential. As the ball subsequently falls to the ground, its potential energy is converted back to kinetic energy. The careful reader may perceive the exchange between kinetic and potential energy as nothing more than an alternate way to describe the interplay between inertia and the force of gravity. This is indeed correct. But notice that the energy approach does not deal explicitly with force, time, or acceleration; there are often very helpful mathematical simplifications accruing from these omissions. Moreover, the idea of potential energy as a "store" of energy, available for conversion to other forms, has considerable conceptual appeal.

An important advantage of the energy concept is that it is possible to identify several different kinds of potential energy, each one associated with one of the forces of nature. The kind of potential energy

I've been describing up to now is specifically *gravitational* potential energy, since it stems from work done to counteract the force of gravity. Another kind of potential energy, one that has particular relevance to many aspects of sports, is *elastic potential energy,* which, as its name indicates, has to do with the energy associated with elastic forces. A spring, or anything that resembles a spring, has the capacity to store elastic potential energy. A spring that has been stretched or compressed will jump into motion the instant it is released, as its internal elastic forces act to restore it to its normal length. In terms of energy, we can describe such events in the following way: the force that stretches or compresses the spring does work that is stored by the spring as elastic energy; when released the spring converts this energy into kinetic energy of motion.

I've often heard good jumpers described as "having springs in their legs." This really isn't far from the truth, because a stretched muscle does act like a spring in that it can store and release elastic energy. Earlier I pointed out that a muscle cannot stretch itself; it can only shorten. It takes an external force to stretch a muscle (very often supplied by the contraction of another muscle—for example, the contraction of the biceps stretches the triceps). The work done by a stretching force contributes to the elastic energy stored by the muscle. When the muscle subsequently contracts, the stored elastic energy adds to the work done in the process of contraction as both are converted to the kinetic energy of motion.

Devices or pieces of equipment that store elastic energy can be found throughout the spectrum of sports. When an archer prepares to shoot his arrow by drawing back the bowstring, he stores elastic energy in the stretched bowstring and in the bow itself—energy that transforms to the kinetic energy of the arrow when the bowstring is released. The bed of a trampoline is made of an elastic material and is bound to its frame by elastic cords or springs. When a gymnast performs on a trampoline, there is a constant interchange between the kinetic energy and gravitational potential energy of the gymnast's body and the elastic potential energy of the trampoline.

One track and field event in which elastic energy storage plays a crucial role is the pole vault, which has probably the most complex technique of any sports activity, requiring an exceptional level of coordination, timing, strength, and speed. Figure 5.1 shows a typical pole-vaulting sequence. First, the vaulter gains speed in a long run-up. In his run, the vaulter must hold the pole (which can be up to 16

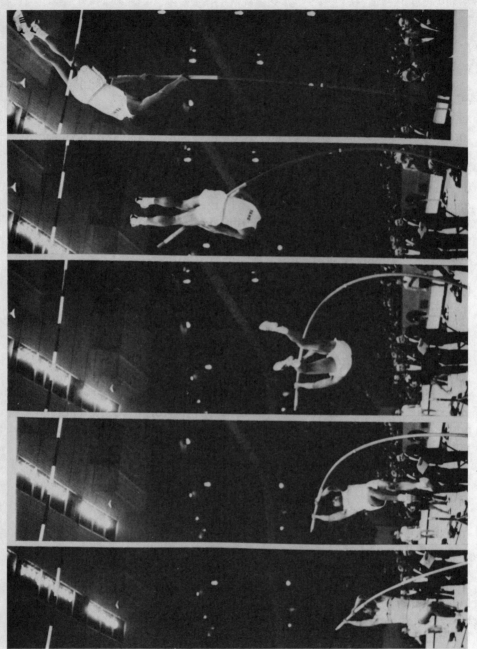

FIGURE 5.1   The pole vault. This sequence shows C. K. Yang competing in February 1964—only a few years after the use of fiberglass poles was sanctioned (*UPI photo*).

feet long) in a roughly horizontal position while trying to achieve a sprinter's speed for the takeoff. At the culmination of his run, the vaulter raises the end of the pole overhead, while jamming the other end forward into the "box" (a small pit just below the bar). The pole now begins to pivot about this end, lifting the vaulter upward. He aids his ascent by pushing upward off the ground at the takeoff. As the pole first begins to pivot, the vaulter is hanging by his hands—but he swings his body parallel to the pole, then thrusts his legs upward to assume a "handstand" position as the pole becomes vertical. The upward swing of his body increases the moment of inertia of the pole-athlete system (by moving mass away from the axis of rotation). According to the law of conservation of angular momentum, this increase in moment of inertia must slow the angular rotation of the pole around its pivot point. Therefore the vaulter must time the upward swing of his body properly—for if it is done too soon the pole will rotate too slowly, and if it is done too late the pole will rotate so rapidly that the vaulter will not have enough time to complete his handstand.

From the handstand position, with the pole nearly vertical, the vaulter completes the jump by twisting his body so that he can arch himself over the bar. As he releases his grip to go over, he pushes off the pole—and also pushes it away to prevent it from hitting the bar. Even the descent is eventful—for in falling from a height of 18 feet the vaulter achieves a landing speed of about 23 mi/hr, and he must orient his body to hit the landing cushion comfortably and safely.

From an energy standpoint, the vaulter is converting the kinetic energy of his linear motion acquired in the run-up to energy of rotational motion as the pole pivots, then to gravitational potential energy as he gains height (the vaulter actually initiates *two* rotational motions —one of the pole around its end, the other of his body around his hands). The effectiveness of his technique essentially decides how much of his initial kinetic energy is ultimately converted into gravitational potential energy, and thereby determines the height he reaches.

About 25 years ago, pole vaulters turned to modern technology to find a way to improve the efficiency of the energy conversion process —and came up with the fiberglass pole. A fiberglass pole is exceptionally flexible; it can easily be bent several feet out of line. The bending of the pole as it is driven into the box on takeoff serves to convert some of the vaulter's kinetic energy into elastic energy. Later on, as the pole becomes more vertical and straightens out, this elastic energy is returned to the vaulter and helps him to go even higher. However, the pole cannot be too flexible or it will return the energy too slowly —that is, it will not spring back in time to help the vaulter over the bar.

Originally, vaulting poles were made of steel, aluminum, or bamboo. With these materials the best pole vaulters could not get much higher than 15 feet. In 1942 Cornelius Warmerdam attained 15'7¾" with a bamboo pole, setting a record that remained intact for 17 years. Vaulters began experimenting with fiberglass poles in the late 1950s. In 1962 their use in international competition was officially sanctioned, and in the following year the first 17-foot vault was achieved. As vaulters have modified their techniques to take full advantage of the properties of the fiberglass pole, their performances have improved dramatically; the world record, set in 1981, is now 19'¾".

There are numerous other illustrations of how equipment designers make use of flexible materials to improve sports performance through effective elastic energy storage and return. A key design consideration is the speed with which stored elastic energy can be returned. This depends on two factors—mass and stiffness. The more massive (or dense) the material is, the slower it responds—greater mass being associated with greater inertia. The stiffer a material is (stiffness being the opposite of flexibility), the more rapidly the energy is returned. However, a stiffer material stores less energy. (Specifically, when subjected to the same force, a stiffer material will distort less and will store less elastic energy than a more flexible material of the same mass.) All of these conflicting effects must be correlated with the performance requirements of the particular piece of equipment.

The principles of elastic energy storage have been put to effective use in tennis racket design. When a tennis ball collides with a racket at high speed, the ball, the strings, and the racket frame itself are distorted by the impact. Consequently, some of the kinetic energy of motion of the ball has been transformed and stored momentarily as elastic energy in the strings and frame. As they spring back to their normal shapes, both the strings and frame ought to return the stored elastic energy to the ball. The strings do recoil rapidly enough to return energy to the ball; however, the racket frame, being more massive, responds more slowly, and the ball has rebounded off the racket before the elastic energy in the frame can be returned to it. (Measurements show that it takes about 15 to 20 milliseconds for the racket frame to rebound, while the ball is in contact with the strings for only about 5 milliseconds.)

Since it is not feasible to design a usable racket frame flexible enough to return its elastic energy to the ball, one approach is to go to the other extreme and make the frame as stiff as possible. A stiff frame will distort less at impact, and will absorb less of the ball's kinetic energy, whereas a flexible frame absorbs more energy—energy that it cannot return to the ball. (The strings, on the other hand, should be made as flexible as possible, a matter that we'll look at more closely in the next chapter.) In recent years, racket designers have turned from the traditional wooden design to newer construction materials such as graphite, boron, aluminum, and fiberglass. One of the main advantages of these substances is their light weight combined with stiffness several times greater than that of wood. But the ability to return more of the impact energy to the ball is not the only criterion for choosing a tennis racket. Considerations of weight, maneuverability, control, and comfort also come into play. Recent advances in technology and design principles, based in part on energy analysis, now provide the tennis player with a much wider range of choices.

The shafts of golf clubs or hockey sticks, which can be manufactured to varying degrees of flexibility, provide additional examples of the use of elastic energy storage. The advantage of a flexible shaft is that it bends slightly during the swing (the end cannot keep up with the handle) and stores elastic energy. This energy is then delivered to the golf ball or hockey puck on impact—provided, of course, that the shaft is not so flexible that it responds too slowly. The result is a greater launching speed—but it must be balanced against the better accuracy and placement that can be attained with a less flexible shaft. Flexibility and elastic energy storage would also be effective in a baseball bat, but size and shape requirements make it difficult to build much flexibility into a wooden bat. Some manufacturers used to advertise that their baseball bats had "flexible whip action." However, it seems highly unlikely that a bat could bend enough when swung to store a useful amount of elastic energy.

Perhaps the most sophisticated use of elastic energy storage in sports to date has been the design of a "tuned" running track at Harvard University. In 1976, when the construction of a new indoor track was being planned, the designers consulted with two mechanical engineers, Thomas A. McMahon and Peter R. Greene, who were doing biomechanical research at Harvard. By analyzing the mechanics of running and the energy interactions between a runner and the track, McMahon and Greene came up with an optimum design for the track surface.

When a runner's foot strikes the track surface, his leg muscles must act to decelerate the downward motion of his body. This action transfers energy to the surface, which, if it is at all compliant, will absorb and store some of the transferred energy as elastic energy. This energy can be returned to the runner during the time his foot remains at that point on the surface (while he is bringing up his trailing leg). McMahon and Greene determined just how flexible or "springy" the surface should be in order to return its stored elastic energy most effectively to the runner.

At one extreme is a very hard surface, like concrete, which has virtually no springiness and returns little or no elastic energy to the runner. At the other extreme is a very compliant, spongy surface, like foam rubber, which absorbs energy but returns it slowly. A runner sinks into this kind of surface when he's running, and is slowed by the excessive time spent rebounding from the surface. The springiness of a "tuned" track lies between these two extremes; it is tuned in the sense that it is designed to return elastic energy at a rate that minimizes the runner's contact time while increasing his stride length— two effects that taken together will maximize his running speed.

The Harvard running track was constructed to have the optimum flexibility predicted by McMahon and Greene's research. How successful was this effort? Runners find the new track to be very comfortable to run on, and the injury rate has declined considerably. Most significantly, during the first year the track was in use, running times decreased by 2% to 3%—enough to knock 5 seconds off a 4-minute mile.

Conservation of Energy

The energy principle can be a rather effective source of conceptual and practical insights. So far we've learned about kinetic energy and two kinds of potential energy—gravitational and elastic. As we've just seen, many of the events that take place at athletic fields and gymnasiums can be understood and analyzed in terms of interchanges between these three forms of energy. However, a problem arises when we try to deal with these interchanges in mathematical terms. Does all of the kinetic energy accumulated by a pole vaulter in his run-up get converted to gravitational energy? If not, then what fraction of the kinetic energy does get converted, and what happens to the rest of it? When a tennis ball strikes a racket, how much of its kinetic energy is converted to elastic energy, and how much of that is returned to the ball? Is there some theoretical way to set up an "energy balance sheet" that accounts numerically for all the energy exchanges that take place?

In a collision between any two objects, there is a conversion of the kinetic energy of their motion to elastic energy during the impact, then back to kinetic energy as the objects rebound. In an ideal collision, all of the elastic energy is converted back to kinetic energy. One object may gain kinetic energy from the other, but their total stays the same; kinetic energy is conserved in the collision. This type of interaction is known as an *elastic collision*.

Most collisions, however, are not elastic. When a ball bounces off a rigid, massive surface like a wall or a floor, it always rebounds with less speed. Less speed means less kinetic energy, so there is a net loss of kinetic energy in the bounce. It is possible for a ball to gain kinetic energy in a collision with a *moving* object, as is well known to any baseball fan; a batter can propel a line drive at a noticeably higher speed than that of the pitch he swung at. However, in this collision the *bat* loses kinetic energy, enough so that the total kinetic energy of bat plus ball always shows a net decrease in the collision.

Any collision in which kinetic energy is *not* conserved is known as an *inelastic collision*. Here all the elastic energy is not returned to the colliding objects. There are some collisions that are nearly elastic, the most notable being the collisions between billiard balls in a game of pool. (In fact, physicists are fond of describing elastic collisions as "billiard-ball collisions.") At the other extreme, imagine a head-on collision between two cars that ends with both coming to a dead stop. This is the ultimate in inelastic collisions, because there has been a total loss of all the kinetic energy that the cars had before they collided.

If kinetic energy is not conserved in an inelastic collision, then where does it go? A careful examination of the net energy balance reveals that the missing kinetic energy has not been stored anywhere as gravitational or elastic potential energy. There appears to be a net loss of energy in the collision. Often energy losses seem to occur even when there hasn't been a collision. Consider a car moving at a modest speed of 25 mi/hr on a city street. The traffic light up ahead turns red, so the driver brakes the car to a stop. Before, the car had a considerable amount of kinetic energy (due to its speed and large mass), and now it has none. The kinetic energy has not been converted to gravitational or elastic energy; it has seemingly disappeared. In order to get the car moving again, the driver must generate a new supply of energy by revving up the engine.

This apparent disappearance of energy in even the simplest of interactions presents a serious problem. The concept of energy is scientifically useful only if energy is conserved, only if we can account for its exchanges and transformations on our balance sheets. A closer examination of the problem reveals that the culprit is *friction*. It turns out that the work done to overcome a frictional force cannot be stored and cannot be converted to any form of potential energy. A moving car is brought to a stop by friction in the brakes and on the tires—and all the energy that is used up to do work against friction is unrecoverable. It can be shown that energy *is* conserved in a perfectly frictionless mechanical system; the interchanges between kinetic, gravitational, and elastic energy always balance. But perfectly frictionless systems do not exist in the world of our experience, as anyone who sets out to build a perpetual motion machine eventually discovers.

Yet anyone who has even the merest acquaintance with science is probably aware that conservation of energy is considered to be the most hallowed, the most valuable, the *central* principle of physics. The general impression, which seems to have been fostered by many science texts and teachers, is that conservation of energy has been known and accepted by scientists since time immemorial. Yet its validity was not firmly established until the middle of the nineteenth century when—through a fascinating interplay of events, personalities, and philosophies—the problem of frictional energy loss was solved, and the energy concept was extended to encompass other forms of energy as well as living things. A brief historical outline of how this came about will set the scene for our study of the human body as an energy-generating and -consuming system.

The eventual development of an all-inclusive conservation of energy principle evolved from the conjunction of two important and well-known scientific facts. The first is that *friction creates heat*—a phenomenon familiar to anyone who has ever warmed his hands, or managed to start a fire with two sticks of wood, by rubbing them together. The second is that *heat can be used to do work*. This is the principle behind steam- and gasoline-powered engines; the heat given off by the burning fuel can be used to drive a piston or turn a wheel. The first steam engines, built in the early 1700s, were highly wasteful devices. But in the 1760s James Watt began his efforts to develop more efficient steam engines. His eminent success in this venture spurred on the Industrial Revolution, and encouraged further development of heat-driven engines. In fact, the demand created by the Industrial Revolution for cheaper and more efficient sources of power may be considered a major stimulant to the eventual formulation of the principle of conservation of energy.

While the connections among heat, work, and energy may now seem self-evident to the modern-day observer, they were not at all obvious to eighteenth-century scientists. The main reason for this oversight was the fact that people thought of heat as a *material substance*—an actual fluid, named *caloric,* which could be stored in objects and transferred from one to another. It was believed that a hot object contained more caloric than a cold one; but when they were placed in contact, caloric automatically fled from the hot object to the cold one. Although this theory has since been discarded, we still use its language today in referring to a "flow of heat" and in measuring heat in calories rather than in the standard units of energy. As long as the caloric theory could successfully explain heat-related phenomena, scientists remained convinced that heat was a material fluid rather than a form of energy.

The overthrow of the caloric theory was triggered mainly by the experiments of American-born Benjamin Thompson (later to be known as Count Rumford) and the Englishman James Joule. Thompson was an extraordinary, larger-than-life character who has been described by one of his biographers as displaying "unswerving honesty in science and unconscionable duplicity in politics." Born in 1753 to considerable poverty in colonial Massachusetts, Thompson married a rich widow 14 years his senior and bought a commission in the Colonial army. When it was discovered that he was collaborating with the British, Thompson fled to England. Here he became wealthy by accepting bribes for the purchase of military equipment for the British army. Accused of giving British military secrets to the French, Thompson shifted his allegiance to the Elector of Bavaria, where he became minister of war—even though, as it turned out, he was serving as a British secret agent. After more than a decade in Bavaria, where he acquired his title, Count Rumford moved to London, then on to Paris, where he became an adviser to Napoleon.

Perhaps the most remarkable feat of Rumford's life is that he managed to find time to produce an impressive output of practical scientific work. Among the many subjects that engaged his interest were the improvement of fireplaces and kitchen stoves, the brewing of coffee, the measurement of the force of gunpowder and the velocities of bullets, and the improvement of the health, comfort, and general living conditions of the poor of Munich. His interest in the theory of heat was stimulated by his experiences while supervising the building of cannon for the Bavarian army. Rumford observed that the drilling tools produced an unlimited supply of heat through friction, and he reasoned that if caloric is truly a material substance, an object could not contain an infinite store of it. Rumford performed several experiments to verify his thesis that the caloric theory could not possibly account for the heat generated by friction, and concluded that heat is actually a form of vibratory molecular motion. In modern terminology, we would say that the heat energy contained in a substance is the sum of the kinetic energies of its randomly moving atoms and molecules, and that heat "flow" is the transfer of energy in one of its many forms from one object to another.

At his death in 1814 Rumford had managed to win a few influential converts to his side, but the majority of scientists still held firmly to the caloric theory. It was well into the 1840s before serious efforts to construct a unified theory of heat and energy began. One of the most important contributions was made by James Joule (1818–1889), scion of a wealthy family whose income derived from the ownership of a brewery (Joule's Beer is still sold locally in the English Midlands). Joule, who remained an amateur scientist throughout his life, made careful measurements of the heat generated by electricity, by chemical reactions, by mechanical processes, and by friction. His results revealed an exact mathematical relationship between work and heat: when a specific amount of mechanical work is done, a specific quantity of heat appears (see Math Box 6, page 177).

The equivalence of heat and work, first demonstrated by Joule, provides the solution to the problem of the disappearance of energy through friction: *the missing energy is converted to an equivalent amount of heat.* When moving objects are brought to a stop by frictional forces, their kinetic energy is transformed to heat energy, stored in the increased motion of its molecules and detected as an increase in temperature. In an inelastic collision between two objects, not all of the elastic energy created at impact is returned to the objects; some of it is converted to heat energy. When a baseball bat collides with a fast ball, some of their combined kinetic energy is changed to heat at the point of impact. Thus a hitter who has been

---

MATH BOX 6: HEAT, ENERGY, AND POWER UNITS

The units used to measure work and energy are the *joule* (metric) and the *foot-pound* (customary). They are related by the conversion factor

$$1 \text{ ft-lb} = 1.356 \text{ joules}$$

Scientists initially believed that heat was a material fluid (caloric), and so they developed special units of measurement for quantities of heat or heat flow. The basic units are the *calorie,* defined as the quantity of heat needed to raise the temperature of 1 gram of water by 1°C, and the BTU (short for British thermal unit), defined as the quantity of heat needed to raise the temperature of 1 pound of water by 1°F. The BTU is a much larger unit than the calorie:

$$252 \text{ calories} = 1 \text{ BTU}$$

The unit used by nutritionists and diet-watchers to measure the energy value of food is the Calorie, equal to 1000 heat calories (1 Calorie = 1 kilocalorie).

In demonstrating that heat is a form of energy, Joule showed that there is a direct equivalence between heat and energy units. The conversions are as follows:

$$4.186 \text{ joules} = 1 \text{ calorie}$$
$$778 \text{ ft-lb} = 1 \text{ BTU}$$

The *rate* of energy generation or consumption has the standard units of power, i.e., the *watt* (1 watt = 1 joule/sec) and the *horsepower* (1 hp = 550 ft-lb/sec). They are correlated with heat rate units as follows:

$$1 \text{ watt} = 0.239 \text{ calories/sec} = 0.86 \text{ Calories/hr}$$
$$1 \text{ hp} = 0.71 \text{ BTU/sec} = 2545 \text{ BTU/hr}$$

---

making contact with the ball and getting a lot of hits has a "hot bat," both literally and figuratively.

Joule first argued for a principle of conservation of energy in 1847, and many other scientists began to follow suit. However, the credit for the formulation of the principle in its most general form belongs to a German scientist, Hermann von Helmholtz (1821–1894). Helmholtz was a scientist of the first rank with an astonishing breadth of interests. He made significant discoveries in the physiology of vision and hearing, and important contributions to the theories of fluid flow and electromagnetism. His command of physiology, physics, and mathematics fused in his work on the conservation of energy. Perhaps the most significant feature of this synthesis was Helmholtz' rejection of the idea that living things possess a "vital force"—a nonphysical essence that powers their activities. Helmholtz contended that *all physiological processes can be explained in terms of physics and chemistry.* All living things, he argued, obey the conservation of energy; the energy that they expend in their activities must be balanced by a source of an equal amount of energy—energy that comes mainly from the digestion of food and not from some mysterious, metaphysical vital force.

Helmholtz published his findings in 1847; buttressed by Joule's measurements and the contributions of several other scientists from the fields of medicine, physics, and chemistry, the principle of conservation of energy began to take hold. By the 1860s, most serious opposition to it had disappeared. The principle has since been extended to encompass several other basic forms of potential energy, particularly those associated with electrical, magnetic, and nuclear forces. Also included are *chemical energy* (the energy absorbed or released in chemical reactions—this is really a form of electrical potential energy, since chemical bonds result from electrical forces) and *radiant energy* (the energy, fundamentally electromagnetic, carried by light and other forms of radiation—infrared, ultraviolet, X rays, radio waves, etc.). All forms of energy are measured in the same units (joules or foot-pounds), and the power output of any energy source— the rate at which energy is being converted—is measured in watts or horsepower. Thus a 60-watt light bulb is converting electrical energy to light and heat at a rate of 60 joules/sec.

The key ideas of conservation of energy may be readily summarized. One idea is that *every process or interaction in nature can be explained as a transformation of energy from one form to another.* Another is that *energy cannot be created or destroyed.* There are no "new" energy sources in nature; we can, of course, discover previously untapped energy sources or find more effective ways to convert less usable forms of energy. But no machine, device, or living thing can generate more energy than it takes in. Most technological inventions are *energy converters* rather than energy sources—a battery converts chemical energy to electrical energy, a toaster converts electrical energy to heat and radiant energy, and so on. It follows that *the total energy of a closed system is constant.* A closed system is anything that is physically isolated from its surroundings; since energy does not enter or leave a closed system, its total energy cannot change. The earth is *not* a closed system, since it receives a great deal of energy from the sun. However, the universe as a whole is a closed system—since, by definition, there is nothing else—so the total energy of the universe must not have changed throughout its existence, going back to the Big Bang.

It's interesting and instructive to follow the energy transformations involved in, say, a game of basketball. In this activity, each player's body uses energy in several forms—kinetic energy for running, potential energy for jumping, and so on. It gets this energy from the chemical reactions involved in the digestion of food—let's say from toast and coffee at breakfast. The electrical energy used to run the toaster and coffeepot came from a huge electrical generator at the local electric company, driven by the heat created by the combustion of oil or coal. These are "fossil fuels"—meaning that they were produced by the decay (chemical transformation) of organic matter that existed hundreds of millions of years ago and was buried in the ground. This organic matter lived and grew by transforming chemical energy and sunlight. The sun, in turn, produces its light through nuclear reactions deep in its core. I could go on, describing the nuclear energy conversion process in the sun, but I think you get the idea.

We seem to have gone far off the subject of sports—but only apparently so. The best way for an intelligent athlete to maintain or improve his athletic performance is to understand how his body works—not just in terms of forces, levers, and muscular strength, but also as an *energy system*. The human body, as Helmholtz first proposed, is subject to the laws of physics and chemistry and obeys the law of conservation of energy. With these guiding precepts, scientists have managed to learn a great deal about human physiology. In recent years, egged on by the growing public awareness and interest in physical fitness, scientists have taken particular interest in how the body responds to stress, specifically that produced by strenuous exercise, and the field of exercise physiology has evolved rapidly as a result. Now we'll take a look at some of the interesting discoveries that they've made.

The Living Energy Machine

The human body produces energy in several forms. Being warm-blooded animals, our bodies maintain a constant internal temperature, so heat energy must be produced to maintain a thermal balance. The movement of our bodies requires the creation of kinetic energy, which can be traced back to the energy inolved in muscle contraction. The body must also supply chemical energy for the reactions that build new cells and destroy old ones, and electrical energy for nerve impulses, which are short bursts of electrical potential energy traveling along nerve fibers. Few scientists still consider the mind to be separate from the body, so thoughts, memories, consciousness itself must necessarily be electrochemical in nature, resulting in the consumption of energy.

The body must generate as much energy as it expends. It does this through the metabolism of food; everything that we take in is digested down to simpler chemical forms and distributed through the body for storage, immediate use, or removal as waste. The rate at which the body generates energy is equal to the rate at which food is metabolized. The oxygen in the air we breathe takes part in the metabolic process, and there is a direct ratio between the rate of oxygen intake and the energy produced. This ratio depends on the type of food consumed; it has different values for carbohydrates, proteins, and fats, and affects the "calorie count" of any portion of food, which is the total amount of energy given off as heat when the food is burned and combines with oxygen.

We generate energy in the form of heat at all times. Awake but relaxed, an average healthy individual takes in about 3.5 milliliters of oxygen per minute per kilogram of body mass, equivalent to a heat output of 0.40 Calories per hour per pound of body weight. (Remember that 1 Calorie, or food calorie, equals 1000 heat calories, as explained in Math Box 6, page 177). This resting energy output is familiarly known as the *basal metabolism* or *basal metabolic rate* (BMR). During exercise, the rate of metabolism rises, going to about 15 times the basal rate during strenuous exercise and even higher in short bursts of activity. Table 5.2 lists representative oxygen intake and heat generation rates for various activities. You may find it interesting to calculate the number of food calories burned off in one of these activities; simply multiply the rate in Cal/hr/lb by your own weight to arrive at the number of Calories consumed per hour.

It's relatively easy to explain the body's heat output; heat is released in the myriad chemical reactions that take place in all parts of the body. But explaining motion is a more difficult task. As I've said before, all body motions can be traced to the contraction of muscle fibers, so the problem reduces down to explaining how muscle fibers

TABLE 5.2: SOME RATES OF ENERGY EXPENDITURE (METABOLIC RATE)

Activity	Oxygen Intake (ml O_2/min/kg)	Heat Rate (Cal/hr/lb)
Sitting (basal rate)	3.5	0.4
Standing	5	0.6
Light work	11	1.3
Easy biking	12	1.4
Walking (3 mi/hr)	13	1.5
Golf	15	1.7
Tennis	24	3.0
Running (5 mi/hr)	28	3.7
Basketball	30	3.9
Running (10 mi/hr)	50	6.9
Running up stairs	50	6.9
Sprinting	100	13.8

contract when they are signaled to do so by a nerve impulse. To understand the contraction of a single muscle fiber, we have to go beyond the cellular level to the molecular level, focusing on the structure, arrangement, and chemical reactions of the protein molecules that exist within the fiber. Remember that a muscle fiber is a single elongated cell, a few millionths of an inch wide. Indeed, the fact that we can actually *see* the structure inside the fiber, let alone determine the molecular arrangements and interactions, is one of the great triumphs of modern science and technology. This quest enlisted the use of electron microscopes, X ray diffraction spectrometers, and sophisticated biochemical techniques—the same basic approach that led to the discovery of the DNA molecule and the genetic code.

The electron microscope reveals a highly ordered structure within the cell walls of each muscle fiber. Under relatively low magnification, the fiber exhibits a pattern of alternating dark and light bands (Fig. 5.2). Moreover, further examination at low magnification reveals that the fiber consists of a bundle of even smaller strands, known as *myofibrils,* embedded in the cellular protoplasm, which contains cell nuclei, mitochondria, and various chemical substances that are needed for the functioning of the muscle cell. Higher magnification shows that the myofibrils are made of parallel rows of interleaved filaments, alter-

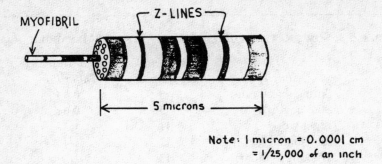

FIGURE 5.2 The banded structure of a muscle fiber.

natingly thick and thin (Fig. 5.3); the dark bands on the muscle fiber turn out to be the places where the thick and thin filaments overlap. The thin filaments are each attached at one end to a structure known as the *Z-line*. In resting muscle, there is a gap between the ends of the thin filaments, but in fully contracted muscle the gap disappears. The thick filaments, which have small projections along their length known as *cross-bridges,* pull the thin filaments toward each other, bringing the Z-lines closer together. This action, taking place simultaneously along the length of the myofibril and in each myofibril in the fiber, results in a shortening of the fiber.

Having identified the mechanical process that occurs in muscle contraction, our curiosity drives us one step further: *what causes the thin filaments to be pulled together?* To answer this question, we have to get down to the molecular structure of the filaments themselves.

The thick filaments are made of a complex protein called *myosin,* which is a rod-shaped molecule with a bulbous head extending from one end. Each thick filament is an assemblage of several hundred myosin molecules aligned together with their heads projecting away from the filaments (Fig. 5.4). These heads, barely visible in an electron microscope, form the cross-bridges that extend toward the thin filaments. Three proteins—*actin, troponin,* and *tropomyosin*—make up a thin filament, which takes the form of a long, twisted braid of molecules. Although the thin filaments are mostly actin, the other two proteins play a pivotal role in the contraction process.

While many of the details are still to be worked out, a basic theory of the muscle contraction process seems to be agreed upon. The central feature is a chemical bond between a cross-bridge (a myosin head)

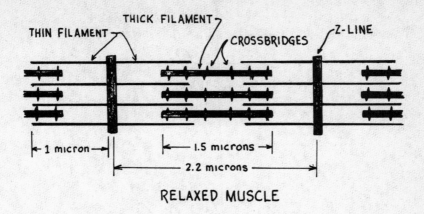

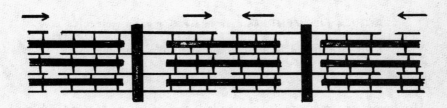

FIGURE 5.3   Schematics of muscle contraction in a myofibril.

and an actin molecule (see Fig. 5.5). But this bond cannot take place when the muscle is in the relaxed state because the alignment of the tropomyosin molecules on the thin filament prevents the myosin head and actin molecule from interacting. Earlier, we learned that muscle contraction is triggered by a stream of nerve impulses, each impulse being a "twitch" of electrochemical activity. It is now known that a nerve impulse stimulates the release of calcium into the gap between the filaments. Although it is not yet clear exactly how this happens, the calcium reacts with troponin and tropomyosin, changing the alignment of the latter and clearing the way for a myosin-actin bond to form.

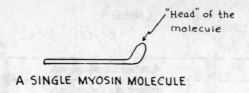

A SINGLE MYOSIN MOLECULE

A THICK FILAMENT: An assemblage of myosin molecules

FIGURE 5.4   The structure of a thick filament.

However, one more factor is needed: the presence of a molecule of *adenosine triphosphate,* more commonly known as ATP. An ATP molecule combines readily with a myosin head, and the combination then reacts with an actin molecule. This happens all along the two filaments, so that each thick filament becomes locked to the adjacent thin filaments, as shown in Figure 5.5a. The ATP immediately decomposes, releasing energy; this energy causes the attached myosin heads to bend backward—and in so doing, they pull the thin filaments together (Fig. 5.5b).

Now a new ATP molecule rapidly attaches to the bent myosin head. This breaks the actin-myosin bond; the myosin head then straightens and reattaches to a new actin molecule (Fig. 5.5c), and the cycle begins again. In each cycle, the bending of the myosin head pulls the thin filaments about a millionth of a centimeter closer, decreasing the distance between the Z-lines by about 1%. There can be many such cycles in the course of a single impulse, leading to a measurable decrease in the overall length of the fiber. When the nerve impulse ends, the calcium is removed (to be reused in future contractions); the thin filament returns to the state in which the actin-myosin bond cannot form; and the muscle fiber then relaxes back to its normal length.

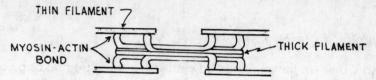

(a): Myosin-ATP-actin bonds are activated.

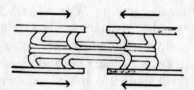

(b): Energized by decomposition of ATP, the bonds bend and pull the thin filaments together.

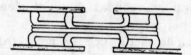

(c): Myosin heads detach, straighten, and reattach to new sites on the thin filaments.

FIGURE 5.5   The sliding filament theory of muscle contraction.

A single muscle fiber always contracts by the same amount, and all the fibers in the same motor unit contract simultaneously during an impulse. The overall strength of the muscle contraction depends on the number of motor units being stimulated and also on the frequency of the impulses.

This "sliding filament" theory of muscle contraction, which was first proposed by the British biologist Hugh E. Huxley in the 1950s, brings our understanding of muscular force right to the molecular level, explaining muscle contraction in terms of chemical reactions. It's difficult to decide which is more remarkable—the fact that the processes I've described actually take place, that we can *will* them to occur whenever we decide to wink an eye or wiggle a finger or shoot a basketball, or the fact that scientists have managed to discover and comprehend these processes.

Muscle Chemistry

Now that we have an idea how muscle contraction takes place, we can return to our original question—namely, how does the body generate the energy for this process? The energy for motion—specifically, the bending of the myosin heads—comes from the chemical decomposition of ATP. The body must constantly replenish its supply of ATP through chemical reactions. Without resupply, the ATP present in living muscle would be used up in a matter of seconds.

There are several pathways by which the body replenishes the ATP in its muscle fibers. It's worthwhile to examine the chemistry of these pathways, because it will lead us to an understanding of how the body withstands the effects of prolonged and intense exercise, and how it adapts to these effects through training. This is one of the most fruitful areas of research in exercise physiology; as we'll see shortly, it leads to a gold mine of valuable information for coaches and athletes at all levels pertaining to training regimes, diet, and many other aspects of exercise and athletic performance.

ATP (adenosine triphosphate) gets its name from the fact that it contains three phosphate groups. (A phosphate group is a particular compound of phosphorus and oxygen.) The chemical bond that holds each group to the molecule is a particularly strong one, and it releases a lot of energy when it is broken. When ATP decomposes, a phosphate group (P) is broken off, and the molecule become adenosine *di*phosphate (ADP):

$$ATP \rightarrow ADP + P + Energy$$

ATP can be reconstructed by reversing the reaction, i.e.,

$$ADP + P + Energy \rightarrow ATP$$

In a contracting muscle cell, ADP and P (the phosphate group) are present from the decomposition of ATP. Thus a quantity of energy must be supplied in order to reconstruct the ATP molecule. This energy is normally supplied through four different processes. (Each of these is actually a rather complicated chain of enzyme-triggered chemical reactions, so the following descriptions have been considerably simplified.) Each of these four methods of energy production can be classified as being either *aerobic* or *anaerobic,* depending upon whether or not oxygen is involved in the reactions. Nowadays we hear a lot about "aerobic exercise." What makes an exercise aerobic?

Simply put, an aerobic exercise is one in which oxygen is used in the production of energy. We'll soon see why this is important.

The four major energy-generating processes are as follows:

1. *The ATP-PC Process:* The basic fuel is a substance known as *phosphocreatine* (PC), which is found in the muscle cell. It decomposes to *creatine* (C) and a phosphate group, releasing energy:

$$PC \rightarrow P + C + Energy$$

This energy triggers the formation of ATP. The interaction can also be described in the following way:

$$ADP + PC \rightarrow ATP + C$$

This process produces ATP very rapidly. Being an anaerobic process, it does not have to rely on a supply of oxygen; all of the fuel (PC) is already present in the muscle cell. However, the supply of PC is depleted in 30 seconds or less, so this process is good only for short bursts of intense muscle activity. After the activity ends, energy must be supplied from some other source to rebuild the cell's store of phosphocreatine.

2. *Anaerobic Glycolysis:* All carbohydrates (starches and sugars) are broken down by digestion to the simple sugar *glucose*. Glucose is stored in the muscles and liver in the form of *glycogen* (a long chain of linked-up glucose molecules). Anaerobic glycolysis is the breakdown of glycogen or glucose in the absence of oxygen. The reaction produces energy for ATP production, but also makes a substance known as *pyruvic acid* as a waste product. If there is no oxygen available, pyruvic acid will immediately be converted to *lactic acid* (this is the substance that gives sour milk its bad taste). Thus the net result of anaerobic glycolysis is

$$Glycogen \rightarrow Glucose \rightarrow Energy + Pyruvic\ acid$$
$$\downarrow$$
$$Lactic\ acid$$

The buildup of lactic acid in the muscles and blood leads to muscle fatigue—specifically, to a decrease in muscle force—and a slowdown in the production of ATP. As a consequence, anaerobic glycolysis is a useful energy source only for about one to two minutes of intense activity.

3. *Aerobic Glycolysis:* In the presence of oxygen, pyruvic acid is decomposed to water and carbon dioxide. Thus the net result of *aerobic* glycolysis is

$$Glycogen \rightarrow Glucose \rightarrow Energy + Pyruvic\ acid$$
$$+$$
$$Oxygen$$
$$\downarrow$$
$$Water + Carbon\ dioxide$$

Water and carbon dioxide are easily removable waste products—and most important, no lactic acid is produced. As a result, aerobic glycolysis can continue indefinitely—or at least until the body exhausts its available supply of glycogen.

4. *Aerobic Fat Metabolism:* Energy for ATP synthesis can also be supplied through the reaction of fat with oxygen:

$$Fat + Oxygen \rightarrow Carbon\ dioxide + Water + Energy$$

Note that in this process the waste products are again water and carbon dioxide. In aerobic exercise, glycogen and fat decomposition both contribute to the resupply of ATP, without producing any limiting waste products. The relative contributions of glycogen and fat vary, depending on the intensity and length of exercise. Notice also that protein metabolism does *not* contribute appreciably to energy production during exercise, except in rare circumstances.

All the chemical reactions that supply the energy for the replenishment of ATP take place in the protoplasm of the muscle fiber—the soup in which the thin and thick filaments are submerged. But the key reactions required for *aerobic* production of ATP occur only in the *mitochondria*—small, subcellular structures that exist by the hundreds in a typical muscle cell.

In an earlier chapter, I described the two different types of muscle cells found in the body: the *fast-twitch* fibers, which respond quickly with a short, strong contraction, and the *slow-twitch* fibers, which provide a slower, more sustained contraction. Both types of fibers produce ATP aerobically and anaerobically. However, the fast-twitch fibers have a higher capacity for anaerobic production; they use up glycogen and build up lactic acid at a faster rate. The slow-twitch fibers, on the other hand, have a higher proportion of mitochondria and extract oxygen more efficiently from the blood, and so they are better suited for aerobic energy production. I also noted earlier that fast-twitch fibers are more suited to use for bursts of effort, while slow-twitch fibers are better for endurance activities. Perhaps you're already beginning to see how all this fits together. In any event, we're now ready to bridge the gap between chemistry and athletic performance.

Energy for Exercise

When we are resting or taking part in any low-level physical activity (anything that would qualify as light-to-moderate exercise), all our energy needs are supplied aerobically via the metabolism of fats and glucose from carbohydrates. At rest, about two thirds of the energy for ATP replenishment comes from aerobic fat metabolism, the remaining one third from aerobic glycolysis. The oxygen requirements are fairly modest; at rest the average individual consumes about a quarter of a liter (roughly a half a pint) of oxygen per minute, rising to about 2 liters per minute in moderate exercise. Up to this level there is no lactic acid buildup in the blood; the anaerobic processes are not being called upon.

When we begin strenuous activity we cross the "anaerobic threshold"; the body cannot immediately supply enough oxygen to meet the energy demands or replenish the rapidly diminishing ATP supply, so the anaerobic processes kick in. As we have seen, the ATP-PC process produces ATP at a high rate but is exhausted after no more than 30 seconds of intense activity. It is this process that supplies most of the energy for short, high-intensity activities like running up several flights of stairs, sudden bursts of acceleration in a game, or sprinting up to 300 meters. Anaerobic glycolysis provides energy at about half the power level of the ATP-PC process, but it can be called upon for up to 2 minutes, during which time the supply of muscle glycogen is depleted and the lactic acid level rises.

During these first few minutes of intense activity the level of oxygen intake is steadily increasing. The athlete breathes more rapidly and his heart beats faster to get more oxygen to the muscle cells. The rate of *aerobic* production of energy rises to take over from the rapidly diminishing anaerobic sources. The extent to which anaerobic and aerobic processes contribute to the athlete's energy supply depends on the energy demanded by the activity and on the athlete's ability to take in oxygen. The maximum rate of oxygen consumption is known as the *aerobic power,* measured in milliliters of oxygen per minute per kilogram of body mass, and represented by the symbol VO_2max. An average untrained male in his 20s has a VO_2max of about 45 ml O_2/

min/kg, but in trained athletes the rate rises into the upper 70s for men and to about 60 for women. The greater the aerobic power, the less anaerobic energy required, the slower the lactic acid buildup in the blood—and the longer and/or faster you can run.

"Running out of breath" is the experience of reaching an uncomfortable level of lactic acid in the blood, usually about 10 to 15 times the resting level. The athlete simply cannot get his body to take in oxygen at a fast enough rate to reduce the lactic acid buildup, and so he must decrease the intensity of the activity or stop altogether. Sometimes the athlete "gets his second wind"; the discomfort and breathlessness suddenly disappear in the midst of the activity. Scientists are not entirely certain what causes this phenomenon; it may result from adjustments in oxygen processing and distribution via the blood, or it may just be the aerobic processes catching up with the demand. However, it seems that highly trained athletes rarely get a second wind, evidently because they have a higher tolerance for fatigue and make the transition from anaerobic to aerobic energy production more smoothly. The second wind is evidently an experience reserved for undertrained athletes.

In order to take part in prolonged but less intense exercise—tennis, basketball, long-distance running—an athlete must rely entirely on aerobic processes. He must attain a "steady state" or equilibrium between oxygen supply and demand so that there is no call for anaerobic energy and no increase in lactic acid. Aerobic exercise is limited in duration by the body's supply of glycogen and fats. Generally, the glycogen gets depleted first; after about 30 minutes of exercise glycogen and fat each contribute half of the energy demand, and the glycogen contribution drops steadily thereafter.

The ability of an athlete to run competitively at a given distance depends on his relative capacity for anaerobic or aerobic energy production. The 100-meter dash takes about 10 seconds to complete and depends entirely on anaerobic energy; there is really no reason to breathe at all during the event. The 200-meter dash falls into the same category, since it derives about 90% of its energy from anaerobic sources. It's not surprising that sprinters who excel at the 100-meter distance also perform well at 200 meters. However, the top sprinters at these distances do not do as well at 400 or 800 meters. These events call for an aerobic energy contribution of 20% to 35%, and they cannot be run at top speed (that is, totally anaerobically) because of muscle glycogen depletion and lactic acid buildup. The athlete must set his pace so that he just reaches his maximum tolerable lactic acid level at the finish line. The same can be said for the 1-mile run and events in the 1- to 3-kilometer range; here the anaerobic and aerobic capacities must be utilized about equally. For longer distances, including the marathon, the primary energy source is increasingly aerobic.

Earlier I pointed out that fast-twitch muscle fibers are better at anaerobic energy production, while slow-twitch fibers have a higher capacity for aerobic production, although both kinds of fibers do produce energy both aerobically and anaerobically. Thus we ought to expect sprinters to have a higher percentage of fast-twitch fibers in their muscles, while distance runners should have more slow-twitch fibers. A number of exercise physiologists have tested this hypothesis by examining small samples (needle biopsies) of calf muscle from different athletes. Sure enough, sprinters, both men and women, averaged 60% to 70% fast-twitch fibers, while marathon runners had 70% to 80% slow-twitch fibers.

Back in Chapter 1, by way of illustrating some of the concepts used to measure motion, I calculated the average speeds for world running records, and plotted the running performance curve, which was a graph of average speed against distance. We are now in a position to understand the characteristics of this curve. First of all, the peak in the curve—the "great divide" between sprinters and runners—marks the transition from anaerobic to aerobic running. We can now understand the decrease in average running speed at distances greater than 200 meters as the consequence of glycogen depletion and lactic acid

---

TABLE 5.3: ENERGY (ATP) PRODUCTION SYSTEMS IN MUSCLES

ANAEROBIC SYSTEMS (No oxygen required):

System	*Fuel*	*Waste Product*	*Speed of Depletion*
ATP-PC	Phosphocreatine	Creatine	Rapid (30 sec)
Anaerobic glycolysis	Glycogen	Lactic acid	Rapid (1–2 min)

AEROBIC SYSTEMS (Oxygen required):

System	*Fuel*	*Waste Product*	*Speed of Depletion*
Aerobic glycolysis	Glycogen	CO_2 and H_2O	Slow
Fat metabolism	Fat	CO_2 and H_2O	Slow

buildup. What remains is to explain why the average running speed still continues to decrease at distances that are almost entirely aerobic.

The physiology of long-distance running has become a very popular subject of research in recent years, spurred on and supported by the still-growing public interest and participation in jogging and marathon running. To study the physiological response of a marathon runner, one does not have to follow him through the streets of Boston or New York taking measurements; the runner can instead perform at a suitable pace on a treadmill in a laboratory setting, where all the relevant quantities—oxygen consumption, lactic acid level, heart rate, etc.—can be easily monitored. One of the top researchers in the field is David L. Costill, who directs the Human Performance Laboratory at Ball State University in Muncie, Indiana. Himself a long-distance runner, Costill has made a host of significant discoveries in this area.

Costill has studied the physiological characteristics and responses of a number of the world's best marathoners in an effort to identify the determinants of top-level performance. Marathoners are able to generate energy at a high rate for more than two hours, and this ability correlates with a high aerobic power. However, no runner ever performs at maximum throughout a race, but instead paces himself to run at a constant *percentage* of his VO_2max. Figure 5.6 shows how the percentage of VO_2max utilized depends on the distance being run, and notice that the graph bears a striking resemblance to the corresponding part of the running performance curve in Figure 1.6.

The explanation for this relationship is fairly well understood. The faster the running speed, the greater the rates of energy production and oxygen consumption have to be. By running at a high percentage of his VO_2max—and a higher average speed—the runner is using up his energy resources (glycogen and fats) more rapidly and therefore will not be able to travel as far. Moreover, running at a high percentage of VO_2max tends to consume glycogen faster than fats, and a rapid depletion of glycogen will lead to early fatigue. By running at a lower percentage of VO_2max, the runner gets a greater fraction of his energy from fat metabolism. This "glycogen-sparing" effect allows the runner to cover a greater distance before the glycogen supplies are depleted. The efficient (and successful) runner is one who can maintain a suitable pace at a *lower* percentage of his VO_2max, for he will then be using up his glycogen reserves more slowly.

The depletion of body glycogen—from the muscles, the blood, and

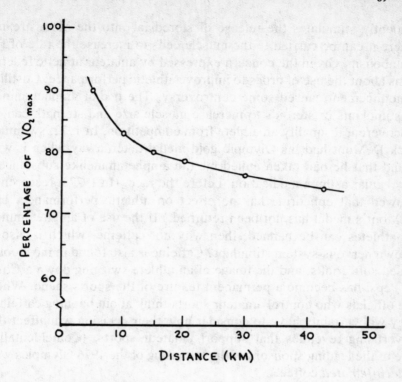

FIGURE 5.6   Percentage of aerobic power used in running different distances. (Data adapted from Costill, D.L., *A Scientific Approach to Distance Running,* Tafnews Press, Los Altos, Calif. 1979, p. 46.)

its storage place in the liver—marks the onset of exhaustion. This point is known to marathon runners as "the wall," and it is usually reached at about 15 to 20 miles. From this point on, the runner must call on all his reserves—his stores of fat, glycogen stored in fast-twitch fibers, even the metabolism of proteins. The body also responds by shifting blood flow from other organs to the muscles, and the decrease in blood supplied to the brain leads to a state of mental confusion that often accompanies exhaustion. "The wall" can be pushed back through glycogen sparing, and this capacity is something that can be acquired through training.

In 1978 Costill reported his discovery that caffeine has a very definite glycogen-sparing effect. He found that the ingestion of two cups of coffee one to two hours before beginning strenuous exercise produced a 19% increase in running time before exhaustion. Caffeine evidently stimulates the release of stored fat into the bloodstream, where it can be carried to the muscle cells to increase the rate of fat metabolism. Given the concern expressed by amateur athletic federations about the use of drugs to improve athletic performance, Costill's announcement caused some controversy. The use of amphetamines as stimulants or steroids to increase muscle size and strength can, if discovered, disqualify an athlete from competition. In 1972, swimmer Rick DeMont had his Olympic gold medal taken away when it was found that he had taken ephedrine (an amphetaminelike substance), his regular asthma medication, before the race. (In 1977 a researcher showed that ephedrine has no effect on athletic performance, but DeMont's medal has not been returned.) If the use of amphetamines by athletes can be banned, then why not caffeine, which is also a known nervous-system stimulant? Caffeine is also found in most cola-based soft drinks, and the image of an athlete swigging down a Coke or Pepsi has become a permanent feature of the sports scene. When the officials who control amateur sports think about banning caffeine, they will certainly have to consider how their decision will affect the advertising revenues that support amateur sports. (Coincidentally, one of the leading sponsors of the televising of the 1976 Olympics was a *decaffeinated* coffee.)

Recovery

As we've seen, strenuous exercise produces severe changes in an athlete's body chemistry. His store of muscle and liver glycogen will have been reduced, the level of lactic acid in his blood elevated, and the supply of PC (phosphocreatine) in his muscle cells depleted. (There are, of course, many other changes in body chemistry that we won't be getting into.) How long does it take for the athlete's body to be restored to its preexercise state, and are there any ways to accelerate the recovery?

After an exercise has been completed, an athlete continues to breathe heavily and have an elevated heart rate for several minutes afterward. During this period, the body is in the first stages of recovery. It is still taking in oxygen at a high rate to pay off its *oxygen debt*. This is the term used to describe the amount of oxygen needed to repair the chemical imbalances produced by anaerobic energy production.

There are two parts to the oxygen debt: Oxygen is used (1) to regenerate PC in the muscle cells and (2) to remove lactic acid from the blood by converting it to water and carbon dioxide. The first of these is repaid rather rapidly, typically within five minutes. Restoring the lactic acid level to its preexercise level takes somewhat longer, usually less than an hour. This process is aided by a "warm-down"—continued jogging or other light exercise after completing the performance—to keep up the oxygen consumption during recovery. Sometimes oxygen is administered to an exhausted athlete to aid his recovery. Surprisingly, studies have shown that this procedure does not speed the rate of recovery. However, by increasing the flow of oxygen to the brain, it may clear the athlete's mind, giving him the impression that he is recovering more rapidly.

Recovery from anaerobic exercise turns out to be relatively speedy. Short bursts of activity, as in sprinting, do not build up a large oxygen debt, so the athlete recovers fairly quickly (typically within an hour). It is for this reason that sprinters can run several heats or enter several events in a one-day track meet without a decline in performance. Recovery from prolonged, aerobic exercise takes considerably longer (a day or more). This is not because the oxygen debt is any larger; in fact, it has been found that if the athlete is running at less than his maximum aerobic capacity (VO_2max), his lactic acid level will usually peak after 10 minutes of continuous exercise and decline somewhat thereafter. If the runner steps up his pace during a race and calls on his anaerobic sources, he will, of course, increase his oxygen debt in the process.

The main reason that prolonged exercise has a much longer recovery period is the glycogen depletion. The body can resynthesize only a small amount of glycogen on its own, and so it must be provided with a new supply. A high-carbohydrate diet over a two-day period is usually sufficient to restore glycogen stores to their preexercise level. (This, for me, is one of the best features of prolonged exercise—in my case, two to three hours of basketball. I can then indulge myself afterward with ice cream, cake, or pasta without gaining weight.)

One rather surprising finding is that a high-carbohydrate diet taken for several days after glycogen depletion results in a supercompensation effect—a higher-than-normal glycogen supply. This technique of *carbohydrate loading* has become very popular with long-distance runners, who incorporate cycles of glycogen depletion and replacement into their training regimes as a means of building up extra supplies of glycogen for a race, thereby increasing the distance to "the wall"—the point of glycogen depletion. Carbohydrate loading can be continued up to three hours before the event, leaving time for the digestive system to convert the food to glycogen.

As a rule, however, it is wise to avoid eating even a light meal within one hour or so before strenuous exercise. A full stomach interferes with breathing, and digestion competes with the muscles for blood supply. Particularly to be avoided are slowly digested foods containing proteins and/or fats. Eating a quick hamburger before any kind of exercise is an invitation to a stomach cramp. The ritual of the pregame steak practiced by football players turns out to be of no value, since meat digests slowly and proteins make virtually no contribution to the energy supply.

One of Costill's many interesting discoveries deals with the effects of taking high doses of sugar right before exercise. Instead of elevating the glycogen level, this tends to *reduce* it. High blood sugar stimulates the release of insulin, which accelerates the removal of glucose from the blood. The combined effects of insulin and exercise tend to reduce glycogen more rapidly, leading to earlier fatigue and possibly hypoglycemia (low blood sugar). However, it is sometimes helpful to take in glucose (in the form of a sweetened drink or fruit juice) *during* exercise to replace losses and stave off exhaustion. The effects, though, are not immediate; it takes some time (usually about 10 minutes) before the glucose reaches the bloodstream in any quantity. Moreover, Costill discovered, the higher the glucose concentration in the drink, the more slowly it is digested and emptied from the stomach. Thus the best drink during exercise is a *low*-concentration sugar-and-water mixture. But the idea of a "quick pick-me-up"—a drink with an *immediate* energy-bolstering effect—has no scientific foundation.

One absolutely necessary substance to be taken during prolonged exercise is water. The body increases its heat generation rate in the muscles by as much as twenty times, and this heat must be released to the surroundings in order to keep the body temperature from rising to a dangerous level. One mechanism for accelerating heat removal is increased blood flow to the skin—hence the flushed and red-faced appearance of an exhausted athlete. The most important cooling mechanism, however, is sweat—to some, the very symbol of an athlete. Through perspiration, the body not only cools itself but also gets rid of some of the waste materials produced by intense activity.

Marathon runners frequently lose up to 8% of their body weight through perspiration in a race, more than 10 pounds of fluid. Dehydration of the body through fluid loss of this magnitude can be quite serious, especially in hot weather. Without sufficient body fluid, cellular reactions are retarded, blood volume decreases, and perspiration stops. In a "no sweat" situation, the body cannot regulate its own temperature and overheats, leading to heat exhaustion or a potentially fatal heatstroke. Athletes must drink water at frequent intervals during strenuous exercise to replace fluid losses.

Up until about ten years ago, many coaches thought that they could toughen up their players by not allowing them to have water during practices. High school athletes in full football uniforms on shadeless athletic fields in August were put through their paces for several hours at a time without being permitted any fluids, and those who dropped from exhaustion were considered too "weak" to be part of the team. Fortunately, exercise physiologists began to identify the many dangers of this practice, and pointed out that acclimatization to the heat *cannot* be achieved through water deprivation. Coaches have now been made fully aware of the importance of fluid replacement and allowing athletes to drink water whenever needed during practices and games. In addition, sponsors and organizers of marathons now make a point of providing frequent stations along the route where runners can get fluids.

Endurance Training

One aspect of exercise physiology that keenly interests scientists, athletes, and coaches is how the human body adapts to a continuing program of aerobic exercise, whether it be a highly structured regimen designed for a competitive athlete or simply a regular schedule of jogging to keep fit. The most obvious result of endurance training is, of course, that you can run faster and longer. This translates physiologically to a sizable increase in maximum aerobic power and efficiency: not only does your VO_2max go up, but you can maintain a given pace at a lower percentage of maximum. In conjunction, the anaerobic threshold (the point at which lactic acid begins to build up) rises; you are also able to tolerate a higher lactic acid level before becoming exhausted. Women respond to endurance training just as well as men do; they show similar rates of improvement in aerobic power and efficiency. The reason that the best women athletes do not attain the same levels of performance as the best male athletes is thus a consequence of fundamental differences in ultimate size and strength, and *not* of different physiological or emotional responses to training, exercise, or competition.

The improvements in performance brought about by endurance training can be correlated with physiological changes of the lungs and heart. There is an increase in lung capacity as well as in the efficiency with which oxygen is removed from the air and diffused into the blood. Like any other muscle, the heart can be strengthened and enlarged by exercise, and endurance training produces a pronounced improvement in its efficiency. There is an increase in the size of the heart, so that more blood is pumped with each stroke, accompanied by a sizable decrease in the resting pulse rate. The net effect is that the heart actually pumps more blood per minute with fewer beats. Whereas the average resting pulse rate for an untrained individual is in the neighborhood of 70 to 80 beats per minute, that of an endurance-trained athlete may be below 40 beats per minute.

The effects of training can also be traced right down to the cellular and subcellular levels. There is an increase in the size and number of blood vessels (leading to a reduction in blood pressure) and in the hemoglobin content and overall volume of the blood. While exercise and training cannot change the ratio of fast-twitch to slow-twitch fibers, it can increase their ability to produce energy aerobically. The muscle cells show an increase in the number of mitochondria and in the enzymes that are needed to produce ATP. The overall effect of these changes is that more oxygen is delivered to the muscle cells, and they in turn have a greater capacity to utilize the oxygen for energy production.

The body of a trained athlete is capable of adapting to various kinds of stress—heat, cold, humidity, etc. One form of stress that may affect physiological response and athletic performance is a relatively sudden lowering of air pressure, as occurs when an individual moves to high altitude. The 1968 Olympics were held in Mexico City, which is at an altitude of 7350 feet above sea level, high enough to have a noticeable effect on athletic performance. The Mexico City Olympics stimulated a lot of research on high-altitude physiology as athletes and coaches sought the best ways to prepare for their events. The basic problem at high altitude is "thinner" air—i.e., lower air pressure and density as compared with sea level. When an individual inhales, his diaphragm pulls down, decreasing the air pressure inside the chest cavity; air enters the lungs until the pressure inside is equal to the atmospheric pressure. Since the atmospheric pressure is low, there will be less air in the lungs—and even though the *relative* amount of oxygen in the air remains at 21%, we consume less oxygen with each breath.

An individual brought to high altitude first adapts to this environment with a faster breathing rate and heart rate to increase the transport of oxygen to the cells. During a prolonged stay, breathing and heart rates return to more normal levels as the body adjusts in other ways (by increasing the number of red blood cells, capillaries, and mitochondria, for example). For the athlete, the major problem to be faced is a decrease in aerobic power; the VO_2max decreases by about 3% for every 1000 feet of altitude above 5000 ft. Thus performance is most affected in aerobic activities, specifically in the longer-distance runs. Predictably, anaerobic performance does not seem to be adversely affected by high altitude—and is actually enhanced by the lower air resistance (for reasons that will be detailed later on). Even after several months of training, running times at the longer distances are poorer than at sea level. It had been thought that an athlete who became acclimated to training at high altitude would perform better when he returned to sea level. However, this theory has not panned out; athletes showed no improvement in their sea-level performance. The evidence seems to be that training at high altitude offers no advantage over training at sea level.

The most pronounced effects of *hypoxia* (insufficient oxygen supply) are felt by mountain climbers, especially those who tackle the Himalayan peaks. Above 20,000 feet the atmospheric pressure is less than half that at sea level; aerobic power and lactic acid tolerance are accordingly below 50% of maximum, even with acclimatization. (It should be noted that the performances of native-born "highlanders" —the inhabitants of the high-altitude villages in the Andes and Himalayas—are significantly better than those of fully acclimatized "lowlanders"—hence the dependence on Sherpa guides and bearers in Himalayan expeditions.) At very high altitudes, any kind of exertion becomes exhausting; climbers progress slowly, stopping frequently to rest even on gradual slopes, and eventually find it necessary to use oxygen masks. At the top of Mount Everest, at an altitude of 29,000 feet, the air pressure is down to about 30% of that at sea level. Remarkably, in recent years a few climbers have actually made it to the summit without any auxiliary oxygen.

The experience of trying to perform even moderate exercise at high altitude is often quite memorable. You don't have to go on a Himalayan expedition to know what it's like; there are quite a few places in the western United States where you can easily get to 8000 feet or higher, most notably in the national parks and mountain passes. One such place is Trail Ridge Road in Rocky Mountain National Park, a paved road that rises to 12,000 feet. If you go there, try some light jogging or climbing; you'll find yourself out of breath rather quickly. (Warning: don't attempt any exercise at high altitude that you don't regularly do at sea level.) At this altitude, where aerobic power is diminished by about 20%, an oxygen debt is acquired rather quickly, and it takes a long time to pay it back when you stop to rest.

When we first looked at the running performance curves of average running speed vs. distance back in Chapter 1, I made a comparison between the world records of twenty-five years ago and today. We saw that there has been a sizable increase in endurance; today's distance runners are going twice as far at a given running speed as their counterparts did twenty-five years ago. I attributed this improvement to better training methods—but now I'd like to qualify this by stating that the improvement is due to *more scientific* training methods. Athletes and coaches now have access to all the research findings of exercise physiologists. There are specific tests that can be used to assess an athlete's potential as a runner (the ratio of slow-twitch to fast-twitch fibers, maximum aerobic capacity, etc.). There is now a scientific basis for establishing a training regime, with specific programs for developing aerobic or anaerobic performance. The principles of proper nutrition and diet during training and competition are well established. Training methods are no longer based on guesswork, hearsay, tradition, or fads.

Racing strategy has also been put on a firm scientific footing. Is it better to take a big early lead, then try to hang on at the end, or should the runner hold back for a late sprint? Is it better to run at a constant rate or to vary the speed? It is now generally agreed that the best running strategy for middle and longer distances is to maintain the fastest possible *steady* pace throughout the race—a pace that allows the athlete to run aerobically, without crossing the anaerobic threshold and building up lactic acid. A fast early pace or a variable pace causes the runner to use his anaerobic energy reserves, thereby creating an oxygen debt. The anaerobic sources can be saved for a final kick lasting about 30 seconds; the ideal race is one in which the runner uses up his glycogen supplies and PC reserves as he crosses the finish line.

Above all, we must recognize that the principles of exercise physiology offer benefits that are not just confined to the specialized world of the top-class athlete and coach. On the contrary, they provide guidelines by which the average *non*athletic individual can improve his health and physical fitness. The value of aerobic exercise arises from the fact that by using oxygen to replenish your ATP supply, you are exercising without building up an intolerable oxygen debt and can therefore continue the exercise for a greater length of time. To achieve a training effect, with its attendant physiological changes in the cardiovascular system (the heart and blood vessels), *you must engage in prolonged exercise*. For disseminating and popularizing this knowledge much credit must be given to Dr. Kenneth H. Cooper of the U.S. Air Force, who first introduced "aerobics" to the general public in 1968. It was largely his efforts that turned the tide against isometrics, calisthenics, and weight lifting in favor of more strenuous exercises that improve cardiovascular fitness rather than physical strength and flexibility.

Although aerobics and exercise physiology seem to be associated mostly with jogging and marathon running, their principles apply to all forms of athletic activity, and performers at all levels throughout sports can and have benefited from them. I've put much of what I've learned in this area to practical use, and I'm now much more able to withstand the rigors of strenuous exercise as a consequence. Moreover, I derive considerable intellectual satisfaction from knowing how and why my body responds to stress; I feel that this information will be of great value to me in maintaining my athletic abilities as I grow older.

Yet knowledge, however valuable, has its limits. Not long ago, I staggered into the house after my regular Sunday morning session of basketball. I had played steadily for nearly three hours and was totally spent. I grabbed the Sunday papers, turned on the TV, and stretched out on the couch, fully intending to remain in that position until suppertime, when I would restore my glycogen supply by consuming a mountain of spaghetti.

I commented to my wife that I could now give a scientific explanation for my state of exhaustion.

"Does it make you feel any better?" she asked.

I had to admit that it didn't.

6 / COLLISIONS

To a physicist, a great deal of the action that occurs in sports can be abstracted and reduced to a common event: a collision between two objects. The collision may take place between two human beings (as in boxing, football, or hockey); between a human body and an inanimate object (soccer, karate, diving); or between two inanimate objects (golf, tennis, bowling). In every instance, we are looking at a situation in which two objects suddenly come into contact and exert relatively large forces on each other for a rather short period of time, bringing about abrupt changes in motion. Collisions in sports are of considerable interest to scientists, especially those who must deal with their physical effects. Their concern may be directed toward the treatment and prevention of injuries, the design of better sports equipment, or the improvement of athletic techniques and performance.

The theory of collisions, which is a relatively simple one as theories go, has proven particularly fruitful throughout the sciences. Its greatest successes have been scored in describing events that take place at the atomic and subatomic levels. It has played a key role in the development of the theory of heat, in the study of chemical reactions, and in the design of devices ranging from steam engines to nuclear reactors. In describing collisions that involve human bodies, bats, rackets, and balls, we'll be using the theory in its simplest form. Nevertheless, in what follows we'll be relying on mathematics more than usual. If you should find it tough going, do try to stick with it; I think you'll be rewarded with some interesting insights and information.

Gathering Momentum

Collisions are analyzed in terms of a very useful quantity known as *linear momentum*. As its name indicates, linear momentum is related to, but distinct from, angular momentum; whereas the latter applies specifically to rotational motion, linear momentum is a property of straight-line or curvilinear motion. The linear momentum of a moving object is defined as the product of its mass and velocity, i.e.,

$$\text{linear momentum} = \text{mass} \times \text{velocity}$$

In symbolic form

$$p = mv$$

p being the letter traditionally used to represent linear momentum. (The units in which linear momentum is measured are kg-m/sec in metric and slug-ft/sec in customary.) This definition makes use of two factors related to motion: the mass of an object—which is a measure of its inertia, its tendency to maintain its motion—and its velocity, or rate of motion. Linear momentum has direction (it's a vector quantity), its direction being the same as that in which the object is moving. We'll learn why this fact is significant later on.

Momentum by itself is one of those words I referred to earlier that has passed beyond its narrow technical meaning into common language. It has, in particular, become a favorite of the sportscasting fraternity, whose members often use it to describe the tempo of a game. After a good start, a team may suddenly begin to "lose its momentum." I once heard a commentator describe an evenly played but somewhat lackluster football game as one in which the "momentum is up for grabs." The word has also been adopted by the news media outside of sports; I'm sure you've heard more than once about a political movement or candidate whose campaign is "gathering momentum." As we look further into the meaning of this word, we ought to get some insight into its popularity, not to mention its value as a scientific quantity. In keeping with common usage, when I use the word "momentum" from here on, I'll be referring specifically to linear momentum, unless otherwise noted.

Our starting point for the theory of collisions is the ubiquitous Newton's second law, F = ma. We'll begin by replacing the acceleration (a) in this equation by an equivalent expression: if the speed of an object changes from an initial value of v_1 to a new value of v_2, then the acceleration (from Math Box 4, page 45) is

$$a = \frac{v_2 - v_1}{t}$$

Substituting this into Newton's second law gives

$$F = ma = m\left(\frac{v_2 - v_1}{t}\right) = \frac{mv_2 - mv_1}{t}$$

We can identify mv_1 as the initial momentum (p_1) of the object and mv_2 as its new momentum (p_2). Thus

$$F = \frac{p_2 - p_1}{t}$$

The quantity $p_2 - p_1$ is the difference between the new and original values of the momentum, and thus represents the *change in momentum*. In words, the equation becomes

$$\text{net force} = \frac{\text{change in momentum}}{\text{time interval}}$$

This equation can be stated in the following way: *the net force is equal to the rate of change of momentum.* This, in fact, was the way that Newton's second law was originally stated in the *Principia,* although Newton had named it the "quantity of motion" rather than "momentum." The equation expresses the idea that a force is needed to change the momentum of an object: a positive (accelerating) force causes the momentum to increase; a negative (decelerating) force causes it to decrease. If the net force is zero, then the momentum must remain constant.

How does this relate to the common-language usage of the word? To bring a moving object to a stop, we have to apply a retarding force large enough to reduce the momentum of the object to zero. Obviously the more momentum an object has, the more force is needed to bring it to a stop in a given amount of time. It is perhaps this aspect of momentum that has helped it to find a place in popular usage: something that has gained or gathered a lot of momentum is difficult to stop, whether it be an idea, a political or social movement, or a physical object. We also see here the merits of the fact that momentum encompasses both mass and velocity. It is difficult (that is, it requires a lot of force or effort) to stop a small, fast-moving object; it is also difficult to stop a huge, massive, slow-moving object. Both types of object have a lot of momentum, but for different reasons.

You can see both of these aspects of momentum at any football game: the fleet-footed but relatively lightweight pass receivers and halfbacks who are hard to bring down once they get up a lot of speed; the slower-moving but heavier fullbacks and even heavier offensive and defensive linemen, whose relatively low-speed charges are equally difficult to bring to a halt. It's a difficult task for a tackler to bring down a fullback who has "gotten his momentum"—reached his top running speed—because he now has both mass *and* speed in his favor. Sportswriters and announcers sometimes describe a team that overpowers and rolls over its opponents, game after game, as a "juggernaut"—evoking an image of a massive, slow-moving, unstoppable object. The word derives from the Sanskrit *jagannatha* (literally, "lord of the world"), which is the name of a huge Hindu shrine on wheels that is moved slowly through crowds of worshipers on festival days (sometimes rolling over and crushing an uncautious or overly pious supplicant). Literally and figuratively, a juggernaut falls into the category of high-mass, low-speed objects with a lot of momentum.

Returning to the original equation linking force to momentum, we can gain a further insight into their relationship by writing it in the following way:

$$Ft = p_2 - p_1$$
$$\text{net force} \times \text{time interval} = \text{change in momentum}$$

The left side of this equation (the product of net force and time interval) is known as the *impulse* of a force. The word "impulse" is commonly used to describe a sudden force of relatively brief duration, and in the scientific sense it describes the effect of a force that acts for a finite (and usually short) period of time, in contrast to forces such as gravity that act continually. The equation, which I'll refer to henceforth as the *impulse-momentum principle,* can be expressed in words as follows: *the impulse of a force is equal to the change in momentum it produces.*

The usefulness of this idea lies in the realization that the same change in momentum can be achieved with a small force acting for a long period of time as with a large force acting for a short period of time. To illuminate this concept, let's compare the consequences of jumping off a 50-foot-high building onto a sidewalk with those of jumping off a 50-foot-high cliff into a deep pool of water. In each case, the jumper attains a speed of nearly 40 mi/hr on impact, and thereafter has his speed reduced to zero. In each instance, the change in momentum upon impact will be the same. However, the sidewalk, being quite rigid, produces this change in a very short time interval by exerting a large (and usually fatal) force on the jumper's body. The water, being more yielding, achieves exactly the same change in momentum, with considerably less disastrous results, by exerting a smaller force over a longer period of time. Our conclusion is aptly summarized by the adage, "It's not the fall that kills you, it's the sudden stop." The point is that the same change in momentum can be achieved by trading force for time, or vice versa, as long as the impulse (the product of force and time) remains the same.

It also follows that the longer a given force is acting, the greater the change in momentum it will produce. This is the principle behind that basic technique common to so many sports, the follow-through. In virtually every sports activity that involves throwing or hitting some object, the participant is urged to "follow through" on his throw or swing. The idea is to keep one's hand, body, bat, racket, or what have you in contact with the object for as long as possible—thereby increasing the impulse of the force and the change in momentum (and final speed) of the object.

We've already looked into similar situations in a different context. As an illustration of Newton's second law in Chapter 2, I discussed the principle of "rolling with a punch"—decelerating an object by using a relatively small force over a proportionally longer interval of time. The impulse-momentum concept presents this same conclusion in a more general way, without making specific reference to the rate of acceleration or deceleration, simply by relating the overall change in momentum to the product of force and time.

A word about the relationship between energy and momentum is in order: a moving object possesses both kinetic energy ($\frac{1}{2}mv^2$) and linear momentum (mv); each of these may be regarded as a measure of the "quantity of motion." It is useful to have two different ways to measure the quantity of motion, because they emphasize different aspects of the relationship between forces and motion. Linear momentum is related to the *impulse* of a force (force × time); kinetic energy is related to the *work* done by the force (force × distance). These two distinct approaches do not contradict each other (they cannot contradict, since both are derived from Newton's laws), but rather they provide two complementary schemes or methods for analyzing various physical phenomena. Certain classes of problems are more easily analyzed in terms of momentum (most notably collisions, as we shall soon discover); others are more readily solved in terms of energy; still others are best understood by considering momentum and energy simultaneously.

Impact Forces

One immediate practical application of the impulse-momentum principle is that it can be used to calculate the forces created in an impact. Let's suppose we want to determine the force exerted by a golf club on a ball as it is being driven off the tee. It is quite difficult to make a direct measurement of the impact force; however, it is possible to determine (1) the impact time (the time interval during which the clubhead and golf ball are in contact), and (2) the speed of the ball after contact is broken. This information is obtained through high-speed photography, either by filming movies or by taking multi-flash still photographs of the impact (Fig. 6.1). In general, movies provide better data. High-speed movie cameras operate at a rate of several thousand frames per second (a standard movie camera takes 24 frames per second), with the result that movements lasting less than a millisecond (0.001 second) can be readily detected. By analyzing the film, scientists can determine the ball speed and impact time (see Table 6.1 for some measured values of the latter). Measurements of a golf club–golf ball impact, made by a number of researchers, show that the impact time is about 1 millisecond, and the speed of the golf ball after impact is about 150 mi/hr (220 ft/sec). These two pieces of information give us the data needed to calculate the impact force. We also need the mass of a golf ball, which is 0.003 slug (based on its standard weight of 1.6 ounces). First we calculate the change in momentum of the golf ball. The ball is initially at rest on the tee, so it has no momentum to start with. The calculation proceeds as follows:

momentum before impact: $p_1 = mv_1 = 0$

momentum after impact: $p_2 = mv_2 = (0.003 \text{ slug}) (220 \text{ ft/sec})$
$$= 0.66 \text{ slug-ft/sec}$$

FIGURE 6.1   Multiflash photo of bat-ball impact. Images have been taken at a rate of 120 per second, corresponding to approximately 8-millisecond intervals (*Dr. Harold Edgerton, MIT, Cambridge, Mass.*).

Now we use the impulse-momentum equation:

$$Ft = p_2 - p_1$$
$$F(0.001 \text{ sec}) = 0.66 - 0 = 0.66 \text{ slug-ft/sec}$$

Solving for F we get

$$F = \frac{0.66 \text{ slug-ft/sec}}{0.001 \text{ sec}} = 660 \text{ lb}$$

Thus the calculation shows that a golf club exerts a force of 660 lb on the ball during the brief (1 millisecond) time of the impact.

This calculation was simplified considerably by the fact that the golf ball is stationary when struck. An added complication arises when the object is moving before the collision and undergoes a change in direc-

TABLE 6.1: SOME MEASURED IMPACT TIMES

The impact time is the interval during which the ball remains in contact with the striking implement. All times are measured in milliseconds (1 msec = 1/1000 sec = 0.001 sec). (Data adapted from Plagenhoef, S., *Patterns of Human Motion,* Prentice-Hall, Englewood Cliffs, N.J., 1971, p. 59.)

Impact	Time (msec)
Golf ball (hit by driver)	1.0
Baseball (hit off tee)	1.3
Softball (hit off tee)	3.5
Tennis (forehand)	5.0
Football (kick)	8.0
Handball (serve)	12.5
Soccer ball (header)	23.0

tion as well as in speed, as a baseball does when a batter connects with a pitch. To show you how we deal with this, I'll propose the following hypothetical situation: a ball with a mass of 0.01 slug (approximately the mass of a baseball) and speed of 100 ft/sec is thrown against a wall and rebounds with the same speed (Fig. 6.2a). The ball undergoes a change in direction, a 180° reversal, so the impact produces a change in the velocity and momentum of the ball, even though there hasn't been any change in its speed. Before the impact, the ball has a momentum of

$$mv = (0.01 \text{ slug})(100 \text{ ft/sec}) = 1 \text{ slug-ft/sec to the right}$$

After the impact the momentum is

$$mv = (0.01 \text{ slug})(100 \text{ ft/sec}) = 1 \text{ slug-ft/sec to the left}$$

To get the change in momentum, the rules of vector arithmetic must be applied. In going from 1 slug-ft/sec right to 1 slug-ft/sec left, the momentum has been changed by 2 slug-ft/sec (Fig. 6.2b). The rule to be used here is that to find the change in momentum when there has been a reversal of direction, we *add* the two momenta instead of subtracting them. This is equivalent mathematically to subtracting a negative number, i.e., $1 - (-1) = 2$. Thus in our hypothetical collision, the ball has had its momentum changed by 2 slug-ft/sec in the

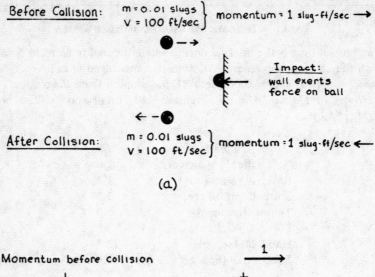

(a)

(b)

FIGURE 6.2   Change in momentum when the direction of motion is reversed.

collision with the wall. Let's make the further assumption that the ball is in contact with the wall for 0.01 second. Using the impulse-momentum equation,

$$\text{impulse} = \text{change of momentum}$$
$$Ft = F(0.01 \text{ sec}) = 2 \text{ slug-ft/sec}$$
$$F = \frac{2 \text{ slug-ft/sec}}{0.01 \text{ sec}} = 200 \text{ lb}$$

During the collision, then, the wall exerts a force of 200 pounds on the ball. This force first decelerates the ball to a momentary stop, then accelerates it back in the direction from which it came.

Now let's apply this procedure to answer the following question: how much force is exerted in the impact when a baseball pitched at 90 mi/hr (132 ft/sec) is hit out of the park for a home run? We need three additional pieces of data: One is the mass of a baseball, which is 0.01 slug (based on a weight of 5¼ oz). The second is the speed of the baseball after it leaves the bat. We'll assume a speed of 100 mi/hr (147 ft/sec); based on aerodynamic calculations (to be described later), a baseball leaving the bat at this speed would travel about 385 feet if launched at the proper angle. The third number we need is the impact time—the amount of time that ball and bat are in contact during the collision. Once again, we turn to the high-speed photography measurements. There do not seem to be any recorded impact times for bats hitting pitched balls (the multiflash photos on p. 208, taken at 8 millisecond intervals, are too widely spaced in time to show how long the ball and bat remain in contact), but an impact time of 1.3 milliseconds has been measured for a baseball hit off a tee. We'd expect the bat to stay in contact a little longer when striking a pitched ball, so a value of 2 milliseconds (0.002 sec) seems reasonable. We're now ready for our calculation:

$$\text{momentum of ball before collision: } p_1 = mv_1$$
$$= (0.01 \text{ slug}) (132 \text{ ft/sec})$$
$$= 1.32 \text{ slug-ft/sec toward batter}$$
$$\text{momentum of ball after collision: } p_2 = mv_2$$
$$= (0.01 \text{ slug}) (147 \text{ ft/sec})$$
$$= 1.47 \text{ slug-ft/sec away from batter}$$

Since the ball changes direction in the impact, we compute the change in momentum by adding:

$$\text{change in momentum} = p_2 - (-p_1) = p_2 + p_1 = 1.47 + 1.32 = 2.79$$
$$\text{slug-ft/sec}$$

The impact force now follows:

$$\text{impulse} = \text{change in momentum}$$
$$Ft = F (.002 \text{ sec}) = 2.79 \text{ slug-ft/sec}$$
$$F = \frac{2.79 \text{ slug-ft/sec}}{.002 \text{ sec}} = 1400 \text{ lb}$$

Our calculation gives a somewhat simplified picture of a ball-bat collision, since it does not take into account the angles at which the ball strikes and rebounds from the bat. Nevertheless, it still gives us a good idea of the force generated by the impact. In general, detailed research studies based on the impulse-momentum principle can supply useful data pertaining to the forces that are generated in various impacts. Such information is valuable for the improvement of performance techniques, the analysis and prevention of sports injuries, and the design of equipment capable of withstanding impact forces.

In most collisions, the impact force is not constant; the change in momentum tells us only what the *average* force is during the impact. The measurement of a force-time graph—showing how the force changes in time during the collision—gives researchers more precise information about the effects of a particular collision. This approach is also useful for interactions that do not seem to be collisions per se, yet involve the same basic principles. One example is the sprinter's start: when a sprinter pushes off from the starting blocks, the blocks must exert equal and opposite forces on his body. These forces, which are exerted for a very short period of time, have a combined impulse that equals the sprinter's change in momentum as he bursts off the starting blocks. By measuring the force-time graph for each of the sprinter's feet while they are in contact with the blocks, researchers can determine whether a particular sprinter is generating the maximum impulse attainable in his start.

Conservation of Momentum

The measurement of a force-time graph or even just the impact time of a collision calls for sophisticated and expensive instrumentation. Yet useful information about a collision can be acquired even if the force and/or time of impact cannot be measured directly. This can be done by making use of a rather important principle of physics known as the *law of conservation of linear momentum*. As its name indicates, this is the counterpart—applicable to linear motion—of the law of conservation of angular momentum that we used earlier to analyze rotational motion.

The conservation of linear momentum is a direct consequence of Newton's third law, the law of action and reaction. The derivation proceeds simply and logically:

1. In any collision (or other interaction) between two objects, the objects exert equal and opposite forces on each other for the same period of time.

2. It follows that the objects experience equal and opposite impulses (force × time).
3. Since the impulses are equal and opposite, then the changes in the linear momentum of each object must be equal and opposite.
4. Consequently if one object has its linear momentum increased by a certain amount in a collision, the linear momentum of the other object must decrease by the same amount.
5. Therefore the combined linear momentum of the two objects has not changed; there has been a *transfer* of linear momentum from one to the other, but no gain or loss in the total linear momentum of the two objects. In the language of the physicist, *linear momentum has been conserved*.

By way of illustration, let's take another look at our golf club-ball collision. When a golf ball is hit off a tee, it gains momentum (I'll drop the "linear" hereafter) from its impact with the moving golf club. But the force of impact on the golf ball is matched by an equal and opposite force that decelerates and decreases the momentum of the golf club, which must lose speed as a result of the collision. The loss of momentum of the club exactly equals the gain of momentum of the ball. In effect, a quantity of momentum has been transferred from the club to the ball, but the total combined momentum of the two objects does not change in the collision. Another way to describe the situation is to say that *a collision cannot create or dissipate momentum; it can result only in the transfer of momentum from one object to another*.

The value of any physical law or principle lies in the power it gives us to explain and/or predict events in nature. From a practical point of view, the value of the law of conservation of momentum is this: if we know how much the momentum of one object changes in a collision, then we automatically know the change in momentum of the other, without having to measure the impact time or force of the collision.

By using this principle, we can make some useful predictions about the outcome of any collision. When two objects collide they must experience the same change in momentum (to be more precise about it, the increase in momentum of one must be numerically equal to the decrease in momentum of the other). Since momentum is mass × velocity, and since the mass of an object normally does not change in a collision, then a change in momentum translates to a change in velocity. Therefore in a collision between any two objects (I'll label them A and B), the change in momentum of A = the change in momentum of B

or

(mass of A) × (change in velocity of A) =
(mass of B) × (change in velocity of B)

We can also express this as a ratio:

$$\frac{\text{change in velocity of A}}{\text{change in velocity of B}} = \frac{\text{mass of B}}{\text{mass of A}}$$

Whichever way you prefer to look at this equation, it leads to the same conclusion: *the change in velocity experienced by each object in a collision is inversely proportional to its mass.* In simple terms, this means that the object with the bigger mass has its velocity changed the least by the collision; the object with the smaller mass has its velocity changed the most. The velocity changes are inversely related to the ratio of the masses; if A's mass is three times greater than the mass of B, then B will experience a change in velocity three times larger than that of A. In a collision between a 5-ounce baseball and a 30-ounce bat, the change in velocity of the baseball will be six times larger than that of the bat (for example, in the multiflash photos of the ball-bat collision on p. 208, the increase in the speed of the ball upon impact—and the considerably smaller decrease in the speed of the bat—are both evident). The relationship between mass and change in velocity underscores the importance of size to a football player: in blocking or tackling a heavier opponent, a lighter player must be prepared to undergo a proportionally larger change in velocity.

This relationship provides some insight into the outcome of any collision. For a collision between a 5-ounce baseball and a 30-ounce bat, we know that the baseball will experience a six-times-larger change in velocity—but what will the actual speed of the baseball be when it comes off the bat? Obviously, the speed of the bat must also be taken into account. But even if the bat speed is known, we still do not have enough information to predict the outcome of the collision. The reason for this shortfall can best be explained by looking at the mathematics. Consider a collision between two objects, A and B, whose masses are known to be m_A and m_B, respectively. Let's assume that their respective velocities before the collision, which we'll represent as v_A and v_B, are known quantities. We want to predict the outcome of the collision—that is, figure out the new velocities (here symbolized as u_A and u_B) that the objects have acquired as a result of the impact.

From the law of conservation of momentum, we know that the total momentum—the sum of the individual momenta of the two objects—does not change in the collision (in adding together the two momenta, we must be cognizant of the fact that momentum is a vector quantity and must take the directions into account). Thus

momentum of A + momentum of B before the collision =
momentum of A + momentum of B after the collision

Substituting the symbols, this becomes

$$m_A v_A + m_B v_B = m_A u_A + m_B u_B$$

This equation contains four known quantities (m_A, m_B, v_A, v_B) and two unknown quantities, u_A and u_B (the respective velocities after the collision). Now it is a basic mathematical tenet that an equation with two unknowns in it cannot be solved. The bottom line is that *the law of conservation of momentum by itself cannot completely predict the outcome of the collision.*

In order to solve the problem, we must have more information about the collision. For example, one possible outcome is that the two objects stick together and move as a single unit after the collision. If this happens, then they have the same postcollision velocity ($u_A = u_B$); the above equation can now be solved and their common velocity calculated. This outcome actually describes at least two types of events in sports. The first is the catch of a projectile (an infielder catching a hard line drive, or a soccer goalie catching a shot on goal), and the second is a football tackle: whether it be head-on, from the side, or from behind, the result of a tackle is that the runner and tackler are locked together and moving with the same velocity for at least a few moments after the impact.

Using conservation of momentum as a guide, we can draw some general conclusions about a head-on collision between a runner and a tackler (Math Box 7, page 216, gives a sample calculation of this type of collision.) Basically, whether the runner or the tackler is driven backward by the impact depends on their respective momenta; after the tackle has been made the two players, now moving as one, will continue to move in the same direction as the one who had the greater momentum before the tackle. Notice that greater *momentum*—rather

MATH BOX 7: COLLISION CALCULATION: A HEAD-ON TACKLE

The Problem: A 224-lb fullback running at a speed of 15 mi/hr (22 ft/sec) is tackled head-on by a 176-lb defensive back running toward him at 17 mi/hr (25 ft/sec). In what direction, and at what speed, do their bodies move upon impact?

The Solution: First let us calculate the momentum of each player before the collision. The mass (in slugs) is calculated by dividing the weight (in pounds) by 32 (see Appendix B for details):

The fullback: mass $m_F = (224 \text{ lb}) \div (32) = 7$ slugs
momentum $p_F = m_F v_F = (7 \text{ slugs})(22 \text{ ft/sec}) = 154$ slug-ft/sec

The defender: mass $m_D = (176 \text{ lb}) \div (32) = 5.5$ slugs
momentum $p_D = m_D v_D = (5.5 \text{ slugs})(25 \text{ ft/sec}) = 137.5$ slug-ft/sec

Next we calculate their combined momentum before the collision, taking their directions into account. The two players are moving in opposing directions; we'll assume that the fullback is moving to the right, while the defender is moving to the left. Therefore their combined momentum is

$$p_F + p_D = 154 \text{ slug-ft/sec} \rightarrow + 137.5 \text{ slug-ft/sec} \leftarrow$$
$$= 16.5 \text{ slug-ft/sec} \rightarrow$$

That is, since they are moving in opposite directions, their total momentum is the *difference* between their respective momenta; if they were moving in the same direction we would have added the two.

After the tackle the two players move as a single unit—in the same direction with the same speed, u. Since their total momentum was to the right *before* the collision, it will be to the right *after* the collision—in other words, the fullback continues to move in the same direction, while the defender is driven backward by the impact. Using the law of conservation of momentum

total momentum before the collision
= total momentum after the collision

$$16.5 \text{ slug-ft/sec} = m_F u + m_D u = 7u + 6u = 13u$$
$$u = (16.5 \text{ slug-ft/sec})/(13 \text{ slugs}) = 1.27 \text{ ft/sec}$$

After the tackle is made, the two players continue to move at a speed of 1.27 ft/sec (0.87 mi/hr) to the right.

than weight, mass, or speed—is the key here. If the lighter player is running faster than the heavier one—fast enough so that he has the greater momentum—then he will drive the heavier player backward in a collision. But if two players are running toward each other at the same speed, the lighter player must necessarily suffer the greater velocity change and be driven backward by the impact. The collision will be even worse for the lighter player if his opponent is moving faster than he is.

Collisions are the very soul of football. Despite all the publicity and glory given to the quarterback, a football team lives or dies by how well its players block and tackle, offensively and defensively. The most talented quarterback cannot perform without good protection; the most gifted running back cannot succeed without others blocking for him. As we've just seen, the law of conservation of momentum underlines the importance of size to a football player. Yet sheer weight isn't everything in football; a heavier player will, in general, be slower and less mobile. Thus there is an optimum weight range for football players that correlates with the relative importance of weight vs. mobility and speed at a given position. A 150-lb running back, receiver, or defensive back is not likely to survive the tackling in professional football, no matter how fast or agile he is. Similarly, one doesn't find too many 300-pounders playing football, even as offensive linemen. The complexities of modern-day football are such that sheer bulk without mobility, and sheer mobility without bulk, are decided disadvantages.

The Coefficient of Restitution

We've seen that when two colliding objects become joined, their mutual speed after the impact can be predicted. But in the great majority of collisions, both within and outside sports, one object rebounds off the other, and the two go their separate ways at different speeds. To predict what these speeds will be, given the initial velocities and masses of the objects, we need more information about the collision. One useful source of information is the principle of conservation of energy. If it is known that the collision is *elastic*—i.e., that kinetic energy has been conserved in the collision—then we can write down a second equation stating that the sum of the kinetic energies of the two objects before the collision is equal to the sum of their kinetic energies after the collision. However, most collisions are decidedly *inelastic*—that is, some of the kinetic and elastic energy is converted to heat during the impact, so that kinetic energy is not conserved.

One way to describe mathematically the loss of kinetic energy in an inelastic collision is through a quantity known as the *coefficient of restitution*. In its simplest version, as applied to an object that is rebounding off an extremely massive and essentially immovable object like a wall or a floor, the coefficient of restitution measures the ratio of the rebound speed to the initial speed. In equation form,

$$\text{coefficient of restitution} = \frac{\text{speed after collision}}{\text{speed before collision}}$$

In a more complex situation, such as an impact between a ball and a moving object, the *relative* speeds of the ball with respect to the object, before and after the collision, are used to calculate the coefficient of restitution. For example, when a baseball thrown at 85 mi/hr collides with a bat approaching it at 60 mi/hr, it is as if the baseball were striking a stationary bat at a speed of 145 mi/hr (in a head-on collision between two objects, their relative speed is the *sum* of the individual speeds). Suppose that after the impact, the ball rebounds with a speed of 100 mi/hr while the bat continues moving forward at a speed of 40 mi/hr: now the ball is moving away from the bat at a relative speed of 60 mi/hr (both are now moving in the same direction). The coefficient of restitution for this collision is thus (60 mi/hr)/(145 mi/hr) = 0.41 (see Math Box 8 pages 220–21 for further details).

Numerically, the kinetic energy loss depends in a fairly complicated way on the masses and speeds of the colliding objects as well as on the coefficient of restitution (I'll call it the COR from here on). The largest possible value the COR can have is 1, which corresponds to an elastic collision in which there is no kinetic energy loss. For inelastic collisions, the COR is always less than 1; the smaller the COR, the greater the loss of kinetic energy. The lowest possible value of the COR is zero, which corresponds to a collision in which both objects stick together or are brought to a stop.

The coefficient of restitution can thus be regarded as a measure of the "bounciness" of a ball. The bouncier a ball is, the more speed with which it rebounds. A ball with a high COR is made of an elastic substance that is not easily deformed and returns rather quickly to its original shape with little loss of energy. (Some years ago, a manufacturer came up with a novelty item known as a "superball." Virtually the same size and shape as a handball, it had an unusually large COR of 0.9, and took an unexpectedly high bounce.) At the other extreme, a ball made of a material that has virtually no elasticity and does not bounce at all (e.g., a ball made of clay or putty) has a coefficient of restitution of zero.

The coefficient of restitution of any ball can be measured very easily by dropping it onto a rigid surface from some specified height (say, 5 feet above the ground) and measuring the height to which it rises after it bounces. If H_{down} is the distance that the ball drops, and H_{up} is the distance that the ball rises after it bounces, then the COR can be calculated from the following formula (the physics behind this formula will become more evident in the next chapter):

$$COR = \sqrt{\frac{H_{up}}{H_{down}}}$$

For example, a tennis ball dropped from a height of 5 feet normally rebounds to half of this height (2.5 ft), so its COR is

$$COR = \sqrt{\frac{H_{up}}{H_{down}}} = \sqrt{\frac{2.5}{5.0}} = \sqrt{\frac{1}{2}} = 0.71$$

In many sports, the coefficient of restitution is written into the official rules, either explicitly or indirectly. The basketball rule book gives this description of a correctly inflated basketball: "When it is dropped to the playing surface from a height of 6 feet, measured to the bottom of the ball, it will rebound to a height measured to the top of the ball of not less than 49 inches . . . nor more than 54 inches." Using the center of the ball as our reference point (a basketball has a diameter of 9.5 inches), we can calculate that the COR of a basketball must fall between 0.76 and 0.80.

The rules of baseball specify that a baseball must have a coefficient of restitution of 0.546. The established testing procedure is to fire a baseball from a cannon at a wall 8 feet away and compare the launching and rebound speeds ("when tested . . . with an initial velocity of 85 ft/sec, the rebound of velocity shall be 54.6% of the initial velocity, with a tolerance of ±3.2%"). The construction of a baseball is a rather complicated layering of cork, two kinds of rubber, three kinds of wool, and two kinds of cotton yarn underneath its cowhide cover. Any change in this recipe alters the coefficient of restitution. During

Math Box 8: The Collision Equations

Most impacts in sports can be represented as a collision between a lighter-weight object (e.g., a ball) and a heavier one (a bat, club, racket, etc.). Before the collision the objects are moving toward each other; after the collision the direction of the lighter object is reversed, while the heavier one normally continues moving in the same direction at reduced speed. For simplicity, it is assumed that the collision is head on: both objects travel on a common straight line before and after they collide.

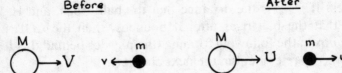

Capital letters have been used to represent the mass (M), initial speed (V), and final speed (U) of the heavier object; the corresponding lowercase letters represent the same properties of the lighter object. According to the law of conservation of momentum

$$MV - mv = MU + mu$$

Notice how the directions have been taken into account in adding the momenta. A second equation is provided by the definition of the coefficient of restitution in its most general form:

$$COR = \frac{\text{relative speed after the collision}}{\text{relative speed before the collision}}$$

The letter e is commonly used as the mathematical symbol for the coefficient of restitution. Once again taking directions into account, we have

$$e = \frac{u - U}{v + V}$$

Usually the masses (M and m), the initial speeds (V and v), and the COR (e) are known quantities, while the postcollision speeds (U and u) are unknowns. Equations for U and u can be obtained by algebraic combination of the conservation of momentum and coefficient of restitution equations. The results are as follows:

$$u = \frac{MV(1 + e) + v(eM - m)}{M + m} \qquad U = \frac{V(M - em) - mv(1 + e)}{M + m}$$

The mathematical symmetry of these equations permits us to use either the weight or the mass for m and M, provided that this is done consistently throughout.

Example: A baseball (weight 5 ounces) thrown at 90 mi/hr strikes a 30-ounce bat at a point where the bat speed is 70 mi/hr. The COR at this speed is 0.55. With what speed does the ball rebound off the bat?

Solution: We can use the weights in place of the masses, and also keep the speeds in mi/hr in these calculations. We will use the following data:

$$M = 30 \text{ oz} \qquad V = 70 \text{ mi/hr} \qquad e = 0.55$$
$$m = 5 \text{ oz} \qquad v = 90 \text{ mi/hr}$$

The speed of the ball after the impact is:

$$u = \frac{MV(1 + e) + v(eM - m)}{M + m}$$
$$= \frac{(30)(70)(1.55) + (90)[(.55)(30) - 5]}{30 + 5} = 123 \ mi/hr$$

The bat speed after the impact is:

$$U = \frac{V(M - em) - mv(1 + e)}{M + m}$$
$$= \frac{(70)[(30) - (0.55)(5)] - (5)(90)(1.55)}{30 + 5} = 35 \ mi/hr$$

Notice that the velocity of the baseball has been reversed in direction and increased in speed from 90 mi/hr to 123 mi/hr. This corresponds to a change in velocity of 213 mi/hr.

World War II baseball manufacturers had to use a lower quality of wool, resulting in a substantial decrease in the COR. Since professional baseball teams also had to make do with lower quality ballplayers during World War II, it's difficult to determine just how much the deadened ball affected play. But there's no doubt about the effect of the change in the composition of the baseball made in 1920, when the ball was intentionally made much livelier to encourage power hitting. Major leaguers increased their home run production from 446 homers in 1919 to 937 in 1921, and the complexion and popularity of the game was radically transformed. Baseball historians look upon 1920 as a watershed year marking the boundary between the "dead ball" and "lively ball" eras.

In general, the coefficient of restitution of any ball is not a constant quantity. As indicated in Table 6.2, the COR tends to decrease in value as the collision speed increases, which is another way of saying

TABLE 6.2: COEFFICIENT OF RESTITUTION OF BALLS USED IN SPORTS

The following coefficients of restitution apply to balls dropped or thrown at a rigid wooden surface. (Data adapted from Plagenhoef, *Patterns of Human Motion*, p. 83.)

| | Coefficient of Restitution | |
Ball	Impact Speed = 15 mi/hr	Impact Speed = 55 mi/hr
Baseball	0.57	0.55
Basketball	0.75	0.64
Golf ball	0.60	0.58
Handball	0.80	0.50
Ping Pong ball	0.80	0.70
Soccer ball	0.75	0.65
Softball	0.55	0.40
Squash ball	0.52	0.40
Superball	0.90	0.85
Tennis ball	0.70	0.50

that a ball rebounds with a smaller fraction of its original speed in a higher-speed impact (physically, a greater proportion of the initial energy is converted to heat in the collision). The COR also decreases with temperature, since rubber and similar substances tend to be less elastic when they are colder. A more obvious variation is that the COR of a given type of ball depends on the surface the ball is bouncing on. A baseball has a higher COR when it hits a concrete wall than when it rebounds off a wooden bat, and it has a higher COR when it bounces on Astroturf than when it bounces on grass. Similarly, a tennis ball has a higher COR on a concrete or asphalt playing surface than it does on clay or grass. Moreover, the COR of any ball normally decreases noticeably with use. All of these variations in the COR, while they are not large numerically, are significant enough to affect the style and strategy of the game.

The Mathematics of Collisions

Now let's return to the problem of predicting the outcome of a collision between two moving objects, given their masses and velocities before the impact. As I noted before, this problem cannot be solved by the law of conservation of momentum alone. However, the coefficient of restitution for the collision provides the additional information needed to arrive at a solution. Specifically, the COR establishes a mathematical relationship between the relative velocities of the objects before and after the collision—which, when coupled with the equation describing the conservation of momentum, allows for a mathematical solution that gives the velocities of both objects after the collision.

The equations for the postcollision velocities are given in Math Box 8, pages 220–21, along with an example showing how they are used. Note that these equations apply specifically to a head-on collision, in which both objects travel on the same straight line before and after they collide. A glancing collision, in which the objects rebound at an angle to their original paths, requires a more complicated computation that takes into account the directional or vector nature of momentum. In this case, the *vector* sum of the momenta of the two colliding objects must be the same before and after the collision. Mathematically, this is equivalent to the requirement that the components of the momentum vectors are conserved in all directions, as shown in Figure 6.3.

The mathematics of glancing collisions is quite complicated, so I won't attempt to go beyond this brief discussion except to take note of one basic conclusion: as Figure 6.3 shows, in a glancing collision the two objects must necessarily rebound to opposite sides of the original line of motion in order to conserve momentum. This result should always be remembered when lining up a shot on a billiards table or a bowling alley—two places where glancing collisions occur with considerable frequency. Novices often forget when lining up a shot that a cue ball or a bowling ball will always be deflected in a glancing collision. For example, in order to hit a "double wood" in bowling (two pins in direct line) the lead pin *must* be hit head-on; if not, the bowling ball and lead pin will automatically both be deflected away from the hidden pin (see Fig. 6.4).

The equations describing a head-on collision between two objects, while considerably simpler than those for a glancing collision, are still

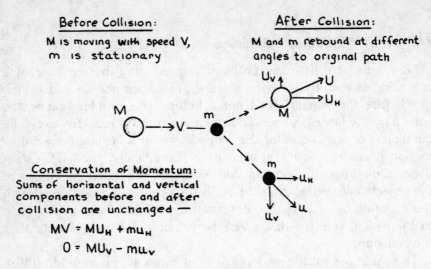

Before Collision:

M is moving with speed V,
m is stationary

After Collision:

M and m rebound at different
angles to original path

Conservation of Momentum:

Sums of horizontal and vertical
components before and after
collision are unchanged —

$$MV = MU_H + mu_H$$
$$0 = MU_V - mu_V$$

FIGURE 6.3 Physics of a glancing collision.

fairly complicated. Nevertheless, it is possible to draw some useful general conclusions from these equations relevant to certain types of collisions that occur in sports, without delving too deeply into the mathematical details.

The type of collision of greatest interest to us in this regard is one between a ball and a "striker"—which could be a bat, golf club,

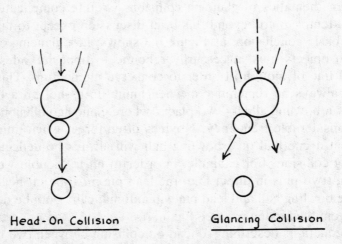

Head-On Collision   Glancing Collision

FIGURE 6.4 Hitting the hidden pin in bowling.

paddle, racket, or even a part of the body. Usually the goal in such a collision is to maximize the speed with which the ball leaves the striker (u in the collision equations). I'll now summarize how this speed is influenced by the factors that affect the outcome of the collision—namely, the masses and speeds of the colliding objects and the COR.

Two of these factors affect collisions in fairly obvious ways. The first is the coefficient of restitution (e in the equations): as a rule, *the greater the COR, the greater the speed of the ball after the impact*. The second factor is the mass of the ball itself (m). Here again the equations bear out the obvious conclusion that (if all the other factors are the same) *the greater the mass of the ball, the smaller the speed of the ball after impact*. This is expected because a heavier ball needs more force to accelerate it.

The next factor to be considered is the precollision speed of the ball (v), the speed with which it approaches the striker. This also affects the speed after the collision in a straightforward manner: *the greater the speed of the ball before the collision, the greater will be its rebound speed*. The basic reason for this can be traced to the elasticity of the ball—the more it is deformed by the impact, the more it will tend to spring back. In other words, the coefficient of restitution fixes a nearly constant ratio between the incoming and outgoing speeds—and even though the COR tends to decrease slightly at higher impact speeds, the basic rule is that *the faster the ball comes in, the faster it goes out*.

This fact is well known to any baseball player or fan. A fast ball is a difficult pitch to hit—but if you do connect with it, the ball will really take off. Slower pitches, on the other hand, may be easier to make contact with but won't travel as far. The same is true in tennis; the faster the ball speed, the faster it rebounds off the racket—and so to keep his returns in the court, the player must control his racket speed in accordance with the speed of the approaching ball. The smallest impact speed comes about when the ball is initially at rest (v = 0); in this case the relative speed of the collision is simply the speed of the striker itself. This describes the act of hitting a golf ball or a tennis serve, "self-hitting" a baseball (throwing it vertically upward and hitting it on the way down), or hitting a baseball off a batting tee. In all of these, the players try to swing with extra force to compensate for the stationary ball. (Note: in serving a tennis ball or self-hitting a baseball, the vertical motion of the ball makes no contribution to its collision speed, since the collision essentially takes place in a horizontal plane.)

The two remaining factors that influence the speed of the ball after impact are the mass (M) and speed (V) of the striker. Taken independently, their effects are easy to recognize. First of all, for a given striker mass, *the greater the speed of the striker, the greater the speed of the ball*. This is an obvious conclusion; the faster you swing a bat, tennis racket, or golf club, the faster the ball will travel when it's hit. Secondly, for a given striker speed, *the bigger the mass of the striker, the bigger the ball speed will be*. This relates back to the idea that the change in velocity experienced by each object in a collision is inversely proportional to its mass, so increasing the ratio of striker mass to ball mass will increase the speed of the ball after impact.

A simple illustration of this idea is proved by the game of bowling. Here we can think of the bowling ball as the striker, colliding with a stationary object—the first bowling pin it makes contact with. (The bowling ball is thus analogous to the head of a golf club striking a teed-up golf ball.) The rules specify that a bowling ball must weigh between 10 and 16 lb, a bowling pin 3 to 3½ lb. If bowling balls of different weight are thrown at the same speed, the heavier ball will impart more speed to the pin; a pin recoils with 10% more speed from a collision with a 16-lb ball as compared with a 10-lb ball. Moreover, a heavier ball will lose less of its own speed in the impact: a 16-lb ball loses about 30% of its initial speed in a head-on collision with a pin, whereas a 10-lb ball loses about 40%. Thus it is to the bowler's advantage to throw a heavier ball; both the ball and the pin will then collide more forcefully with the other pins in the ensuing collisions. The catch is that a physically weaker bowler typically has more difficulty throwing a heavy ball with sufficient speed and accuracy. But a bowler who is strong enough to throw a ball of any weight with appropriate speed and control will always do better with a 16-lb ball.

Effective Mass

Up to now, we've looked at collisions that involve only two objects, in which a transfer of momentum from one to the other takes place. But collisions in sports often involve more than two objects, and other forces besides the force of impact can come into play. In such circumstances, the transfer of momentum is a more complicated affair. A stationary football player can brace himself against an impending collision by digging his feet into the turf. This introduces another force into the collision (the friction force between his feet and the ground) and allows some of the momentum to be transferred to a third object —namely, the earth. When a tennis ball collides with a racket, some of the momentum of the collision is absorbed by the arm of the player holding the racket. This is the case whenever any striking implement —golf club, baseball bat, hockey stick—collides with another object; the body of the person holding the striker is the third participant in the same collision.

To deal with this situation, biomechanics researchers have introduced the concept of an *effective mass* (also known as the *striking mass*). The effective mass is the combined mass of the striking implement and those parts of the holder's body that participate in the interaction. The effective mass cannot be predicted beforehand, but it can be measured: high-speed photography can be used to determine the speeds of the ball and striker before and after the impact, and by comparing the change in velocity of each, the effective mass can be calculated.

In the late 1960s a study of the effective mass for impacts in a number of sports was conducted by Stanley Plagenhoef of the University of Massachusetts. His results, many of which are summarized in his book *Patterns of Human Motion,* demonstrate the importance of maintaining a tight and rigid grip on the striker: the stronger the grip, the greater the effective mass; in effect, more of the holder's body becomes part of the striker.

In general, the shorter the impact time, the smaller the contribution made by the athlete's body to the effective mass. Moreover, the more rigid the ball is, the less time it spends in contact with the striker— hence, a rigid ball has a short impact time, leading to a correspondingly smaller effective mass. Because a football is not a very rigid object, the impact time in kicking a football is relatively long. Here the kicker's foot is the striking implement, and the effective mass includes his foot and lower leg. Plagenhoef compared the soccer-style kick (in which the ball is hit with the side of the foot at the instep) with the more traditional straight-on toe kick. He found that the effective mass was several kilograms larger for the soccer-style kick, and higher ball velocities were achieved as a consequence. Plagenhoef's measurements were made on only one individual, but his results nevertheless may explain the success of soccer-style place-kickers in professional football.

In another study, Plagenhoef photographed and analyzed the golf drives of a number of top men and women professional golfers. We would expect the contribution of the golfer's body to the effective mass to be relatively small in a golf drive, in view of the high rigidity of a golf ball and the short impact time for the ball-club collision. Predictably, Plagenhoef's measurements show that the effective mass in driving consists mainly of the head of the club itself, with the club shaft and the golfer's hands making only a minor contribution. (Interestingly, because of its greater length and the fact that its mass is concentrated in the clubhead, a driver imparts more momentum to the ball at impact than an iron does, even though a driver weighs less than an iron.) The men golfers did exhibit higher effective masses at impact than the women did—but it was only 84 grams (equivalent to about 3 ounces) more. The study also showed that the men golfers attained clubhead speeds at impact averaging 24 mi/hr higher than those of the women. This difference can be easily attributed to the greater physical size and strength of the men in the study.

The Baseball Bat

In any activity that involves hitting a ball, you might think that the best results would be obtained by using as massive a striking implement as possible or by otherwise increasing its effective mass at impact. However, the problem with this analysis is that the mass and the speed of the striker are not necessarily independent of each other, for the simple reason that *the heavier the striker is, the harder it is to accelerate it*. Thus an athlete who swings a more massive striker may sacrifice speed as a consequence. In selecting the weight of a baseball bat, tennis racket, golf club, etc., each athlete must take into account the competing factors of mass and speed as they relate to his own level of physical strength.

The balance between mass and speed is really crucial when choosing the weight of a baseball bat. A lighter bat is more maneuverable; the batter can get it up to speed in a shorter time, so he can delay his decision to swing at a pitch a bit longer than with a heavier bat. A heavier bat has the advantage of transferring more momentum to the ball at impact, but to gain this advantage a batter must make a greater effort in order to accelerate the bat to the same speed that he would achieve with a lighter bat.

To simplify the comparison, let's suppose that a batter expends the same amount of energy in swinging bats of different weights, trading speed for mass and vice versa: is it better to swing a lighter bat at higher speed, or a heavier bat at a lower speed? The calculations required to answer this question are too complex to present here, so I'll summarize the main conclusion. Between the two extremes of an exceptionally light bat swung at high speed and a very heavy bat that makes contact with the ball at low speed, there is an optimum bat weight that maximizes the speed of the baseball as it rebounds off the bat. Surprisingly, this optimum weight turns out to be much smaller than you would expect.

A baseball weighs 5 to 5¼ ounces and is thrown by major league pitchers at an average speed of 80 to 90 mi/hr. The bats used by major league hitters normally range from 30 to 36 ounces in weight, and a typical bat speed, measured at the point of contact, is about 70 mi/hr (remember that since the bat is undergoing rotational motion, not all points along the bat are traveling at the same speed). From these numbers, it follows that the momentum of the bat is approximately 5 times larger than that of the ball. Under these conditions, the calculated optimum bat weight, leading to the best combination of bat weight and speed for the highest rebound speed of the ball, is only about 20 ounces! How do we reconcile this with the fact that baseball players, through a process of trial and error over many years, have found 30- to 36-ounce bats to be most effective?

This question was first raised twenty years ago by Paul Kirkpatrick, a physics professor at Stanford University. In an *American Journal of Physics* article entitled "Batting the Ball," Kirkpatrick developed a theory for optimum bat mass that led to a value of 17 to 18 ounces. His only comment on this strange result was that "apparently the principle . . . is not fully binding upon athletes who are much more interested in effectiveness than in efficiency."

I have to thank my younger son, the baseball expert, for seeing beyond the mathematics and solving this perplexing mystery. The answer is really quite simple: *a 20-ounce bat would be much too short to use*. A professional baseball bat must be made from solid wood, and a 20-ounce bat of any reasonable thickness could not be much longer than 22 inches—a length suitable at best for a seven-year-old. In contrast, the bats used by college and professional ballplayers are typically 34 to 36 inches long. (The shortest bat ever used by a major leaguer was 30½ inches long and belonged to Willie "Hit 'em Where They Ain't" Keeler, one of the greatest hitters of the dead ball era.)

Thus a theoretical analysis of the bat-ball collision leads to the conclusion that it is more effective for the batter to put his effort into swinging a lighter bat at higher speed—or, in other words, that bat speed is a more important consideration than weight. However, light bat weight can be achieved only at the expense of length. As I pointed out earlier, it is to the batter's advantage to use a long bat, not only to better cover the strike zone, but also to attain greater bat speed at the point of contact. However, greater bat length contributes to greater weight and moment of inertia, which makes the bat more difficult to accelerate.

Under these circumstances, it would seem that the best way to achieve lightness without sacrificing length is to use a relatively long, skinny bat. But a thin-barreled bat has less hitting surface—that is, the thinner the barrel, the harder it is for the batter to make contact when he swings at the pitch. Yet the fatter the barrel, the greater the weight and moment of inertia of the bat. Moreover, the fact that a bat must be of solid wood gives the batter (and bat manufacturer) little flexibility in balancing weight against length and thickness. As a general rule, the weight of a wooden bat in ounces is equal to its length in inches, give or take about 2 ounces—for example, a standard 34-inch bat won't weigh less than 32 ounces nor more than 36 ounces. Some players have even tried illegal means to produce lighter bats for their length—by hollowing out the bat barrel and putting in a cork insert.

It's clear, then, that the search for an optimum bat involves conflicting goals that cannot be satisfied simultaneously. The choice of a bat is therefore governed by the batter's strengths and preferences, as well as by game situations. A "contact" hitter—one who bats for accuracy rather than distance—is better off with a lighter and more maneuverable (but necessarily shorter) bat. To gain more bat control, some hitters like to "choke up" on a bat—grip the bat higher on the handle. The bat can be moved more quickly this way (its moment of inertia has been decreased because of the shorter axis of rotation), but the shorter radius of the swing translates to a lower bat speed at the point of contact.

An exceptionally strong player can get away with using a longer, thicker (and heavier) bat without sacrificing too much bat speed. Babe Ruth normally used a 44-ounce bat, and on occasion used bats as heavy as 54 ounces. Ruth was, of course, the most renowned home-run hitter in baseball history. Yet his fame as a home-run hitter has obscured the fact that he was an all-around hitter with a lifetime batting average of .342, a remarkable achievement in view of the fact that he used an unusually heavy, and presumably less maneuverable, bat.

Despite the practical restrictions on bat weight and length, there are a number of major leaguers who manage to perform their jobs successfully using a bat that may weigh as little as 25 ounces. This relatively thin-barreled model is known as a *fungo* bat (American language experts have never been able to identify the origin of this word), and it is used by coaches during fielding practice to hit fly balls to the outfielders. Since the balls are self-hit rather than thrown by a pitcher, and since the coach wants to aim his hits to the outfielders, the light and maneuverable fungo bat is perfectly suited to its role. Frank Howard, formerly the manager of the New York Mets (and reputedly one of the strongest men ever to play baseball), informed me of yet another of its advantages: in pregame practice, a coach may bat out a hundred or more fly balls—a task that becomes considerably more tiring when a heavier bat is used.

The dilemma that a batter faces in choosing between lighter weight (to achieve higher bat speed) and greater length and barrel thickness (to improve his chances of making contact with the ball) is just one of the many trade-offs that maintain the contest between pitcher and batter at a constant level. Even the slightest variations in the rules and equipment—changing the height of the pitcher's mound by a few inches, or using a different type of wool in the manufacture of the baseball—can tip the delicate balance between offense and defense in a very marked way.

Indeed, much of the infinite variety, the unpredictability, and the excitement of the game of baseball is due in large measure to the simple and often overlooked fact that a baseball bat has a round barrel. The maximum allowed barrel diameter is 2.75 inches, whereas the diameter of the baseball itself is 2.90 inches. When a batter swings at a ball that not only is approaching him at high speed but may also be sinking, rising, or curving, it is extremely difficult for him to control the alignment of bat and ball at impact. The ideal, of course, is a head-on collision in which the force of the impact acts through the center of gravity of the ball and along the path of the pitch. If the contact point is a fraction of an inch lower, the ball will be popped up; a fraction of an inch higher and the ball will be hit toward the ground. A deviation of more than 3 inches in distance (the result of starting the swing about 3 milliseconds too early or too late) between the paths of the bat and ball results in a complete miss. In contrast to the baseball bat, a cricket bat has a flat surface, 4¼ inches wide; with this implement a batter—or rather a batsman, according to cricket terminology—can direct his hits more easily in almost any direction he chooses.

Baseball is a game from a pretechnological era. Many modern Americans are bored or annoyed by its leisurely pace, its devotion to the past, its lack of concern for the passage of time. Indeed, the game

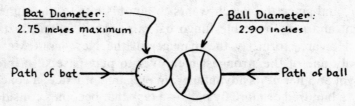

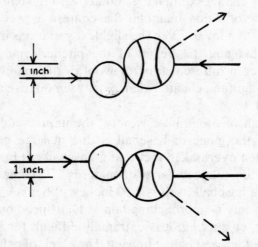

FIGURE 6.5   Possible outcomes of a bat-ball collision.

has put up a valiant and admirable struggle against the onslaught of technological change, succumbing to some of its blandishments (e.g., Astroturf, domed stadiums, computerized scoreboards), while rejecting others (electronic aids for umpires). One particularly threatening technological intrusion that has thus far been resisted by professional baseball is the aluminum bat.

The most obvious advantage of an aluminum bat is an economic one; wooden bats break fairly easily, while aluminum bats are virtually indestructible. As a result, the aluminum bat has almost completely taken over the market at the high school and college baseball levels, where equipment budgets are restricted. Yet an even more significant advantage is that aluminum bats can be constructed in a much wider range of weight and length combinations. For example, an aluminum bat of the same length and shape as a 34-inch, 33-ounce wooden bat could be made to weigh as little as 28 ounces. Moreover, since an aluminum bat is hollow, its weight is more evenly distributed; it will not be as top-heavy as its wooden counterpart. Thus the aluminum bat will have a lower moment of inertia and will be easier to accelerate. In addition, aluminum bats can be manufactured with a thicker barrel without adding appreciable weight or "top-heaviness" to the bat. With an aluminum bat, a hitter does not have to make a choice between lightness of weight, length, and thickness; he can have all three in a single bat.

Manufacturers of aluminum bats claim that baseballs rebound off aluminum and wooden bats at the same speed. Yet many players contend that a baseball or softball will travel 20 to 30 feet farther when hit with an aluminum bat. In an effort to settle this argument, a group of engineers at Arizona State University did a study comparing the performance characteristics of wooden and aluminum bats. With six players from the college team as subjects (Arizona State has traditionally had one of the top college baseball programs in the country), the researchers measured the speeds of batted balls with a radar gun. They found that line drives hit with an aluminum bat averaged about 4 mi/hr faster than those hit with a wooden bat—a difference that corresponds to about a 10% increase in the distance that the ball travels. This improvement can be attributed in part to the better physical properties of aluminum compared with wood (i.e., greater rigidity and strength), and in part to the higher bat speeds that can be achieved when swinging an aluminum bat.

Today, aluminum bats predominate at all levels of amateur baseball and softball. As a direct consequence of the changeover from wood to aluminum, there has been a dramatic rise in batting averages and a drop in pitching effectiveness (as measured by earned-run averages) among college baseball players. Thus all of the scientific evidence, coupled with the experiences and statistics of baseball players who have used them, points clearly to the superiority of aluminum over wooden bats. Yet at the present time their use is prohibited in professional baseball. Recognizing that aluminum bats would give too much of an advantage to the hitters and wreak havoc on the records and statistics so dear to baseball fans, the rules-makers have wisely chosen, at least for the moment, to resist this technological advance.

On the other hand, aluminum bats have proved a welcome addition to fast-pitch softball. Using the windmill-style delivery, many softball pitchers are able to achieve throwing speeds in the 90-to-100-mi/hr range; and since the pitching distance is 46 feet (instead of 60½ feet as in baseball), the batter has even less time to react to the pitch as compared with baseball. As a result, the game has traditionally been dominated by the pitchers; the most outstanding windmill pitchers have amassed incredible (at least by baseball standards) records for strikeouts and no-hitters. But in recent years, the introduction of the aluminum bat—with its obvious advantages of lighter weight, easier acceleration, and greater bat speed—has helped the batters considerably, and has done much to create a more competitive balance between pitching and hitting.

The Sweet Spot

There is yet another aspect of a baseball bat to be considered—namely, where along the length of the barrel should contact be made? As I emphasized earlier, when a bat is swung the linear speed along the bat increases with distance from the handle. Therefore the bat speed is greatest if the point of contact is at the end of the bat, and smallest if it's near the handle. It goes without saying that the handle is the worst place to make contact with the ball, not only because of the low bat speed but also because it's the thinnest and weakest part of the bat. On the other hand, when the ball hits at the very end of the bat the ball does not seem to travel as far, and the contact also produces a stinging sensation in the hands. There is, however, one spot on the barrel of the bat where, if you make contact there, the ball seems to jump off the bat; there is almost no sensation at the hand, no tugging at the grip; the collision feels smooth, effortless, and true. This spot is known to ballplayers as the *sweet spot*. This experience is not confined to baseball; golfers and tennis players also know the sensation of hitting the ball at the sweet spot of the club or racket.

There is, needless to say, a scientific explanation for this phenomenon; in fact there are *three* possible explanations. The most popular theory is that the sweet spot is a point known to physicists as the *center of percussion*. When a sudden force (more precisely, an impulse) is applied at the center of percussion of a rotating object, there is no reaction at the pivot point.

To understand this concept, let's take a look at what happens when a long stick receives a sudden impulse, as shown in Figure 6.6. If the line of the force acts through the center of gravity, the stick will move in a straight line, but if the force is applied anywhere else, the stick will acquire a rotational motion around its CG in addition to the linear motion. Notice that in this case there is a stationary point on the stick where the linear and rotational motions exactly cancel. As a result, the stick pivots around the stationary point rather than its CG.

Now suppose that the stick is fixed so that it can only pivot at its

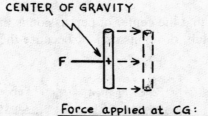

CENTER OF GRAVITY

Force applied at CG:
Only linear motion produced (no rotation about CG)

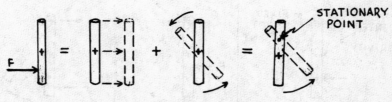

STATIONARY POINT

Force not applied at CG:
Linear and rotational motions are produced —
they combine to create a stationary point

FIGURE 6.6   The effect of an eccentric force on the motion of a stick.

end (Fig. 6.7). If a force is applied at the right spot, it makes the stationary point coincide with the fixed pivot point. The stick would then swing freely without exerting any force on the pivot. This particular point of application of the force is the center of percussion. (The center of percussion must necessarily be located to the side of the CG away from the pivot.) If the force is applied anywhere else, there will be a reaction force at the pivot tending to push it one way or the other.

When a baseball bat, in the hands of a batter, makes contact with the ball, the pivot point during impact is the top of the batter's grip— that is, at the location of his right index finger (assuming he's a right-hander and not batting cross-handed). The exact position of the center of percussion depends on the location of the pivot point; if you choke up on the bat, the center of percussion moves closer to the end of the bat. If the ball hits the center of percussion of the bat, then there will be no reaction force at the pivot point, and the motion of the pivot point will be undisturbed by the impact. If the ball hits between the center of percussion and the handle, the batter will feel a force tending to push the bat into his palms; if the ball hits between the center of percussion and the end of the bat, the batter will feel a force tending to open his grip by pushing on his fingers. The two-handed grip acts to counteract these forces (they are more noticeable when hitting one-handed).

It has been proposed that the center of percussion is the sweet spot of a baseball bat, golf club, or tennis racket, because the holder feels

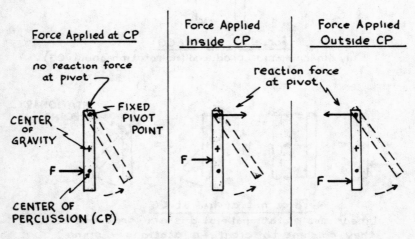

FIGURE 6.7 The center of percussion.

the least amount of force on his hand when he hits the ball at that point. For most baseball bats held in the conventional way, the center of percussion is located about 6 to 8 inches from the fat end of the bat (Fig. 6.8). On a golf club, the center of percussion is located right on the face of the club. The location of the center of percussion of a tennis racket is a matter that we'll return to in short order.

The second theory of the sweet spot has to do with the vibrations that are set up along the length of the bat whenever it is struck. Every material object has a natural tendency to vibrate when it is distorted or disturbed in a particular way; these vibrations travel through the object, carrying energy in the form of waves. When any fixed solid object such as a coiled spring, a stretched wire, or a clamped metal rod is disturbed, the waves move back and forth along its length, producing a vibration pattern that is determined by the properties of the object—its mass, length, elasticity, etc.—and also by the manner in which it is being held. In every circumstance, the object has a natural frequency with which it vibrates. If the object is a guitar string, for example, its natural frequency corresponds to the sound—the particular note on the musical scale—that it gives off when it is plucked. This frequency changes according to the length of the string (adjusted by holding it down with a finger) and also depends on the tension in the string. Furthermore, every vibrating object has one or more locations along its length that will not vibrate at all when the object is struck in an appropriate manner. These dead spots, which are points where the waves that travel back and forth along the object always cancel each other out, are called *nodes*.

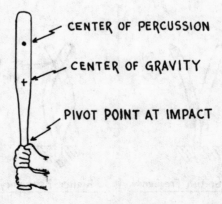

FIGURE 6.8   Center of percussion of a baseball bat.

A baseball bat also has a natural frequency when struck, and while it does not resonate as beautifully as a guitar string does, it still can be induced to "sing"—in fact, an aluminum bat can be made to hum as loudly as a tuning fork. It's very easy to demonstrate this phenomenon for yourself; all you need are some baseball bats and something to hit them with (preferably something made of hard rubber that won't make an annoying "ping" or a dent whenever you hit the bat). Simply suspend the bat loosely, gripping it between your thumb and index finger about 5 to 6 inches from the handle end, and tap it at various places along its length. The position of the node will be very apparent. With a wooden bat the vibrations can be easily sensed by your fingers, but with an aluminum bat the vibrations can also be heard as a fairly loud, resonant ringing—except when the bat is struck at its node.

A baseball bat gripped at its handle has two main patterns of vibration, similar to those of the clamped stick shown in Figure 6.9. The first pattern corresponds to the natural vibration frequency of the bat. The second pattern—which is a higher multiple of its natural frequency and is equivalent to the overtone of a musical note—has a node located between the bat's center of gravity and its end. When the bat is struck anywhere along its length *except* at the node, it will vibrate in a combination of the two patterns, producing both the natural frequency (which is normally too low in pitch to be audible or to be felt as a vibration) and its higher-frequency, audible overtone. However, if the bat is struck at the node, only the lower frequency is created; the higher frequency overtone does not appear. This suppression of the higher-frequency vibration is readily apparent to the holder

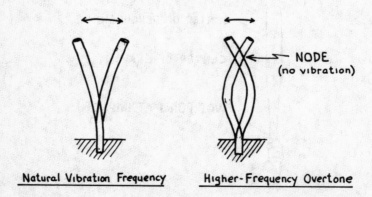

Natural Vibration Frequency   Higher-Frequency Overtone

FIGURE 6.9   First two vibration patterns of a clamped stick.

of the bat; not only is there no audible sound, but also no vibration is felt at the handle when the bat is struck at the node. The vibrations that occur when a ball hits the bat at a point far from the node are felt as a stinging sensation in the hands.

We can easily understand why the node is a "sweet spot" in an energy context: when the baseball strikes the bat away from the node, some of the ball's kinetic energy is transformed into the energy of vibration of the bat—energy that is not returned to the ball as it rebounds. When the ball strikes the node, however, less energy is lost to vibrational motion. Thus the second theory states that the sweet spot is the node of the bat's natural vibration; hitting the ball at this point feels good because the high-frequency vibrations that sting the hands are not generated; the ball rebounds with more speed because less energy is diverted into useless vibrational motion. On a baseball bat the center of percussion and the vibration node are quite close to each other. They're not that easy to tell apart, the main difference being that when the ball hits the center of percussion no *force* is felt at the handle, and when the ball hits the node no *vibration* is felt. Thus the sweet spot phenomenon is probably a combination of both of these effects.

Some baseball players claim that an aluminum bat seems to have a larger sweet spot. Others qualify this by saying that a ball jumps off a wooden bat only if it hits the sweet spot, but it seems to travel equally well if it hits any part of an aluminum bat. This may have more to do with the greater rigidity of aluminum compared with wood than with the nature of the sweet spot. However, the group of researchers at Arizona State who compared the two types of bats did find that the sweet spot of an aluminum bat is about two inches wide, while the sweet spot of a wooden bat is basically a single point. It is not clear from their report whether they were measuring force, vibration, or both. My guess is that they were measuring both and that the greater width of the sweet spot is due to the fact that the center of percussion and the vibration node are farther apart on an aluminum bat than on a wooden bat.

The third theory of the sweet spot holds that it is located at the point or region where the coefficient of restitution for the collision between the ball and striker has its largest value. This theory has particular relevance for a tennis racket, since the COR depends on the string tension and is not uniform over the whole face of the racket.

Howard Brody, a physicist at the University of Pennsylvania, has studied the physics of the tennis racket rather thoroughly and considered all three theories of the sweet spot. He was particularly interested in comparing the relative merits of the conventional tennis racket and the oversized Prince racket devised by racket designer Howard Head. On a conventional tennis racket, the center of percussion is not at the center of the strings, but is actually about 2 inches below the center, toward the handle. Thus hitting the ball at the center of percussion reduces the force on the player's hand, but the player gives up the advantages of hitting at the center (better accuracy) or at the top end of the racket (greater speed at the point of contact). The Prince racket is the same length as a conventional racket, but its string area has been increased by about 20% by extending the head toward a shortened handle. As a result, its center of percussion coincides with the center of the head.

Like a baseball bat, a tennis racket has a vibration node; and when the ball strikes the node, no vibrations are transmitted to the handle. On both the conventional and Prince rackets, the node is located about 5 inches from the tip of the racket—close to the center of the strings on a conventional racket, but above the center of a Prince. On either racket, the vibration node is located about 4 to 5 inches away from the center of percussion.

This brings us back to the third theory, which proposes that the sweet spot is the region of the highest coefficient of restitution. This is the definition used by Head to support his claim that a Prince racket has a larger sweet spot than a conventional racket. On the other hand, Brody prefers to refer to this region as the "power region" of the racket. In any case, the COR does vary considerably over the face of the racket; it is lowest near the tip of the racket and highest close to the bottom of the head, near the handle. The COR also tends to decrease sideways away from the center axis (the continuation of the line of the handle) of the racket head. Moreover, measurements show that the COR of a tennis ball is greater bouncing off the racket strings (COR ≈ 0.85) than off a solid object (COR ≈ 0.7) and that the COR depends strongly on the tension of the strings at the point of contact. In addition, the COR tends to be smaller when the ball impacts at higher speeds.

These facts can be explained in terms of the elastic energy storage in the strings and racket frame. Earlier we learned that some of the ball's kinetic energy is transformed on impact to elastic energy in the strings and frame. The racket frame responds too slowly to return any of this energy to the ball, but the stiffer the frame is, the less elastic energy it will absorb in the first place. Any racket frame, no matter what it's made of, is always more flexible near the tip and stiffest near the handle. As a result, slightly more energy is absorbed by the frame when the ball hits near the tip. Consequently the COR will be lower there, and higher toward the stiffest part of the racket.

The strings, on the other hand, rebound more quickly and return much more of their elastic energy to the ball. The fraction of energy returned depends on the extent to which the strings are unevenly distorted by the impact. A collision at higher speeds, or one that occurs away from the center line of the racket, produces more distortion, less energy return, and a lower COR. In general, the more flexible the strings are, the more energy they return to the ball. What this means is that *a tennis racket acts more effectively at lower string tension*. Brody compared two Prince rackets—one strung with 70 lb tension, the other with 50 lb tension—and found that the impact time was about 0.4 millisecond longer and the COR measurably larger for the 50-lb tension. This information should be especially useful to tennis players at all levels who are undecided as to how tightly their rackets should be strung. Brody's message is: *looser is better*.

Each of the three different definitions of the sweet spot of a tennis racket points to a different location. Moreover, there doesn't seem to be much basis for choosing any one of them as better than the other two. Ultimately, the best definition of the sweet spot is a subjective one—namely, it's the place where it feels good when you hit the ball there.

The Physics of Karate

Among the collisions that take place in sports, perhaps the most dramatic are the ones where the striker is a human hand. Such collisions are, of course, a prominent feature of boxing. This is a sport that has been criticized because of its inherent brutality; but at its best, boxing features remarkable displays of speed, reflexes, and stamina. From the scientific point of view, it is of considerable interest to compare boxing with its Oriental counterparts—namely, karate ("empty hand" in Japanese) and its Chinese and Korean variants, *kung fu* and *tae kwon do*.

The differences between the ways that blows are delivered in boxing and in karate are a reflection of their purpose. In boxing, punches are thrown primarily to knock the opponent off balance. Most punches are characterized by a long follow-through which continues the pushing action started by the impact. The force of the blow is distributed over a wide area (the front surface of the boxing glove). As a result, the effect of a punch in the head is not primarily physical damage to any part of the face, but rather a rapid rearward acceleration of the head. A well-delivered and unresisted blow to the head can cause an acceleration on the order of 80 times the acceleration of gravity—a jolt that can easily separate the receiver from his senses.

The main purpose of a karate blow, on the other hand, is to focus the force of impact on a small area so as to do damage—break bone or tissue—at the point of contact. In the course of any punch, the arm is first rapidly accelerated, then decelerated as it becomes fully extended and collides with its target. Maximum speed is attained about 75% of the way through the motion. A karate blow is designed to make contact when the hand reaches its maximum speed, thereby effecting the maximum transfer of energy from the hand to the target (to achieve this goal, the participant tries to aim his blow to terminate at an imaginary point a few inches beyond the target). Contact is made with the knuckles, the side of the hand, or the edge of the foot to concentrate the force of the blow. A karate punch is delivered with the wrist, elbow, and shoulder rigidly locked—creating a high effective mass and a large transfer of momentum and energy to the target.

Karate was originally devised for weaponless hand-to-hand combat, but nowadays it is practiced mainly as a sport. In karate competitions no contact is allowed; the blows are aimed to terminate just before hitting the opponent, and the emphasis is on form and technique. By far the most dramatic and impressive displays of karate techniques are those in which experts break wooden boards, bricks, or concrete blocks with their bare hands or feet. More than a few physicists—some of them karate experts themselves—have been sufficiently intrigued by these demonstrations to conduct research studies of karate blows to determine how these impacts can take place without bodily damage.

The physics of a karate blow is fairly straightforward; it requires a knowledge of the strengths of different materials under tension, compression, and bending forces. In the collision, the wooden board or concrete block is being bent by the force of the blow, while the bones of the hand or foot are being compressed—and human bone can withstand compressive forces better than wood or concrete can withstand bending. This explains, in simple terms, how a karate expert can break a board or block without damaging his hand.

In a typical board-breaking demonstration, the board is supported at its ends, and the blow is aimed to strike midway between the supports. The board is bent by the impact, being stretched (experiencing a tension force) on its lower surface and compressed on its upper surface (see Fig. 6.10). Both wood and concrete are weakest under tension, so the board (or a concrete block) will then begin to crack at its lower surface. The crack quickly expands upward as the hand follows through, completing the total break.

The amount of force required to break a wooden board depends on the width and thickness of the board, the distance between its support points, and the type of wood used. The narrower and thinner the board and the greater the distance between the supports, the less force is required. The board is always struck parallel to the grain of the wood, where it has less strength. A standard pine board ¾" thick by 6" wide, with supports 10" apart, requires a force of about 150 lb at its center to break; the crack will begin to form when the center has been deflected about ¼" out of line. Concrete, being more rigid, need be deflected by only about ¹⁄₄₀" to begin to crack—but this requires a larger force (about 650 lb for a concrete slab 1½" thick).

High-speed photographs of various karate blows have shown that hand speeds as high as 30 mi/hr are reached in a downward strike (when the hand is swung downward in a vertical arc on to the target). Impact times generally are in the 5- to 10-millisecond range. Under

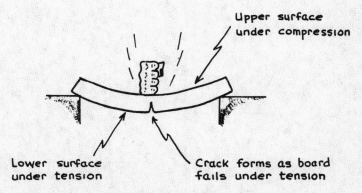

FIGURE 6.10   Breaking a board with a karate punch.

these conditions, the force exerted by the hand can approach 800 lb, more than enough to shatter a wood block or concrete slab of appropriate thickness. In terms of energy requirements, about 10 to 15 joules of energy are needed to break a wooden board, about 35 to 40 joules to break a concrete block. The kinetic energy of the hand in a properly executed downward strike is typically 50 joules or more.

Upon impact, the hand is decelerated rapidly and is subjected to a rather large force. However, this force is not enough to shatter the bones in the hand if the blow is thrown correctly. Bone can withstand compression forces rather well, and even under bending forces it is 40 times stronger than concrete. It is possible to break an opponent's rib with a well-thrown karate punch or kick because the bones of the hand or foot can withstand compression better than the rib can withstand bending. It is, of course, also possible to break your hand with a poorly thrown blow.

There are some individuals who are so awed by karate demonstrations that they become convinced a superhuman effort is required, a summoning up of mystical powers not known to science or attainable through Western modes of thought. Assuredly, a considerable amount of training and self-discipline is required to accomplish such feats. But the fact is that scientists who have studied the physics of karate have shown that the achievements of karate experts are well within the capability of anyone with normal physical strength.

7 / GRAVITY

It was a wintry Saturday morning, and I was in the college gym waiting my turn to play a game of three-man basketball. The game in progress was being dominated by a slender, long-limbed, black teenager who seemed to be able to hover in the air at will while he effortlessly plucked rebounds from over the outstretched hands of taller opponents. I expressed my admiration to the fellow who was sitting next to me.

"That guy is an amazing jumper," I said.

My companion agreed wholeheartedly. "Yeah," he replied. "He sure can *rise up*."

As a person whose leaping ability sometimes borders on the pathetic, I have always viewed the abilities of great jumpers with considerable jealousy. In truth, there are some performers who seem to be able to defy gravity, and I stand in absolute awe of their talents. One of these is Julius Erving, whose floating, soaring drives to the basket present an exquisite combination of grace and strength. Another is Mikhail Baryshnikov, much admired in the ballet world for his *ballon,* which the dictionary describes as "the lightness of movement that allows a dancer to appear to remain in the air unusually long during a jump."

Despite the apparent evidence provided by our own eyes, the laws of physics say that it is impossible to defy gravity. Yet how can we account for the ability of some athletes to "rise up" and hang in the air for relatively long periods of time? Is it an optical illusion, a rare natural talent, or a skill that can be acquired by any athlete who learns and practices the proper techniques?

There is a scientific explanation for great jumping ability. It begins, obviously enough, with the theory of gravity. After all, it is the force of gravity that we must counteract when we jump, and it is this same force that brings us so inevitably back to earth. Gravity plays a significant role in virtually every sport: it affects our ability to run, to catch a fly ball, to shoot a 15-foot jump shot, to reach the green in three strokes on a par-5 hole. The athlete, coach, or sports fan who knows how gravity works can appreciate the limitations that it places on athletic performance, and can understand what is possible or impossible with regard to jumping, or to hitting or throwing a ball. So a survey of scientific attempts to understand gravity is now in order.

Falling Bodies

The very greatest scientific minds—Aristotle, Galileo, Newton, Einstein—have each attempted to understand the nature of gravity. As we learned earlier, Aristotle did not think of gravity as a force, but as an innate tendency of objects to return to their natural resting place —the surface of the earth. He believed that the rate at which an object falls depends on two factors: its elemental composition (the relative proportions of earth, water, fire, or air) and the resistance offered by the medium through which the object is falling. Aristotle thought of the weight of an object as simply a measure of its tendency to fall: the faster it falls, the more it must weigh. It follows from this idea that a heavy object should fall faster than a light object, in proportion to their weights.

When Galileo began his research on motion in the early 1600s, this proposal caught his attention. He pointed out that if Aristotle's claim were true, then a 100-pound stone should fall a hundred times faster than a one-pound stone. So if the two stones are both released at the same instant from a height of, say, 100 feet, the 1-pound stone would have fallen only a distance of 1 foot by the time the 100-lb stone hit the ground. Galileo pointed out that this proposition could be easily disproved by direct experiment, since a 100-lb stone actually hits the ground only a few inches ahead of the lighter one.

In grade school, I was taught that Galileo actually performed this experiment himself by dropping two stones of unequal weight from the Leaning Tower of Pisa. (The Tower is really the bell tower of Pisa's cathedral, and it began to lean even before its completion in the year 1350.) Galileo did live in Pisa for a few years, and the tower would have been an ideal location for the experiment. What a perfect illustration of the romance of science! One can so easily imagine the triumphant look on Galileo's face as the two stones crashed to the ground before a stunned group of Aristotelian scholars assembled at the foot of the Tower. So I must admit to being sadly disillusioned when I learned some years ago that the story is probably a myth. Science historians, in fact, have not found any evidence that the experiment was ever performed anywhere. Moreover, they have learned that Galileo's own theories on falling bodies during the time he lived in Pisa did not differ markedly from those of Aristotle. Galileo did conduct many experiments to disprove Aristotle's theories, but these were mostly done some forty years after he left Pisa. So much for the romance of science.

Galileo, like Aristotle, believed that the speed of a falling object depends on the resistance it experiences as it falls. The extent of this resistance depends not only on the medium through which the object is falling but also on such factors as the weight, size, and shape of the object itself. But Galileo contended that in the absence of any resistance, *these factors no longer affect the rate of fall*. Take a stone and a sheet of paper, hold them at the same height, then release them at the same time: the stone falls rapidly, while the sheet of paper flutters slowly to the ground. But crumple the paper into a tight ball and repeat the experiment; now the stone and ball of paper hit the ground at virtually the same moment. Crumpling the paper did not change its weight, but it did reduce its surface area, thereby decreasing the force of air resistance considerably.

This simple experiment illustrates the important principle that *in the absence of resistance, all objects fall at the same rate*. In other words, objects of different weight, size, shape, or composition fall with precisely the same motion *provided* they experience no resistance from the medium they are falling through. Since every medium produces some resistance, the statement is strictly true only if there is no medium at all—that is, if the object is falling in a vacuum. Of course, one does not often encounter objects falling in a vacuum—this is a privilege generally reserved for astronauts—so this principle may seem a bit abstract. However, in many situations the effect of medium resistance is very slight, and the motion is virtually the same as if the object were falling in a vacuum.

Galileo performed experiments in which he was able to reduce the resistance to motion to insignificance. In this way, he could measure more precisely the motion of an unaffected falling object. He discovered that when medium resistance is not a factor, falling objects experience a steady increase in speed as they fall. In other words, *all objects fall with a constant acceleration.* Galileo's measurements, translated into modern-day units, showed that an object falling in a vacuum at the earth's surface will increase its speed of fall by approximately 32 ft/sec (about 22 mi/hr or 9.8 m/sec) with each passing second of time.

To clarify these ideas, let's suppose that a stone is released from a substantial height and allowed to fall freely. At the instant of release, the stone is momentarily motionless. But it immediately picks up speed; after one second has elapsed the stone will have accelerated to a speed of 32 ft/sec. During the following 1-second interval the stone will increase speed by an additional 32 ft/sec, so that after 2 seconds its speed will be up to 64 ft/sec. At the end of 3 seconds, the speed will be 64 + 32 = 96 ft/sec, and so on. As long as air resistance is not a factor, the stone will continue to increase its speed at the same uniform rate until it hits the ground. Moreover, in a vacuum *any* falling object—a feather, a grain of sand, a human body—will pick up speed in precisely the same manner. That is, it will gain speed at a steady rate of increase of 32 ft/sec every second. Based on the definition of acceleration as rate of change of velocity, we can say that the acceleration of a falling object is 32 ft/sec/sec—read as 32 feet per second, per second—and abbreviated to 32 ft/sec^2 (see Math Box 3, page 43, if you need to refresh your memory about the units for measuring acceleration).

Galileo's findings can be condensed into a single statement, known as *the law of falling bodies:*

In a vacuum, all bodies on the earth fall with a constant acceleration of 32 ft/sec^2.

Anything that is falling in a vacuum (or under conditions in which air resistance is not significant) is said to be in *free fall.* The acceleration of a body in free fall, 32 ft/sec^2, is usually represented by the letter g and is known as *the acceleration of gravity*. The value quoted here of g = 32 ft/sec² is approximate; its precise value varies slightly over the surface of the earth from 32.09 ft/sec² to 32.26 ft/sec², for reasons that will be explained later. In metric units, g is approximately 9.8 m/sec².

The motion of an object falling in air rather than in a vacuum is considerably more complicated. We'll be examining the consequences of air resistance in some detail later on, so at this point I'll just briefly summarize its main effects. In general, the faster an object falls, the more resistance it encounters from the air. As a result, its acceleration is not constant, but steadily decreases as the object picks up speed and the resistance force grows. Thus the speed of fall increases, but not at a steady rate. Eventually the speed levels off to a constant value known as the *terminal speed*. Generally speaking, the motion of any heavy object will not be noticeably affected by air resistance in the first 2 to 3 seconds of fall. During this time the object falls with very nearly a constant acceleration, but air resistance gradually becomes more and more of a factor thereafter.

Quantities such as the distance that a freely falling object traverses in a given period of time, or the amount of time required for an object to fall a given distance, can be readily calculated using the standard equations of motion (see Math Box 9, page 250). Figure 7.1 shows how the distance and speed of fall increase with time. Since a freely falling object descends with ever-increasing speed, it will cover progressively greater distances in successive time intervals. Note that it falls 16 feet during the first 1-second interval, 48 feet in the next second, and 80 feet in the third second of fall. After 3 seconds, an object in free fall has dropped a total distance of 144 feet (about the height of a 12-story building) and is traveling at a speed of 65 miles/hr. A dramatic demonstration of this was shown in a TV commercial on traffic safety, sponsored a number of years ago by an oil company in its never-ending quest to serve the American public. In the commercial a car was pushed off a 10-story building. From this height the freely falling car hit the ground at a speed of about 60 mi/hr. The car was, of course, totally demolished. The commercial very effectively demonstrated what it would be like to drive your car into a solid wall at 60 mi/hr.

The ability to calculate speeds and distances for falling bodies often leads to interesting insights into sports techniques. For example, one of the standard heights used in platform diving competitions is 10

MATH BOX 9: EQUATIONS OF MOTION FOR AN OBJECT IN FREE FALL

The motion of a freely falling object can be described mathematically by the standard equations of motion (presented previously in Math Box 4, page 45):

$$v_2 = v_1 + at$$

$$d = v_1 t + \frac{1}{2}at^2$$

where
v_1 = initial speed $\quad\quad$ t = elapsed time
v_2 = speed after time t $\quad$ d = distance traveled
a = acceleration

Since an object in free fall has an acceleration of 32 ft/sec² (g) and usually starts from rest, we can simplify the above equations by letting $v_1 = 0$ and $a = g = 32$ ft/sec², as follows:

$$v_2 = gt = 32t$$

$$d = \frac{1}{2}gt^2 = 16t^2$$

In these equations (where we're using customary units) t is always measured in seconds, d in feet, and v in ft/sec. In metric units, g = 9.8 m/sec², d is in meters, and v in m/sec.

The following is a simple illustration of how these equations are used.

The Problem: How long does it take to fall 100 feet? With what speed does the falling object hit the ground?
The Solution: Since d = 16t² and d is 100 feet, we have

$$t^2 = \frac{d}{16} = \frac{100}{16} = 6.25$$

$$t = \sqrt{6.25} = 2.5 \; seconds$$

The speed after 2.5 seconds is $v_2 = gt = (32)(2.5) = 80 \; ft/sec$. (This speed is equivalent to 55 mi/hr—see the conversion chart in Appendix A.)

meters (32.8 feet). A diver falling from a height of 10 meters will hit the water in about 1.4 seconds at a speed of approximately 30 mi/hr. This is sufficient time for the diver to execute various combinations of somersaults and twists. However, the 30-mi/hr impact speed underscores the importance of hitting the water with the diver's body as

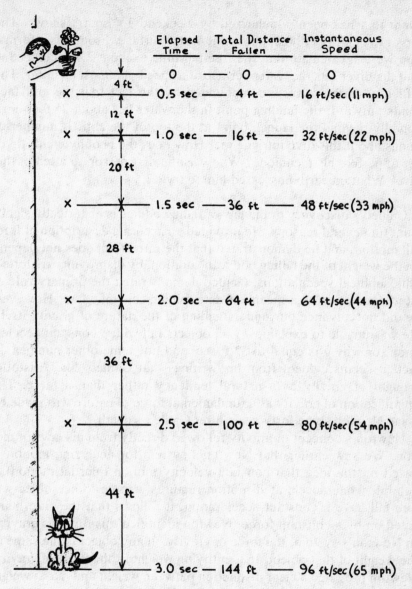

	Elapsed Time	Total Distance Fallen	Instantaneous Speed
	0	0	0
4 ft	0.5 sec	4 ft	16 ft/sec (11 mph)
12 ft			
	1.0 sec	16 ft	32 ft/sec (22 mph)
20 ft			
	1.5 sec	36 ft	48 ft/sec (33 mph)
28 ft			
	2.0 sec	64 ft	64 ft/sec (44 mph)
36 ft			
	2.5 sec	100 ft	80 ft/sec (54 mph)
44 ft			
	3.0 sec	144 ft	96 ft/sec (65 mph)

FIGURE 7.1   Motion of a freely falling object during the first three seconds of fall.

vertical as possible. A vertical entry is required not just for esthetic reasons; it is the least painful way to break the surface of the water when one is traveling at 30 mi/hr.

A more dramatic example is provided by the Acapulco cliff dive, an event that has been popularized by weekend TV sports shows. The top of the cliff is 118 feet above the water surface. From this information we can calculate that the free-fall time is about 2.7 seconds and that the diver hits the water surface at a speed of almost 60 mi/hr. The difficulty of this dive is compounded by the fact that the cliff face slants outward; the landing point in the water lies about 25 feet horizontally beyond the launch point at the top of the cliff. A number of things about this dive intrigue me. How does the neophyte cliff-diver get to perfect his technique? Who was the first person to attempt this dive? What on earth possessed him to try it?

Galileo's discovery of the law of falling bodies is historically significant for several reasons. He provided an accurate description of free-fall motion, and he demonstrated that the rate of fall does not depend on the weight of the falling body. In addition, by disproving Aristotle's philosophical speculations, Galileo demonstrated the primary role of experimentation as a means of determining scientific fact. However, he did not advance our understanding of the nature of gravity itself. He was unable to explain *why* all objects fall with a constant acceleration, or why g is equal to 32 ft/sec^2 and not some other number. In fact, it seems evident from his writings that Galileo, like Aristotle, thought of gravity as a natural tendency rather than a force. The identification of gravity as a fundamental force of nature was made by Isaac Newton some forty years after Galileo's death.

Newton's concept of gravity followed directly from his laws of motion. We saw earlier that Newton's system for analyzing motion is based on the idea that constant-velocity motion (inertial motion) is natural, while accelerated motion requires a force. Since objects in free fall have a constant acceleration, it follows that they are being acted on by a constant force. Newton identified this force as gravity. In Newton's system, the force of gravity on any object is the same as the weight of that object. In identifying weight as the force of gravity, Newton provided a clear distinction between weight and mass: weight is a force, whereas mass is a measure of inertia, or resistance to force. (See Appendix B for the mathematical details.)

To gain a deeper understanding of the nature of gravity, Newton turned to the heavens. Around 1600, the German astronomer Johannes Kepler had worked out the laws that describe the motions of the planets around the sun. However, Kepler could not explain the cause of planetary motion. According to Newton's laws of motion, only straight-line motion is natural or force-free; an object moving on a curved path is necessarily being accelerated by a force. Newton reasoned that since planets travel on curved paths around the sun, their motion is accelerated; therefore they are being acted on by a force of attraction emanating from the sun. Newton identified *this* force as gravity, as well. Using Kepler's laws of planetary motion as a guide, Newton mathematically deduced a formula for the force of gravity. He discovered that the gravitational force between two bodies gets weaker as the distance between them increases.

Newton then used the moon to check his hypothesis. The moon, as it orbits the earth, is being accelerated by a force which Newton identified as the earth's gravity, weakened by the 240,000-mile distance from the earth to the moon. He thereby showed that the earth's gravity extends at least as far as the moon; the same force that causes bodies to fall to the earth's surface also causes the moon to orbit the earth.

By identifying gravity as a force that exists between all bodies in the universe—and not just at the earth's surface—Newton dramatically advanced our understanding of the cosmos. Using his theories of motion and gravitation, Newton was able to account for the specific orbits of the moon and planets, the motions of comets, the existence of tides in the earth's oceans, and many other natural phenomena whose causes were not previously understood. His theories foretold the coming of artificial satellites, travel to the moon, and the other wonders of the space age. And as we shall soon discover, Newton's theories can also be used to help us understand the role of gravity in sports.

But before we go on: to the average nonscientist, mention of the name of Newton usually evokes an image of the genius sitting under an apple tree, deep in thought. Suddenly an apple falls and . . . Eureka! Surely, no discussion of gravity would be complete without at least a brief discussion of this vital historical question: was Newton really inspired to discover gravity by an apple falling from a tree? Historians have researched this with some care. The story originated with Newton himself, who told it to his biographer, William Stukeley, in 1726. Newton claimed that the event took place in the year 1666, on a day when he was sitting in his garden trying to figure out the cause of gravity. However, recent studies of Newton's correspondence by science historians seem to show that he did not arrive at his theory of gravity until 1683! Evidently, Newton made up the apple story to establish a prior claim to the theory over rival scientists who proposed some ideas about gravity in the 1670s, ideas that Newton used to develop the theory of gravitation. Of course, Newton's fear of having to share the glory with others turned out to be unfounded. Despite his idiosyncrasies, Newton's place among the greatest creative geniuses of human history is justifiably and permanently established.

Projectiles

For the most part, Newton's theory of gravitation did not disprove or contradict Galileo's discoveries; instead it offered a means to understand and extend them. The theory of gravity, coupled with Newton's laws of motion, enables us to analyze more complicated motions, including motions that are common to many sports. At this point we can begin to deal with the question posed at the beginning of this chapter—namely, what is the secret of good jumping ability? The key to understanding jumping is to recognize that *it is a form of projectile motion:* a high jumper going over the bar or a basketball player going up for a rebound is moving in essentially the same way as a baseball or golf ball in flight. Their motions are governed by the same physical laws and are described by the same equations.

To the physicist, a projectile is any object that is thrown, pushed, or in any way launched upward and thereafter has no means of self-propulsion. Its motion is governed by inertia, gravity, and any resistance forces it encounters in flight. Everyone knows that "what goes up must come down"—but what decides how high a projectile rises, or how long it stays in the air? As we learned in our earlier discussion of inertia, a projectile must be accelerated by an external force before it is launched. This period of acceleration begins with the object at rest and ends when the accelerating force is removed. For a thrown baseball the acceleration begins at the start of the throw, with the ball resting in the thrower's hand, and ends at the instant the ball is released. The accelerating force arises from contractions of the arm and shoulder muscles, culminating in a push on the ball provided by the thrower's hand. For a jumping basketball player, the acceleration begins at the moment when he begins to push against the floor, and ends at the instant when his feet break contact. Muscles in the feet, legs, and back combine to create a downward push on the floor—and according to the principle of action and reaction, the floor must then push upward on the jumper with an equal force. It is this reaction force, exerted by the floor on the jumper, that accelerates him upward.

Once the object—ball or jumper—loses contact with the source of the force, it is now effectively in free fall. To simplify matters, we'll assume that the effects of air resistance can be ignored, so the only force that can influence the motion of the projectile from here on is gravity. We know that an object released from rest will immediately accelerate downward—but what if the object starts out moving upward? Newton's laws predict that the downward pull of gravity will oppose the upward motion and *decelerate* a rising object at a rate of 32 ft/sec^2. In other words, the object *loses* speed as it rises at a rate of 32 ft/sec every second. Eventually, the instantaneous speed becomes zero, and the object is momentarily suspended in the air. From then on, it falls as any other falling object does—*increasing* speed at a rate of 32 ft/sec^2.

When an object is launched vertically upward, with no sideways or horizontal motion, its subsequent motion is easily analyzed: it decelerates on the way up and accelerates on the way down, at a rate of 32 ft/sec^2, as just described. But let's suppose the object is launched at an angle to the ground—as a baseball is when it comes off a bat—so that it is moving horizontally and vertically at the same time. An important principle of motion, discovered by Galileo and reinforced by Newton's theories, is that *the horizontal and vertical motions proceed independently of each other*. That is, the object continues to move vertically as if it had no horizontal motion, and moves horizontally as if it had no vertical motion.

There's a standard way to test your willingness to accept this principle. Imagine two people—one of them holding a rifle, loaded with a single bullet, in a perfectly level position, the other holding an identical bullet in his hand at exactly the same height above the ground as the rifle barrel. As the rifle holder pulls the trigger, the bullet holder releases his bullet and allows it to fall to the ground. Let's suppose that the two bullets start moving at precisely the same instant from the same height, and that air resistance is not a factor. The question is: which bullet hits the ground first?

Logically, you might argue that the dropped bullet travels a much shorter distance than the one fired from the rifle, and therefore the dropped bullet should hit the ground first. But in fact both bullets hit the ground at exactly the same time! The scientific principle behind this apparently strange result is that horizontal and vertical motions proceed independently, so the fired bullet should fall vertically as if it had no horizontal motion. The fired bullet and the dropped bullet each start out with no initial vertical motion; they are both accelerated downward by gravity; and they are falling from the same height. Therefore they have the same time of fall—and they must hit the ground at the same instant. True, the fired bullet travels a greater distance—but only in the horizontal direction, as a result of the large but purely horizontal speed it acquires as it accelerates down the barrel of the rifle. But this has no effect on the rate of fall of the bullet. This argument holds only if the rifle is held exactly level, however. If the rifle is angled upward, for example, the bullet will leave the barrel with some speed in the vertical direction, and it will then take longer to hit the ground than the dropped bullet (which starts out with no initial vertical speed).

The idea that a horizontally fired projectile falls just as fast as one that is dropped is one of those scientific concepts that are difficult to believe wholeheartedly. Nevertheless, its truth can be readily demonstrated. Here's one illustration. If you let a stone drop from a height of 4 feet, it will fall vertically to the floor in a half-second (Fig. 7.2a). Now suppose you drop the same stone from the same height inside a

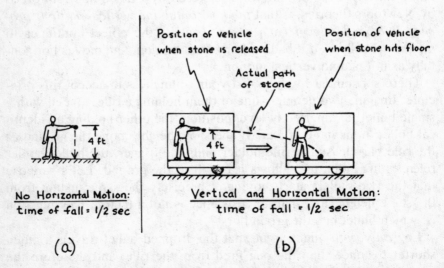

FIGURE 7.2 The independence of vertical and horizontal motion.

moving vehicle: you'll still see the stone fall vertically to the floor in a half-second (Fig. 7.2b). But because of inertia the stone was also moving horizontally, at the same speed as the vehicle, as it fell. Yet it had the same time of fall as in *a*, when its motion was purely vertical. Evidently the horizontal motion of the stone had no effect on its vertical motion. This is a clear demonstration of the independence of horizontal and vertical motion, an essential principle for predicting the path of any projectile.

When air resistance is not a factor, a projectile has a trajectory that can be described in relatively simple mathematical terms. Since gravity is a purely vertical force, it will affect only the vertical component of the projectile's motion. That is, in the vertical direction the projectile will decelerate as it rises and accelerate as it falls, at the usual rate of 32 ft/sec^2. But the horizontal motion is *not* affected by gravity. In fact, in the absence of air resistance there aren't any forces that would affect the horizontal motion. According to Newton's law of inertia, when there are no forces acting on an object, it moves with a constant speed in a straight line. Thus projectile motion consists of free fall in the vertical direction combined with constant-speed motion in the horizontal direction.

The combination of the two motions produces a path that is known to mathematicians as a *parabola*. A typical parabolic trajectory is shown in Figure 7.3. Here the position of the projectile is shown at one-second intervals to illustrate the combination of its vertical and horizontal motions. Note that the projectile covers equal distances in the horizontal direction (because it's moving at constant speed horizontally), while in the vertical direction it slows down as it rises and then speeds up as it falls, as does any object in free fall. Note also that near the peak of the trajectory (from 2 seconds to 4 seconds on the diagram), the height of the projectile does not change very rapidly, because the vertical speed is close to zero. If the projectile takes off with a relatively large horizontal speed, it will travel a good distance horizontally near the peak of its trajectory, while its vertical position changes very little. This feature contributes to the illusion of a jumper "hanging in the air," as if he had willfully suspended himself in flight. Of course, the jumper is not defying the law of gravity, but instead is obeying it rather scrupulously.

I happen to find a parabola a particularly pleasing thing to look at, as geometric figures go. It's much more interesting and esthetic than a simple arc or rainbow (which are just portions of a circle). Also, it is

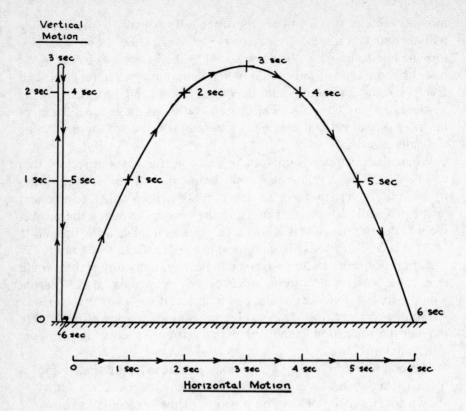

FIGURE 7.3 The parabolic trajectory of a projectile.

one of the few things in sports that the spectator can enjoy more than the participant. To appreciate a parabola, you have to see it from the side. In baseball, the batter and fielder can't see the parabolic shape of a fly ball because they're looking at it end on; the best view is had by the people in the stands. In a basketball game, it's also difficult for the players to see the parabolic path of a 15- or 20-foot shot because they tend to look at the basket rather than the ball, and their concentration is (and should be) focused on getting into position for the action to follow. You can't usually see parabolas on televised sports because the standard camera angles don't show them; perhaps the only exception is the path of a football on a kickoff or punt, if the camera pulls back to show the whole field. No, the best place to see a parabola is at the game, in the stands. Once in a while, take your attention off the movements of the players and just watch the flight of the ball itself, just to enjoy the beauty of a parabola.

Parabolas come in a variety of shapes, ranging from tall and skinny to low and flat. The basic size and shape of a parabolic trajectory depend on the launching velocity—the speed and direction of the projectile at the instant the accelerating force is removed. For example, when an artillery shell is fired from a gun, the speed with which the shell leaves the gun and the angle that the gun makes with the horizontal together determine the height, range, and time of flight of the shell. The launching angle, which can have any value between 0° and 90°, in effect divides the launching velocity into vertical and horizontal components. If the launching angle is 90° to the ground, then the projectile is being sent straight upward; all the speed goes into vertical motion and there is no horizontal component. At the other extreme, a launching angle of 0° means that the projectile is being shot horizontally; here all the speed goes into horizontal motion. When launched at a 45° angle, the projectile starts out with equal amounts of vertical and horizontal speed. If the angle is greater than 45°, the initial vertical component will be larger than the horizontal; the resulting trajectory will tend to be relatively high and more sharply peaked. If the launching angle is less than 45°, then the initial horizontal speed is greater than the vertical, producing a relatively low, flat path.

Because of the independence of horizontal and vertical motion, the height to which any projectile rises (Fig. 7.4) and the amount of time it spends in the air—the "hang time"—are both determined by a single factor: the *vertical speed at the instant of launching*. It follows from the laws of motion that all projectiles launched in a vacuum with the same vertical speed will rise to the same height in the same amount

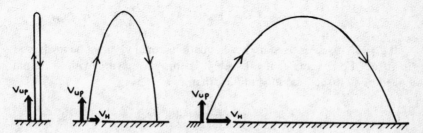

FIGURE 7.4 Maximum height of a trajectory. Projectiles launched with the same vertical speed (v_{up}) attain the same maximum height and time of flight, even if their horizontal speeds (v_H) are not the same.

MATH BOX 10: HEIGHT AND HANG TIME OF A PROJECTILE

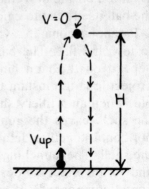

A projectile is launched with an initial vertical speed, v_{up}. It decelerates as it rises, losing speed at a rate of 32 ft/sec² until its instantaneous speed is zero. At this point, the projectile begins to fall back to the ground. The equations of motion (from Math Box 4, page 45)

$$v_2 = v_1 + at$$

$$\text{and} \quad d = v_1 t + \frac{1}{2}at^2$$

can be applied to the two parts of the trajectory. For the rising part, $t = t_{rise}$, $v_1 = v_{up}$, $v_2 = 0$, $d = H$, and $a = -g = -32$ ft/sec2 (the projectile is decelerating as it rises). Substituting these values into the above equations gives us

$$0 = v_{up} - gt_{rise}$$

$$\text{and} \quad H = v_{up}t_{rise} - \frac{1}{2}gt_{rise}{}^2$$

For the falling part of the trajectory, $v_1 = 0$ and $a = g = 32$ ft/sec²; thus

$$H = \frac{1}{2}gt_{fall}{}^2$$

The total time of flight, the hang time, is: $t_H = t_{rise} + t_{fall}$.
The above equations can be combined mathematically to give the following:

$$H = \frac{v_{up}{}^2}{2g} \quad \text{and} \quad t_H = \frac{2v_{up}}{g}$$

If $g = 32$ ft/sec² is used in these equations, then v_{up} must be measured in ft/sec. For example, if a baseball is thrown upward with an initial speed of 80 ft/sec (about 54 mi/hr), then

$$H = \frac{v_{up}{}^2}{2g} = \frac{(80)^2}{2(32)} = 100 \text{ feet}$$

$$t_H = \frac{2v_{up}}{g} = \frac{2(80)}{32} = 5 \text{ seconds}$$

of time, even if they have different weights and different horizontal speeds. Math Box 10, page 260, shows how the height and hang time are related mathematically to the vertical speed.

Vertical Jumping

Now let's apply what we've learned to jumping. As we saw previously, any object, including a human body, moves as if all its mass were concentrated at its center of gravity. Once a jumper loses contact with the ground and becomes a projectile, his center of gravity will follow a path that is mathematically fixed by the launching velocity. There is nothing that the jumper can do, once he is in the air, to change the motion of his center of gravity. There is no way that he can extend his hang time or delay his fall to the ground. One occasionally sees a jumper bend his legs sharply, bringing his heels to the back of his thighs, *after* he's left the ground, in the mistaken notion that this will increase the height of his jump. Basketball fans may remember Dick Barnett, who played for the New York Knicks in the sixties, as one who used this technique whenever he took a jump shot. Not long ago, I had the opportunity to ask Barnett why he always bent his legs after he left the ground. He said that it was a habit he developed as a youngster, and while he recognized that it didn't make him jump any higher, he felt that it helped him to maintain his balance in midair. (There may be some truth to this: according to the principle of angular momentum conservation discussed earlier, bending the knees in midair should rotate the upper body slightly backward in reaction.)

In any case, no arm or leg motions initiated after the jumper is airborne can have any effect on the motion of his center of gravity. Nevertheless, we know for a fact that some athletes can jump higher and stay in the air longer than others. This means simply that the better jumpers have a higher initial vertical speed when they leave the ground. So their success depends not on what they do *after* they leave the ground, but what they do *before* they leave.

Let's begin by analyzing a purely vertical jump (one without any horizontal motion). To start, the jumper bends his knees, drops into a crouch, and swings his arms downward so that his hands are approximately behind his thighs (see Fig. 7.5). From this position, he is ready to begin the upward acceleration of his body. Pushing down forcefully on the floor, he straightens his body at the knees and hips, and swings

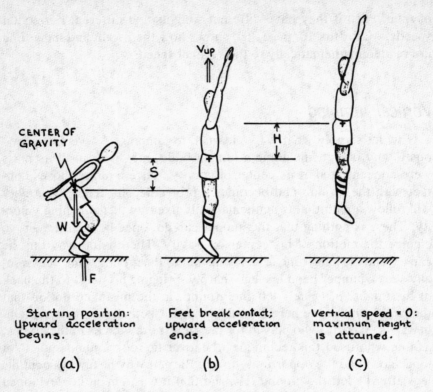

CENTER OF
GRAVITY

W

F

v_{up}

S

H

Starting position:
Upward acceleration
begins.

Feet break contact;
upward acceleration
ends.

Vertical speed = 0:
maximum height
is attained.

(a)

(b)

(c)

FIGURE 7.5   The stages of the vertical jump.

his arms above his head. These actions accelerate his center of gravity upward, increasing its speed until his body is fully extended and his feet leave the floor. The speed attained at this point is the launching speed (v_{up}) that determines how high he will rise and how long he will spend in the air.

From the physiologist's point of view, jumping is an activity that involves many different muscles. It is powered mainly by the contraction of the quadriceps muscle, which extends down the front of the thigh and over the kneecap, and is attached to the lower leg just below the kneecap. When the quadriceps contracts, it straightens the knee and hip joints. To the physicist, the jumper's body is simply an object whose motions can be analyzed mathematically using Newton's laws. The body is acted on by two forces—its weight, W (the force of gravity), acting downward, and the upward reaction force, F, exerted by the floor. When a person is standing relaxed on the floor, these two forces are exactly equal. If the reaction force can be made to exceed the weight, then there will be a net upward force and the body will accelerate upward; the more the reaction force exceeds the jumper's weight, the greater will be the upward acceleration. However, the launching speed depends not only on the amount of acceleration but also on the time interval and distance over which the acceleration occurs.

The interval in which the jumper is accelerating upward—I'm going to call it the *contact time*—is the time that it takes for the jumper to move from his initial crouched position as shown in Figure 7.5a to a stretched-out position (b). During this interval the jumper's feet are pushing downward on the ground, generating the reaction force F. In the same interval, the jumper is straightening his body, raising his center of gravity a distance S, as shown. At this point, the jumper's feet leave the ground, and he becomes a projectile. His CG continues to rise a vertical distance H, which I've named the *jumping height*.

Equations linking the jumping height and hang time to the jumper's launching force and weight can be obtained through an uncomplicated application of Newton's second law (see Math Box 11, page 264). The conclusion is that the jumping height is directly proportional to two factors: (1) the center-of-gravity rise, S, and (2) the force-to-weight ratio, F/W.

The first of these factors, S, depends on how deeply the jumper bends before he begins his jump, and it is a function of the body proportions, jumping style, and strength of the individual. It follows from the physics of jumping that the deeper you crouch (making S larger), the higher you should be able to jump. But crouching too deeply eventually becomes counterproductive; it's rather difficult to jump vertically from a deep squat. There are physiological reasons behind this—one having to do with the process of muscle contraction. A muscle exerts its maximum force when it is slightly stretched— normally when it is about 20% longer than its resting length. Also, the torque exerted by a muscle to rotate a bone at a joint depends on the angle of the joint, since this angle affects the moment arm of the muscle force. So if you start a jump from too deep a crouch, your jumping muscles will be overstretched and will not contract with maximum force or torque. Thus, after a point, the advantage gained by lowering your CG (increasing S) is counteracted by a weaker accelerating force.

For best results, then, the idea is to bend the knees deeply enough

MATH BOX 11: THE PHYSICS OF VERTICAL JUMPING

We begin with Newton's second law, $F = ma$. In jumping, there are two opposing forces, so the net force that accelerates the jumper's body is equal to the upward reaction force, F, minus the weight, W, of the jumper:

$$F - W = ma$$

Here m and a are the jumper's mass and upward acceleration, respectively. The jumper's center of gravity accelerates upward, starting from rest, during the time (t_c) his feet are in contact with the ground. The vertical launching speed v_{up} attained during this interval (using $v_2 = v_1 + at$) is

$$v_{up} = at_c$$

The distance S traveled by the jumper's center of gravity while accelerating upward (using $d = v_1 t + \frac{1}{2}at^2$) is

$$S = \frac{1}{2}at_c^2$$

The distance that the jumper's center of gravity rises after launching, H, and the hang time, t_H (from Math Box 10, page 260), are

$$H = \frac{v_{up}^2}{2g} \qquad \text{and} \qquad t_H = \frac{2v_{up}}{g}$$

We also must make use of the relationship between weight and mass:

$$W = mg$$

Combining these equations, we can obtain the following:

$$H = (F/W - 1)S$$

and

$$t_H = \sqrt{\frac{8H}{g}}$$

In the above, we have assumed a constant force and constant upward acceleration, even though these quantities change during the jump. However, the same result is obtained if we assume F to represent the *average* force exerted during the contact time.

to lower the CG a significant distance, but not so deeply that the leg muscles generate a lot less than their maximum force. You can verify this conclusion through some simple experimentation: see how high you can reach by jumping vertically from a standing start, and then make note of how much you have to bend your knees in order to maximize the height of your jump. If you bend your knees too little, the distance that your CG rises will be too short, and if you bend your knees too much, you will not be able to generate a good accelerating force. There is an optimum knee angle that gives the best result.

The second factor that determines jumping height is the force-to-weight ratio, F/W. This is the launching force (equivalent to the force with which the jumper pushes on the ground during takeoff) divided by his body weight. The launching force arises from muscle contractions as the jumper extends his body; biomechanical measurements show that this force is not constant, but tends to increase until just before the feet leave the ground. Thus the force that enters into the calculations is the *average* force exerted during the contact time. The importance of the force-to-weight ratio reflects the obvious fact that heavy people are not good jumpers—the more you weigh, the more muscle force you have to exert to reach a given jumping height.

There are a few ways for a jumper to increase the upward accelerating force beyond that generated by his own leg muscles. One contributing factor is the upward swing of the jumper's arms as his body rises. The usual purpose of this motion is, of course, to extend one's reach at the top of the jump, but it also contributes to the accelerating force through the action-reaction principle. The upward force exerted by the shoulder and back muscles on the arms in lifting them creates an equal downward reaction force on the body, and this force is transmitted through the muscles and skeleton to the ground. To be fully effective, however, the arm swing must be completed before the feet leave the ground. A jumper can also increase the height of his jump by taking a brief run-up or two-step hop just before the main jump. The effect of the run-up is *not* to convert horizontal motion to vertical motion—because they are independent of one another, this is not possible. However, it does increase the accelerating force in several ways. As the jumper's body descends on the step before the main jump, its downward motion must be decelerated before the upward acceleration of the jump can begin. The deceleration causes the stretching of the same muscles that will be used in the jumping process. "Prestretching" the muscles increases the number of fibers involved in the subsequent contraction, and leads to some elastic energy storage in the muscle—consequently, muscles that have been stretched prior to use tend to contract with even greater force. There may also be a rebound effect from the floor: if the surface has any resiliency, it will be distorted when the jumper lands on the last step of the run-up and will contribute some of its stored elastic energy to push the jumper upward. The extent of this force will depend on the nature of the surface; basketball players who play outdoors on asphalt or concrete and indoors on a wooden floor normally find that they can jump an inch or so higher indoors.

Table 7.1 lists some typical numerical values (calculated from the equations shown in Math Box 11, page 264) showing how the jumping height and hang time are related to the force-to-weight ratio. To simplify matters, I've assumed that the jumper lowers his CG 15 inches before beginning his jump; for most jumpers S ranges between 12 and

---

TABLE 7.1: VERTICAL JUMPING

The following values were calculated assuming that S (the center-of-gravity rise) is 15 inches. For a given force, larger values of S will increase the jumping height, hang time, and contact time proportionally.

H (ft)	F/W	t_c (sec)	v_{up} (ft/sec)	t_H (sec)
0.5	1.40	0.44	5.66	0.35
1.0	1.80	0.31	8.00	0.50
1.5	2.20	0.26	9.80	0.61
2.0	2.60	0.22	11.31	0.71
2.5	3.00	0.20	12.65	0.79
3.0	3.40	0.18	13.86	0.87
3.5	3.80	0.17	14.97	0.94
4.0	4.20	0.16	16.00	1.00
4.5	4.60	0.15	16.97	1.06

H = jumping height (distance center of gravity rises after feet leave ground)
F/W = ratio of launching force to weight of jumper
t_c = contact time (total time in acceleration stage)
v_{up} = launching speed (vertical speed at launching)
t_H = hang time (total time in flight after launching)

18 inches. Also included in the table are calculated values for the vertical launching speed v_{up}, and the contact time, t_c. Looking at the table, we can see that the larger the launching force, the less time the jumper spends accelerating (the contact time gets shorter) and more time in the air (the hang time gets longer). The evident conclusion, then, is that the secret of good jumping is to generate as large a force-to-weight ratio as possible.

Biomechanical research on jumping has shown that a typical athlete can generate an average force of about 2 to 3 times his own weight as he pushes off the ground. According to Table 7.1, a force-to-weight ratio between 2 and 3 corresponds to a jumping height ranging from somewhat more than 1 foot to about 2½ feet. These distances seem rather puny—after all, the world record for the high jump is 7'9", and there are basketball players who are able to place coins on the top of the backboard, 13¼ feet above the floor. However, these accomplishments are deceptive. The typical world-class high jumper is tall, thin, and long-legged—so his center of gravity is already 3 to 4 feet above the floor even before he begins to jump. Similarly, the ability of a basketball player to reach the top of the backboard does not take into account the initial height of his center of gravity or the length of his arms.

Great Jumpers

The best measure of jumping ability, then, is how high a jumper can raise his CG in a standing jump. This can be determined by measuring the difference between a person's jumping reach and his standing reach, with his arms fully extended upward. (This is sometimes called a *Sargent jump:* Dudley Sargent, one of the pioneers of American physical education earlier in this century, found that it was a reliable test of physical ability.) The average jumping height attained in this manner by college students is about 20 inches. This is not an event for which official records are kept—nevertheless, *The Guinness Book of World Records* reports that a standing vertical jump of 4 feet was achieved by basketball player Darrell Griffith in 1976. Since Griffith weighs about 200 lb, this means that during his takeoff he was pushing down on the ground with an average force of about 750 lb.

A calculation of the power requirement for vertical jumping reveals that this activity requires a rather prodigious output. From the definitions of power and work given in Chapter 5, it's possible to estimate the power rating of Griffith's jump at about 12 hp, approximately 9 kilowatts. Of course, the duration of this output is extremely brief, lasting less than 0.2 second.

Even greater vertical leaps have been made by high jumpers. A high jump is, of course, not a purely vertical leap. The jumper needs some horizontal motion to carry him forward over the bar—he gets it from a run-up of several strides—so the path of his center of gravity is a parabola. Nevertheless, the emphasis in this event is on vertical height, so the jumper tries to achieve as large a vertical speed on takeoff as he can. The run-up helps the jumper to create more vertical force. Also, once the jumper plants his takeoff leg, he swings his free leg and both arms upward before he leaves the ground to increase the reaction force. The result is that a somewhat larger accelerating force can be generated in a high jump than in a standing vertical jump. A high jumper tries to clear the bar with his CG as low as possible. For this reason, the jumper must roll his body horizontally over the bar. There are several different techniques for doing this. One is the *straddle style,* in which the jumper goes over face down with his head-to-foot axis parallel to the bar. At the peak of his trajectory, the jumper tries to drape his body over the bar, keeping as much body mass (i.e., his arms and legs) below the level of the bar as he can. Another style is the *Fosbury flop*—named for Dick Fosbury, who won the 1968 Olympics with what was then considered to be a highly unorthodox style (it's now used by many high jumpers). A "flopper" jumps by twisting his body at takeoff so that he goes over head first, but with his back to the bar (Fig. 7.6). By arching his body backward over the bar, the jumper may actually be able to make his CG (which would be outside his body) pass *under* the bar. By perfecting this technique, a flopper may be able to gain a 2- to 3-inch advantage over a straddle-style jumper. One drawback of either style is that the high jumper must use some of his jumping force to give his body the rotation it needs to roll over the bar (in other words, the line of action of the upward accelerating force must be directed slightly away from the jumper's CG).

Now let's see how much a high jumper actually raises his CG in a jump. A typical high jumper is about 6 feet tall. If his CG is located at 58% of his body height (higher than for the average person), then it will be about 3½ feet above the ground. To go over the bar at 7'6", the jumper must raise his CG about 4 feet. In this respect, the most

FIGURE 7.6 Dwight Stones demonstrates the "flop" technique of high jumping. Does his center of gravity go over or under the bar? *(UPI photo.)*

remarkable jumper around is Franklin Jacobs, whose best effort to date is 7′7″—even though he is only 5′8″ tall. His admirers like to point out that he has jumped nearly 2 feet over his own head. But this is not the most appropriate measure of his prowess, because it does not tell us how high he raised his CG. It turns out to be a prodigious 52 inches—which ought to qualify Jacobs as the best high jumper of his time, even if he does not hold the world record.

Many scientists believe that there is a definite upper limit to the height attainable in the high jump, based on such considerations as maximum muscle forces, bone stresses, and power generation. Today's high jumpers may be very close to this limit. Between 1952 and 1962, the record for the high jump advanced from 6′8″ to 7′5″, but in the past twenty years it has increased only a few inches more, to 7′9″. Will anyone ever high jump 8 feet? I'd be willing to bet that it won't happen in this century.

Armed with the knowledge we have gained from an analysis of jumping, we can now make some generalizations about the characteristics of good jumpers. First of all, there is a certain body type that is conducive to natural jumping ability. Obviously, it's a distinct advantage to have long legs; and since the jumper's own weight counteracts the upward acceleration, it helps to be relatively light in weight. In particular, the upper body is essentially dead weight in jumping, so a slender build is a definite asset. These two factors—long legs and a slender upper body—combine to give the jumper a higher center of gravity, which means that he starts his jump at a relatively higher point above the ground. Finally, since the most important muscles for jumping are in the thigh, it obviously helps to have strong thigh muscles. This is an area where the jumper can work to improve his jumping ability, through appropriate weight-training exercises that develop the important jumping muscles.

Is there a racial component to jumping ability? Among most basketball players it is taken almost as an accepted fact that blacks are better jumpers than whites. Some ballplayers refer mockingly to the "white man's disease"—the inability to jump. (Paradoxically, the best high jumpers are Russians and eastern Europeans, evidently a triumph of intensive training and scientific technique.) Understandably, sports scientists are reluctant to study racial differences in athletic performance. Nevertheless, there are physiological variables that would contribute to better innate jumping ability—for example, there are statistical studies showing that black males tend to have proportionally longer legs and lighter upper bodies compared with their white counterparts. One physiological factor that contributes to innate jumping ability is the proportion of fast-twitch to slow-twitch fibers in the jumping muscles. You'll recall that the fast-twitch fibers generate a larger force for a relatively short time, while the slow-twitch fibers produce a more sustained but smaller force. Obviously, the fast-twitch fibers are best suited for good jumping. It's been shown that the best jumpers have a higher ratio of fast-twitch to slow-twitch fibers in their jumping muscles. Scientists generally believe that this ratio is determined by heredity. Could the genetic factor that controls this ratio be racially linked?

Despite all that we have said so far about the scientific aspects of jumping, there still remains the fact that the greatest jumpers—the Baryshnikovs and Ervings—are able to create the *illusion* of extended hang time (Fig. 7.7). Our calculations show (see Table 7.1) that the actual hang time for even an expert jumper is about one second or less. Yet it is what the great jumpers can do with their bodies during this brief moment that creates the illusion. Mikhail Baryshnikov hardly fits our profile of the ideal jumper—he is neither tall nor slender. He has, however, received incomparable training which has provided him with powerful muscles and tremendous body control—and body control is the key. It is the number and quality of different "moves" that the jumper makes while he is in the air that create the illusion of extended hang time; with excellent body control the jumper can make the most of the brief flight time allotted to him by gravity. Through carefully designed and flawlessly performed movements—sharply extending his arms and legs horizontally at the peak of the jump, for example—Baryshnikov can make us think that he has defied gravity.

With his long arms and legs, and huge hands that can hold a basketball as easily as you or I can hold a grapefruit, Julius Erving can create similar illusions. His exceptional body control enables him to make that extra move during a jump that convinces us he can hang in the air. Erving's best moves are made when he takes off from a running start, so that he covers a considerable horizontal distance while airborne. I once saw a game in which Erving got ahead of everyone on a fast break. He began his leap near the free-throw line, about 12 feet from the basket, and as he soared toward the hoop he suddenly spun 180° in midair and dunked the ball over his head, with his back to the basket. My knowledge of the science of jumping enabled me to see that Erving's jump was not unusually long or high—but I could also recognize his midair move as a work of art, a piece of theatre, the creation of an illusion.

Gravity on the Earth

The principles that we've used to analyze vertical jumping and projectile motion in general can be applied to a great many areas of sports, and we'll be devoting the next chapter to this subject. But first I'd like to introduce a few more scientific ideas related to gravity—ideas that lead to subtle and surprising facts about athletic performance. Our subject will be the somewhat mysterious quantity g, the acceleration of gravity, which appears in virtually every equation relating to falling bodies and projectile motion.

Earlier in this chapter, we learned that the numerical value of g, 32 ft/sec², was obtained by Galileo through extensive and careful experi-

FIGURE 7.7   Great jumpers. (ABOVE) Mikhail Baryshnikov *(photo by Nina Alovert)*; (OPPOSITE) Julius Erving *(UPI photo)*.

mentation. Left unexplained were the reasons why g has a value of 32 ft/sec² and not some other number, and why all objects fall to the earth with the same acceleration, regardless of their mass. To resolve these mysteries, we'll have to look at Newton's theory of gravitation in

more detail. This will involve some mathematics, but it will be worth the effort to follow it through.

Newton identified gravity as the force that causes objects to fall to the earth, the moon to revolve around the earth, and the earth and the other planets to revolve around the sun. He concluded from this that gravity is a force of mutual attraction between all bodies in the universe. Using the available astronomical data, Newton worked out a mathematical formula for the strength of this force, deducing that it depends upon the masses of the attracting bodies as well as on the distance between them. Let's suppose that there are two objects—stars, planets, baseballs, whatever you like—identified as "A" and "B," with masses m_A and m_B, respectively, whose centers of gravity are a distance, d, apart. Newton's law of gravity describes the force of gravitational attraction (F_{grav}) between the two objects as follows:

$$F_{grav} = \frac{Gm_A m_B}{d^2}$$

Let's see what this means. First of all, the quantity G that appears in the equation is called the *universal constant of gravitation*. Basically, it's a conversion factor that is used to change the units of mass and distance on the right side of the equation to the units of force on the left (just as we use conversion factors to change from miles to kilometers, for example). The numerical value of G, determined by actual measurement, turns out to be very small—it equals 0.0000000343 in customary units, and 0.0000000000667 in metric units. In words, then, the force of gravity between two objects is calculated by multiplying their masses, dividing by the square of the distance between them, then multiplying this result by the constant G.

In describing the effects of gravity at the earth's surface, Newton identified the weight of any object as the gravitational force of attraction between that object and the earth itself. This force depends on the mass of the object, represented by m, and the mass of the earth, M_E. Newton had shown that the appropriate distance to use to calculate the force of gravity is the distance between the centers of gravity of the two objects. In this case, the distance from the center of the earth to the center of an object on the surface is simply the radius of the earth, R_E (which is approximately 4000 miles). If we make these substitutions ($m_A = m$, $m_B = M_E$, $d = R_E$) in the law of gravity we get an equation for the weight (W) of an object at the earth's surface:

$$W = F_{grav} = \frac{GmM_E}{R_E^2}$$

The weight of an object is related to its mass by the equation $W = mg$ (as a consequence of Newton's second law, $F = ma$; see Appendix B). If we replace W by mg in the preceding equation, we get

$$mg = \frac{GmM_E}{R_E^2}$$

Now, since m, the mass of the object, appears on both sides of the equation, we can divide it out, leaving us with

$$g = \frac{GM_E}{R_E^2}$$

This is a rather important result, because it relates the acceleration of gravity, g, to the mass and radius of the earth (the universal constant of gravitation G appears in the equation to balance the units of measurement). This answers our question as to why g equals 32 ft/sec^2 and not some other number: *the numerical value of g depends on the specific values of the mass and the radius of the earth.* If the earth had a different mass or radius, g would have a different value.

Newton's theory also explains why all bodies fall to the earth with the same acceleration, regardless of their mass: g does not depend on the mass of the object because m appears on both sides of the equation, and cancels out. We can understand this in nonmathematical terms in the following way. The force of gravity acting on any object depends on its mass; more massive objects are attracted to the earth with a greater force. But the more mass an object has, the greater its inertia or resistance to force. The greater gravitational force and greater inertia exactly counterbalance, so all objects wind up falling with the same acceleration.

As far as sports is concerned, the most notable consequence of Newton's explanation of the value of g is the discovery that *g depends on the distance to the center of the earth.* The earth is not perfectly spherical, so all points on the surface are *not* the same distance from the center; therefore g does not have the same value everywhere on the earth. Since the flight of a projectile depends on g, it follows that athletic performance in any sport or event involving projectile motion will depend on the location. In fact, some scientists have suggested that athletic records, particularly in track and field events, ought to be adjusted to take account of the value of g at the place where the record is set.

Let's see if there's any merit to this suggestion. Are the differences in g from place to place on the earth really large enough to give an athlete a significant advantage or disadvantage? There are basically two sources of variation in g: one is the altitude of the location, and the other is its latitude (position with respect to the equator). The variation with altitude comes from the fact that the higher the altitude of a location above sea level, the farther it is from the center of the earth. Thus the higher the altitude, the lower g will be. The following table shows how g changes with altitude, assuming a value of g at sea level of exactly 32.200 ft/sec^2:

Altitude (ft above sea level)	g (ft/sec^2)	% Decrease in g
0	32.200	—
2000	32.194	0.019
4000	32.188	0.037
6000	32,182	0.056
8000	32.175	0.078
10,000	32.169	0.096
12,000	32.163	0.115

There are only a few large cities at high altitudes where athletic competitions might be held. Bogota, Colombia, is 8500 ft above sea level; Addis Ababa, Ethiopia, is at 8000 ft; Mexico City (site of the 1968 Olympics) is at 7350 ft; Santa Fe, New Mexico, is 7000 ft above sea level. In these locations, the acceleration of gravity is only about 0.06% to 0.08% smaller than at sea level. As a result, the advantage to the athlete is rather small. For example, any projectile that travels 200 ft at sea level would travel about 2 inches farther at a 7500-ft altitude due to the lower gravity.

A more substantial variation in g occurs as a result of the earth's daily rotation. Each day, every point on the earth's surface is carried on a circular path around the earth's north-to-south axis. However, points that are on or close to the equator traverse a larger circle in the course of a day, while points that are closer to the north or south pole travel on smaller circles. Accordingly, the speed of daily rotation varies along the earth's surface from a maximum of about 1040 mi/hr at the equator to zero at the poles.

The natural tendency of any object is to travel in a straight line. Because of the earth's rotation, any object on its surface would naturally fly off into space if it were not held down. Earlier we learned that a centripetal force is needed to keep any object moving in a circle—and in this case, it's the earth's gravitational pull that provides the centripetal force. The result is an effective weakening of the force with which objects are held to the earth, since a portion of the gravitational force of attraction must be used for centripetal force. Because the rotational speed is highest at the equator, more centripetal force is needed there than anywhere else on the earth's surface. As a result, the measured force of gravity—and consequently the acceleration of gravity—is smallest at the equator and largest at the poles, where no centripetal force is required. A further variation in gravity arises from the fact that the earth's rotation causes it to bulge outward at the equator and flatten at the poles. Since the poles are closer (by about 13 miles) to the center of the earth than the equator is, the acceleration of gravity at the poles will be correspondingly greater.

Thus the rotation of the earth makes the acceleration of gravity at any point on the surface dependent on its distance from the equator, as measured by its *latitude* (lines of latitude are parallel to the equator; they range from 0° at the equator to 90° at the poles). The following table shows how the value of g changes with latitude:

Latitude	g (ft/sec²)	% Decrease in g
90° (the poles)	32.258	—
80°	32.253	0.016
70°	32.238	0.062
60°	32.215	0.133
50°	32.188	0.217
40°	32.158	0.310
30°	32.130	0.397
20°	32.108	0.465
10°	32.093	0.512
0° (the equator)	32.088	0.527

As you can see, the variations in g due to latitude are more substantial than the altitude variations. An athlete definitely gains an advantage by performing at sites closer to the equator. For example, a 70-foot shot put made in Oslo, Norway (latitude 60°N), would travel 70′1″ in Montreal, Canada (45°N), 70′2″ in Cairo, Egypt (30°N), and 70′3″ in Caracas, Venezuela (10°N). A 300-foot javelin throw in Moscow, USSR (56°N), would travel 301 feet in Lima, Peru (12°S). Should these differences be taken into account in validating world records? Before answering this question, let's take a look at what ought to represent the most extreme advantage ever given to world-class athletes—the 1968 Olympic Games in Mexico City. This site is not only close to the equator (its latitude is 19°N) but it is also at high altitude (7350 ft). As a result, the acceleration of gravity is only 32.085 ft/sec² —0.41% lower than in Helsinki, Finland (60°N), site of the 1952 Olympics, and 0.28% lower than in Munich, Germany (48°N), where the 1972 Olympics were held. In any event involving projectile motion—i.e., all the throwing and jumping events—athletes gained about 4 additional inches per 100 feet of distance because of the lower gravity as compared with sea level. The advantage ranged from an extra ½ inch in the high jump to a full foot in the javelin throw.

Should Olympic and world records be adjusted to take differences in gravity into account? In events such as the shot put or hammer throw, the athlete is essentially pitting his strength against the force of gravity, and it seems only fair to equalize the competition for a world record by making sure that all participants are competing against the same amount of gravity. For example, a javelin throw of 310 feet in Helsinki would actually represent a greater effort than a throw of 310'10" in Mexico City, yet the latter would be considered as the better achievement.

Nevertheless, the idea of adjusting world records for differences in gravity has attracted virtually no support. I suspect that most people find it difficult to believe that the advantages of a lower gravity are large enough to merit consideration, even for the relatively extreme situation that prevails at Mexico City. In fact, there is a more compelling reason for adjusting world records for differences in altitude. The air becomes thinner at higher altitudes; at 7500 feet, the atmospheric pressure is only 75% of its sea-level value. There are physiological disadvantages to performing at high altitude, as we discussed earlier. On the other hand, projectiles as well as the athletes themselves experience less air resistance, enabling them to throw and jump greater distances.

The consequences of lower air resistance, unlike those of lower gravity, are not easy to calculate with any precision. Later, I'll assess the extent to which track and field athletes are aided by performing at high altitude. At that point we'll return to the question of whether or not world records should be adjusted to take into account such external factors as altitude, temperature, wind, and gravity.

There is, however, a circumstance under which athletic records would undoubtedly have to be adjusted for gravity. This requires a bit of fantasizing, a look into the next century, when people from the earth have begun to colonize the moon and planets. The time will come when one group of workers decides to challenge the guys who work over in the next crater to a game of softball. Eventually, the middle managers and upper-echelon administrators will want to set up tennis courts or a golf course. Before the end of the next century, we might see a major league team on the moon, or the first Olympics on Mars. But what kinds of problems will interplanetary athletes have to contend with?

Experts generally agree that the moon and Mars are the only bodies in the solar system that could support extensive colonization by earthlings. Since Mars has an extremely thin atmosphere and the moon has none at all, the colonists would have to work in space suits or in enclosed, air-filled, pressurized bubbles. This means that athletic events would have to be held in domed stadiums with artificial playing surfaces.

But what is the force of gravity like on these bodies? Before the days of Galileo and Newton, there was no scientific basis for even speculating about gravity on other planets. But thanks to Newton's theory of gravity we can now *calculate* a value for g for any celestial body. The moon is a large, massive body, so it must exert a gravitational force on any objects at or near its surface. The strength of this force will depend on the mass and radius of the moon in exactly the same way that gravity on the earth's surface depends on the mass and radius of the earth.

Astronomers have been able to make reliable measurements of the moon's mass (it's about 1/80 of the earth's mass) and radius (1078 miles, about 27% of the earth's radius). From these data the value of g can be calculated. It turns out that

$$g_{moon} = 5.33 \text{ ft/sec}^2 = (1/6) g_{earth}$$

Similar data are available for the planet Mars, where g turns out to have a value of 12.3 ft/sec^2, about 38% of g on the earth. On the moon, where gravity is one-sixth as strong as on earth, all objects will weigh one-sixth as much as they do on the earth (so a 240-lb defensive end will tip the scales at 40 lb!). However, the *mass* of any object—its resistance to force—remains the same. According to Newton's second law, the force required to accelerate an object depends on its *mass* rather than its weight. It would therefore take the same amount of force to produce a given acceleration on the moon as on the earth —so our 40-lb defensive end will be just as difficult to push aside. For the same reason, runners will not be able to accelerate more rapidly on the moon, even though they weigh less.

But projectile motion will be affected considerably. For the same launching speed and angle, a projectile will travel six times farther, rise six times higher, and remain in flight six times longer than on the earth. Under these conditions, athletics will be transformed completely. For example, anyone who can raise his center of gravity 3 to 4 feet in a vertical jump on earth will raise it 18 to 24 feet on the moon —so a 25-foot high jump would be commonplace. The game of basketball would be totally confused by this ease of jumping, and by the fact that both the players and the basketball would take six times longer to go up and to come down. How could baseball be played if a routine fly ball travels one-third of a mile and stays in flight for 30 seconds? Baseball stadiums would have to be as big as golf courses, and golf courses would occupy a whole county. In the first Lunar Olympics, there would be a 450-foot shot put, a 175-foot long jump, and a 1600-foot hammer throw. Will these feats be recorded on an equal basis with those of earthbound athletes?

8 / WHAT GOES UP MUST COME DOWN

Slowly drifting backward, an outfielder settles under a high fly ball. A quarterback throws a long pass to his receiver speeding down the sidelines. From the top of the free-throw circle, a basketball player arcs a jump shot cleanly through the hoop. A golfer lofts a shot from the fairway onto the green, 100 yards away. These are common scenes from our most popular sports—events that seem unremarkable to the typical sports fan, belying the years of practice required before such plays can be made routinely.

The events I've described have a common link: they all depend on the ability of the athlete to judge the trajectory of a projectile. This is a skill that takes a long time to master, and it is essential to success in many sports. Whether the athlete is launching a projectile or catching one, whether he uses all his strength to send a projectile as far as possible or controls his effort to send it a specific distance, the basic principles that govern its flight are always the same. These principles can be readily identified and used to pinpoint the factors that determine the trajectory of any projectile. On this basis, one can understand the techniques used to launch or catch projectiles in sports, and may even discover ways to improve them. With these goals in mind, we'll first look at the basic theory of projectile motion, and then survey some of the sports in which it plays a part.

Trajectories

Let's begin with a brief review of the main scientific concepts on which the theory of projectile motion is based:

1. Objects fall because they are attracted to the earth by the force of gravity. This force causes all objects to accelerate toward the earth with a constant acceleration of 32 ft/sec^2 (g).
2. Once a projectile is launched and is moving freely, its motion is affected only by inertia (its natural tendency to move at constant velocity) and gravity. The horizontal component of the motion (governed by inertia) and the vertical component (governed by gravity and inertia) proceed independently of each other.
3. The trajectory of any projectile is a parabola whose size and shape depend entirely on the launching speed and launching angle. Since the earth's gravity accelerates all objects at the same rate regardless of weight, the trajectory of a projectile does not depend on its weight, size, or shape.
4. The foregoing principles hold true only when the projectile is moving in a vacuum or is not significantly affected by the resistance of the medium through which it is moving.

In studying projectile motion, we are generally interested in three aspects of the trajectory. These are the *maximum height* (the vertical distance from the ground to the peak of the parabola); the *horizontal range* (the horizontal distance from launch point to landing point); and the *time of flight* (the elapsed time from launching to landing), also known as the *hang time*. Up to now, we've been stressing the vertical aspects of projectile motion (as it pertains to jumping) and have been mainly concerned with the maximum height. However, for most sports and athletic events, the horizontal range is the most important factor: the goal is to make the projectile travel some specific distance (golf, basketball) or go as far as possible (shot put, long jump). Sometimes the main goal is to make the time of flight as large as possible—one example being the football punt, where the idea is to have a long hang time so that the punting team can get downfield to stop the runback. There are also situations where the goal is to get the best combination of two of these factors.

Each of the three quantities—maximum height, horizontal range, and time of flight—depends in a specific mathematical way on the launching speed and launching angle. (The exact equations are given in Math Box 12, below). Without getting into the details, I'll describe how each of these factors affects the trajectory.

The influence of the launching speed is a fairly obvious one: the greater the launching speed, the longer and higher the trajectory will be. Thus for a specific launching angle, the maximum height, horizontal range, and time of flight will all increase as the launching speed is

---

MATH BOX 12: THE EQUATIONS OF PROJECTILE MOTION

The mathematical derivation of the equations of projectile motion from basic principles is straightforward but lengthy. Accordingly, I have simply presented the final equations without explaining their origins. (The more mathematically inclined and interested reader can look up their derivation in any introductory college physics textbook.) A summary of the basic ideas of trigonometry (as well as a table of values for the sine, cosine, and tangent) can be found in Appendix C.

We'll assume that the projectile is launched with an initial velocity v_0, directed at an angle A with the horizontal, as shown:

The velocity vector can be resolved into vertical and horizontal speed components, as follows:

vertical: $\quad v_{up} = v_0 \sin A$
horizontal: $v_H = v_0 \cos A$

The equations that describe the characteristics of the parabolic trajectory of a projectile traveling over level ground are as follows:

Maximum height: $\quad H = \dfrac{v_{up}^2}{2g} = \dfrac{1}{2g} (v_0 \sin A)^2$

Time of flight: $\quad t_H = \dfrac{2v_{up}}{g} = \dfrac{2}{g} (v_0 \sin A)$

Horizontal range: $\quad R = \dfrac{2v_{up}v_H}{g} = \dfrac{2v_0^2}{g} (\sin A)(\cos A)$

increased. In field events such as the shot put or hammer throw, where the goal is to throw a heavy weight as far as possible, the athlete's main task is to generate a large force to accelerate the weight —the larger the launching speed, the longer and higher the projectile will travel. Yet in the throwing events, having the strength to achieve a large launching speed is not the only consideration; the direction of the throw is almost equally important. In fact, the ability to throw a projectile consistently at the best launching angle can often override considerations of strength.

Now let's see how the launching angle affects the trajectory. If the launching speed is held fixed, what angle produces the greatest height, range, and time of flight? It turns out that the greatest maximum height will be attained if the launching angle is 90°, thereby putting all the speed into the vertical direction. Interestingly, the time of flight also depends on the launching angle in exactly the same way—the projectile stays in the air longest when it is launched vertically. As the launching angle is made closer to the horizontal (0° angle) the trajectory becomes lower and flatter, and the time of flight becomes shorter.

The way in which the launching angle affects the horizontal range is a bit more complicated. If the launching angle is high (close to 90°), the projectile stays in flight for a relatively long time, but doesn't travel very far horizontally. If the launching angle is low (close to 0°), the speed is concentrated in the horizontal direction, but the time of flight is relatively short, so the projectile doesn't get to travel very far before it hits the ground. Evidently, the greatest horizontal range is obtained for a launching angle somewhere between the two extremes of 0° and 90°. In fact, a detailed mathematical analysis of the problem shows that *the greatest horizontal range is achieved with a launching angle of 45°.*

To help you get a feeling for the way the launching angle affects projectile motion, I've drawn some graphs showing how the maximum height, horizontal range, and time of flight all depend on the launching angle (Fig. 8.1). The graphs show clearly how the maximum height and time of flight both get larger as the launching angle becomes more vertical, and how the horizontal range gets larger as the launching angle gets closer to 45°. Notice also that the horizontal range is the same on either side of 45°: the projectile covers the same horizontal range for 30° as it does for 60°, for 20° as for 70°—in general, the range is the same for any pair of angles that add up to 90°. Some typical trajectories (all with the same launching speed) are shown in Figure 8.2.

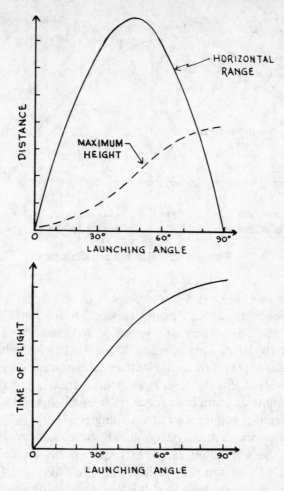

FIGURE 8.1 Dependence of trajectory features on the launching angle.

The fact that a launching angle of 45° produces the greatest horizontal range is a very useful piece of information. If the launching speed is fixed, but the projectile can be aimed at any angle—and the goal is to send it as far as possible—then the projectile will travel the greatest horizontal distance if it is sent off at a 45° angle. But very often the goal is not to have the projectile go as far as possible, but rather to have it travel a specific distance—for example, when an artillery shell is being aimed at a target 1000 yards away, or in a simple game of catch where you are throwing to someone 100 feet away from you. How can this be done with the least amount of effort? By turning the basic principle around, we find that *to cover a specific distance using*

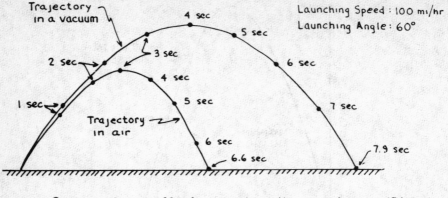

Launching Speed : 100 mi/hr
Launching Angle : 60°

Trajectory in a vacuum

Trajectory in air

4 sec
5 sec
2 sec
3 sec
4 sec
6 sec
1 sec
5 sec
7 sec
6 sec
6.6 sec
7.9 sec

Range in Air :   323 ft   Max. Height in Air :   174 ft
Range in Vacuum : 581 ft   Max. Height in Vacuum : 252 ft

FIGURE 8.2   Parabolic trajectories.

the smallest launching speed, the projectile should be launched at a 45° angle. For instance, to throw a baseball to a point 200 feet away, the thrower must give the ball a speed of 86 ft/sec if it is thrown at a 60° angle, or 100 ft/sec if thrown at a 20° angle. But if the ball is thrown at a 45° angle, a speed of only 80 ft/sec is required to make it travel the same 200 feet. So the lowest launching speed, and therefore the smallest amount of launching force, is needed to send a projectile a given distance if it is launched at a 45° angle.

These conclusions must be qualified somewhat. A 45° launching angle gives the maximum range or requires the smallest launching speed provided that the projectile is traveling over level ground—in other words, *the launching and landing points must be at the same elevation.* If the projectile is being shot up an incline, the launch angle needed to achieve the greatest horizontal range must be greater than 45°—producing a higher trajectory to compensate for the fact that the ground is sloping upward to meet the projectile. But if the ground is sloping downward, a flatter trajectory, with more horizontal speed, can be used, so the launching angle for maximum range will be less than 45°.

It is possible to show mathematically that the launching angle for maximum horizontal range on an incline differs from 45° by an amount equal to half the angle of the incline (see Math Box 13, page 287). The difference is *added* to 45° if the projectile is launched uphill, and *subtracted* from 45° if the projectile is going downhill. For example, suppose that a projectile is being launched up a 10° incline: then max-

MATH BOX 13: EQUATIONS FOR PROJECTILE MOTION ALONG AN INCLINE

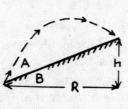

Uphill Launch

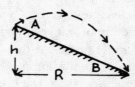

Downhill Launch

Optimum launch angle (for maximum horizontal range, R):

$$A_m = 45° + \frac{1}{2}B \qquad\qquad A_m = 45° - \frac{1}{2}B$$

where tan B = h/R

Maximum horizontal range (when launch angle = A_m):

$$R = \frac{V_o^2}{g}\sqrt{1 - 2gh/V_o^2} \qquad\qquad R = \frac{V_o^2}{g}\sqrt{1 + 2gh/V_o^2}$$

Horizontal range (for any launch angle):

$$R = \frac{V_o^2}{g}\sin 2A \times \qquad\qquad R = \frac{V_o^2}{g}\sin 2A \times$$

$$\left(1 + \sqrt{1 - 2gh/(V_o \sin A)^2}\right) \qquad \left(1 + \sqrt{1 + 2gh/(V_o \sin A)^2}\right)$$

imum horizontal range will be attained by launching at an angle of $45° + \frac{1}{2}(10°) = 50°$. If the same projectile were to be launched down a 10° incline, the launching angle for maximum range would be $45° - \frac{1}{2}(10°) = 40°$. One last point: these angles maximize the *horizontal* distance from launch point to landing point, not the distance along the incline.

This particular feature of projectile motion may seem, at first, hardly worth our notice, but it does have relevance in a few sports. One example is the shot put (the shot is launched from the thrower's hand, which is higher than the landing point); another is basketball shooting, where the launch point (the shooter's hand) is usually lower than the landing point (the 10-foot-high basket). Knowing the best launching angle in such activities can lead to improved performance, as we shall see later.

Over the past few pages, I've tried to present, as simply as possible, some of the important results of the theory of projectile motion. Once again, let me emphasize that these conclusions are strictly correct only for projectile motion in a vacuum—for example, a 45° launching angle does *not* produce the greatest horizontal range if air resistance measurably alters the trajectory. In such circumstances, we can only make some very general statements about the motion of the projectile and defer discussion of the details until the next chapter. But if the motion is affected by air resistance only slightly or not at all, then we can use our results—including the equations of projectile motion found in Math Box 12, page 283—to make predictions and draw conclusions that turn out to be useful and fairly accurate.

The flight of a golf ball is very strongly affected by air resistance, not only because of the small size and weight of the ball, but also because of the backspin that is imparted to the ball when it is hit properly. (For reasons that will be explained later, a backspinning ball tends to stay in the air somewhat longer than it would otherwise.) Since air resistance is such an important influence, we can't use the projectile motion equations with any validity. However, we can still make some general observations. In fact, the contents of a bag of golf clubs reveal the extent to which the principles of projectile motion are put to use. The faces of the clubs are inclined at various angles, so that each club produces a different launching angle when it hits the ball. The woods, which are used for long-distance drives from the tee or fairway, have faces that are inclined only slightly—about 10° to 15° —from the vertical (we will see why this is so in the last chapter). Progressing from the 1-wood (the driver) to the 4-wood, the face angle becomes a bit more inclined, thereby increasing the launching angle. As a result, the 4-wood tends to produce drives that are higher and shorter than those obtained with the other woods. The irons, on the other hand, are used for accuracy and placement rather than distance. The progression from the 1-iron to the 9-iron is marked by successively greater inclination of the face of the club, ranging from about 20° for the 1-iron to 45° for the 9-iron. If the golfer swings every iron in exactly the same way, always imparting the same force to the ball, then the trajectory of the shot will vary according to the choice of club; the drives will get successively higher and shorter as higher-numbered (and more steeply angled) irons are used. Generally, each iron produces a drive that is about 10 to 15 yards longer than that of the next higher-numbered iron in the sequence. The golfer who knows the distances he can get with each of his clubs should be able to develop considerable accuracy on his shorter drives and approach shots.

The relationship among launching speed, launching angle, and the horizontal range and time of flight also plays a part in football kicking strategy. On a punt or kickoff, the kicker has two goals in mind: one is to kick the ball as far downfield as possible, and the other is to have a long hang time to cut down the kick return. However, the theory of projectile motion shows that these goals can't be satisfied simultaneously: the greatest distance occurs when the football is kicked at a 45° angle, and the greatest hang time is achieved by kicking at a 90° angle. If the football is kicked at a 45° angle to gain distance, the time of flight will be relatively short, inviting the danger of a long runback. If the football is kicked at a 90° angle it will have a long hang time—but it will come down at the same point from which it was kicked. So the problem for the kicking team becomes: how much hang time should be sacrificed in order to kick the football a significant distance downfield?

Unfortunately, the trajectory of a football is significantly altered by air resistance, so the projectile motion equations cannot provide us numerical answers for solving this dilemma. Later on, when we treat the effects of air resistance in some detail, we'll see how kickers arrive at the best strategic compromise between distance and hang time.

The Long Jump

Projectile motion is a feature of a number of track and field events. In the long jump, the projectile is the athlete himself. The jumper is allowed a long running start—a distance of 120 to 160 feet is usual—up to the takeoff point. At takeoff, the jumper pushes off and launches his body into a parabolic trajectory. While airborne, the jumper is a projectile; there is nothing he can do to increase his distance or time of flight. Whatever motions he makes while in flight serve only to maintain his stability and to prepare for the landing. The jumper tries to land with his feet forward of his body—but not too far forward, for if he falls backward upon landing, the jumping distance will be measured to the point where his seat hits the ground. His goal is to pitch forward after landing.

The long jump has a venerable history, dating back to the ancient Olympics in the seventh century BC. At that time, athletes jumped while holding weights in each hand. The purpose of these weights is not entirely certain. Some think that they were thrown backward by the jumper in midflight, giving him an added push forward through the principle of action and reaction. Other scholars believe that the weights were not thrown, but were held in the hands to be swung backward or forward to maintain balance in flight.

The long jumper's main problem with balance is that he acquires some forward rotation (and angular momentum) at the takeoff. Since he can't stop this rotation entirely once he is airborne (because of the conservation of angular momentum), the jumper must at least counteract its effects. A forceful forward swing of the arms will cause his legs to rotate forward—a maneuver that would be enhanced by holding weights in the hands to increase the moment of inertia of the arms.

The world record for the long jump is 29'2½", set by Bob Beamon at the Mexico City Olympics in 1968. Beamon's jump is considered to be one of the most astounding sports feats ever—not only because it broke the existing world record by nearly 2 feet, but also because no one, not even Beamon himself, came close to this distance in the ensuing 14 years. (Some track and field enthusiasts have discredited Beamon's record because it was set in the rarefied air of Mexico City —a matter we'll consider more closely in the final chapter.) Only a few other long jumpers have ever exceeded 28 feet. One of these is Carl Lewis, who jumped 28'10¼" in June 1983, the second best long jump ever. Based on his progress to date, Lewis could very likely break Beamon's record before too long.

Since the goal of the long jumper is to travel as great a horizontal distance as possible, we would expect the jumper to try to launch his body at a 45° angle. Surprisingly, world-class long jumpers typically have launch angles between 20° and 22°. Are they unaware of this important physical principle? The answer is that it is impractical, if not impossible, to launch a successful long jump at a 45° angle. When any projectile is launched at a 45° angle, its horizontal and vertical speed components are equal—so to achieve a 45° takeoff, a long jumper must provide a vertical speed to match the horizontal speed he has gained in his run-up. Let's assume that our athlete can jump as well as a top-class high jumper, and is able to raise his center of gravity about 3½ feet. Consulting Table 7.1, we find that to jump 3½ feet vertically requires a vertical launching speed of nearly 15 ft/sec. So to launch himself at a 45° angle, our jumper would have to attain a horizontal speed of 15 ft/sec in his run-up. But if we calculate the length of the jump achieved at these speeds (using the equation for horizontal range in Math Box 12, page 283), we find that the distance will be only 14 feet—less than half of the world record.

The explanation for this poor performance lies in the fact that the typical long jumper can run a lot faster than 15 ft/sec. A more likely running speed is 30 ft/sec—equivalent to running a 100-yard dash in 10 seconds. With a horizontal speed of 30 ft/sec and a vertical speed of 15 ft/sec at takeoff, the jump would cover a distance of 28 feet— most definitely a winning effort. With these speeds, the launching angle would be 26.6°, and it is quite evident that the higher launching speed more than compensates for the fact that the angle is much less than the optimum 45°. Of course, it would be even better if the jumper could match his horizontal speed of 30 ft/sec with a vertical speed of 30 ft/sec—but this speed translates to a vertical leap of 14 feet, which is quite beyond the ability of any human.

The horizontal and vertical speeds of 30 ft/sec and 15 ft/sec, respectively, that I've ascribed to our hypothetical long jumper by way of illustration differ somewhat from the actual speeds achieved by the best performers in this event. Olympic-level long jumpers generally attain horizontal speeds of about 32 ft/sec and vertical speeds at take-off of about 13 ft/sec (raising the jumper's CG by about 2.6 feet). At these speeds the calculated horizontal distance is 26 ft. However, this represents just the distance covered by the jumper's CG. He can add more than 2 feet to this distance by landing with his feet ahead of his body. On the other hand, the jump will always be shortened somewhat by the effect of air resistance.

Thus to be outstanding in the long jump, an athlete must be a great sprinter as well as a great jumper. (Bob Beamon ran the 100-yard dash in 9.5 seconds, and Carl Lewis has run the 100 meter in 9.96 seconds, only 0.01 second off the world record.) However, it is the jumper's ability to gain vertical speed that determines the hang time and length of a long jump. He cannot convert any part of his horizontal speed into vertical speed; he generates his vertical speed only by accelerating upward at takeoff—a feat that is particularly difficult because the jumper's great horizontal speed limits the contact time that he needs to accelerate his body vertically. Thus the jumper must compromise his speed somewhat in order to provide a little more time to accelerate vertically.

The Shot Put

There are four major Olympic throwing events—discus, javelin, shot put, and hammer throw. The flight of a discus or a javelin is significantly shaped by air resistance, so we will defer a discussion of their motions to a later chapter. In the shot put, the aim is to propel a 16-pound, 5-inch-diameter ball (the "shot") as far as possible. The shot is not thrown in the usual way; rather the shot-putter starts with his arm bent and the shot tucked behind his ear, and then pushes the shot up and out by extending his arm. The shot must be launched (or "put") from within a circle 7 feet in diameter, and the shot-putter gains a small amount of horizontal speed by moving across the circle with a two-step run-up prior to the put. But most of the speed acquired by the shot as it is being accelerated comes from the force applied by the shot-putter's arm.

A formidable amount of force is required to put the shot. World-class shot-putters typically achieve distances of 70 feet (the present official world record is 72′8″). For a projectile to cover this distance (assuming the optimum launching angle and no air resistance), it must be launched with a speed of about 45 ft/sec. As the shot-putter extends his arm (a distance of about 3 to 4 feet) he must apply enough force to accelerate the shot from 5 ft/sec (his approximate run-up speed) to 45 ft/sec. Using the basic equations of motion and Newton's second law, we can calculate that a force of roughly 150 lb is required. Thus the effort needed to put a shot 70 feet is equivalent to that required to press a 150-lb dumbbell with one hand. This is why shot-putters are built like weight-lifters, with bulky, heavily muscled bodies.

The optimum launching angle for the shot put is *not* 45°, because the launch point is higher than the landing point. The shot becomes a projectile at a point that is usually 7 to 8 feet above the ground—so it is, in effect, traveling down an incline. As noted previously, the optimum launching angle will be 45° less half the angle of the incline. For a 70-ft put launched 7½ feet above the ground, the angle of incline is about 6°—so the shot should be launched at a 42° angle to get the best distance.

Because of the weight and size of the shot, the trajectory of a shot put is not seriously affected by air resistance. If air resistance is ignored, then the distance of the put will depend on just three factors: the launching speed, the launching angle, and the height of the release point. Which of these factors is most important? With a few calculations we can tell how each factor affects the length of the put, and we can identify the aspects of technique that a shot-putter should concentrate on to get better distance.

First, let's check out the importance of the launching angle. We'll assume a fixed launching speed of 45 ft/sec for a release point 7½ feet above the ground, and calculate the distance for a number of different launching angles (using the equations from Math Box 13, page 287):

Launch Angle	Distance
36°	69'2"
39°	70'1"
42°	70'5"
45°	70'1"
48°	69'1"

We can see the advantage of launching at the optimum angle of 42°. If the shot-putter's launch angle is off by 3°, he will lose 4 inches on his put—often the difference between a gold and a silver medal. It would be interesting to know what launch angles are used by the best shot-putters to see if they have learned, consciously or unconsciously, to use the optimum angle. Unfortunately, there hasn't been much research on the launch angles of shot-putters. The few reported results available point to an average launch angle of 38°. If these results are generally true, then most shot-putters could gain a few inches by launching at slightly higher angles.

Next, let's see how the height of the launch point (i.e., the height of the shot-putter's hand at the moment of release) affects distance. We'll choose a launching speed of 45 ft/sec and a launching angle of 42°, and try a few typical heights:

Launch Height	Distance
7 ft	69'11"
7½ ft	70'5"
8 ft	70'10"
8½ ft	71'3"

Here we see clearly that the greater the launch height, the greater the distance of the put. It's to the shot-putter's advantage to have as high a release point as possible—and since the height of the release point depends on the size of the shot-putter, what this amounts to is that a taller shot-putter has a natural advantage over a shorter one.

Finally, we can calculate the effect of increasing or decreasing the launching speed. For a fixed launching angle of 42° and a launch height of 7½ feet, the results are as follows:

Launching Speed	Distance
43 ft/sec	64'10"
44 ft/sec	67'7"
45 ft/sec	70'5"
46 ft/sec	73'3"

These results are rather dramatic: an increase in launch speed of a mere 1 ft/sec leads to an increase in distance of nearly 3 feet! So the shot-putter's greatest payoff comes when he tries to improve his launching speed—either by increasing the speed of his run-up or by developing greater strength in his arm and shoulder.

The Hammer Throw

Perhaps more than any other track and field event, the shot put requires sheer, brute strength—or so the shot-putters tell us. But my own candidate for the most demanding event in terms of physical strength is the hammer throw. The "hammer" is really a shot (a 16-lb ball) with a 4-foot-long steel wire and handle attached. The peculiar name dates back hundreds of years to the days when the contestants threw an actual sledgehammer having a long wooden handle and iron head. In the early 1900s the handle was replaced by a wire and the event was standardized, but the original name was retained. (The old version is still a popular event at the annual Scottish Highland Games.)

The thrower accelerates the hammer by swinging it around in a horizontal circle. He starts out by circling the hammer twice overhead, with his feet in place, and then whirls his body two or three more times before the release. The thrower must do this while remaining within a ring 7 feet in diameter (Fig. 8.3). This event has been

FIGURE 8.3 The hammer throw. Former Olympic champion Harold Connolly in the midst of his windup *(UPI photo)*.

almost the exclusive province of eastern European behemoths in recent years, and is not very well known to American athletes or sports fans. I once conducted an informal poll, asking sports-knowledgeable people what they would guess to be the world record for the hammer throw. No one came within 50 feet of the right answer; everyone was amazed (as I was when I first found out about it) to learn that the record is 275½ feet. This is nearly 92 yards—farther than any quarterback can throw a football. The record for the discus throw is only 233 feet—and a discus weighs only 4 pounds and acquires aerodynamic lift, like an airplane wing, when it is airborne.

Let's figure out the physical requirements for a 275½-foot throw.

To achieve maximum distance, the hammer must be launched at a 45° angle. (The point of release is higher than the landing point, but the angle of incline is very slight because of the great horizontal distance.) With air resistance effects ignored, the launching speed required for this distance turns out to be about 64 mi/hr.

A hammer-thrower accelerates the hammer by pulling on it, rather than pushing it as in the shot put. As the hammer circles around, the thrower must pull forward on it to make it pick up speed, and also pull inward (Fig. 8.4). This inward pull is the centripetal force (described in Chapter 3) needed to maintain circular motion by counteracting the natural tendency of any object to fly off on a straight line. In order to maintain a steady forward pull on the hammer, the thrower has to rotate his body fast enough so that his arms are always ahead of the hammer. The thrower must pivot his feet, hips, and shoulders at an ever-increasing rate in order to keep up a steady angular acceleration of the hammer. Since the thrower has five revolutions in which to bring the hammer up to its launching speed, the demand is not too excessive—to achieve a speed of 64 mi/hr in five revolutions requires an average forward acceleration of 20 ft/sec^2, which corresponds to an average force of about 10 lb.

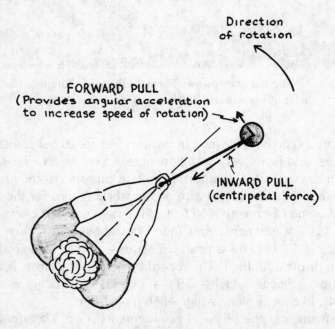

FIGURE 8.4   Forces in the hammer throw.

The centripetal force that the thrower must provide is another matter. The equation for centripetal force ($F = mv^2/R$) shows that as the speed of the revolution increases, the force increases in proportion to the square of the speed. Thus as the thrower accelerates the hammer, he must pull with a progressively larger inward force. In the equation, R is the radius of the circular motion; with the thrower's arms fully extended and the wire being 4 feet long, R will be about 7 feet. The hammer has a mass of 0.5 slug (based on its weight of 16 pounds). When a speed of 64 mi/hr (94 ft/sec) is reached, the centripetal force will be 630 pounds!

This force represents the maximum force, at the instant of release, that the thrower exerts for a 275½-ft throw. Even for more modest distances, a hammer-thrower may experience a force exceeding 500 lb during his last revolution. This is the pull that the thrower exerts on the hammer with his two arms. Now according to Newton, for every action there is a reaction—so if the thrower is pulling inward on the hammer with a force of, say, 500 lb, then the hammer is pulling outward on the thrower with an equal 500-lb force. This force tends to pitch the thrower outward. He must resist this force to maintain his balance, and there are only two counterforces available to him—his weight and the friction between his feet and the ground. To compound the difficulty, the thrower must launch the hammer at a 45° angle—so during the last revolution he must incline his swing upward. Now the hammer is pulling upward as well as outward on him, and if the upward component of this force is larger than the thrower's weight, he will be lifted off the ground. For example, if the centripetal force reaches 600 lb at a 45° angle, the upward component of the force on the thrower will be 425 lb—so it is inevitable that he will be lifted off the ground once he inclines the hammer upward. The thrower must not allow this to happen too early in the throw, because once his feet break contact with the ground he can no longer accelerate the hammer or keep his balance.

Since hammer-throw competitions are usually won by throws well over 200 feet, it's easy to find one reason why this event is not seen very frequently—namely, the amount of space it takes up. Training must be a problem, also—there aren't too many empty football-field-sized areas around where a hammer-thrower can go to practice. And holding this event indoors is, of course, out of the question. To get around these difficulties, many hammer-thrower types have turned to a related event—the 35-lb weight throw. Like the hammer, the 35-lb ball has a handle attached to it, but the handle is attached directly to the ball without a long wire. As a result, the thrower's turning radius is much shorter than for the hammer throw, about 4 feet as compared with 7 feet. Also, the mass of the 35-lb weight is a bit more than twice that of the 16-lb hammer. Both of these factors serve to reduce the distance that can be attained—specifically, for the same 600 lb of centripetal force, a 35-lb weight will go about one-fourth as far as a 16-lb hammer. Competitions are usually won with throws of about 70 feet or so, which makes the 35-lb weight throw a less space-consuming event, suitable for both indoor and outdoor meets.

It's clear from our brief analysis that a successful weight- or hammer-thrower must possess prodigious strength in the arms, shoulders, and legs, and also considerable agility and coordination. Incidentally, the world record for the 35-lb weight throw, 76 feet, is held by Yuri Sedykh of the USSR. Sedykh is a two-time Olympic gold medalist in the hammer throw, winning the 1980 Olympics with a throw of 268'4". Second place went to Sedykh's countryman, Sergei Litvinov, who subsequently set the present record of 275'6" in June 1982.

In March 1982, the U.S. intercollegiate indoor track and field competition in the 35-lb weight throw was won by Bill Borden of Southern Connecticut State College, with a throw of 67'8". When interviewed by reporter Frank Litsky of *The New York Times,* Borden made a comment that gives an interesting insight into the psychology and strategy of weight-throwing. He gave as the reason for his success the fact that he had switched from three turns to two:

"You can get more animal with two turns. When I used three turns, I was thinking my foot goes here, my arm goes here, my toe goes here. If I'm thinking technique, I'm not going to throw that far. Now I'm just fired up. I can go berserk."

Throwing a Baseball

The most essential features of the game of baseball—throwing, fielding, batting, pitching—all involve projectile motion to a substantial degree. As an illustration, let's see what the theory of projectile motion can tell us about the simple and basic act of throwing a baseball. When a fielder makes a throw during the course of play, his goal is rarely to make the ball go as far as possible. In almost every game situation, players have to make the ball travel a specific distance in the shortest time possible. The question is, should baseball throws be launched at a 45° angle? A projectile launched at 45° has the greatest horizontal range for a given launching speed; it also requires the least amount of force to throw the ball a given distance if the throw is sent off at a 45° angle. But a 45°-launching angle does not result in the shortest time of flight. Consequently, there are very few circumstances during the course of play when a player would want to throw the ball at a 45° angle.

A baseball throw is the opposite of a football punt, in the sense that we want the time of flight to be as short as possible. The shortest time of flight is achieved when the launching angle is 0°—in other words, when the ball is thrown horizontally. However, any projectile thrown horizontally is going to fall as fast as if it were only dropped. As a result, most baseball throws cannot be launched horizontally because the ball would hit the ground before reaching its target.

Consider, for example, the throw from third base to first base. On a baseball diamond the bases are 90 feet apart and the diagonal distance from third to first is 127 feet. Allowing for the normal fielding positions and the first baseman's stretch to catch the throw, a typical throw made by a third baseman travels about 120 feet. A third baseman must have a particularly strong throwing arm, so it's not unreasonable to expect him to throw a ball as fast as a typical pitcher can—about 85 mi/hr would be a good estimate. Since 85 mi/hr is equivalent to 125 ft/sec, we can quickly calculate that the time of flight would be 0.96 second: distance/speed = 120 ft/(125 ft/sec) = 0.96 sec. But in this interval of time, a freely falling object should drop a distance of 14.7 feet. Conclusion: it is impossible for a third baseman to throw a ball horizontally to first base on a fly; the ball would hit the ground well before reaching the base.

In order to make this throw the third baseman must launch it at a slight upward angle. For a horizontal range of 120 feet and a launching speed of 125 ft/sec, the projectile motion equations show that the required launching angle would be about 7°. With this angle, the time of flight is slightly longer, about 0.97 second instead of 0.96. In throwing at this angle, the third baseman is actually aiming at a point 15 feet above the first baseman's glove. Of course, he does not consciously aim his throw at this point; he looks and throws at the first baseman, but angles his throw upward. Longer throws naturally require even steeper angles. Every infielder learns by practice and experience how much he has to angle his throw to reach first base—a factor that will depend on the length of the throw, the fielder's throwing speed, and the game situation.

Air resistance slows the speed of the ball in flight substantially—so real throws require somewhat higher launching angles and have longer flight times than the calculated values. For example, a third-to-first throw at 85 mi/hr actually takes about a tenth of a second longer than the value previously cited. With greater distances and flight times, air resistance becomes even more of a factor.

Sometimes an outfielder will purposely throw the ball on a flatter trajectory so that it will reach home plate on a bounce—either to compensate for a weak throwing arm or to permit the throw to be cut off by an infielder. However, it has always been a cardinal rule of baseball that throws to first base from the infield must be made on a fly—until recently. The development of artificial playing surfaces like Astroturf (first introduced in the Houston Astrodome because the groundskeepers weren't able to grow grass in an indoor stadium) has changed this. When a batted or thrown baseball bounces on grass or dirt, it loses a considerable amount of speed and may take a ''bad hop''—i.e., an unpredictable change of direction. But on an artificial surface, the ball takes a true bounce, losing little speed. To compensate for the faster speeds of ground balls, infielders must play deeper positions, requiring them to make longer throws to first base. Infielders have discovered that on an artificial surface the deeper throws sometimes can be made more effectively by purposely throwing the ball on a bounce to the first baseman. In throwing the ball more horizontally, the fielder takes advantage of the shorter time of flight— and since there is little loss of horizontal speed when the ball bounces, there really is no great advantage to trying to reach the first baseman on a fly.

The change from grass to artificial turf has affected many aspects of baseball play. It is much more difficult to bunt successfully, for example, but easier to hit a ball through a drawn-in infield. In the outfield, balls hit between the fielders are more likely to go through to the wall, resulting in more extra-base hits. An outfielder has to be cautious about charging in on short fly balls, because there is a good chance that the ball will bounce over his head if it is not caught.

There are a lot of baseball fans today who deplore the trend toward artificial surfaces and indoor stadiums. I grew up playing baseball on bumpy, dusty, weed-infested and rock-strewn sandlots where fielding a grounder cleanly required an act of God. Not too long ago, I had an opportunity to play baseball regularly on Astroturf. In contrast to the experiences of my childhood, playing the infield became an absolute pleasure. I quickly became confident that I could field any ball hit to me, because I didn't have to worry about tricky hops or bad bounces. But then a lot of balls were hit by me so fast that I had absolutely no chance to catch them. I developed a considerable fondness for Astroturf as a result of this experience, and I imagine that future generations of baseball players and fans will wonder how the old-timers could have ever played the game on such unpredictable surfaces as dirt and grass.

The art of pitching depends crucially on the effects of air resistance. The path of any pitch is strongly influenced by the spin on the ball and its interaction with the surrounding air. In the next two chapters we will learn all about the aerodynamics of curves, sinkers, knucklers, and the like. However, it's interesting to figure out what the path of a pitched ball would be in the absence of air resistance. The ball would, of course, follow a parabolic trajectory and curve downward. On a standard baseball diamond the pitching rubber is located 60½ feet from home plate. But while the pitcher starts his windup from this point, by the time he releases the pitch the ball is 6 to 7 feet closer to the plate. So let's take, as a round number, 54 feet as the actual distance the baseball travels as a projectile. As for the speed of the ball—while there are a few major-league pitchers who can throw a baseball at 95 mi/hr, a more typical speed for a fast ball is 85 to 90 mi/hr. For comparison, we'll look at the difference between a pitch traveling at 85 mi/hr (125 ft/sec) and one at 100 mi/hr (147 ft/sec). The travel time (= distance/speed) from point of release to home plate is 0.43 second for an 85-mi/hr pitch, and 0.37 second at 100 mi/hr. The extra 0.06 second that the batter has available to react to the slower pitch turns out to be, for most batters, the difference between a hittable and an unhittable pitch.

How much does the pitch drop naturally (due to gravity) as it comes to the plate? Assuming that the ball is thrown horizontally, it will fall as much as any other dropped object would in the same amount of time. We can calculate (using the equation $d = \frac{1}{2} gt^2$) that a 100-mi/hr pitch would drop about 2'2", while an 85-mi/hr pitch would drop nearly 2'7" over the 54-foot throwing distance. Without air resistance, the path of a pitched ball would be very predictable, and a lot easier to hit.

Judging a Fly Ball

Of all the skills that a baseball player must master, the one that intrigues me most is the art of judging a fly ball. Almost immediately after the batter swings and makes contact, as the ball is rising up and away from home plate, the fielder must decide where the ball is going to come down, and then he must run to that spot at an appropriate speed to make the catch. What the fielder has to do, in effect, is to make an estimate of the direction, range, and time of flight of the complete trajectory of the ball, based on the motion of the ball during the early part of its flight. The more of the initial trajectory that the fielder watches—i.e., the longer he takes to make his decision—the less time he has to get to the landing point. The best outfielders are able to make a rapid assessment, based on a rather short viewing of the initial trajectory, that is so accurate that they can virtually turn their backs to the ball, run to a spot, and wait for the ball to arrive there.

Judging a fly ball does not require strength, or unusual coordination, or quick reflexes—and yet it is not an easy skill to master. (Please note that I am referring to the problem of *judging* a fly ball—figuring out where the ball will land—and not the act of *catching* it when you get there.) What makes it unique is that there does not seem to be any way to teach this skill or to put into words a description of a method or technique that can be used to judge a fly ball. Thus there are no *verbal* rules or hints that one can give to aid the learning process. When standing in the batter's box, a hitter can think useful thoughts —keep your eye on the ball, keep your swing level, etc.—but when trying to judge a fly ball, thinking about what to do doesn't seem to help at all. So the skill must be completely self-taught on a nonverbal level.

If there is no recognized, conscious technique for judging a fly ball, then how is it done at all? Like most athletic skills, it is acquired through practice and experience, constant repetition, trial and error, until a subconscious reflex pattern is established—in this case, one that relates the first stages of any trajectory to the projected landing point. This pattern must depend, of course, on the stream of sensory information that the fielder receives as he views the flight of the ball. This raises an interesting question: what information is most useful in predicting the trajectory of the ball? To state it another way, what cues are used subconsciously by the fielder to figure out where the ball is going to land?

Other scientists besides myself have puzzled over this question. In 1968, the *American Journal of Physics* published an article by Seville Chapman, a physicist at the Cornell Aeronautical Laboratories, entitled "Catching a Baseball." To answer the question, Chapman mathematically analyzed the path of a fly ball as seen by the fielder. He dealt specifically with a ball that is hit directly toward the fielder so that he must move either forward or backward, but not sideways, to make the catch. While it may seem that the fielder has a simpler decision to make—whether the ball will land in front of or behind his present position—this type of fly ball is actually the most difficult to judge. When the ball is hit to the fielder's side, he is able to see the curvature of the trajectory, making it easier to visualize where the ball will come down. But if the ball is hit directly at him, the parabolic arc is not visible; the ball only appears to rise and fall in a vertical plane.

Paradoxically, while the straight-on fly ball is the most difficult to judge, it is the easiest to analyze mathematically. Chapman looked at the changes that take place in the *angle of elevation* of the ball (the angle between the ground and the fielder's line of sight to the ball) as the fly ball approaches the fielder (Fig. 8.5). In general, the angle of elevation increases as the ball approaches (in other words, the ball appears to rise higher and higher in the sky). However, if the ball is going to land in front of the fielder, the angle will suddenly begin to decrease just before it hits the ground. The key to whether or not the flight of the ball is being judged correctly, Chapman found, is based on trigonometry—specifically, the *tangent of the angle of elevation* (the ratio of the height of the ball to the horizontal distance from the ball to the fielder, as shown in Fig. 8.5). If the fly ball is coming directly to the fielder (so that he does not have to move to catch it), the tangent of the angle will *increase at a steady rate*. If the ball is going to be over the fielder's head, the tangent of the angle will increase at an *increasing* rate (i.e., the tangent will change by successively larger amounts in equal intervals of time). If the ball is going to land in front of the fielder, the tangent of the angle will increase at a *decreasing* rate. Therefore, Chapman claimed, the fielder judges a fly ball by moving either forward or backward so as to make the tangent of the angle of elevation appear to increase at a uniform rate. Chapman concluded that this is the only physical quantity that changes in a simple and regular way while the ball is in flight.

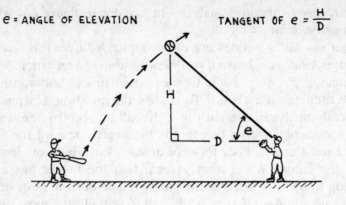

e = ANGLE OF ELEVATION   TANGENT OF $e = \dfrac{H}{D}$

The angle of elevation increases as
the fly ball approaches the fielder —

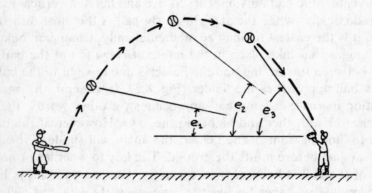

FIGURE 8.5   The angle of elevation of a fly ball.

Chapman's theory of "trigonometric outfielding" was based on the assumption that air resistance does not affect the flight of a baseball in any significant way. Unfortunately, this assumption turns out to be incorrect. My own calculations (which I'll be discussing more fully in the next chapter) show that air resistance does modify the trajectory substantially. For the typical speeds and times of flight that occur under game conditions, a batted baseball travels about 60% as far as it would in a vacuum, and the shape of the trajectory is no longer a perfect parabola. When air resistance forces are accounted for, the tangent of the angle does *not* increase at a constant rate as seen by a fielder who has judged the flight of the ball correctly.

Having shown that the tangent of the angle of elevation is not a useful cue for judging a fly ball, I examined several other geometrical and trigonometric features of the trajectory. None of them showed any characteristic variations that would tell an outfielder which direction he has to move to catch the ball. Evidently, the information used subconsciously in judging a fly ball lies at a deeper level than mere geometrical or trigonometrical factors.

In fact, the mystery of how a fielder judges a fly ball turns out to be one manifestation of a much larger problem—namely, how an individual determines the location in space of a rapidly moving object and coordinates this information with the movement of his body. At the present time, psychologists and physiologists have only a partial understanding of the factors that contribute to this process. Binocular vision is certainly one of these factors; it aids in depth perception by providing two slightly different views of the object (one from each eye) as it moves against the background. However, depth perception with a single eye is also possible; a one-eyed outfielder can, with practice, learn to judge fly balls.

In addition to the visual cues, however, there is one course of *nonvisual* sensory feedback that is used in tracking the motion of an object. It is the vestibular system of the inner ear—the sensory apparatus used to maintain balance, distinguish up from down, and detect acceleration. This system responds very rapidly to movements of the head, and you can demonstrate its powers for yourself with a simple test. Hold up one finger in front of your face, and focus your gaze on it. Holding your gaze fixed, turn your head rapidly from side to side; notice how your finger stays sharply in focus. Next, hold your head steady, and move your finger rapidly from side to side; notice that you now cannot move your eyes fast enough to follow the motion of your finger and keep it in sharp focus.

In the first part of this test, in order to keep your gaze fixed on your finger you had to move your eyes rapidly from side to side to compensate for the motion of your head. It turns out that this compensatory counterrotation of the eyes is directed by signals from the inner ear, generated by the motion of your head. In the second part of the test, your head was stationary and the eye motion required to follow your moving finger was triggered by purely visual feedback. The fact that you could keep your finger in focus in the first part of the test, but not in the second part, demonstrates that the inner-ear signals are processed much more rapidly by the brain than visual signals are. These signals are, in fact, processed by different parts of the brain; inner-ear signals are processed rapidly by the "lower brain" (the cerebellum), while visual signals are processed—more slowly—by the cortex.

What does this have to do with judging a fly ball? When a fly ball is hit, the fielder's very first response is a jerking backward of his head to follow the flight of the ball. I've proposed a theory (which I first presented at the January 1983 meeting of the American Physical Society) which states that the response of the inner ear to this motion may be responsible for the rapid reactions displayed by an experienced outfielder. Through a process of trial-and-error learning, the nervous system of an outfielder becomes programmed to respond to the vestibular signals generated by the movement of his head when the ball is hit. This sensory input becomes coordinated with the body motions needed to direct the player to the landing point.

In presenting this hypothesis, I stated—quite facetiously—that when an experienced outfielder judges a fly ball, he's really playing it by ear. Some of the people who have commented on my proposal have taken this statement too literally, and pointed out in support that an outfielder seems to react to the sound of the "crack of the bat." While the vestibular system is located in the inner ear, it has no relation to the process of hearing. Moreover, an outfielder can judge a *thrown* fly ball just as easily as a batted one. I think it's clear that the sound of a fly ball plays little or no part in the judgment process.

Whether or not my hypothesis will stand up to rigorous testing and the weight of evidence remains to be seen. Even if it does, it will still not make it easier for anyone to learn how to judge fly balls. In any event, my studies have served to deepen my appreciation for the capacity of the human body to master this difficult and mysterious skill.

The Science of Basketball Shooting

Basketball is yet another sport in which projectile motion is a central feature. To the uninitiated, basketball seems like a sport demanding only that its participants be tall. But to those who know it well, basketball is a rather subtle and sophisticated game requiring speed, stamina, agility, and the development of a wide variety of skills. Of these, the most fundamental skill is the ability to "put the ball in the hoop"—i.e., to shoot the ball accurately at distances ranging from 2 to 20 feet.

In the most basic terms, to shoot a basketball successfully one must launch the ball on a trajectory that will make it pass through an 18-inch-diameter hoop mounted 10 feet above the floor. The basketball is a projectile that is being launched for accuracy rather than maximum distance, so the launching speed and angle must be carefully controlled by the shooter. The shot is usually taken while the shooter is moving, jumping, or reacting to the defensive maneuvers of an opposing player, making the task that much more difficult. He must determine the type of shot to use and select the appropriate launching force and direction in a fraction of a second, with a minimum of conscious thought. However, the shooter does have some margin for error in the trajectory of his shot because the basketball, at 9½ inches in diameter, is smaller than the hoop—and the ball may bounce off the rim and/or backboard and still go through for a basket.

Many players and coaches seem to subscribe to the theory that "pure shooters," the ones who can hit 15- and 20-foot shots consistently, are born and not made. Formal basketball coaching emphasizes the development of ball-handling skills, defensive techniques, team play, etc. But it is rare for a coach to attempt to tamper with a player's shooting style. This is considered to be an innate talent; you either have it or you don't.

I contend that pure shooters *can* be made—that it is possible to develop and improve one's ability to shoot a basketball accurately by taking a scientific approach to basketball shooting. I feel specially qualified to make this claim, having written the first research paper on the physics of basketball ever to be published in the *American Journal of Physics*, and having put my own theories into successful practice on the basketball court. (Admittedly, I was not motivated to do this research entirely by scientific curiosity; I wanted to rise above the level of mediocrity I had sustained for so many years as a basketball player.)

My scientific analysis of basketball shooting centers on a study of the most effective trajectory for a shot, making use of many of the ideas about projectile motion previously discussed in this chapter. The laws of physics require the path of a basketball shot to be a parabolic arc whose shape is defined by the launching speed and angle (air resistance is not a significant factor in basketball shooting). For a specific distance from the basket, there are any number of different trajectories that connect the shooter's hand to the center of the basket, each one calling for a different combination of launching speed and angle. The choice of trajectory usually depends on the player's preferred shooting style as well as on the conditions under which the shot is being taken. At one end of the spectrum is the low-angle, flat-trajectory, "line-drive" shot, and at the other end is the steeply angled, high-arching, "rainbow" trajectory. Is there any natural advantage for one type of trajectory over another? In other words, is there a "best" trajectory, an optimum launching angle, that offers the greatest probability for a successful shot?

One way to decide on the best trajectory is to consider the amount of force needed to launch the shot. It is to the shooter's advantage to use as little force as possible. The smaller the force needed to launch the shot, the more quickly and effortlessly it can be released by the shooter. Modern-day basketball is a very fast-paced game. The old-fashioned two-handed set shot, taken with both feet planted on the floor, is rarely seen; the game is dominated by the jump shot, launched at the top of a vertical jump while the shooter is facing the basket, or turning, or even moving toward or away from the basket. Obviously, this kind of shot must be launched with a minimum of effort. A quick release is particularly important to the good shooter who finds himself being guarded closely and given only brief opportunities to get off a clear shot.

The force with which a shot is launched determines its launching speed. Thus the trajectory that requires the smallest launching force is the one that calls for the smallest launching speed to reach the basket—and this, in turn, is related to the launching angle. We've already seen that the smallest launching speed needed to cover a given distance is achieved when the projectile is launched at a 45° angle—provided that the launch point and the landing point are at the same elevation. This is normally not the case in basketball shooting, because the launch point (the place where the shooter's hand leaves the ball) is usually lower than the 10-foot height of the basket. In effect, the shooter is launching the projectile up an incline (Fig. 8.6). This means that the launching angle calling for the smallest launching force is *not* 45°—unless you happen to be tall enough to release your shots at the same level as the basket.

The ball becomes a projectile when it breaks contact with the shooter's fingers; even if the shooter is as small as 5'9", this point will be at least 7½ feet above the floor. So the vertical rise of the incline (h in Fig. 8.6) is normally not more than 2½ feet. In a game, the vast majority of shots are taken within a 25-foot range of the basket (in professional basketball, the line for a three-point shot is 22 to 23¾ ft

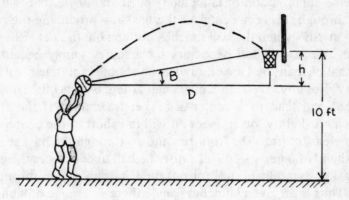

B = ANGLE OF INCLINE   TANGENT OF B = $\frac{h}{D}$

FIGURE 8.6   Angle of incline for basketball shooting.

from the basket). On the other hand, when a player is within about 10 feet from the basket, he is more likely to try to bank his shot off the backboard than to try to shoot it in directly. Accordingly, for the kinds of shots we're dealing with, the horizontal distance to the basket is typically 10 to 25 feet, and the angle of incline (B in Fig. 8.6) turns out to be 14°, at most. We learned earlier that when a projectile is being launched up an incline, the launching angle for maximum range or minimum force is equal to 45° plus half the angle of the incline, or 45° + B/2 (see Math Box 13, page 287). Since B is never more than 14°, it follows that the minimum-force launching angle for a basketball shot will be between 45° and 52°, depending on the distance and height of the point of release.

Unfortunately, there is no single launching angle that gives the minimum force in every situation. It is larger for short-range shots than for long-range ones, and closer to 45° for taller shooters than for shorter ones. Nevertheless, in every instance the minimum-force angle always lies between the two extremes of line-drive and rainbow shot, although it tends to be more of a high-arch shot than a flat one. Both line-drive and rainbow shots require relatively more force to launch, and they also travel at higher speeds and tend to rebound harder if they hit the rim or backboard. The best shooters are admired for having a "soft touch" or a "soft shot." The softest shot is the one that is launched at the minimum-force angle.

There is yet another advantage to shooting at the minimum-force angle. As I noted earlier, a player has a certain margin for error in launching his shots. For *any* trajectory, minimum-force or not, there is a precise combination of launching speed and angle that will send the ball through the very center of the basket—producing the much-desired "swish" when the ball touches nothing but the net. However, a perfect trajectory is not necessary for a score, simply because the ball is smaller than the basket, giving the shooter some leeway in his trajectory. For any given launching angle, there is a specific launching speed that will lead to a center-of-basket trajectory. If the shot is launched at a slightly lower speed, it will fall short of the center—but may still clear or graze the front rim and go through the basket. Similarly, a slightly higher speed will cause the ball to overshoot the center of the basket, but fall short of (or hit) the back rim and go through for a score. Thus for a given launching angle there is a range of launching speeds that will result in a basket. I've called this range the *margin for error in speed*. In the same way, for a given launching speed there is a range of launching angles that will make the ball land somewhere between the front and back rims of the basket. I refer to this as the *margin for error in angle*.

My mathematical analysis of the two margins for error required some fairly extensive mathematical calculations that eventually called for the use of a computer to complete. I'll spare you the gory details and summarize my findings. First of all, I found that the margin for error in speed is biggest when the shot is launched at as high an angle as possible. This result gives the edge to the rainbow trajectory over the line drive. In other words, with a flat trajectory the range of speeds leading to a basket is relatively narrow, so you're more likely to be a consistent scorer by shooting with a higher trajectory, where the margin for error in speed is wider. A more significant result, however, is that the margin for error in angle turns out to be greatest when shooting a minimum-force shot. The corresponding launching speed for this shot (which is the lowest launching speed for the given distance) provides the widest range of launching angles for a successful shot.

To illustrate this idea, let's consider a 15-foot shot—about the distance of a shot launched from a point between the free-throw line and the top of the circle—taken by a 6-foot-tall player (whose point of release will be about 8 feet above the floor). For this distance and height, the launching speed for a minimum-force shot turns out to be 23.5 ft/sec. For this speed, the launching angle needed for a perfect, center-of-basket trajectory is 49°. However, any launching angle between 46° and 53° will result in a basket—a margin for error in angle of 7°. Now let's compare this with a line-drive shot, taken at an angle of 43°. The required launching speed is slightly higher (23.7 ft/sec), and the margin for error in angle is only about 1°, which means that the launching angle must be between 42.5° and 43.5° for a basket. Again, let's compare these results with a rainbow shot, taken at a 54° angle, also requiring a speed of 23.7 ft/sec for a center-of-basket shot. In this case, the margin for error in angle is about 4°—any angle between 52° and 56° will lead to a basket.

These numbers clearly illustrate the advantage of shooting minimum-force shots. I don't mean to imply that this is the only trajectory that will be successful; it is possible to score baskets with rainbows and line drives, but it's more difficult to do so consistently, because of the narrow margins for error. My results also show that it's better to err on the side of too much arch than too little—i.e., rainbow shots are easier to make than line drives. There have been a few consistent line-drive shooters in the professional ranks, but they had to have exceptionally precise control of their shooting speeds and angles. If you watch the best outside shooters in the NBA—George Gervin, Brian Winters, Andrew Toney, to name a few—you'll see that they all shoot relatively high-arched shots. Even the tallest players—seven-footers such as Kareem Abdul-Jabbar and Robert Parrish—arch their shots rather than shoot them on a line toward the basket.

My calculations also revealed the level of precision needed to shoot consistently, even when using the most favorable trajectories. The amount of force needed to launch a 15-foot shot at a 54° angle is only 2% greater than the minimum force (at 49°) for this distance—but this difference is quite noticeable to the shooter. Even finer distinctions can be made. Let's suppose that a player is taking 15-foot shots with a 49° launching angle, and his shots are consistently falling short and hitting the front of the rim. To adjust his shot so that the ball goes in cleanly, the shooter must use a little more force. It turns out that the amount of extra force needed to make this adjustment is about one *ounce*—corresponding to an increase of less than one-tenth of a percent! Yet this slight difference can definitely be felt and controlled. These numbers show dramatically the exceptional level of skill required to have a good "shooting touch."

The main purpose of my study was to show how the principles of mathematics and physics could be used to analyze something seemingly unscientific—namely, basketball shooting. But there is a practical side to this work; I believe that the results can be useful to basketball players and coaches. A shooter ought to be able to improve his scoring accuracy by learning to launch shots at the right speed and angle. But how can a player or coach put these calculations to good use? Obviously, you can't memorize the proper launching angle for every shot, especially since it changes with height and distance, but even if you do know what the best launching angle is for a given shot, how are you to tell whether you are actually releasing your shots at this angle?

The answer is that a player can learn the best launching angle by the way it looks and the way it feels. If you practice taking the same shot at different launching angles, you can easily feel the difference in the amount of force needed to launch the shot. The angle that feels the most effortless is the best one. Another way to judge the launching angle is to look at the height of the ball at the peak of its trajectory in relation to the top of the backboard. Figure 8.7 shows some possible trajectories to use for a 15-foot shot released 8 feet above the floor. The minimum-force trajectory (the solid line) is launched at a 49° angle. For comparison, the dotted lines show the paths of shots launched at angles of 41° and 57°, each requiring about 5% more launching force than a 49°-angle shot. The minimum-force trajectory has its high point about 2¾ feet above the plane of the rim, or about a half a foot below the top of the backboard. In comparison, the rainbow launched at a 57° angle has its peak about a foot *above* the top of the backboard. A coach or fellow player, standing to the side so he

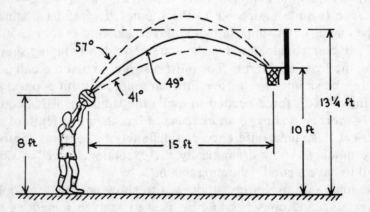

FIGURE 8.7 Judging the minimum-speed trajectory.

can see the trajectory of the shot, can help a shooter to adjust his launching angle to the proper arch.

My own experience with this technique proved to be extremely satisfying. I had been playing basketball for more than twenty years without developing any ability as a shooter. I had occasional streaks of success amid long spells of inconsistent, if not terrible, shooting. The problem was that I had always been a line-drive shooter, and that turned out to be the key to my failures. I changed my shooting style to a higher-arch shot, and after a few weeks of practice my shooting accuracy began to improve dramatically.

I have also learned how to cure shooting slumps and maintain consistency through scientific thinking. You'll often hear experts talk about the proper "mechanics" of a golf swing or of pitching a baseball. They're referring to the correct performance of a sequence of motions that allow the activity to be done most effectively. But I've never heard anyone talk about the proper mechanics of basketball shooting. Just as there is a successful "groove" for a golf swing or a pitching delivery, there is a groove for basketball shooting—and the way to avoid shooting slumps is to know how to stay in that groove.

There are a number of aspects of good shooting mechanics to be aware of. First and foremost is the trajectory—learn to deliver a soft, effortless, high-arch shot. Above all, avoid line-drive shooting; don't aim the ball *at* the basket, but aim it high so that the ball *descends* into the basket. A second important feature is the proper rotation of the ball. Your shots are not always going to swish cleanly through the hoop; very often they will hit the rim or backboard. The speed and especially the direction of the rotation on the ball will influence the ball's path after it hits. We learned in Chapter 3 about the value of backspin: a backspinning ball always loses speed when it strikes a surface. Obviously, backspin will help a basketball shot. What must be avoided is any sideways rotation (when the ball appears to rotate clockwise or counterclockwise as seen by the shooter). With this kind of rotation, the ball will veer sideways when it hits the rim or backboard. This action may be helpful for layups or bank shots, but will be detrimental to a longer distance, straight-in shot. To give a shot the proper rotation, the ball should be positioned on the tips of all five fingers (with the thumb extended to the side and the other fingers pointed upward) and released with a slight downward snap of the wrist. The shooter should be careful not to rotate his wrist when releasing the shot. I cured one shooting slump when I discovered that

I was taking my thumb off the ball before releasing the shot, thereby giving the ball a slight clockwise rotation when I pushed it off with my other fingers.

The third part of good mechanics has to do with arm action. Some shooters generate the launching force with their wrist; others use the wrist and forearm. I prefer to use my whole arm, starting the shot from my shoulder. Whatever style is used, the important thing is to launch the ball so that it isn't off line to the right or left of the basket. A useful rule is to "keep your elbow under the ball." In other words, if you try to shoot the ball with your elbow sticking out away from your body, it will be pretty difficult to get the shot on line to the basket. I always try to remember to tuck my elbow against my side before starting the shot. Finally, there is the follow-through, which is just as important in basketball shooting as it is in many other sports. In releasing the shot, your arm should be stretched out toward the basket to guide the ball onto its proper trajectory. Knowing the proper mechanics can take the mystery out of those stretches of bad shooting that plague even the best players. By running through a mental check-list of the essentials, it becomes relatively easy to pinpoint and focus on the one small change in your motion that may be throwing you off.

Understanding the physics of basketball has really given me a unique way of seeing the game. As a player, it has helped me to improve my performance and to keep it at a consistent level. As a spectator, I can watch other players—even the top college and professional stars—and spot the reasons why they are or are not accurate shooters. If only I were twenty years younger and a foot taller!

9 / MOVING THROUGH FLUIDS

Air resistance affects an athlete's speed of movement and alters the paths of projectiles. Its absence would make it impossible to throw a curve ball or to hook a tee shot. In sports as diverse as auto racing, downhill skiing, and Frisbee throwing, the effects of air resistance dictate the techniques, equipment, and strategy used in competition. The same is true for all water-based sports, since objects moving through water are affected in the same manner as objects moving through air, but to a far greater extent.

Up to now, I've avoided describing resistance effects in any detail. If a projectile is *not* affected by air resistance, the equations that describe its motion are relatively easy to understand and use, but once we include the forces created by the medium (air or water) through which the projectile is moving, the mathematics become devilishly difficult. Exact formulas for the range or height of the trajectory cannot be obtained; in fact, all sorts of elegant and clever mathematical techniques must be used just to yield good approximate trajectories. In their efforts to make really accurate predictions, scientists have found the mathematics to be so intractable that they have had to fall back on computers to do the dirty work of grinding out the large number of computations needed to trace out a trajectory, point by point.

The yearnings of mathematicians, physicists, and engineers to describe the motion of an object through a resisting medium have been spurred by both intellectual and practical needs. These efforts have a long history that goes back to Aristotle's philosophical speculations on the motions of falling bodies. Isaac Newton devoted considerable effort to the problem—with an interesting purpose in mind. About fifty years before Newton, the great French philosopher-scientist Rene Descartes had proposed a theory of the universe which envisioned the sun, planets, and stars as embedded in an all-encompassing fluid of "celestial matter." According to Descartes, the rotation of this fluid set up huge whirlpools that carried the planets in their paths around the sun. Newton's studies—which appear in the *Principia* under the title of "The Motion of Bodies in Resisting Media"—disproved Descartes' hypothesis, thereby clearing the way for Newton's own theory of gravitation as the most plausible explanation for planetary motion.

After Newton, the study of resistance effects became concentrated into two main areas—*aerodynamics* and *ballistics*. The science of aerodynamics is concerned with identifying and describing the forces that are created when any object moves through air. It has progressed substantially because of its powerful motivation—mankind's longtime desire to fly. Some of the individuals who made the most significant contributions to aerodynamics—George Stokes, Osborne Reynolds, Frederick Lanchester, Ludwig Prandtl, Theodore Von Karman—are far from being household names, but it was their theoretical contributions that made the development of the airplane possible. When we consider the rate at which progress has been made—from the Wright brothers' first powered flight to the 747, the SST, and manned spaceflight in a span of less than seventy years—we can begin to appreciate the remarkable accomplishments of the many largely unknown scientists who contributed to the growth of aerodynamics.

The science of ballistics, on the other hand, is often viewed as a somewhat unsavory enterprise. Its main purpose has traditionally been the analysis and prediction of the trajectories of bullets, artillery shells, bombs, and missiles for the military. Thanks to the inspiration furnished by a nearly unbroken chain of wars and international rivalries, ballistics scientists have made considerable progress. For that matter, the science of aerodynamics made its greatest advances in response to the need for military aircraft in the two world wars.

Motivations—noble or ignoble—aside, the achievements of aerodynamics and ballistics science are of considerable practical value in the world of sports. We'll begin with an outline of the basic scientific principles, and then see how these concepts can be used to help us understand many aspects of athletic performance. For our purposes, we will be concerned with the forces acting on objects that are immersed in and moving through either air or water. These two substances may seem at first to be quite different, but to the scientist they are both examples of fluids. In contrast to solids, which generally maintain a fixed, rigid shape, fluids move easily in response to any disturbance and tend to take on the shape of their container. All gases (of which air is one example) and liquids (including water) are considered to be fluids. Air and water thus have many properties in common, and as a result the resistance forces that they exert on objects moving through them can be described in terms of a single theory, even though these forces may differ considerably in strength.

In general, an object moving through a fluid may experience any of four distinct effects—*drag, lift, buoyancy,* and *hydrostatic pressure.* The first of these, the drag force, always acts to oppose the motion— that is, the direction of the drag force is exactly opposite to the direction of the velocity of the object. The lift force, on the other hand, acts perpendicularly to the motion and tends to deflect the object sideways from its original path. While there is always a drag force on a moving object, the lift force appears only under special circumstances—specifically if the object is spinning or is not perfectly symmetrical.

The other two forces, buoyancy and hydrostatic pressure, exist even when an object is stationary in a fluid. The force of buoyancy is an upward (gravity-opposing) force that acts on any object partially or totally immersed in a fluid. The buoyant force thereby tends to counteract the weight of the object, making it lighter. It is this force that enables people to swim easily and that causes balloons to rise in the air. Since performance in water sports and recreational activities such as swimming, diving, and boating depends very strongly on the effects of hydrostatic pressure and buoyancy, let's take a closer look at these forces.

Bodies in the Water

Hydrostatic pressure arises because a fluid must support its own weight. Think of a fluid as divided into horizontal layers: each layer rests on the layer immediately below, which in turn rests on the layer below it, and so on, so that any given layer of fluid must hold up all the layers of fluid above it. In other words, each layer must exert an upward force that exactly counterbalances the weight of all the layers above. It is customary to describe this effect in terms of pressure rather than force. Pressure is defined in physics as the ratio of force to area—the applied force divided by the total area of surface on which the force acts (see Math Box 14, below, for details). Thus the hydrostatic pressure is the pressure (force/area) exerted by the fluid to support its own weight or the weight of any object that is immersed in the fluid. It follows that the total force exerted on any surface in a fluid is equal to the hydrostatic pressure multiplied by the

---

MATH BOX 14: PRESSURE AND DENSITY

Pressure is defined as the ratio of the strength of an applied force to the area over which the force is directly distributed:

$$\text{pressure} = \frac{\text{force}}{\text{area}} \quad \text{or} \quad p = \frac{F}{A} \qquad \textit{Units:} \text{ lb/in}^2; \text{ lb/ft}^2; \text{ N/m}^2$$

Density is a measure of the compactness or concentration of matter. If two objects have the same size, the one made of denser material will weigh more. Density can be defined in two ways: as the ratio of mass to volume (the mass density, represented by the Greek letter ρ (rho) or as the ratio of weight to volume (the weight density, d):

$$\text{mass density} = \frac{\text{mass}}{\text{volume}} : \rho = \frac{m}{V} \qquad \textit{Units:} \text{ slugs/ft}^3; \text{ kg/m}^3; \text{ gm/cm}^3$$

$$\text{weight density} = \frac{\text{weight}}{\text{volume}} : d = \frac{W}{V} \qquad \textit{Units:} \text{ lb/ft}^3; \text{ N/m}^3$$

Note that since $W = mg$, then $d = W/V = (mg)/V = (m/V)g$, so that

$$d = \rho g$$

The densities of air and water at 60°F:

	ρ (slugs/ft³)	d (lb/ft³)
Water	1.94	62.4
Air	0.00237	0.0762

Hydrostatic pressure: The hydrostatic pressure at a depth h below the surface of a fluid of weight density d (mass density ρ) is

$$p = dh = \rho g h$$

total area of the surface. In order to maintain a state of equilibrium at any point in a fluid, the hydrostatic pressure must be exerted equally in all directions.

The deeper we submerge ourselves in a fluid, the greater will be the hydrostatic pressure—because there will be more overlying layers of fluid to support. This means that *the pressure in any fluid increases with depth*. The rate at which the pressure increases depends specifically on the density of the fluid. Thus the denser the fluid, the more weight that has to be supported, and the greater the pressure will be at a given depth (see Math Box 14, page 318). As we move about on the surface of the earth, we are actually submerged in—in fact, at the bottom of—an "ocean of air": the earth's atmosphere. Each layer of the atmosphere must support the weight of all the air above it; consequently the pressure of the atmosphere increases with depth. From the point of view of anyone on the surface of the earth, this is equivalent to saying that the atmospheric pressure decreases with increasing altitude. In any case, atmospheric pressure is greatest at sea level, where it has an average value of 14.7 lb/in². Thus the total force exerted by the atmosphere on the top of the average person's head amounts to about 1500 pounds!

Our bodies have evolved to withstand and function under the weight of the atmosphere, so that when we are subjected to significantly different pressures our ability to carry out normal activities may be seriously impaired. Such conditions may occur at high altitudes, where the air is noticeably less dense and at lower pressure, or underwater, where the pressure becomes progressively higher with increasing depth. Water is, of course, many times denser than air; as the table in Math Box 14, page 318, shows, one cubic foot of water weighs 62.4 lb, while a cubic foot of air weighs only 0.0762 lb. Consequently, the pressure increases with depth much faster in water than it does in air. In fact, the hydrostatic pressure in water grows by "one atmosphere" (14.7 lb/in²) with every 34 feet of added depth. (In salt water, which is slightly denser than fresh water, the pressure increases by 1 atmosphere for every 33 feet of depth.)

We've already learned about the problems associated with exercise at high altitude, all of which stem from the fact that less air is taken into the lungs in one breath because of the lower pressure. When the body is subjected to higher-than-normal pressure—as it is underwater —a different set of problems arises, also associated with breathing.

It's possible for an individual to remain underwater for about a minute or so while holding his breath. (In 1973, Jacques Mayol actually dove to a depth of 282 feet on a single breath—a rather bizarre way to get one's name into the record books, in my opinion.) But to remain underwater for an extended period of time, one must have a *self-contained underwater breathing apparatus* (hence the term "scuba" diving). In order for air to enter the lungs, however, it must be at the same pressure as the hydrostatic pressure on the diver's body.

The continued breathing of air at high pressure creates a number of potentially dangerous conditions. Air is 78% nitrogen—but this substance plays no role in respiration and is normally an inert gas as far as the body is concerned. But it does get dissolved into the blood, and the higher the pressure, the more nitrogen is forced into solution in the bloodstream. This in itself is not dangerous, but if it is continued for a prolonged period, a state known as *nitrogen narcosis* may occur in which the diver becomes confused, disoriented, and irrational—the effect on the nervous system of excess nitrogen in the blood being somewhat similar to that of alcohol.

A much greater threat to a diver's health and safety comes about when he rises to the surface, however. As the hydrostatic pressure decreases, the nitrogen comes out of solution; and if the diver rises too rapidly, the nitrogen will form gas bubbles in the bloodstream and body tissues. This leads to the painful and sometimes fatal illness known as decompression sickness or "the bends." To avoid this condition, divers must rise to the surface slowly to allow the dissolved nitrogen to leave the bloodstream at a more moderate rate. Although scuba divers have descended to depths of more than 400 feet (where the hydrostatic pressure is nearly 12 atmospheres), it is generally considered dangerous to remain below 200 feet for a prolonged period of time.

In contrast, the force of buoyancy represents one of the more benign consequences of hydrostatic pressure. To understand how they're connected, consider the submerged object shown in Figure 9.1: the fluid exerts hydrostatic pressure on the top, sides, and bottom of the object, but since the bottom of the object is deeper in the fluid than the top is, and since the hydrostatic pressure exerted by the fluid increases with depth, it follows that there is a greater pressure acting on the bottom of the object than on its top. The result is a net upward force on the object—and this is the buoyant force. In other words,

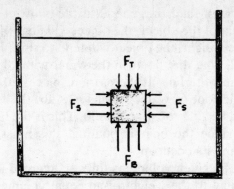

Hydrostatic force = Hydrostatic pressure × surface area

F_T = Hydrostatic force on top
F_s = Hydrostatic force on sides
F_B = Hydrostatic force on bottom

BUOYANT FORCE = F_B - F_T

FIGURE 9.1   The buoyant force on a submerged object.

the buoyant force represents the *difference* between the hydrostatic forces (the hydrostatic pressure times the surface area) exerted on the top and bottom of the object.

There is a basic principle that can be used to determine the strength of the buoyant force on any submerged object, regardless of its shape:

The buoyant force on any object is equal to the weight of the fluid it displaces.

This is *Archimedes' principle,* named—as you might have suspected—for the great Greek scientists Archimedes (287–212 BC) The basis of the principle is as follows: when an object is partially or fully submerged in a fluid, it pushes aside (displaces) a volume of fluid equal to the submerged volume of the object. For example, when a ship is floating in water it displaces a volume of water equal to the volume of the part of the ship that is below the waterline. In order for the ship to float, its entire weight must be supported by the hydrostatic pressure exerted by the water on the submerged part of the ship. According to Archimedes, the buoyant force on an object is equal to the weight of the displaced volume of fluid. In general, if the buoyant force equals or exceeds the weight of the object, the object will float. If the buoyant force is less than the weight, the object will tend to sink. For example, let's imagine a small boat that floats in the water with 20 cubic feet of its volume below the waterline. It therefore displaces 20 cubic feet of water. Since 1 cubic foot of water weighs 62.4 lb, the weight of the displaced water will be $20 \times 62.4 = 1248$ lb. This is the buoyant force on the boat—and since the boat is floating, this must also be the weight of the boat and its occupants.

When an object of a given volume is fully submerged in a fluid, the buoyant force is equal to the weight of an equal volume of the fluid. Whether the buoyant force is less than, equal to, or greater than the weight of the object itself depends on the relative densities of the object and fluid. If the object is denser, it will outweigh an equal volume of fluid; its weight will exceed the buoyant force and it will sink. If the object is less dense than the fluid, the buoyant force will exceed its weight and the object will rise in the fluid. A small, helium-filled balloon—the kind that you might buy for a child at the circus or the zoo—rises very rapidly in air because helium is considerably less dense than air. The famous Goodyear blimp, so familiar to TV sports fans, is actually a huge, helium-filled, propeller-driven balloon. The balloons used by most recreational balloonists are usually filled with hot air (produced by on-board heaters): since the density of air decreases as its temperature increases, the hot air contained in the balloon will be less dense than the air outside, and the balloon will rise. The observation that "hot air rises" is explained by the fact that a parcel of any hot gas within cooler (and therefore denser) surroundings will experience a buoyant force that exceeds its weight.

In general, the projectiles used in sports do not experience a significant buoyant force in air. The reason is simply that most projectiles are much denser than air, so that the buoyant force (the weight of the air they displace) is much smaller than their weight. This is true even if the projectile is air-filled like a basketball, football, or Ping-Pong ball. Despite its apparent lightness, the weight of a Ping-Pong ball is about 100 times greater than its buoyant force in air. But for those sports and activities that take place in water, the buoyant force is a dominant factor. The design of all watercraft—canoes, rowing shells, kayaks, sailboats, speedboats, etc.—must pay close attention to weight distribution and water displacement, since these factors determine how well the craft will float.

In dealing with buoyancy, it is helpful to use the term *specific gravity,* which is defined as the ratio of the density of a given substance to the density of water. Thus an object with a specific gravity of 2 is two times denser than water and will sink—as will any object whose specific gravity is greater than 1. Similarly, anything with a specific gravity less than 1 is less dense than water, and will float.

To a swimming instructor, the world is divided into "sinkers" and "floaters." Some people find it very easy to float in water, while others must exert considerable effort to keep from sinking. The underlying reason for this range of floating ability is that the human body has a specific gravity very close to that of water. But different parts of the human body have different specific gravities. The specific gravity of fat is about 0.8; that of muscle around 1.0; of bone, between 1.5 and 2.0. Thus the ability of any individual to float depends upon his body type—a higher proportion of body fat tends to give a lower overall specific gravity, making it easier to float (for this reason, women usually are able to float more easily than men).

If you're floating face down in the water and you relax your body completely, your arms and legs will begin to sink. This is because they have a higher specific gravity than the rest of the body. The torso, especially the chest, has the lowest specific gravity, especially when the lungs are full of air. The average torso with little or no air in its lungs has a specific gravity slightly greater than 1, and will sink. Taking a deep breath to fill your lungs with air expands the chest and increases the body volume, simultaneously decreasing your overall specific gravity and increasing the buoyant force by displacing more water to keep you afloat. Nevertheless, there are still some individuals who will be almost fully submerged when floating with their lungs filled—and a small percentage who sink no matter what they do. To what extent does an inability to float limit one's performance as a swimmer? Being a "sinker" might make it more difficult for an individual to *learn* to swim, but it has little or no effect on his ability to propel himself through the water.

Many people who cannot float in ordinary fresh water find that they are able to float in salt water. In general, it is easier to float in salt water because it has a slightly higher density (about 2.5% higher) than fresh water. According to Archimedes' principle, if equal volumes of fresh and salt water are displaced, the salt water, being heavier, will exert the greater buoyant force. Floating objects tend to float higher in salt water than in fresh water, because they don't have to displace as much liquid to achieve a balance between their weight and the buoyant force. There are two well-known bodies of water on the earth —the Dead Sea between Israel and Jordan, and the Great Salt Lake in Utah—which have a considerably higher salt and mineral content than the ocean. Some people like to swim in these waters because of the supposed health value of the dissolved minerals. Anyone can float in these waters without difficulty—but accidentally swallowing a mouthful of the stuff can be a truly awful experience.

The Drag Force

We now turn to the most significant consequence of movement through a fluid—the drag force that directly opposes and retards motion. For a projectile moving through air, the drag force constitutes the bulk of what we have been referring to all along as "air resistance." We can reasonably expect the size of the drag force to depend on the nature of the fluid, the properties of the object itself (its size and shape), and the velocity with which the object is moving through the fluid.

With regard to velocity, the key idea (first stated by Newton) is that the drag force depends on the *relative* velocity of the object in the fluid. An object that is being carried along by the fluid, like a log floating downstream, is not moving relative to the fluid and does not experience a drag force. A ball launched at 50 mi/hr against a 10-mi/hr wind has a velocity of 60 mi/hr relative to the air—and thereby feels a greater drag force than one that is launched at the same speed with the wind (resulting in a relative velocity of 40 mi/hr). Moreover, an object standing still in a 60-mi/hr wind is subject to the same drag force as if it were moving at 60 mi/hr through still air. This is the principle behind the wind tunnel, a device that has proven to be extremely useful to scientists and engineers in aerodynamics research. An airplane, automobile, or any object to be tested can be placed in a wind tunnel and subjected to any desired air speed. By using smoke, colored dyes, or attached streamers, the airflow around the object can be made visible, and various types of instrumentation can be used to measure drag forces, vibrations, stresses, or anything else of interest.

The two properties of a fluid that most strongly affect the drag force are its *density* and *viscosity*. As a general rule, the denser the fluid the more resistance it produces. Changes in the temperature, pressure, and humidity of air each affect its density differently. I'll briefly summarize their effects in turn.

Temperature: As the air temperature *increases,* the air density *decreases.* Air is 12% less dense at 95°F than at 30°F. Consequently, the drag force on a moving object decreases as the temperature rises.

Pressure: As the air pressure *increases,* the air density also *increases.* At any one place on the earth, the air pressure doesn't vary day-to-day by more than 3% to 4%. However, air pressure does decrease significantly with altitude, dropping approximately 3% for every 1000 feet of elevation. Thus a moving object experiences less drag at higher altitudes than at sea level.

Humidity: As the humidity—the percentage of water vapor in the air—*increases,* the air density *decreases.* You may find this surprising, since the air often feels "heavy" on humid days—but this feeling arises from body physiology (perspiration evaporates more slowly when the air is damp) and not from the actual density of the air. In damp air, oxygen and nitrogen molecules are replaced by lighter-weight water molecules. Thus damp air weighs less than dry air at the same temperature and pressure. Changes in air density due to humidity are normally not very large, however—for example, at 86°F and 80% humidity the air is about 1% less dense than dry air at the same temperature and pressure. Nevertheless, moving objects are subject to less drag at higher humidity.

Everything else being equal, a projectile will travel farther on a hot day than on a cold one, farther at higher altitude than at sea level, farther in humid air than in dry air.

Viscosity is a measure of a fluid's resistance to flow and also of its stickiness—how well it will adhere to any object or surface. Substances such as molasses, ketchup, and motor oil have relatively high viscosities; gasoline and benzene are among the less viscous liquids. As you would expect, the viscosities of all gases are substantially smaller than those of liquids—typically about a hundred times less.

Gases become slightly more viscous as their temperatures increase. However, the reverse is true for liquids—for example, the viscosity of water decreases by about 15% when its temperature goes up from 50°F to 150°F. This feature is an important consideration in the choice of motor oil used in automobile engines, given the wide range of temperatures they are subject to. At low temperatures, the oil will be particularly viscous and sluggish—but as the engine warms up, the oil thins out as its viscosity decreases. The Society of Automotive Engineers grades motor oil by its viscosity—SAE 40 being more viscous than SAE 30, which is more viscous than SAE 20, etc. The motor oil most commonly used in automobiles is a mixture of several different grades of oil that compensates for the wide temperature range. For example, motor oil marked as "10W-40" contains a low-viscosity oil for low temperatures (SAE 10W, the W for "winter") combined with a higher-viscosity oil (SAE 40) for high-temperature operation.

When an object is moving through a fluid, or when a fluid flows past a stationary object, the fluid, because of its viscosity, interacts with the surface of the object. The fluid literally sticks to the surface, thereby forming a very thin *boundary layer*. The fluid in the boundary layer is slowed down as it passes by a stationary object; if the object is moving, it will drag some of the boundary layer fluid along with it. This results in an action-reaction force very similar to friction—the object pushes on the fluid, and the fluid pushes on the object. This interaction creates one form of retarding drag force—known as *viscous drag* or *surface drag*—that opposes motion through a fluid. Naturally, a fluid of relatively high viscosity will generate a proportionally greater drag force. Moreover, the larger the object is (the more surface area exposed to the flow) the greater the drag will be. The drag force also depends on the *flow velocity,* which is another name for the relative velocity of motion of the object in the fluid. As the flow velocity increases, the drag force increases.

The flow velocity determines how the object interacts with the fluid. To show how, we'll take as an example a spherical object moving in a fluid—a choice that, if the fluid is air, has obvious relevance to sports. If the flow velocity is very small—and once again let me emphasize that it doesn't matter whether it's the object or the fluid that's actually moving—then the fluid will flow smoothly around the sphere, as shown in Figure 9.2a. The lines in the diagram are called *streamlines*; they show the direction of the flow at any point, and represent the actual paths taken by small parcels of fluid as they move around the object (in a wind tunnel the streamlines can be marked by smoke or dyes and can then be photographed and analyzed). The type

(a): LAMINAR (TYPE I) FLOW

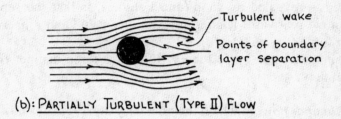

Turbulent wake

Points of boundary
layer separation

(b): PARTIALLY TURBULENT (TYPE II) FLOW

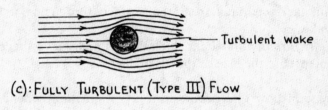

Turbulent wake

(c): FULLY TURBULENT (TYPE III) FLOW

FIGURE 9.2   Fluid flow around a sphere.

of motion shown in Figure 9.2a is known as *streamlined* or *laminar flow*—"laminar" because the fluid moves around the object in uniform layers of differing speeds (the slowest-moving layers being those closest to the surface).

Streamlined flow cannot be maintained at high flow velocities. The smoothness of the flow is disturbed; the streamlines become distorted and jumbled, and the flow becomes turbulent. Sometimes turbulence is caused just by the shape of the object, particularly if it has an abrupt edge or a sharp contour. Because of its inertia, the moving fluid is unable to follow the contour and stick to the surface, and so the boundary layer separates from the surface (Fig. 9.2b). This effect produces a region of turbulence behind the object commonly known as the *wake*. The wake of a moving object is a region of low pressure; and since the pressure in front of the object is greater than the pressure behind it, there will be a net pressure force on the front of the object (the side facing the flow). This constitutes a second type of drag force known as *pressure* or *form drag*. As the flow velocity increases, the point where the boundary layer separates from the object moves frontward (upstream), resulting in an even larger wake and greater drag. As the flow velocity increases further, a stage is reached where the entire boundary layer becomes turbulent. This actually *reduces* the tendency of the boundary layer to separate—and the surprising outcome, as revealed by wind-tunnel studies, is that the separation points move rearward, leading to a *smaller* value and a *decrease* in the drag force (Fig. 9.2c).

To summarize the basic theory, there are three distinct types or stages of flow:

I. *Laminar flow,* in which the boundary layer remains attached to the surface

II. *Partially turbulent flow,* in which the boundary layer (itself still laminar) separates from the surface, producing a turbulent wake

III. *Fully turbulent flow,* in which the boundary layer becomes turbulent, but the size of the wake decreases

The type of flow that occurs in a given situation depends on five factors: the size, shape, and surface roughness of the object; the viscosity of the fluid; and the flow velocity. Laminar (type I) flow occurs when the object is small and smooth, the viscosity is high, and/or the flow velocity is small. In this stage, the drag force consists entirely of viscous drag. At some higher flow velocity a transition to partially turbulent (type II) flow will take place. The flow velocity at which this transition begins is relatively small if the object is large and has a rough, irregular surface, or if the fluid has a low viscosity—i.e., under any conditions that make it difficult for the fluid to stick to the surface. In type II flow, form drag occurs in addition to viscous drag; as the flow velocity increases and the wake grows in size, the form drag soon becomes the larger of the two. The same factors also determine the critical flow velocity at which the transition from type II to type III (fully turbulent) flow takes place. There is at first a sharp drop in the form drag when this transition takes place, but thereafter the drag force continues to grow as the flow velocity increases.

The transition from type I to type II flow, with its corresponding increase in drag, can be forestalled by making the surface smoother or by changing the shape to reduce sharp bends and edges—in other words, by giving the object what is commonly referred to as a "streamlined" shape. For example, if we compare a sphere with a teardrop shape, as shown in Figure 9.3, we see that the turbulent wake virtually disappears for the latter—so the drag force is diminished considerably.

The transition from type II to type III flow can also be pushed up to a higher flow velocity by streamlining and smoothing the surface—but since this transition results in a *decrease* in drag force, it's sometimes more useful to make it occur at a lower flow velocity. In other words, if the normal speed of the object puts it close to the transition point, it's better to give it a rougher surface so as to push it into type III flow and take advantage of the lower drag. This is one of the effects produced by the fuzz on tennis balls, the dimples on golf balls, and the seams on a baseball—for the speeds these objects normally travel at in a game, an irregular surface will put them into type III flow, and they actually experience less drag than they would if their surfaces were smooth. Contrary to what you expect—but nevertheless verified by experiments and experience—a dimpled golf ball or a scuffed-up baseball actually travel faster and farther than smooth-surfaced balls of the same size and weight.

The determination of the type of flow that is taking place and the calculation of the drag force are rather complicated procedures. Theoretical predictions are generally imprecise; the best results are invariably obtained through wind-tunnel measurements. To illustrate the limitations of the theoretical approach, I've outlined in Math Box 15, page 330, the methods used to calculate the drag force on a sphere, which is just about the simplest body to analyze theoretically. The method centers on a very useful quantity called the Reynolds number (R) that depends on the flow velocity, sphere diameter, and fluid viscosity. A low value of R (less than 1) indicates a relatively slow flow in which viscous forces dominate; a large value of R (it can

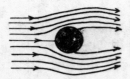 

FIGURE 9.3   Reducing turbulence and drag by streamlining.

MATH BOX 15: DRAG FORCES ON A SPHERE

Viscosity is a measure of the resistance of a fluid to flow (its precise mathematical definition is too complicated to present here). The symbol most commonly used for viscosity is the Greek letter η (eta).

Common units of η: lb-sec/ft^2; N-sec/m^2 (a more frequently used metric unit is called the *poise:* 1 poise = 0.1 N-sec/m^2).

At 60°F, the viscosity of air is 3.74×10^{-7} lb-sec/ft^2
the viscosity of water is 2.34×10^{-5} lb-sec/ft^2

The *Reynolds number* is a characteristic of fluid flow around an object, and is used to determine whether the flow is laminar or turbulent. It depends on the flow velocity (v), on the mass density (ρ) and viscosity (η) of the fluid, and on the diameter (D) or other significant dimension of the object. The Reynolds number (R) is a pure number and thus does not carry any units. It is defined as

$$R = \frac{vD\rho}{\eta}$$

Dependence of flow type on Reynolds number:

R < 1: Laminar flow (type I)—viscous drag only
R $\approx$ 1: Transition to type II flow
1 < R < 1000: Turbulent wake grows—viscous and form drag
1000 < R < 200,000: Turbulent wake grows—form drag dominates
R $\approx$ 200,000: Transition to type III flow—form drag decreases
R > 200,000: Fully turbulent flow—form drag dominates
Note: The transition from type II to type III flow occurs at R $\approx$ 200,000 for a *smooth* sphere, and there is about a 60% decrease in the form drag thereafter. The transition will occur at a lower Reynolds number for a rough sphere, but the decrease in form drag is not as large.

Equations for drag force on a smooth sphere:

Viscous drag: $F_v = 3\pi D\eta v$ D = sphere diameter
Form drag: $F_f = \frac{\pi}{8} C_D D^2 \rho v^2$ v = flow velocity
                                          ρ = fluid density
                                          η = fluid viscosity

C_D = the drag coefficient: for type II flow, $C_D \approx 0.5$
for type III flow, $C_D \approx 0.2$

go up into the millions) indicates turbulent flow. In addition, the calculation of the drag force calls for a *drag coefficient* (C_D), whose value varies with the Reynolds number (and also depends on the surface roughness) in a not easily predictable way. Despite all these difficulties, it's still possible to make some reasonably good predictions of speeds and trajectories, especially if you happen to have access to a computer.

I've supplied a rather hefty dose of basic aerodynamics theory in the last few pages. Don't be concerned if you didn't follow or absorb all the details; if you've at least gained an understanding of the way that the drag force is affected by such factors as the size and shape of the object, the viscosity of the fluid, etc., then you ought to be able to appreciate the relevance of the theory as it pertains to sports. The objects that experience drag forces in sports fall into three categories: projectiles (most of which are spheres); vehicles (racing cars, speedboats, bobsleds, etc.); and the athletes themselves (runners, skiers, swimmers, and so on). The only fluids of interest to us are, of course, air and water. We can begin to appreciate the influence of aerodynamic drag on sports performance by using the theory we've just developed to assess the effects of the drag force on the motion of a falling body and on the trajectory of a projectile.

Falling Bodies, Reconsidered

When an object is released and allowed to fall through a fluid, its weight (the force of gravity pulling the object toward the earth) is opposed by the motion-resisting drag force exerted by the fluid. When the object is first released, its weight will be greater than the drag force and it will accelerate downward. However, as the speed increases the drag force grows, and the object will not accelerate as rapidly (its speed will continue to increase, but at a slower rate). Eventually a speed will be reached at which the drag force equals the weight: since the opposing forces are now exactly balanced, the object will no longer accelerate—but it will continue to fall at a constant speed. This is the *terminal speed* that I referred to earlier.

Any object falling through air or water will almost immediately experience turbulent flow. Because of the relatively low viscosities of air and water, laminar flow cannot be maintained unless the object is microscopically small (less than one-thousandth of an inch in diameter), or else has a low density and thereby experiences a significant buoyant force. Accordingly, any object of reasonable size falling through air or water will be more greatly affected by form drag (characteristic of turbulent flow) than by viscous drag (characteristic of laminar flow). The balance of force between weight and form drag makes it possible to set up an equation to determine the terminal speed (see Math Box 16, page 333).

We've learned that all objects fall at the same rate in a vacuum (with a constant acceleration of 32 ft/sec^2), regardless of weight, size, shape, composition, etc. But as we now know, this is not the case for objects falling through air. Given two objects of the same size but different weight, the heavier one will have a greater terminal speed and will fall faster. For example, a lead ball 6 inches in diameter weighs 46 pounds and has a terminal speed of 640 ft/sec, but a wooden ball of the same diameter would weigh about 3½ pounds and would have a terminal speed of 170 ft/sec. If both were to be dropped simultaneously from a height of 180 feet (about the height of the Tower of Pisa), the lead ball would hit the ground first, landing about 10 feet ahead of the wooden ball. Although neither ball would actually reach its terminal speed during the fall, the wooden ball (being lighter) would be more affected by air resistance and would fall at a slower rate.

Similarly, if we take two iron balls—one weighing 100 pounds, the other weighing 1 pound—and drop them from the same height, the 100-pound ball would fall at a faster rate. When the 100-pound ball hits the ground, the 1-pound ball would be about 3 feet behind. Aristotle, as you may recall, had theorized that the 100-pound ball would fall 100 times faster. Galileo, on the other hand, wrote that the 100-pound ball lands only 2 inches ahead of the 1-pound ball. This discrepancy is taken as strong evidence that Galileo never actually did the Tower of Pisa experiment. Thus both Aristotle and Galileo guessed incorrectly—and while Galileo was a lot closer to the truth, we should still give credit to Aristotle for stating correctly that a heavier object falls faster than a lighter one *through a medium*.

The gentleness of falling rain is a direct consequence of aerodynamic drag. When it rains, the raindrops fall from clouds that are several thousand feet above the earth. If raindrops were to fall freely, with a constant acceleration of 32 ft/sec^2, from a height of, say, 3000 feet, they would be traveling at 300 mi/hr when they hit the ground—making it decidedly unsafe for anyone to be outside. But because of

MATH BOX 16: CALCULATING THE TERMINAL SPEED

A sphere falling through a fluid reaches its terminal speed when the drag force is equal to its weight—resulting in a net force of zero and no further acceleration. Assuming that the drag force is due mainly to form drag, and using the equation for form drag given in Math Box 15, page 330, we arrive at the following equation:

$$\text{weight} = \text{form drag}$$

$$W = \frac{\pi}{8} C_D D^2 \rho v_T^2$$

where W = weight of sphere ρ = fluid density
  D = sphere diameter v_T = terminal speed
  C_D = drag coefficient

Solving the above equation for v_T results in

$$v_T = \sqrt{\frac{8W}{\pi C_D \rho D^2}}$$

It is common practice to define the drag factor K, as follows:

$$K = \frac{\pi C_D \rho D^2 g}{8W}$$

so that $v_T = \sqrt{g/K}$

Those readers who know enough mathematics to be familiar with hyperbolic functions (sinh, cosh, tanh) can calculate the speed and distance covered by a falling body starting from rest by using the following equations:

$$v = v_T \tanh (gt/v_T)$$

$$d = \frac{v_T^2}{g} \log \cosh (gt/v_T)$$

where v and d are the speed and distance fallen, respectively, after a time t.

their small size and weight, raindrops falling through air reach their terminal speeds very quickly and do not accelerate thereafter. A typical raindrop about 1/10 inch in diameter has a terminal speed in air of a more reasonable 15 mi/hr. The theory also predicts correctly that bigger raindrops fall with a greater speed than smaller ones.

Table 9.1 lists the properties of some of the balls used in sports. I've calculated a terminal speed for each one—but keep in mind that

TABLE 9.1: PROPERTIES OF COMMON BALLS IN AIR

Ball	Weight (pounds)	Diameter (inches)	K (Drag Factor)	v_T (Terminal Speed in mi/hr)
16-lb shot	16.0	4.72	0.00014	325
Football	0.91	11.1 × 6.8	0.0015	100
Baseball	0.32	2.90	0.0016	95
Golf ball	0.10	1.68	0.0018	90
Softball	0.40	3.82	0.0024	80
Handball	0.14	1.88	0.0026	75
Tennis ball	0.13	2.56	0.003	70
Squash ball	0.07	1.77	0.0048	55
Soccer ball	0.94	8.75	0.0051	55
Basketball	1.31	9.47	0.007	45
Volleyball	0.59	8.43	0.012	35
Ping-Pong ball	0.006	1.47	0.04	20

Drag force: $F = mKv^2$

Drag factor: $K = \dfrac{\pi C_D \rho D^2 g}{8W}$

these are not really that precise, because there is some uncertainty as to the proper value of the drag coefficient (C_D) that should be used to calculate the form drag on a sphere. For a *smooth* sphere in type II flow, $C_D = 0.5$. But the balls listed in the table have varying degrees of surface roughness; furthermore, during the course of play many of these projectiles may enter type III flow, where C_D may be as low as 0.2. Since a football is not spherical, its drag coefficient depends on whether it is moving nose first or end-over-end. For any projectile, the only reliable way to get a drag coefficient is by wind-tunnel studies —and lacking such data I've used what I believe are reasonable estimates for each of the balls listed. The terminal speeds entered in the table are probably not in error by more than 15%.

In looking over this table, there are a couple of important points to consider. Keep in mind that the higher the terminal speed, the smaller the effect that air resistance has on the ball's motion. (An object falling in a vacuum has an infinite terminal speed—in other words, its speed continues to accelerate as long as the object keeps falling.) Mathematically, the drag force $F_D = mKv^2$, where m is the mass, v the speed of the ball relative to the fluid, and K is a quantity called the *drag factor* (see Math Box 16, page 333). The drag factor in turn depends on the nature of the ball, its drag coefficient, and the density of the air. As a rule, the bigger the drag factor is, the more aerodynamic drag affects motion.

It should come as no surprise that of all the balls listed, the 16-pound shot has the highest terminal speed—indicating that its motion is least affected by air resistance. In general, the terminal speed depends on a combination of weight and size—notice that a squash ball and a soccer ball, though decidedly different in weight and diameter, have about the same terminal speed. The listed terminal speed of 95 mi/hr for a baseball may seem confusing, since it is well known that pitched and batted baseballs can and do travel at speeds in excess of 100 mi/hr. The explanation is that *the terminal speed is not the maximum possible speed that an object can have*—rather, it is the speed that it attains after it has been *falling* through a fluid for a sufficiently long period of time. A ball can be launched at a speed greater than its terminal speed—but it will slow down to the terminal speed as it falls.

In 1908, catcher Gabby Street of the Washington Senators attempted to catch baseballs dropped from the top of the Washington Monument—a difficult and hazardous stunt, considering the 555-foot height of the monument. (He caught only one of the thirteen balls dropped.) From this height, a baseball would take almost 7 seconds to fall and would reach a speed of 87 mi/hr—not quite attaining its terminal speed of 95 mi/hr. A speed of 87 mi/hr is a little less than that of a good fast ball—but it's much easier to catch a ball thrown horizontally than one falling vertically. More recently, a number of players have attempted to catch baseballs dropped from planes or blimps as high as 1000 feet above the ground. In fact, the greater altitude doesn't add that much to the speed of the ball, since it won't exceed 95 mi/hr.

Out of curiosity, you might be wondering how terminal speeds in water compare with those in air. Actually, nearly all of the balls listed in the table do not have a terminal speed in water—the reason being that they float. The only sinkers on the list are the golf ball, handball, and 16-lb shot (many people are quite surprised to learn that a baseball floats). As for golf balls—any golfer who has ever dumped his shot into a water hazard is well aware that they sink. Because of the density of water and the substantial buoyant force it exerts on a golf ball, the terminal speed of a golf ball in water turns out to be a modest 1 ft/sec.

We've seen how air resistance affects the motion of a falling object —but what happens when a ball is thrown vertically upward into the air? When the ball is rising, its motion is opposed by both gravity and the drag force (see Fig. 9.4)—so it decelerates more rapidly than it would in a vacuum. When the ball descends, the gravitational force and drag force now act in opposite directions (Fig. 9.4b). The result is that the ball will rise to its highest point in less time than it takes to fall back to the ground. By way of illustration, I've computed the maximum height, time to rise and fall, and final speed for a baseball, tennis ball, and Ping-Pong ball, each launched vertically into the air with an initial speed of 96 ft/sec (about 65 mi/hr), and compared them to the corresponding values in a vacuum.

	In a Vacuum:	*In Air:*		
	Any ball	Baseball	Tennis Ball	Ping-Pong Ball
Maximum height	144 ft	118 ft	104 ft	31 ft
Time to rise to maximum	3.0 sec	2.6 sec	2.4 sec	1.1 sec
Time to fall back to ground	3.0 sec	2.8 sec	2.7 sec	1.7 sec
Final speed on impact	65 mi/hr	54 mi/hr	48 mi/hr	18 mi/hr
Terminal speed	No limit	95 mi/hr	70 mi/hr	20 mi/hr

These numbers clearly demonstrate how the motion is altered by air resistance. They verify the fact that a baseball can be thrown higher than a tennis ball, and much higher than a ping-pong ball, for the same effort.

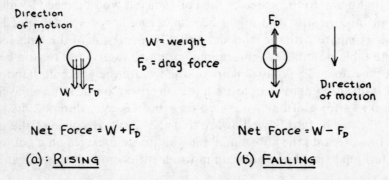

FIGURE 9.4   Forces on a ball moving vertically in air.

Trajectories in Air

At this point, we can begin to consider how air resistance alters the trajectory of a projectile that has been launched at an angle to the ground. Its horizontal speed will not be constant, as it would be in a vacuum; instead it is being steadily decreased by the drag force. Also, as we've just seen, the vertical motion is no longer symmetrical; the projectile will take less time to rise to its peak than it will to fall. The overall result is that the trajectory is shortened, lowered, and blunted (the fall is steeper than the rise) by air resistance, as shown in Figure 9.5. The perfect symmetry of the parabolic trajectory is lost—although to the eye, the trajectory still looks parabolic, so its esthetic qualities may still be appreciated.

The calculation of trajectories has been the central problem of ballistics science for several centuries. As I've said before, this is a trivial problem when air resistance is *not* a factor, but the introduction of a drag force (not to mention a lift force, which we haven't discussed yet) into the equations of motion changes the picture entirely. It then becomes impossible to get an exact solution to the equations of motion, so there are no simple formulas that can be used to calculate the range, height, or shape of the trajectory. In response, mathematicians have developed a variety of methods to get approximate solutions. In the past, the accuracy that one could achieve with these methods was

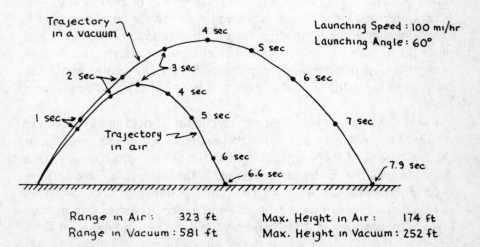

FIGURE 9.5   Effect of air resistance on the trajectory of a baseball.

limited mainly by one's tolerance for doing long, laborious computations for hours on end. But this is just the kind of work that computers are designed to do.

As a scientist who received most of his education before the computer revolution began, I am terribly envious of the advantages today's students have. Throughout high school and college I did all of my calculations using books of mathematical tables and a slide rule. When I was first introduced to computers in the early 1960s, they were relatively slow, limited in capacity, and huge in size. Most of all, they were inaccessible—it wasn't at all easy to get time on a computer to do one's research (or one's homework). But remarkable changes have taken place in twenty years. The evolution of versatile hand-held calculators has released students from the bondage of laborious computations. An even more significant development is the desk-top computer with a capacity that is comparable with that of the IBM dinosaurs of the 1960s. What's more, today's youngsters, having been introduced to computers at a very early age, are developing a familiarity and affinity for them that I find truly inspiring.

Not long ago, I relented to the impassioned pleas of my two sons, who claimed that they would suffer emotional deprivation, loss of esteem with their peers, and possible failure in school without a home computer. It has proven to be an extremely worthwhile investment, not only for them but for myself as well. Using the equations and techniques that it took mathematicians two centuries to develop, and with some assistance from my sons (who graciously allotted me a few hours of computer time), I wrote a program to compute a point-by-point trajectory for any chosen projectile. Given the launching speed, launching angle, and the drag factor, the computer calculates and plots the trajectory in less than a minute. Accordingly, I can now present a host of previously unpublished facts and figures about the flight paths of balls that I'm sure will be of interest to any sports fan.

I don't intend to claim that my calculations yield highly accurate results. The deficiency lies not in the mathematics, or the program, or the limitations of the computer, but in the aerodynamic theory. One difficulty which I've already addressed is the uncertainty in determining a drag coefficient for each projectile. Secondly, the theory does not take into account the effects of wind or the lift forces that may be created by any spin that the ball may have. So in what follows I'll try to assess the extent to which the accuracy of my conclusions might be limited by each of these factors.

In all of my calculations, I've assumed that the air temperature is 60°F, and the atmospheric pressure is 14.7 lb/in². As I noted earlier, the drag force depends on the air density, which depends in turn on the air temperature, pressure, and humidity. Under the normal range of conditions under which sports are played, the air density doesn't fluctuate by more than 10%. A 10% decrease in air density would increase the range of a fly ball by about 2% (e.g., it would add 7 feet to the length of a 350-foot fly ball).

Actually, there are only a few athletic events in which the drag force noticeably changes the trajectory of the ball. In many sports, the ball is usually not in flight long enough or else is not traveling fast enough for the drag force to produce significant effects. This is certainly the case with wall sports, in volleyball, and in tennis—although in the latter the lift force does play an important role, as we'll see later. The shot put has a substantial trajectory, but because of the low drag factor, its motion is virtually unaffected: a 70-foot put is shortened only 5 inches or so by air resistance.

Basketball shots do not have very high speeds (most are launched at speeds under 20 mi/hr), nor do they have long flight times. Nevertheless, a basketball has such a large drag factor that its trajectory, even though short, is still affected somewhat by air resistance. In fact, the drag force actually improves the likelihood of making a basket because it slows down the speed of the ball in flight and makes the ball descend more vertically toward the basket. Otherwise, air resistance effects do not appreciably affect the course of play in basketball.

In soccer, most kicks are relatively short and close to the ground. But a ball will occasionally be kicked for distance rather than accuracy during a game—often by a goalie on a long clearing kick after an unsuccessful attempt on goal. Through high-speed photography, biomechanics researchers have ascertained that soccer players can kick a ball up to speeds of 60 mi/hr. This is just above the calculated terminal speed of 55 mi/hr for a soccer ball, so its trajectory on a long kick ought to be noticeably changed by aerodynamic drag. A ball launched in a vacuum at a 45° angle with a speed of 60 mi/hr would travel 240 feet and remain in flight for nearly 4 seconds. The calculated distance for a soccer ball launched in air with this speed and angle is only 135 feet, with a time of flight of 3 seconds.

There are really only three major sports in which the ball is repeatedly launched on long trajectories—golf, baseball, and football. In each of these sports, air resistance effects shape the course of play and even influence the techniques and strategies used.

The official rules of golf specifically state that a golf ball should be made so that it cannot exceed a speed of 255 ft/sec (174 mi/hr) when struck. Measurements show, however, that the top golfers give a ball a maximum impact speed significantly less than that—about 150 mi/hr using a driver or 120 mi/hr with an iron. The distance that a golf ball will travel when struck depends not only on the launching speed but also on the launching angle. We learned previously that a launching angle of 45° produces the greatest horizontal range when air resistance is not a factor. When the ball is subject to a drag force, however, the optimum angle always turns out to be less than 45°. To demonstrate how the drag force alters the trajectory of a golf ball, I used the computer to determine the optimum launch angle and maximum range for several different launching speeds, with the following results:

	Launching Speed (mi/hr)			
	100	125	150	175
Optimum launch angle	41°	39°	38°	36°
Time of flight (sec)	5.0	5.6	6.2	6.6
Maximum range (yd)	123	158	189	217
Range in a vacuum (yd)	220	340	484	652

The table reveals the extent to which the optimum launch angle is reduced below 45° by the effect of drag. Notice also how much the maximum range in a vacuum is reduced by drag—roughly from 50% to 70%, depending on how long the ball is in flight. Upon closer inspection, however, these results might prove puzzling to a knowledgeable golfer or fan. First of all, the face of a driver is inclined about 10° to the vertical, and consequently launches the ball on a low, flat trajectory. Yet the optimum launch angles shown above are in the 36°-to-41° range. Secondly, the computed distances (in the third row of the table) are decidedly smaller than what a golfer can achieve. Many golfers can hit a drive 250 yards off the tee and 200 yards with an iron from the fairway.

As it turns out, the reason for both of these contradictions lies in the fact that the lift force has not been taken into account. Aerodynamic lift makes a large contribution to the flight of a golf ball, drastically changing the shape of its trajectory and adding considerable yardage to its range. We'll return to this subject in the next chapter.

The Airborne Baseball

I'd expect the computer to predict better trajectories for a baseball, for two reasons: first, the lift force on a baseball is normally insufficient to influence its flight to the extent that it does a golf ball; second, wind-tunnel studies have established a fairly reliable value for the terminal speed of a baseball. My computer calculations show that to obtain maximum horizontal range, a baseball should be launched at an angle of about 39° to 42°, depending on its speed (the higher the speed, the lower the optimum angle). The following table shows how the maximum range in air compares with the range in a vacuum, for different launching speeds:

Launching Speed (mi/hr)	Maximum Range in Air (feet)	Max. Range in a Vacuum (feet)	Time of Flight in Air (sec)
80	290	425	4.4
90	340	535	4.7
100	385	660	5.1
110	435	795	5.4
120	480	945	5.7
130	525	1105	5.9
140	565	1280	6.2

It is a rare and noteworthy event when a batter hits a baseball more than 450 feet on a fly. We can see from the table that to do this without the aid of the wind would require a launching speed off the bat in excess of 110 mi/hr. Such a speed is well within the capability of a major league hitter who makes perfect contact with a fast ball (see the results of the calculation in Math Box 8, page 220).

When it comes to throwing a baseball, the maximum *pitching* speed attained to date is Nolan Ryan's 100.9 mi/hr, but the average major leaguer's throwing speed is probably around 85 mi/hr. A pitcher, who must throw from a fairly fixed position, uses mainly his arm and upper body to accelerate the ball. However, if a player is allowed to run forward with the ball before throwing it, he could add perhaps 5 to 10 mi/hr to the speed of the ball. Taking all this into consideration, I estimate that a major league ballplayer who is trying to throw for distance rather than accuracy might be able to attain a top launching speed of 100 mi/hr. If the ball is launched at the optimum angle—which is 41° for this speed in air—it ought to travel 385 feet. The *Guinness Book of World Records* reports a throw of 445′10″ by out-fielder Glen Gorbous, who had a brief major league career with the Reds and Phillies in the 1950s. No details are given as to the conditions under which the throw was made—but one can assume that Gorbous took a substantial run-up before releasing the throw, and may have had the wind at his back.

As I pointed out in the previous chapter, fielders normally try to make their throws in the shortest possible time during a game. For short throws, the effects of air resistance can be ignored; but the longer a ball is in flight, the more its motion is affected by air resistance. The following table shows the minimum time required to make a throw of a given distance in air, assuming a throwing speed of 85 mi/hr:

Distance (feet)	Time (sec)	Launching Angle
100	0.88	6.7°
125	1.12	8.6°
150	1.38	10.7°
200	1.96	15.6°
250	2.67	21.9°
300	3.69	32.0°

One of the most exciting plays in baseball is when a runner tries to tag up after the catch and score from third base on a short fly ball. Depending on his speed, it could take him as little as 3 seconds to run the 90 feet from third to home, although an average runner would probably take about 3.7 seconds. If the outfielder catches the ball within 300 feet of home plate and makes a perfect throw, he could beat the average runner, but this is not very likely if the distance is any greater than 300 feet. The table also points out the advantages of a relay throw: two 150-foot throws together take 1.38 + 1.38 = 2.76 seconds, compared with 3.69 seconds for a single 300-foot throw. Of course, we have to add in the amount of time it takes for the relay man to catch the throw, turn, wind up, and throw. If this takes more than a second, then there's no advantage to the relay. For distances much longer than 300 feet, however, a properly executed relay should definitely take less time than a single throw. This is one of many instances where the strategy of baseball is unconsciously dictated by the effects of air resistance.

For those of you who prefer softball to baseball, I've computed the maximum ranges for a softball and a baseball, assuming the same launching speed. Because of its greater weight and size, a softball experiences 50% more drag than a baseball does. The results clearly show the effects of the greater drag force.

Launching Speed (mi/hr)	Maximum Range (feet)	
	Baseball	Softball
80	290	250
90	340	290
100	385	325
110	435	360
120	480	395
130	525	425
140	565	455

Thus we see, for example, that it takes as much effort to hit or throw a softball 360 feet as it does to hit or throw a baseball 435 feet. Notice how the difference grows as the launching speed gets bigger—a consequence of the fact that the drag force increases as the speed of the ball increases.

Footballs in Flight

The flight of a football is also shortened substantially by aerodynamic drag. The problem with attempting to calculate its effects is that the drag force on a football in the air depends on the way the ball is thrown or kicked. A properly thrown football always spirals—that is, it rotates around its long axis as it travels. As we learned earlier, this spin gives the ball a gyroscopic action that prevents the ball from tumbling or wobbling in flight and keeps it moving nose first. Moreover, a football has the best aerodynamic shape—even better than a sphere, in fact—when it is spiraled. When a football is kicked, however, it doesn't always spiral in flight, and it may tumble end-over-end. Moving in this manner, a football has the poorest aerodynamic properties and experiences a much greater drag force.

To kick for distance, the kicker must make sure that his foot hits the center of gravity of the ball; it will then "sail" without tumbling. An off-center kick, with the impact point above or below the center of gravity, produces rotation, causing the ball to tumble in flight. Not only will the ball have a smaller initial speed (since some of the force goes to producing rotation), but it will also be subject to more drag in flight. The one strategic advantage of an end-over-end kick is that it is difficult to catch, bounces unpredictably, and is thus more likely to lead to a fumble.

What effect does the orientation of the ball in flight have on the distance it travels? As a reasonable estimate, I'd expect the drag factor to be about four times larger for an "end-over-end" football as compared with a "nose-first" one. The following table shows how the distance that a football travels is affected by different amounts of drag (I've assumed a launching speed of 55 mi/hr, typical of a good college or professional kicker):

Launching Angle	Distance in yards		
	End-Over-End (K = 0.006)	Nose-First (K = 0.0015)	In a Vacuum (K = 0)
45°	37	55	67
50°	36	54	66
55°	34	51	63
60°	31	47	58

As the table clearly shows, the difference in distance between the two extremes is rather large: a nose-first kick goes about 50% farther than an end-over-end kick for the same launching speed and angle.

By assuming a drag factor (K) of 0.0015 for a nose-first football—only a bit lower than that of a baseball, incidentally—I've been able to get a good match between aerodynamic theory and real football kicking. Biomechanical studies have shown that good kickers can consistently give the ball a launching speed between 50 and 60 mi/hr. My computer calculations predict that a football launched with a speed of 60 mi/hr at the optimum angle, 43° in this instance, should travel about 64 yards on a fly. These calculations do not take into account the effects of the wind or of aerodynamic lift on the flight of a football—nevertheless, the results obtained agree fairly well with what one sees in actual football games.

In the previous chapter, I presented the dilemma faced by a kicker or punter who must choose between distance and hang time. Kicking at a higher launching angle will increase the hang time—but it also decreases the distance, as the previous table shows. High-speed photography demonstrates that the launching angles used by most kickers fall in the 50°-to-55° range. Why is this range of angles considered to be the most effective? One simple way to find out how football strategists solve the distance-vs.-hang time problem is to watch a few football games, stopwatch in hand, to time the punts and kickoffs. The results turn out to be fairly consistent: the best kicks—the ones that are returned for little or no yardage—have hang times of 4 seconds or better and travel 60 yards or more in the air. The following table, which I computed for nose-first kicks, shows how the distance and hang time are related to the launching speed and angle:

Launching Angle	Launching Speed = 58 mi/hr		Launching Speed = 60 mi/hr	
	Distance (yards)	Hang Time (sec)	Distance (yards)	Hang Time (sec)
43°	60	3.38	64	3.49
50°	58	3.78	62	3.90
55°	55	4.03	59	4.16
60°	51	4.25	54	4.39

We can see that to achieve a hang time close to 4 seconds, the ball must be kicked with a launching speed close to 60 mi/hr and a launching angle of 50° or more. We can also see the extent to which distance is sacrificed to gain hang time—a football launched at a 55° angle falls about 5 yards short of the maximum distance attainable, but yields nearly 0.7 second in extra hang time. Increasing the launching angle to 60° adds an additional quarter second of hang time, but at the expense of another 4 to 5 yards. Based on the speed with which the kicking team can get downfield to stop the return, a 55° angle seems to give the best compromise. The good punter always tries to avoid low, line-drive kicks; for launching angles much less than 43°, they provide neither long distance nor long hang time.

Finally, a few comments on football passing: a football cannot be thrown with as much speed as a baseball—not because of its size so much as because of the way it must be thrown. A fast ball is thrown with the pitcher's full force going almost entirely into the forward speed of the baseball. A football must be spiraled, so it will not have as much forward speed (in fact, the throwing motion for a football is similar to that used by a pitcher to throw a curve ball). The available data point to a top launching speed of about 100 ft/sec (68 mi/hr) for a forward pass. My computer tells me that a football thrown with an initial speed of 100 ft/sec and launched at the optimum angle of 43° should travel 231.9 feet (77.3 yards) in the air. This prediction agrees quite reasonably with real football experience; a strong-armed quarterback is capable of throwing a football up to 80 yards.

10 / *LIVING WITH RESISTANCE*

In the preceding chapter, I attempted to show that aerodynamic theory can be used to make fairly accurate predictions of the trajectories of baseballs, footballs, and the like. But when you get right down to it, the practical consequences of this information are limited. It may be interesting to the curious or statistically minded sports fan to know how fast or how far the top athletes can throw or hit a ball, but it really isn't that useful to the athletes themselves or their coaches. After all, most of this information is acquired by experience—through the process of trial and error—in competition or on the practice field.

Nevertheless, aerodynamic theory does play a very active and direct role in sports. In racing competitions, especially those conducted at high speed, the ability to control and reduce the drag on the athlete or his vehicle often makes the difference between winning and losing. Accordingly, the design of equipment and techniques must be firmly based on the conclusions drawn from theoretical analyses and wind-tunnel measurements of drag forces.

Up to this point, we've been looking at resistance forces only as hindrances to motion, as barriers to be reduced or overcome. However, there is one type of resistance force that is actually an *aid* to the athlete in many areas of sports. This is the force of *lift,* which, if suitably harnessed, can be employed to prolong flight or to cause a projectile to curve in flight in a controlled manner. Thus in this chapter we'll be considering ways in which scientific principles can be used to help the athlete live with, and make the best of, the forces of resistance.

The Energy Cost of Air Resistance

As a force that opposes motion, air resistance does negative work against a moving object, and much of the energy expended by an athlete or vehicle to maintain its motion goes to counteracting the drag force. In this respect, the most important features of this force are as follows:

1. Aerodynamic drag increases in proportion to the square of the speed. A moving object experiences 4 times more drag at 20 mi/hr, and 9 times more drag at 30 mi/hr, than it does at 10 mi/hr.
2. Aerodynamic drag depends on the size of the object. The drag force is directly proportional to the *frontal area*—the amount of surface that directly impacts with the onrushing air.
3. Aerodynamic drag depends on the shape and smoothness of the object, both of which determine the drag coefficient. By altering the contours of the surface to produce a streamlined shape, the drag coefficient can be made smaller.

While the drag force itself depends on the *square* of the speed, the power drain (the rate at which energy must be expended to move against the force) depends on the *cube* of the speed (see Math Box 17, page 349). Thus when the speed of any moving object is doubled, the power drain goes up $(2 \times 2 \times 2 =)$ 8 times. This is the main reason why it is wasteful and inefficient to drive a car at high speed—the amount of power used against air resistance is 2½ times higher at 75 mi/hr than at 55 mi/hr. At 75 mi/hr, a typical pre-1975 passenger car uses about 35 hp of its output just to overcome air resistance, as compared with 14 hp at 55 mi/hr. This rather large power drain emphasizes the importance not only of driving at lower highway speeds but also of streamlining the contours and reducing the frontal area of the automobile to reduce drag and improve driving efficiency.

Back in the days when gasoline was plentiful at 35¢ a gallon, the manufacturers of passenger automobiles were really unconcerned with the aerodynamic shapes of their models. But now that gasoline

MATH BOX 17: POWER CONSUMPTION TO OVERCOME AIR RESISTANCE

Power is defined as the rate at which work is being done or energy is being expended:

$$\text{power} = \frac{\text{work}}{\text{time}} = \frac{\text{force} \times \text{distance}}{\text{time}} = \text{force} \times \frac{\text{distance}}{\text{time}} = \text{force} \times \text{speed}$$

or
$$P = Fv$$

This equation states that the power (P) required to move an object at a constant speed (v) against an opposing force (F) is equal to the force multiplied by the speed.

The drag force (due to form drag) on a moving object is proportional to the square of the speed (v^2):

$$F = mKv^2$$

Here m is the mass of the object, and K is the drag factor (from Math Box 16, page 333). Hence the power expended to overcome air resistance when moving at a constant speed v is proportional to the cube of the speed (v^3):

$$P = Fv = mKv^3$$

economy has become the watchword, streamlining has become a virtual necessity. As an example, consider the two designs shown in Figure 10.1: Car A, with its flat nose and chopped-off back, generates two areas of turbulence when in motion. By tapering the front and back of the car, both areas of turbulence can be reduced considerably, leading to a significant decrease in form drag and in the rate of energy expended against air resistance.

One technique used by racing drivers to conserve energy during a long race is to stay directly behind and close to the car in front of them. As we learned earlier, the wake of a moving object is a region of relatively low pressure. By staying in the wake or "slipstream" of the car in front, a driver reduces considerably the force of air resistance on his own car.

The Aerodynamics of Winter Sports

High-speed performance is characteristic of those winter sports that take place on ice or snow—downhill skiing, speed skating, and sled-

A (THE GAS GUZZLER)

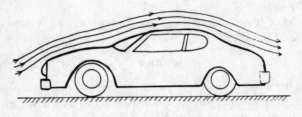

B (THE SPORTY ECONOMY CAR)

FIGURE 10.1 Automobile streamlining.

ding. In nearly all of these events, the athletes do not compete head-to-head, but make individual runs against the clock. Since the athletes do not have the opportunity to pace themselves against their competition, as they do in track, they must go all-out to achieve as much speed as they can within the bounds of safety. Olympic gold medals and world championships have been decided by margins as small as hundredths of a second.

The next time that you see any of these events, look for the techniques that are used to reduce drag. If you're watching speed-skating competitions, for instance, you'll notice the characteristic stance used by the skaters—upper body bent over so that it is nearly parallel to the ground, and one arm tucked behind the back while the other swings rhythmically (Fig. 10.2). The purpose of this stance is to reduce the skater's frontal area. The skater must swing at least one arm to maintain good balance—but the other arm is tucked out of the way to reduce the drag. Notice also that the skater is covered from head to toe with a form-fitting racing suit to keep his body surface as

FIGURE 10.2 Olympic speed-skating champion Eric Heiden's stance and clothing are designed to minimize air resistance *(UPI photo)*.

smooth as possible. (As you watch, you might also consider some of the other scientific principles discussed earlier that come into play—how the skater uses his skate blades to push on the ice and accelerate; how he deals with centripetal force on turns; how he maintains his balance; and so on.)

Speed skaters show a decrease in average speed with distance similar to that of long-distance runners. However, the endurance curve for skating does not drop as sharply as for running, the rate of fatigue being smaller for skaters than for runners. Speed skaters achieve top speeds approaching 35 mi/hr in sprints; their average speeds in the longer races are around 25 mi/hr. (Skaters move nearly twice as fast as runners at the middle distances.) At these speeds, the effects of drag, while substantial, are not as all-important as they are at higher speeds of, say, 60 mi/hr or more. Accordingly, some of the steps taken by skaters to reduce drag may be of more benefit psychologically than physically.

Olympic sledding events come in two categories—bobsledding and luge. A bobsled is a covered sled designed for either a two-man or four-man crew, whereas a luge is an open or "skeleton" sled, for one or two riders, that is basically a souped-up version of the common sled used by children (a high performance "Flexible Flyer," so to speak). Bobsled runs consist of several thousand feet of sharp, steeply banked curves and downhill stretches where speeds up to 90 mi/hr may be reached. A bobsled can weigh up to 500 pounds and is made of steel to maintain its stability and structural integrity on the run. The members of a bobsled team steer and control the speed of the sled by shifting their weight in unison or by braking. At these speeds, aerodynamic design of the bobsled is essential to minimize drag. A luge is ridden in a sitting position, legs extended forward; to increase speed, the rider will lie almost flat on his back so as to reduce his frontal area and the attendant drag. Speeds of 60 mi/hr or more are attained on a luge run. Lugers characteristically suffer from back problems, headaches, and other consequences of the vibrations they experience on a run.

Skiing is certainly the most popular winter sport—and the kind of skiing most people do bears the same resemblance to top-level competitive downhill skiing as children's sledding does to luge. The top skiers *average* over 60 mi/hr on a downhill run, with peak speeds near 90 mi/hr (the record for speed skiing, as I mentioned earlier, is 125 mi/hr). The aerodynamic drag on the skier's body is all-important and depends very markedly on his stance, clothing, and equipment. Considerable research has gone into the development of racing suits that will reduce drag while keeping the racer's body warm and shielded from the wind. Some years ago, designers came up with a plastic fabric that was aerodynamically very smooth—but dangerous to wear. The problem was that if a skier fell and began to body-slide down the slope, the smoothness of the fabric produced so little friction that the skiers could not slow themselves, and they continued to slide into the barriers or down the slope at skiing speeds. Eventually the fabric had to be banned by the international skiing federation.

More than twenty years ago, skiing coaches began to use wind-tunnel studies to determine the best stance for high-speed skiing. Skiers were placed in wind tunnels and subjected to winds of various speeds. They tried out different stances, changing the positions of their body and equipment while the drag force on them was measured. This led to the development of the "egg position" (Fig. 10.3). This is a very deep, compact crouch in which the thighs and upper body are roughly parallel to the ground, with the elbows tucked inside the knees, and the hands positioned near the chin. Measurable increases in drag are observed if, for example, the elbows are pointed out away from the body or if the arms are extended in any way. One surprising finding is that the boot buckles, by protruding slightly from the front and sides of the skier's feet, create sufficient turbulence to add about 0.3 second per minute to a downhill run. The baskets at the ends of the ski poles are another measurable source of drag. To reduce this effect, aerodynamic covers have been designed for the ski boots and

FIGURE 10.3 Erwin Stricker of Italy demonstrates the egg position for minimizing air resistance in downhill skiing. Note also the aerodynamically designed helmet *(UPI photo)*.

pole baskets; bent ski poles are also used so that the baskets can be tucked behind the skier's body and out of the airflow. These advancements in skiing technique and equipment provide one of the most striking examples of the application of scientific principles to the improvement of sports performance.

The egg position used by downhill skiers is an effective stance because it makes the skier's frontal area as small as possible, thereby minimizing the drag force. The principle of reducing drag by reducing frontal area is also used by cyclists and jockeys. There is one sport, however, in which the participant tries to *increase* the air resistance on his body. The sport I'm referring to is sky diving—one of those "recreational" activities where the exhilaration of the activity—in this case, the experience of floating freely through the air—is heightened (for some people, at least) by the very real possibility that you could get killed in the process.

In sky diving, the control of air resistance can mean the difference between life and death. When a human body falls through air, it reaches its terminal speed—somewhere between 100 and 200 mi/hr— in about 15 to 20 seconds, during which time it falls several thousand feet. The terminal speed, as we've seen, depends directly on the weight of the body (heavier bodies fall faster) and also on the frontal area—which is the only element of control that the sky diver has. In a head-first "nose dive" the frontal area is smallest, and terminal speeds approaching 200 mi/hr are possible. The smallest terminal speed (about 100 mi/hr) is achieved in the spread-eagle position— body parallel to the ground with arms and legs extended outward. By changing his frontal area between these two extremes, a sky diver is able to control his rate of descent. Also, by changing the angle of his body he can alter the direction of the drag force to produce sideways motion. In this way he can aim his descent toward a specific landing point on the ground.

The Aerodynamics of Running and Jumping

Track and field athletes must also contend with aerodynamic drag. The drag force acting on a runner is entirely form drag, and there is little that he can do to reduce it—it is, after all, rather difficult to run competitively in the egg position. But sometimes athletes are aided by an external factor—namely, a following wind. Running with the wind leads to a decrease in aerodynamic drag (the runner's velocity relative to the air is decreased by the wind speed). According to international rules, a track record will be disallowed if it was set with the aid of a trailing wind whose speed was greater than 2 m/sec (about 4.5 mi/hr). It is difficult to calculate precisely how much advantage a sprinter gains from a trailing wind; one estimate is that a wind speed of 1 m/sec will reduce a top sprinter's time for the 100-meter dash by 0.12 second. In this particular event, 0.12 second is a substantial amount of time—to date, about ten different runners have come within 0.12 second of breaking the long-standing world record of 9.95 seconds, set by Jim Hines in 1968 at Mexico City.

The 1968 Mexico City Olympics still stick in the craw of track and field purists. World records were set in the 100-, 200-, and 400-meter runs. Despite the intense competition that prevails at these distances, two of these records (Hines' 9.95 sec in the 100 and Lee Evans' 43.86 sec in the 400) still stand after 15 years. Tommie Smith's 19.83 sec in the 200 lasted until 1979, when Pietro Mennea ran this distance in 19.72 seconds—also in Mexico City. And then, of course, there is Bob Beamon's fabulous long jump of 29'2½". The purists claim that all of these performances were tainted because of the lower air resistance at Mexico City's altitude.

As I noted earlier, Mexico City is 7350 feet above sea level; its elevation and proximity to the equator conspire to give an acceleration of gravity of 32.085 ft/sec^2, which is 0.36% lower than the standard sea level value of 32.2 ft/sec^2. The lower gravity contributed very little to Beamon's long jump (an inch, at best) and nothing to the sprint records—but to what extent did the lower air resistance contribute to these performances?

The atmospheric pressure in Mexico City is 77% of the sea level pressure—hence the air density and the drag factor (K) are correspondingly lower. A sprinter thus experiences a 23% smaller drag force than he would running at the same speed at sea level. This turns out to be the same as if he were running with the aid of a trailing wind of 1.4 m/sec—within the accepted limit of 2 m/sec, but a decided advantage nevertheless. As a reasonable estimate, Jim Hines' time for the 100 meters was probably shortened by 0.17 second because of the lower air resistance; and Mennea, who had the advantage of a real trailing wind in addition to high altitude, may have gained as much as 0.45 second over 200 meters.

Now we come to Bob Beamon's long jump. His performance was

aided by the Mexico City altitude in three ways: lower gravity; lower air resistance during the jump; and lower air resistance during his run-up. Considering Beamon's body as a projectile with its mass concentrated at its center of gravity, I used my computer program to calculate the effects of each of these three factors. The results were as follows:

1. The 23% smaller drag force at the elevation of Mexico City adds about 1½ inches to the length of the jump as compared with sea level.
2. The lower gravity of Mexico City ($g = 32.085$ ft/sec², as compared with the standard sea level value of 32.2 ft/sec²) increases the length of the jump by 1 inch.
3. The distance covered in a long jump depends very strongly on the horizontal speed of the jumper at the takeoff. Beamon could run 100 yards in 9.5 seconds at sea level. At the higher elevation, he would be able to run faster; assuming that he gained 0.1 second over 100 yards, he would have increased his running speed by about 1%. A 1% increase in launching speed at the elevation of Mexico City adds 2 inches to the length of the jump.

Adding it all up, we find that Beamon gained a maximum of 4½ to 5 inches by jumping at Mexico City instead of at sea level. If we adjust Beamon's record jump by this amount, it is reduced to 28'9½". Even at this distance it remains a truly phenomenal performance.

The question of whether or not track and field records should be adjusted for wind, altitude, gravity, etc., can be argued endlessly. I'll confess that I can't make up my mind—and so I plan to come down firmly on both sides of the issue. The present system is replete with inconsistencies and inequities. Why should one sprint record be disallowed because a 2.1-m/sec trailing wind was blowing, while another is accepted with a 1.9-m/sec wind? Why is there a wind-speed limit in some events and not in others? There is no wind restriction in the discus throw, for example—and as we shall see shortly, wind velocity has a very decided effect on the flight of a discus.

A few years ago, Bert Nelson, editor of *Track and Field News*, began a campaign to have all sprint times adjusted for wind and altitude. His proposal does have some merit—after all, a 10.07 time for 100 meters at sea level is actually a better performance than a 9.98-second run in Mexico City with a trailing 1-m/sec wind. But how should this adjustment be made? The corrections for wind and altitude are imprecise, and vary according to the runner's size, weight, and running speed. And if we are going to penalize a runner for having a trailing wind, shouldn't we then reward him—by lowering his time— if he has to run *into* the wind?

What about more minor influences, such as gravity, air temperature, and atmospheric pressure? Surely their effects are too small to merit an adjustment, you say. But consider this: times in all races are measured electronically to a precision of 0.01 second. Distances and heights in throwing and jumping events are measured (with tape measures!) and recorded by officials to a precision of 0.01 meter—i.e., 1 centimeter, or about ⅜ inch (Beamon's long jump is officially recorded as 8.90 meters, for example). Thus an athlete can break a record by running 0.01 second faster or by throwing a projectile 1 centimeter farther than the previous best—a difference that could very easily be attributed to lower gravity or variations in air density brought about by moderate changes in air temperature or pressure.

It's possible to make a pretty good case for adjustment of records —provided, of course, that acceptable correction formulas can be established for all the relevant external factors. Nevertheless, the proponents of adjustment have not made many converts. It appears that most athletes and track fans are willing to put up with the inequities of the present system for one simple and compelling reason: the setting of records should not be done by mathematicians or statisticians, but by the athletes themselves, on the field, in the heat of competition.

Resistance in the Water

All objects that move through the water, from swimmers to aircraft carriers, must overcome substantial viscous and form drag. In addition, they may experience yet another type of resistance known as *wave drag*. This is a force that arises whenever an object moves at or near the boundary between any two substances—air and water, for instance. An undisturbed water surface is normally exposed to the 14.7 lb/in^2 hydrostatic pressure of the atmosphere. A boat or swimmer moving through the water and pushing it aside also exerts a pressure on the water surface. Subject to these conflicting forces, the surface begins to bob up and down, producing waves, which can very readily be observed moving away from a sprinting swimmer or a boat traveling at even moderate speeds. The interaction of the moving object with its own waves produces a retarding force—hence the name "wave drag."

At higher speeds, the pressure exerted by a boat on the water produces a reaction that acts to lift the nose of the boat out of the water. Since less of the boat's surface is now in contact with the water, the viscous and form drags are correspondingly reduced. The boat then skims along on the water surface—an effect commonly known as *hydroplaning*. A boat with a relatively flat, slightly rounded bottom is more likely to hydroplane, a fact that has been put to use in the design of speedboats. Because of the high speeds attained and the fact that less of the boat's surface is in contact with the water, a hydroplaning speedboat can become unstable rather easily—as evidenced by the high mortality rate among speedboat racers.

Surprisingly, swimmers experience a relatively large wave drag, particularly when using the butterfly or breaststroke. In fact, at racing speeds, the wave drag on a swimmer is greater than the viscous and form drag—thus it is to the swimmer's advantage to keep as much of his body below the water surface as possible. The breaststroke can be done faster if the swimmer remains completely underwater—a discovery that was made by swimmers in the 1950s. However, the rules of competitive swimming now require this stroke to be done with the swimmer's head breaking the water surface.

There has been a considerable amount of research done on various aspects of swimming technique. It has been found, for example, that swimmers using the free-style (crawl) stroke get at least 75% of their propulsive force from their arms. The main purpose of kicking one's feet, as it turns out, is not to aid in propulsion but to raise the legs and keep the body horizontal in the water, thereby reducing the frontal area and the form drag. Another way to reduce form drag is by improving the smoothness of the surface in contact with the fluid. To achieve this end, women swimmers have taken to wearing form-fitting swimsuits, while some of the men swimmers shave off all their exposed body hair (including on their head) in preparation for a meet.

There are four different strokes used in swimming competition; the free-style is the fastest, followed in order by the butterfly, backstroke, and breaststroke. The present world record for the 100-meter free-style is 49.36 seconds—which corresponds to an average speed of 4.5 mi/hr. The fastest breaststrokers achieve about 3.5 mi/hr (the best 100-meter time to date being 1:02.86). Top-class swimming meets can be very exciting to watch—so it comes as somewhat of a surprise to learn how slowly swimmers move in the water.

The Lift Force

Now we'll turn our attention to the last of the four forces produced by motion through a fluid—the *lift force*. Lift is the most significant force in aerodynamics. Without it, the science would have never gotten off the ground, literally or figuratively. This is the force that makes airplanes fly—and baseballs curve, golf drives hook, and Frisbees hang in the air. The lift force is not necessarily a "lifting" (i.e., gravity-opposing) force; in general, it acts laterally—at right angles—to the path of an object moving through a fluid. It may be directed up, down, left, or right, depending on the circumstances.

Lift is produced by any break in the symmetry of the airflow around an object. This can be accomplished in a number of ways: by giving the object an asymmetrical shape; by tilting a flat object so that it is inclined to the flow; or by giving the object a spin. The effect is to make the air moving over the top (or around one side) of the object follow a different path from the air moving under the bottom (or around the other side) of the object. This creates a pressure difference —from top to bottom or side to side—which translates into a force that deflects the object laterally.

To illustrate how this works, I've diagrammed in Figure 10.4 the flow around an *airfoil*—which you'll recognize as the cross section of

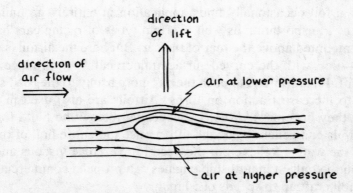

FIGURE 10.4 Lift on an airfoil.

an airplane wing. The crowding of the streamlines near the top of the airfoil indicates that the air flowing over the top is moving at a higher speed than the air underneath it. The rather complicated mathematical theory of this effect (which was first developed between 1900 and 1910) demonstrates that the formation of the boundary layer around the airfoil actually causes the oncoming air to accelerate over the upper surface—hence the increase in its speed. Here another physical principle, proposed by the Swiss mathematician Daniel Bernoulli in 1738, comes into play. Bernoulli's principle, which was based on ideas first suggested by Newton, states in mathematical terms that when the velocity of a moving fluid increases, the pressure exerted by the fluid decreases, and vice versa. In this case, the upward pressure of the slower-moving air below the wing is greater than the downward pressure exerted on the wing by the faster-moving air above it. The result is a net upward pressure which acts to lift the airfoil vertically.

The buoyant force and the lift force both arise from a difference in pressure between two surfaces. To clear up any confusion you might have about the similarity of these forces, let me reiterate that the buoyant force derives from a difference in density and always acts upward (opposing gravity). The lift force is the result of differences in fluid speed; it occurs only when the object is moving relative to the fluid; and it can act in any direction. On an airplane, the upward-acting lift on the airfoil-shaped wings is sufficient to overcome the weight of the plane and keep it in flight. But downward- and sideward-acting lift forces are also needed to control the flight—to change direction, altitude, and so on. The "control surfaces" on an airplane—the flaps, ailerons, and rudder—are used to alter the size and direction of the lift forces on the wings and tail for this purpose.

The airfoil occasionally finds application in entirely ground-based forms of transportation as well. Certain types of racing cars have an airfoil mounted above the rear of the car. But here the airfoil is upside down—i.e., with the curved surface underneath—to produce *downward* lift. Its purpose is to push the car more firmly to the road surface so as to increase traction on turns. Airfoils are also used in water, where they become *hydrofoils*. Suspended below the hull of a boat, hydrofoils can generate enough lift to raise the entire hull of the boat out of the water. Relieved of the need to overcome viscous and form drag on the hull, standard ship engines can propel a commercial-sized hydrofoil craft up to speeds of 50 mi/hr.

An airfoil, like any other object moving through a fluid, experiences a motion-retarding drag force. The goal of airfoil design is to find a shape that produces the highest lift and smallest drag. Thus the *lift-to-drag ratio* becomes an important aspect of an airfoil—the higher this ratio, the more effective the airfoil is in flight. Normally, the lift-to-drag ratio depends on the angle that the airfoil makes with the oncoming air. Increasing this angle—which is known as the *angle of attack* —from the horizontal position raises both lift and drag on the airfoil; but initially there is a much greater increase in lift, so the lift-to-drag ratio rises. However, if the angle of attack becomes too steep, a state is reached where the airflow over the top becomes highly turbulent (see Fig. 10.5), bringing about a sharp drop in the lift-to-drag ratio. In other words, increasing the angle of attack of an airplane will at first improve the lift-to-drag ratio and allow the plane to climb rapidly; but if the angle becomes too large, the sudden decrease in lift-to-drag ratio will cause the plane to *stall*—i.e., lose both its lift and forward motion —a condition that may be followed by a rather precipitous, often uncontrollable (and fatal) dive. A typical airfoil will stall when the angle of attack exceeds 15° to 20°.

Even a perfectly flat object will generate lift if it is angled to the airflow. You can demonstrate this for yourself rather convincingly just by extending your arm out of the window of a moving car with the palm of your hand held horizontally and facing downward. Rotate your hand slowly into the airflow and you will feel the lift force (at a speed of 30 mi/hr or more, the force is very noticeable). If you angle your hand too steeply, you'll begin to feel more drag than lift. Without too much difficulty, you ought to be able to find an angle that provides the optimum lift-to-drag ratio on your hand.

The principle of adjusting the angle of attack to maximize the lift-to-drag ratio plays an important role in a number of sports—unexpectedly so, because the projectiles involved bear little or no resem-

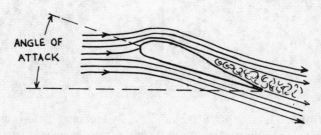

ANGLE OF
ATTACK

FIGURE 10.5   Airflow past an inclined airfoil.

blance to an airfoil. In ski jumping, the projectile is the skier himself, and he uses his skis to provide aerodynamic lift. As the ski jumper leaves the chute and becomes airborne, he angles his skis upward (to provide lift) and also leans his body forward so that it is parallel to the skis to reduce the drag on his body (see Fig. 10.6). The skis used in jumping are longer and wider than usual; the more surface area they have, the greater the lift.

Recently, some ski jumpers have modified this basic technique by rotating their skis to the side (at an angle to their path). The idea is to use the jumper's body itself as an airfoil and thereby gain additional lift. With the skis in the standard position, the jumper's body is shielded from the airflow; by turning the skis to the side, the jumper allows the oncoming air to hit directly on his body. By inclining his body forward at the proper angle, he can attain a favorable lift-to-drag ratio. If this is done properly, and the jumper gains lift from his body

FIGURE 10.6 Gaining lift in ski jumping. By inclining his skis and body at the correct angle to the airflow, Willi Puerstl of Austria maximizes the lift-to-drag ratio during his jump *(UPI photo).*

as well as from his skis, he can add several feet to the length of his jump.

The Javelin Throw

A javelin, despite its seemingly nonaerodynamic shape, experiences a lift force in flight that opposes the force of gravity and adds noticeably to its distance when thrown. The javelin throw has its roots in prehistoric times, when the spear was the most effective means of bringing down an adversary—human or animal—at a long distance. As a weapon, the spear has been made obsolete by the gun, but the javelin throw remains as one of the traditional track and field events, going back to its first appearance in the Olympic Games of 708 BC. At that time, incidentally, the competition was decided on the basis of accuracy—the javelin was aimed at a distant target—rather than on the distance of the throw.

The rules governing the dimensions of the javelin are fairly specific. It must have a mass of at least 800 grams (1¾ lb), a minimum length of 260 cm (8′6⅜″), and a diameter at its thickest point of between 25 and 30 cm (1 to 1³⁄₁₆ inch). Moreover, the center of gravity of the javelin must be located 90 to 110 cm (about 3 to 3½ feet) from its front tip. Within these restrictions there is still much that can be done to improve the aerodynamic characteristics of the javelin—namely changing its taper and weight distribution. In fact, prior to 1961 the rules were less stringent. Around 1955, javelin manufacturers started to make use of aerodynamic design principles, and javelin-throwers began to make rather substantial improvements in their throwing distances. The modern "aerodynamic" javelin, standardized in 1961, can be thrown about 35 feet farther on the average than the pre-1955 "nonaerodynamic" version because of its better lift-to-drag characteristics. The present world record for the javelin throw, incidentally, is 317′4″—nearly 6 yards longer than the length of a football field.

To date, little has been done in the way of theoretical analysis of javelin aerodynamics; most of the improvements have come about through trial-and-error testing. The length of a javelin throw depends, as for any projectile, on the launching speed and launching angle. An additional factor is the *angle of attack* of the javelin—the angle that the shaft of the javelin makes with its flight path (see Fig. 10.7a). The optimum launching angle seems to be around 35°. A higher launching

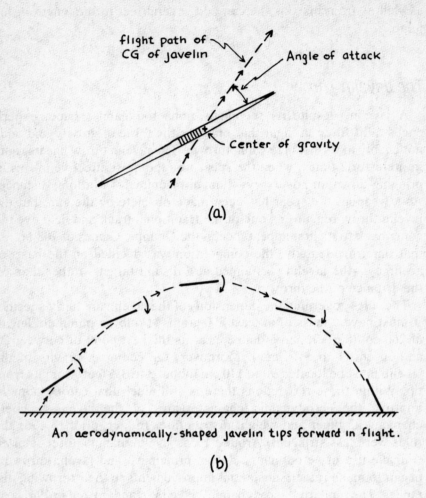

FIGURE 10.7   The flight of a javelin.

angle, closer to 45°, might be expected to increase the horizontal range, but it actually provides a less favorable lift-to-drag ratio. Javelins are usually launched with a zero angle of attack (the javelin shaft is aligned with its flight path); however, some throwers prefer a small angle of attack of up to 10°. If a wind is blowing, both the launching angle and the angle of attack must be adjusted according to the wind speed and direction; if the javelin is being thrown into the wind, a flatter launching angle will be more effective.

One of the ways in which aerodynamic design can improve the flight characteristics of a javelin is to shape it so that there is slightly more lift on its rear than on its front half. The effect will be to make the javelin tip forward about its center of gravity. The nose of the javelin will thereby tend to drop in flight, keeping the axis of the javelin closely aligned with its flight path (Fig. 10.7b). If the nose were to rise instead of fall, the increasing angle of attack of the javelin could cause it to stall in flight.

The Discus Throw

Another traditional Olympic event, with a history as old as that of the javelin throw, is the discus throw. The discus started out as a flat stone plate roughly a foot in diameter, weighing anywhere from 3 to 12 pounds. It has since evolved and been standardized into its present form as a wood-and-metal disk, 8¾″ in diameter, about 1¾″ thick at the center and tapered toward the edge, weighing 4.4 pounds. The discus is launched from a circle about 8 feet in diameter, and is thrown with a pivoting motion somewhat similar to that used in the hammer throw. Launching speeds as high as 55 mi/hr are attained. The world record for the discus throw currently stands at 233′5″.

Despite the venerable history and tradition of this event and the interesting aerodynamics of the discus in flight, little serious research has been done on the subject. Measurements of the lift and drag forces were made by Richard Ganslen at the University of Arkansas in the early 1960s, and in 1981 a very thorough theoretical examination of discus aerodynamics by Cliff Frohlich of the University of Texas appeared in the *American Journal of Physics*. Otherwise, nothing of any significance has been written on the subject in the past twenty-five years. The following is a survey of their main conclusions about the flight of the discus.

Figure 10.8a shows how the plane of the discus is oriented in flight. Angle A is the *angle of attack*—the angle between the plane of the discus and its trajectory. Angle B is the *attitude angle*—the angle that the plane of the discus makes with the horizontal. To calculate the aerodynamic forces, the velocity of the discus must be measured relative to the air: the speed and direction of the wind must be taken into account by adding together (as vectors) the velocity of the wind and the velocity of the discus relative to the ground.

A discus is thrown with a substantial spin—around 400 rpm is typi-

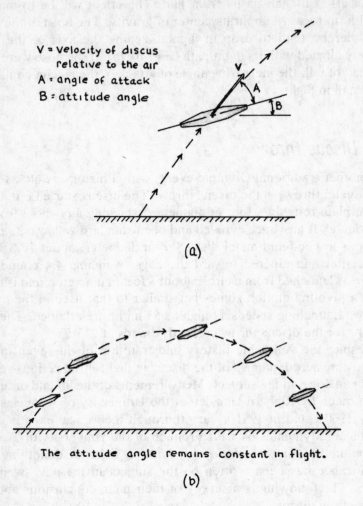

V = Velocity of discus
relative to the air
A = angle of attack
B = attitude angle

(a)

The attitude angle remains constant in flight.

(b)

FIGURE 10.8 The flight of a discus.

cal—giving it a gyroscopic action which stabilizes it against tumbling in flight. The discus consequently maintains a nearly constant attitude angle in flight, as shown in Figure 10.8b. When there is no wind, the most favorable attitude angle is about 25°. During the latter half of the flight the air will be hitting the discus on its underside, producing the greatest amount of vertical lift. However, if the discus is too steeply inclined on its descent—if the angle of attack exceeds 30°—it will stall in flight, rapidly losing forward speed and altitude.

One of the most interesting facts about the discus—confirmed by both experience and theory—is that it will travel a greater distance when thrown *into* the wind. Surprisingly, a discus will travel about 25 feet farther when thrown against a 25-mi/hr wind than it would if thrown with the same wind. The reason is that the air speed relative to the discus is higher when the discus is thrown into the wind, resulting in a greater lift-to-drag ratio. In fact, the effect of lift is so pronounced that a discus will actually travel farther when thrown into a 40-mi/hr wind than it would in a vacuum.

When there is no wind, the optimum launching angle is about 38°. When throwing a discus into the wind, the greatest horizontal range is attained by using a smaller launching angle (25° to 35°, depending on the wind speed) and attitude angle (10° to 20°)—thus giving the discus a lower, flatter trajectory. With a tail wind, a discus will go farther if it is given a higher, more inclined trajectory. Despite the importance of wind speed and direction—and unlike the situation in sprinting— there is no maximum allowed wind for the establishment of records in the discus throw, as I noted earlier. Thus no record is ever disallowed in this event because of excessive wind—a rather curious situation, under the circumstances.

The aerodynamic lift and drag on a discus depend on its size and mass, and also on the density of the air. Unlike most other projectiles, a discus will travel slightly farther in denser air (the denser the air, the greater the lift force). The size and mass become even more significant factors when the wind is blowing—a lighter, bigger discus is more likely to "sail" in the wind and travel a greater distance. The discus used by women throwers is somewhat smaller in diameter and half the weight of the men's discus—with the interesting consequence that the world record in the women's discus throw (235'7") is longer than that for the men's event.

Despite its long and distinguished history, the discus throw certainly does not rank high among the top participation or spectator sports. Yet it is a close relative to one of the most popular recreational activities in America—Frisbee throwing. A standard Frisbee is the same diameter as the men's discus but is much lighter, weighing only about 3 ounces. Like the discus, the flight of a Frisbee is stabilized by gyroscopic action arising from its spin. The thickened rim not only provides a place to grip and catch a Frisbee, but also shifts its weight distribution outward to give it a larger moment of inertia and greater stability against tumbling in flight. Aerodynamically, the discus and Frisbee are rather similar, but the large weight difference makes them respond quite differently to lift and drag forces. A Frisbee reacts very much like a discus thrown into a stiff wind: the best results are obtained by throwing it with a low launching angle and a flat trajectory. And if you launch a Frisbee at even a moderately inclined angle, it will very obligingly demonstrate for you the phenomenon of aerodynamic stall.

The Aerodynamics of the Curve Ball

I've saved for last what is clearly the most important contribution of the lift force to sports—the curved flight of a spinning ball. The game of baseball lives and dies by this phenomenon; virtually all of the subtle strategy and art that permeates the game at its highest level —and makes it so fascinating for the knowledgeable fan—ultimately depends on the ability of the pitcher to throw (and the batter to hit) a variety of "breaking pitches"—curves, screwballs, sliders, etc. This same phenomenon can turn a game of golf into a miserably frustrating experience for the weekend duffer—yet it adds considerably to the performance of the top-flight golfer if properly harnessed.

Let's begin with an examination of the aerodynamics. At the most basic level, the viscosity of air is the cause of curved flight. Viscosity leads to the formation of the boundary layer—the thin layer of fluid whose motion is retarded by any object obstructing its flow. Although it is not strictly true, for our purposes we can think of the boundary layer on a rotating ball as being attached to (and rotating with) the ball as it moves through the air. The interaction of the rotating boundary layer with the oncoming air disturbs the flow pattern around the ball. (Remember that we can consider a ball moving through the air as entirely equivalent to a state in which the ball is stationary and the air is moving.)

Figure 10.9a shows the airflow around a spinning ball in a relatively slow airstream (so that the flow is still laminar). As shown in the figure, the ball and its boundary layer are rotating clockwise. The airflow is coming from the top—the same as if the ball were moving from bottom to top in still air. Notice how the streamlines are crowded together on the right side of the ball (where the boundary layer is

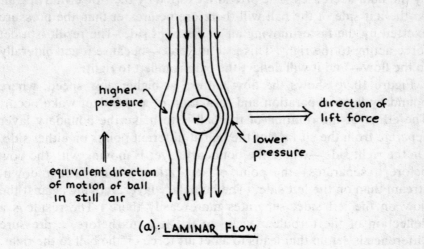

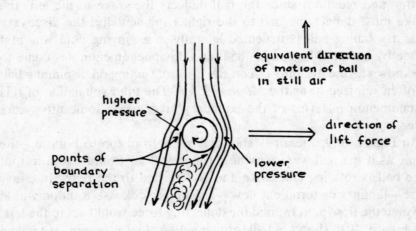

FIGURE 10.9   Airflow around a spinning ball.

moving with the flow) and spread out on the left side (where the boundary layer is moving into and against the flow). The result is that the adjacent air on the right side of the ball has a higher speed than the air passing by on the left side. Now we invoke Bernoulli's principle: as the speed of a parcel of fluid increases, the pressure exerted by the fluid decreases. The pressure exerted by the slower-moving air on the left side of the ball will therefore be greater than the pressure exerted by the faster-moving air on its right side. The result is a net force acting to the right. This is a lift force—because it acts laterally to the flow—and it will deflect the ball from left to right.

Figure 10.9b shows the flow pattern at higher flow speed, where boundary layer separation and formation of a turbulent wake occur. The effect of the rotation of the ball is to make the boundary layer separate from the surface of the ball at different points on either side. On the right side—where the boundary layer is moving with the flow before it separates—the point of separation will be farther downstream than on the left side. (The boundary layer, moving against the flow on the left side, separates more easily there.) The result is a deflection of the turbulent wake to the left. As before, a pressure difference is set up that leads to a net lift force on the ball to the right. (You can also understand this result in terms of Newton's law of action and reaction: since the ball deflects the wake to the left, the wake must deflect the ball to the right.) Incidentally, the discovery that a spinning ball is deflected laterally in a moving fluid was first made by Gustav Magnus in 1852, and this phenomenon has come to be known as the *Magnus effect*; the lift force acting on a spinning ball is often referred to as the *Magnus force*. The full explanation of this phenomenon in terms of the boundary layer came some fifty years later.

In Figure 10.9, the air is shown moving from top to bottom—the same as if the ball were moving through still air from bottom to top. The ball is rotating clockwise and is deflected to the right. In either case—laminar or turbulent flow—a counterclockwise rotation would reverse the flow pattern, and the deflecting force would act to the left. As Figure 10.10 shows, a ball thrown with a *clockwise* spin (as viewed from above) should curve to the *right*; a ball thrown with a *counterclockwise* spin should curve to the *left* (Fig. 10.10a and b). By the same principle, a backspinning ball should rise in flight (Fig. 10.10c); a ball moving with a topspin should sink (Fig. 10.10d). Notice that in each case the front of the ball is turning in the same direction that the ball is curving. This provides a simple rule for deciding which way a ball will curve in flight: namely, the ball curves toward the same direction that the front of the ball is turning.

Up to now, I've not mentioned the effect of gravity, for the very good reason that gravity has nothing to do with the Magnus effect.

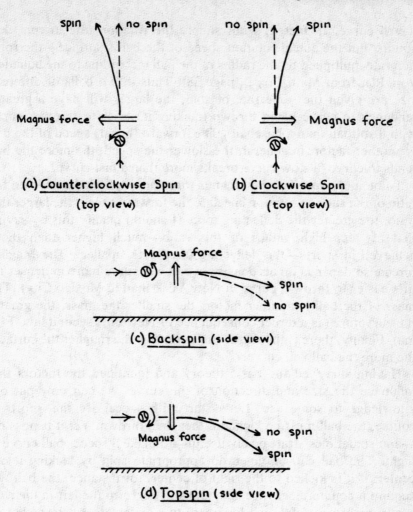

FIGURE 10.10   Spin and the curve ball.

However, a spinning ball in flight has two sources of curvature—one is the necessarily downward curvature caused by gravity; the other is the curvature caused by lift (i.e., the Magnus force), which can be in any direction. The actual trajectory of the ball is a combination of these two curvatures, leading to an infinite variety of paths.

What factors determine the size of the Magnus force and the amount of curvature of the trajectory? It seems obvious that the spin rate should be important—the more spin you put on a ball, the more it will curve. In fact, it's not simply the rotation rate in rpm that counts, but the actual rotation speed of the ball's surface—the rotation rate multiplied by the radius of the ball (according to the equation $v = R\omega$, from Math Box 2, page 38). Thus if two balls of different size are given the same rate of spin, the larger will have a greater tendency to curve when thrown (making it easier to throw a curve with a softball than a baseball). The forward (linear) speed of the ball is another factor; in general, the slower the speed, the more the ball tends to curve (a slow curve breaks more than a fast curve).

To be more specific, the Magnus force on a sphere depends on the ratio of the surface rotation speed to the forward speed; the larger this ratio, the greater the deflecting force (I should qualify this by saying that at very high values of this ratio—much higher than those achieved in sports—the deflecting force gets smaller). The Magnus force also depends on air density; a ball will curve more in denser air (it's easier to throw a curve in New York than in Mexico City). The mass of the ball is another factor; the smaller the mass, the greater the curvature (as a direct consequence of Newton's second law, $F = ma$). Finally, there is the surface smoothness: the rougher the surface, the more the ball will curve.

Having surveyed the basic theory and identified the factors that influence the size and direction of the curve, we can now put our knowledge to some use. Let's start with soccer. In this sport, of course, the ball must be kicked rather than thrown. Yet it is possible —and sometimes strategically useful—to make a soccer ball curve in flight. The ball can be given an appropriate spin by kicking it off-center: if it is kicked to the right of center, for instance, the ball will acquire a counterclockwise spin and will curve to the left in flight. A curve might be useful on a long pass to a teammate, or for a shot on goal, but it is particularly effective on a corner kick (Fig. 10.11). By

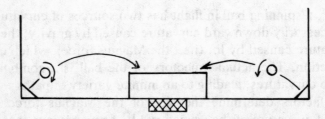

FIGURE 10.11 Curving the corner kick.

giving the ball the proper spin, it can be made to curve in toward the goal mouth, where it could be kicked or headed in by a teammate.

The control of spin is an essential feature of a tennis player's repertoire of shots. We've already learned how spin affects the way the ball bounces, but now let's focus on how it affects the flight of the ball and the strategy of play. Tennis players like to put topspin on their ground strokes—not only because of the high bounce it produces, but also because of the way it affects the trajectory. Topspin produces a downward force which makes the ball sink in flight. A topspin drive does not have to be hit on a low trajectory; even if it crosses over fairly high above the net, it will drop sharply afterward. Topspin is also essential to a high-speed serve: it is virtually impossible for a ball served at a speed of 120 mi/hr or more to drop fast enough due to gravity alone to clear the net and still bounce in the service court. The added downward force contributed by topspin makes it possible.

In contrast, a ball hit with a backspin tends to rise in flight, prolonging its hang time—and usually providing more advantage to the receiver than the hitter. A ball can also be hit at an angle to give it a degree of sidespin so that it will curve sideways. Normally, a right-handed player gives the ball a counterclockwise spin (as seen from above) with an overhead stroke, so that the ball will curve from his right to left (or to the receiver's right). The main advantage of this type of spin lies not so much in the curvature in flight (which is not too pronounced unless the ball is hit slowly) but in the angle that the ball takes when it bounces.

All of the effects of spin in tennis also occur in table tennis, as well. However, they are much more pronounced in table tennis because of the lighter weight and slower speed of the ball. The strength of the Magnus force on a spinning table-tennis ball is nearly equal to the weight of the ball itself, and as a result the curvature of its path in flight is often very obvious to the eye.

In the previous chapter I alluded to the importance of lift to the flight of a golf ball. When hit in the proper way, a golf ball gets a lot of backspin from the impact. The horizontal grooves found on the face of a golf club increase the friction force between the ball and the clubface, and greatly enhance the amount of spin imparted to the ball. It's possible for spin rates as high as 8000 rpm to be attained; at this rate a point on the surface of the ball is traveling at a speed of 40 mi/hr. Since this is a sizable fraction of its linear speed, and a golf ball has a relatively small weight, the lift produced by backspin is substantial. Because this force acts upward and counteracts the ball's tendency to fall, the ball can be launched on a flatter trajectory to gain more horizontal distance. As a consequence, the flight time may be extended by several seconds and the range by as much as 30 yards. The optimum launching angle for maximum range turns out to be between 10° and 20°, as compared with 36° to 41° when lift is not a factor. This, then, is the solution to the mystery of why the face of a driver is inclined only slightly to the vertical—it is, in fact, sloped at just about the right angle to launch a golf ball for maximum distance, when both vertical lift and drag affect its motion.

In order to impart sufficient backspin, it is essential to hit the golf ball squarely with the face of the club. If the face is angled at the moment of impact, the ball will be given a sideways spin—leading to either of those twin enemies of the golfer, a hook or a slice. If the clubface is turned inward (I'm assuming that the golfer is right-handed) the ball will receive a counterclockwise spin and will hook to the left. If the clubface is angled outward, the ball gets a clockwise spin and slices to the right. The better golfers know how to use a controlled hook or slice to hit a drive around an obstacle.

The importance of the dimples on a golf ball is really surprising. The earliest golf balls—the game, in fact, dates back to Roman times —had a smooth leather cover and were stuffed with feathers. Around 1850, the "featherie" (as it was known) was replaced by a solid ball made of a rubberlike substance known as gutta-percha. Around this time it was discovered that if the surface of the ball were covered with nicks and grooves, the ball would carry a lot farther in flight. Around 1900, the gutta-percha ball was replaced by one with rubber thread wound around a liquid or rubber core, encased in a hard, dimpled skin. With some modifications, this is the form in use today.

Without its dimples, a golf ball would travel only about three-fourths as far. By increasing the surface roughness, the dimples cause the airflow around the ball to be more turbulent. This has the effect of decreasing drag (as noted earlier) and also of increasing the Magnus effect. If given a backspin, a dimpled ball has greater lift. But the ball also has a greater tendency to hook or slice.

In 1975, two California scientists, physicist Fred Holmstrom and chemist Daniel Nepela, began experimenting with the dimples. They hit upon a design in which the dimples were confined to a band around the ball's equator, with no dimples at the poles. If the ball is set on the tee with the band of dimples aligned vertically, with one of the undimpled poles facing the golfer, it shows a remarkable tendency to travel in a straight line in flight. Holmstrom and Nepela claimed that their ball reduced the tendency to hook or curve by 75%, while decreasing the distance (because there are fewer dimples on the ball) by about 10%. Their new ball became known as the "happy non-hooker."

Unfortunately, Holmstrom and Nepela's invention has not been a total success. Their ball, which is formally named the Polara, has been banned by the United States Golf Association from use in tournament play. Claiming that the Polara would "reduce the skill required to play golf and threaten the integrity of the game," the USGA changed its rules to specify that a golf ball must have equal aerodynamic properties in all directions. To no one's surprise, Holmstrom and Nepela have sued the USGA; to my knowledge, their case has still not been settled.

The Science of Pitching

Last, but certainly not least, is baseball. As I see it, the real key to the game, the pitcher's secret weapon, is the presence of raised seams and stitches on the baseball. Without them, it would be very difficult to make the ball curve. The seams not only give the pitcher something to push on to give the ball a spin, but also increase turbulence by interrupting the smoothness of the surface.

A good pitcher can make a baseball curve in a number of different directions by changing his grip and angle of delivery. A pitcher can easily give the ball a rate of spin of up to 1800 rpm. (This may sound like a lot, but in fact the ball will make less than 15 rotations on its way to home plate.) Because of the way that the human wrist is constructed, it is much easier for a right-hander to make the ball spin clockwise (as seen by the pitcher). The reverse is true for a left-hander, who finds it easier to spin the ball counterclockwise. Because of the different spin directions, the curve balls of a lefty and a righty will move in opposite directions.

A curve ball thrown by a right-hander will break from left to right, as seen by the batter. The ball will curve away from a right-handed batter, and into a left-handed batter; this type of pitch is much easier for a left-handed batter to hit. If the pitcher is left-handed, his curve will break from right to left—away from a left-handed batter, toward a right-handed batter. Therein lies the reason behind much of the maneuvering done by baseball managers in a close game—bringing in a lefty pitcher to face a left-handed batter (who is then pinch-hit for by a right-handed batter); "platooning" two players, one righty, one lefty, at a position; stacking a lineup with right-handed batters against a lefty pitcher, and so on.

One way for a pitcher to overcome the righty-lefty percentages is to develop a "screwball"—a pitch that breaks in the opposite direction of his natural curve. To do this, the pitcher must rotate his wrist in its less flexible direction—a motion that not only is uncomfortable, but also puts considerable strain on the pitcher's forearm and elbow. As you might expect, this is a difficult pitch to throw; because it is harder to release the pitch with as much spin as on a curve, a screwball will not curve as much as a normal curve ball does.

A curve ball thrown with a sidearm motion will sweep horizontally while also dropping because of gravity. A pitcher can accentuate this motion by throwing the ball from the "three-quarters-overhand" position (with his arm about 45° above the horizontal). This pitch, if thrown by a righty, will then break down and away from a right-handed batter. If the pitcher comes "over the top"—i.e., swings his pitching arm in a vertical plane—the ball is being given a topspin, and the pitch will be deflected downward, accentuating its drop due to gravity. Experienced batters attempt to see the rotation on the ball as it approaches them (a difficult task made somewhat easier by the distinctive red color of the stitches), so that they can predict the curvature of the pitch. As a countermove, many pitchers have perfected the slider, which is basically a late-breaking curve. The pitch is thrown with less rotation than a curve; it approaches the batter like a fast ball—but then begins to curve (though not as sharply) just before it crosses the plate.

There are, of course, a great number of variations on these basic pitches—depending on the pitcher's throwing motion and grip, his pitches will break in a fairly individualistic way. The underlying principle in all cases, however, is the direction and rate of spin on the ball when it is thrown.

It is also possible to throw a pitch with some backspin on it. One way is to hold the ball across the seams with the fingertips and release it with a downward snap of the wrist. (Many pitchers naturally throw their fast ball this way.) Backspin produces upward lift. However, it would require a spin of almost 5000 rpm—well beyond the capacity of any pitcher—to make the upward lift force exceed the weight of the ball. Thus the ball cannot actually rise in flight; it merely does not drop as much as it would under gravity alone. This creates the *illusion* of a "rising" fast ball.

There is some debate as to whether the sharp "break" of a curve ball is real or an optical illusion. The baseball player's description of a good overhand curve is that it looks like it's "falling off a table." Although this may be partly an illusion, there is some truth to it. A curve does bend more sharply at the end of its trajectory than it does at the beginning, and there is a physical reason why this is so. A spinning baseball is subject to a fairly constant lateral force (i.e., the Magnus force) which produces a corresponding acceleration lateral to its path. So as the pitch comes to the plate it is accelerating sideways: therefore it will be gaining lateral speed and covering greater distances sideways the closer it gets to the plate. The curvature should become greater as the pitch approaches the batter. Theoretically, however, the curvature should be smooth, and the ball ought not to break sharply, as claimed.

There are two possible theoretical explanations for the sharp break of a curve ball, assuming it is real. One has to do with the difference in the drag force on a ball according to whether it is in type II (partially turbulent) or type III (fully turbulent) flow. In the previous chapter we learned that as the flow velocity increases, a ball will undergo a change from type II to type III flow, a change that is accompanied by a *decrease* in the drag force. A baseball loses speed as it travels through the air, and if it undergoes the reverse transition—from type III to type II—as it slows down, it should experience a sudden *increase* in drag. There would be a correspondingly sharp change in the relative strengths of the lift and drag forces on the ball, which would then lead to a sudden change in the curvature of its trajectory. It has been proposed that if a baseball is thrown at the right speed, it will slow down through the transition and break sharply as it nears the batter. Since the speed of the ball decreases by only about 10 mi/hr during its trip from pitcher to batter, its speed would have to be very precisely controlled to produce the same effect every time. Unfortunately, no measurements have as yet been made to determine the speed at which a baseball undergoes this transition. Thus it is not clear that this explanation can fully account for the sharp break of a curve under all circumstances.

The second explanation—and the one that I find more acceptable —has to do with the way that the seams on a baseball interact with the airflow. The erratic behavior of a knuckleball illustrates the extent to which this interaction can affect the path of a pitch. To throw a knuckleball, a pitcher grips the ball with his fingernails or knuckles and throws it with not too much speed and little or no rotation. A knuckleball breaks unpredictably in almost any direction. It is a difficult pitch to hit and to catch (most catchers of knuckleball pitchers use oversized mitts). It is also a difficult pitch to throw effectively—but once a pitcher has mastered the knuckleball, he can throw it on nearly every pitch and still be able to fool the hitters. Because the pitch does not require much speed, many older pitchers have prolonged their careers by developing an effective knuckleball. The classic example is Hoyt Wilhelm, an outstanding knuckleballer who was still pitching in the major leagues at the age of 49.

In an effort to understand the behavior of the knuckleball, two mechanical engineering professors at Tulane University, Robert G. Watts and Eric Sawyer, performed wind-tunnel studies on a baseball. They discovered that a lateral deflecting force appears *even when the ball is not rotating*. They identified the cause of this force as the seams, which create an unsymmetrical wake. At certain orientations of the baseball with respect to the airflow, boundary layer separation occurs right at the seam—and sometimes the point of separation fluctuates rapidly from the front to the back of the stitches. When the ball is rotating quickly, these fluctuations are too short-lived to affect its flight. (Nevertheless, the sudden break at the end of a curve ball may be attributable to a change in the orientation of the seams as the ball loses speed and rotation on its way to the plate.) But if the ball has a very slow spin, as a good knuckleball should, the slowly changing orientation of the seams can lead to sizable and seemingly erratic fluctuations in the lateral force on the ball. Watts and Sawyer concluded that a knuckleball will be most effective if the ball makes less than one rotation on its way to the plate. However, if the pitch is thrown with no spin at all, it will curve somewhat, but will not show the erratic motion characteristic of a knuckleball.

The key to the unpredictable behavior of a knuckleball, it seems, is the creation of an unsymmetrical and varying wake. For many years, pitchers have unknowingly tried to accomplish this same goal in a variety of illegal ways. The foremost example, of course, is the spitball. The pitcher doesn't actually have to spit on the ball; he just transfers some moisture from his fingers—and other substances such as Vaseline will do just as well. Some pitchers (and catchers) have been known to cut the ball on a sharpened belt buckle or scuff up some part of its surface just before delivering the pitch at a crucial point in a game. The creation of a slick, wet, or rough spot on any part of the ball serves to produce an uneven surface which can influence the boundary layer and wake.

Most American sports fans have, at best, a rudimentary knowledge of the English game of cricket, so it may come as a surprise to discover that the art of the cricket bowler is at least as intricate as that of a baseball pitcher, if not more so. Both can vary the speed, spin, and direction of their throws—but the cricket bowler has an added dimension available to him in that he can make his throws on a bounce, and thus can vary their length. A bowler uses spin for two purposes—to make the ball angle in different directions when it bounces, and to make the ball "move through the air," that is, curve in flight. (In cricket terminology, a curve ball is known as an "inswing" or an "outswing," depending on whether it breaks toward or away from the batsman.) The cover of a cricket ball is made of two hemispheres of leather seamed together by four parallel rows of raised stitches. The bowler varies his deliveries by gripping the seam in different ways, using different spin directions and orientations of the seam to the line of flight to produce a considerable variety of combinations of in-flight curvature and angles off the bounce. By disturbing the boundary layer and changing the shape of the wake, the seam on a cricket ball produces the same aerodynamic effects as the stitches on a baseball. In addition, the seam digs into the ground when the ball bounces, often enhancing the sharpness of the bounce. Thus in cricket, as in baseball, the seam on the ball is the key to much of the subtlety of the game.

As a youngster, I was never able to throw a curve ball. We used to play stickball in the local schoolyard, using a smooth, pink rubber ball known as a "spaldeen" (the name of the manufacturer, Spalding, was stamped on its surface). I am happy now to be able to attribute my inability to make this ball curve to its smooth, seamless, turbulence-retarding surface. I had more success pitching with a tennis ball—undoubtedly because of its rougher surface. But I must confess that I couldn't throw a curve with a baseball, either. Recently someone pointed out my error: I was gripping the ball in the palm of my hand, when I should have been holding it with my fingertips. Ever since then, I've been able to throw a dandy overhand curve. With my understanding of baseball aerodynamics, I've also managed to develop a knuckleball that has made an impression on quite a few Little Leaguers. Unfortunately, these newfound skills may have come to me a little late in life. But then I've never really abandoned my childhood dream to be a major league baseball player. Would anyone out there like to take a chance on a 44-year-old rookie pitcher?

APPENDIX A

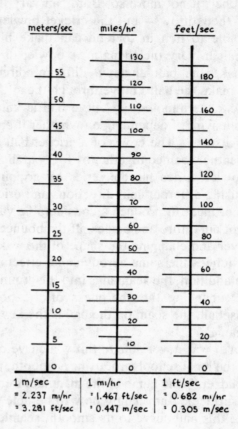

meters/sec	miles/hr	feet/sec
1 m/sec	1 mi/hr	1 ft/sec
= 2.237 mi/hr	= 1.467 ft/sec	= 0.682 mi/hr
= 3.281 ft/sec	= 0.447 m/sec	= 0.305 m/sec

SPEED CONVERSION TABLE

mi/hr	m/sec	Time for One Mile	mi/hr	m/sec	Time for One Mile
10	4.47	6:00	17	7.60	3:32
11	4.92	5:27	18	8.05	3:20
12	5.36	5:00	19	8.49	3:09
13	5.81	4:37	20	8.94	3:00
14	6.26	4:17	21	9.39	2:51
15	6.71	4:00	22	9.83	2:44
16	7.15	3:45	23	10.28	2:37

APPENDIX B:
WEIGHT AND MASS

The weight of any object is the gravitational force exerted on it, while its mass is a measure of its inertia or resistance to force. The mathematical relationship between weight and mass follows from two basic physical principles. One is Newton's second law, $F = ma$ (discussed in Chapter 2). The other is that an object falling freely at the surface of the earth has a constant acceleration of approximately 32 ft/sec² (discussed in Chapter 7).

The force that causes an object to accelerate toward the earth is its weight, W (the force of gravity). This force produces an acceleration symbolized by g. Substituting W for the force, F, and g for the acceleration, a, in Newton's second law gives us

$$W = mg$$

This equation relates the weight of any object to its mass. The standard units of weight and mass in the customary and metric systems are as follows:

	weight	*mass*	*g*
Customary:	pounds	slugs	32 ft/sec²
Metric:	newtons	kilograms	9.8m/sec²

The following conversion factors are useful:

    1 slug = 14.59 kg (1 kg = 0.0685 slug)
    1 pound = 4.448 newtons (1 newton = 0.2248 lb)

On the earth's surface, the weight of

    1 slug ≈ 32 lb
    1 kilogram ≈ 2.2 lb

APPENDIX C:
BASIC TRIGONOMETRY

The three trigonometric functions known as the *sine, cosine,* and *tangent* of an angle can be defined in terms of ratios of the lengths of the sides of a right triangle, as shown:

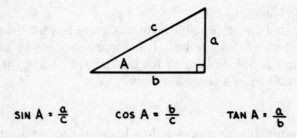

$$\text{SIN } A = \frac{a}{c} \qquad \text{COS } A = \frac{b}{c} \qquad \text{TAN } A = \frac{a}{b}$$

As the accompanying table shows, the sine and tangent of an angle get larger as the angle increases from 0° to 90°, whereas the cosine gets smaller. The sine and cosine are never numerically greater than 1, while the tangent becomes infinitely large as the angle approaches 90°.

A	sin A	cos A	tan A
0°	0	1.000	0
15°	0.259	0.966	0.268
30°	0.500	0.866	0.577
45°	0.707	0.707	1.000
60°	0.866	0.500	1.732
75°	0.966	0.259	3.732
90°	1.000	0	infinite

BIBLIOGRAPHY

General References

Dyson, G., *The Mechanics of Athletics,* U. of London Press, London, 1962.

Fox, E. L., & Mathews, D. K., *The Physiological Basis of Physical Education and Athletics,* W. B. Saunders, Philadelphia, 1981.

Griffing, D. F., *The Dynamics of Sports,* Mohican Publishing, Loudonville, Ohio, 1982.

Hay, J. G., *The Biomechanics of Sports Techniques,* 2nd ed., Prentice-Hall, Englewood Cliffs, N.J., 1973.

Jerome, J., *The Sweet Spot in Time,* Summit Books, New York, 1980.

McWhirter, N., editor, *Guinness Book of World Records, 1982 Edition,* Sterling Publishing, New York, 1982.

Schlossberg, D., *The Baseball Catalog,* J. David Publishing, New York, 1980.

Wells, K., & Luttgen, K., *Kinesiology,* 6th ed., W. B. Saunders, Philadelphia, 1976.

Introduction

Michener, J., *Sports in America,* Random House, New York, 1976.

Novak, M., *The Joy of Sports,* Basic Books, New York, 1976.

Weston, A., *The Making of American Physical Education,* Appleton-Century-Crofts, New York, 1962.

Chapter 1

Henry, F. M., & Trafton, I., The Velocity Curve of Sprint Running, *Res. Q.* (AAHPER) *23,* 409 (1951).

Keller, J. B., A Theory of Competitive Running, *Physics Today 26,* 43 (Sept. 1973).

Lietzke, M. H., An Analytical Study of World and Olympic Racing Records, *Science 119*, 333 (1954).

Riegel, P. S., Athletic Records and Human Endurance, *Am. Sci. 69*, 285 (May 1981).

Ryder, H. W., Carr, H. J., & Herget, P., Future Performance in Footracing, *Sci. Am. 234*, No. 6, 109 (1976).

Chapter 2

Dijksterhuis, E. J., *The Mechanization of the World Picture,* Oxford U. Press, Oxford, 1961.

Franklin, A., Principle of Inertia in the Middle Ages, *Am. J. Phys. 44*, 529 (1976).

Chapter 3

Alexandrov, I., & Lucht, P., Physics of Sprinting, *Am. J. Phys. 49*, 254 (1981).

Hopkins, D. C., & Patterson, J. D., Bowling Frames: Paths of a Bowling Ball, *Am. J. Phys. 45*, 263 (1977).

Manuel, F. E., *A Portrait of Isaac Newton,* Belknap Press, Cambridge, Mass., 1968.

Walker, J., In Judo and Aikido Application of the Physics of Forces Makes the Weak Equal to the Strong, *Sci. Am. 243*, No. 1, 150 (1980).

Chapter 4

Brody, H., Physics of a Tennis Racket, *Am. J. Phys. 47*, 482 (1979).

Frohlich, C., Do Springboard Divers Violate Angular Momentum Conservation? *Am. J. Phys. 47*, 583 (1979).

————, The Physics of Somersaulting and Twisting, *Sci. Am. 242*, No. 3, 154 (1980).

Jones, D. E. H., The Stability of the Bicycle, *Physics Today 23*, 34 (April 1970).

Lowell, J., & McKell, H. D., The Stability of Bicycles, *Am. J. Phys. 50*, 1106 (1982).

Post, R. F., & Post, S. F., Flywheels, *Sci. Am. 229*, No. 6, 17 (1973).

Walker, J., The Essence of Ballet Maneuvers Is Physics, *Sci. Am. 246*, No. 6, 146 (1982).

Chapter 5

Costill, D. L., *A Scientific Approach to Distance Running,* Tafnews Press, Los Altos, Calif., 1979.

Frisanchio, A. R., Functional Adaptation to High Altitude Hypoxia, *Science 187,* 313 (1975).

Hock, R. J., The Physiology of High Altitude, *Sci. Am. 222,* No. 2, 52 (1970).

Huxley, H. E., The Mechanism of Muscular Contraction, *Science 164,* 1356 (1969).

Margaria, R., The Sources of Muscular Energy, *Sci. Am. 226,* No. 3, 84 (1972).

McMahon, T. A., & Greene, P. R., Fast Running Tracks, *Sci. Am. 239,* No. 6, 148 (1978).

Murray, J. M., & Weber, A., The Cooperative Action of Muscle Proteins, *Sci. Am. 230,* No. 2, 58 (1974).

Wilson, M., Count Rumford, *Sci. Am. 203,* No. 3, 158 (1960).

Chapter 6

Blum, H., Physics and the Art of Kicking and Punching, *Am. J. Phys. 45,* 61 (1977).

Brody, H., Physics of the Tennis Racket II: The "Sweet Spot," *Am. J. Phys. 49,* 816 (1981).

Connolly, W. C., & Christian, V., Locating the "Sweet" Spot, *The Physical Educator 37,* 21 (1980).

Feld, M. S., McNair, R. E., & Wilk, S. R., The Physics of Karate, *Sci. Am. 240,* No. 4, 150 (1979).

Kirkpatrick, P., Batting the Ball, *Am. J. Phys. 31,* 606 (1963).

Plagenhoef, S., *Patterns of Human Motion,* Prentice-Hall, Englewood Cliffs, N.J., 1971.

Walker, J., Karate Strikes, *Am. J. Phys. 43,* 845 (1975).

Chapter 7

Adler, C. G., & Coulter, B. L., Galileo and the Tower of Pisa Experiment, *Am. J. Phys. 46,* 199 (1978).

Caspar, B. M., Galileo and the Fall of Aristotle: A Case of Historical Injustice? *Am. J. Phys. 45,* 325 (1977).

Cohen, I. B., Newton's Discovery of Gravity, *Sci. Am. 244,* No. 3., 166 (1981).

Kirkpatrick, P., Notes on Jumping, *Am. J. Phys. 25,* 614 (1957).

Offenbacher, E. L., Physics and the Vertical Jump, *Am. J. Phys. 38,* 829 (1970).

Chapter 8

Bizzi, E., The Coordination of Eye-Head Movements, *Sci. Am. 231,* No. 4, 100 (1974).

Bloch, R., The Origin of the Olympic Games, *Sci. Am. 219,* No. 2, 78 (1968).

Brancazio, P. J., The Physics of Basketball, *Am. J. Phys. 49,* 356 (1981).

Chapman, S., Catching a Baseball, *Am. J. Phys. 36,* 868 (1968).

Lichtenberg, D. B., and Wills, J. G., Maximizing the Range of the Shot Put, *Am. J. Phys. 46,* 546 (1978).

Litsky, F., Borden Captures Weight Throw, *New York Times,* March 7, 1982.

Regan, D., Beverley, K., & Cynader, M., The Visual Perception of Motion in Depth, *Sci. Am. 241,* No. 1, 136 (1979).

Chapter 9

Coulter, B. L., & Adler, C. G., Can a Body Pass a Body Falling Through the Air? *Am. J. Phys. 47,* 841 (1979).

Hart, F. X., & Little, C. A., Student Investigations of Models for the Drag Force, *Am. J. Phys. 44,* 872 (1976).

Rouse, H., *Elementary Mechanics of Fluids,* J. Wiley & Sons, New York, 1946.

Chapter 10

Alley, L. E., An Analysis of Water Resistance and Propulsion in Swimming Using the Crawl Stroke, *Res. Q.* (AAHPER) *23,* 253 (1952).

Brearly, M. N., The Long Jump Miracle of Mexico City, *Mathematics Magazine 45,* 241 (1972).

Briggs, L. J., Effect of Spin and Speed on the Lateral Deflection (Curve) of a Baseball; and the Magnus Effect for Smooth Spheres, *Am. J. Phys. 27,* 589 (1959).

Erlichson, H., Maximum Projectile Range with Drag and Lift, With Particular Application to Golf, *Am. J. Phys. 51,* 357 (1983).

Frohlich, C., Aerodynamic Effects on Discus Flight, *Am. J. Phys. 49,* 1125 (1981).

Lafrance, P., Ship Hydrodynamics, *Physics Today 31,* 34 (June 1978).

Maugh, T. H., Introducing the Happy Non-Hooker, *Science 187,* 941 (1975).

Mehta, R., & Wood, D., Aerodynamics of the Cricket Ball, *New Scientist* (Aug. 7, 1980).

Nelson, B., Of People and Things, *Track & Field News 30,* No. 10, 42 (1977); *32,* No. 9, 50 (1979); *32,* No. 10, 54 (1979).

Raine, A. E., Aerodynamics of Skiing, *Science Journal 6,* No. 3, 26 (1970).

Watts, R. G., & Sawyer, E., Aerodynamics of a Knuckleball, *Am. J. Phys. 43,* 960 (1975).

INDEX